WHAT EVERY AMERICAN SHOULD KNOW ABOUT WOMEN'S HISTORY

D0972409

WHAT EVERY AMERICAN SHOULD KNOW ABOUT WOMEN'S HISTORY

200 Events that Shaped Our Destiny

Christine Lunardini, Ph.D.

ADAMS MEDIA CORPORATION
Holbrook, Massachusetts

Copyright ©1997, Christine Lunardini. All rights reserved.
This book, or parts thereof, may not be reproduced in any form
without permission from the publisher; exceptions are made for
brief excerpts used in published reviews.

Published by Adams Media Corporation
260 Center Street, Holbrook, MA 02343

ISBN: 1-55850-687-X

Printed in Canada.

J   I   H   G   F   E   D   C   B   A

Library of Congress Cataloging-in-Publication Data
Lunardini, Christine A., 1941-
What every American should know about women's history : 200 events that shaped our
destiny / Christine Lunardini.
       p.   cm.
Includes bibliographical references and index.
ISBN 1-55850-687-X (pbk.)
1. Women—United States—History. I. Title.
HQ1410.L86   1997
305.4'0973—dc20   96-27818
                                                                                                            CIP

This publication is designed to provide accurate and authoritative information with regard to the subject matter covered. It
is sold with the understanding that the publisher is not engaged in rendering legal, accounting, or other professional advice.
If legal advice or other expert assistance is required, the services of a competent professional person should be sought.
                     — From a *Declaration of Principles* jointly adopted by a Committee of the American Bar Association
                                                                               and a Committee of Publishers and Associations

JACKET PHOTO CREDITS: Billie Holiday, Library of Congress; "Soldiers without Guns" poster, Library of Congress; Annie
Oakley, Library of Congress; Sojourner Truth, Library of Congress; Jacqueline Bouvier Kennedy, Library of Congress; Billie
Jean King, Archive Photos; Suffragettes, Archive Photos.

This book is available at quantity discounts for bulk purchases.
For information, call 1-800-872-5627 (in Massachusetts, 617-767-8100).

Visit our home page at http://www.adamsmedia.com

To
Emily Jane Thompson
University of Pennsylvania
Class of 1998

As you set out for Ithaca,
hope the voyage is a long one,
full of adventure, full of discovery

Contents

                        WHAT EVERY AMERICAN SHOULD KNOW

WHAT EVERY AMERICAN SHOULD KNOW

Acknowledgments

As most authors would readily admit, the cover credits on almost all books should read, "Written by [Author's Name]...and the Countless People Without Whom the Author Would Not Have Had a Prayer of Completing this Book." Of course, most of us prefer to take full credit on the outside, and settle for a list of acknowledgments on the inside. But those to whom we are indebted know full well the extent of their contributions, whether substantive or supportive. First and foremost, I would like to thank and acknowledge Edward Watts Morton Bever, Ph.D. A classmate and colleague from Princeton, Ed was unfailingly generous both in contributing his skills as a researcher and in drafting entries. That the project was completed in a timely fashion is due in no small part to his assistance. I would also like to thank the many historians whose works I consulted and the city of New York for maintaining one of the best public libraries in the country. My agent, Elizabeth Knappman of New England Publishing Associates, ever on the lookout for appropriate projects, led me to Adams Media Corporation, who offered me the opportunity to do the book. The editors and staff at Adams Media Corporation, including Brandon Toropov and Chris Ciaschini, were more than helpful. It was definitely my good fortune that Miccinello Associates did the copyediting, for I am sure they saved me from more than one egregious mistake. On a personal note, I owe more than I can ever repay to a host of friends and loved ones who offered consistent support, encouragement, suggestions, and criticisms, as well as their good will: Maureen Callahan, Steve Victore, Catherine Clinton, Noah Callahan-Bever, Chloe Callahan-Flintoft, Sheila Callahan-Victore, Maureen Keating Tsuchiya, Sheila and Kit Thompson, Pat Donahue, Donna, Jonathan, and Abigail Lunardini, and Elyn Rosenthal. Thank you one and all.

Introduction

Not too long ago, I received a newspaper clipping from a friend who thought I might enjoy reading about a conference held recently in Pennsylvania. The article was entitled "Putting Women in Their Historic Place," and it described the conference, which was intended to focus attention on the contributions to history that have been made by women, with the hope that written histories would begin to reflect that perspective more frequently. I quickly read the article and laid it aside, only to be drawn back to it later on. But I was really thinking about the woman who sent me the article—a gracious lady who graduated from the University of Pennsylvania when it was still unusual for women to attend any university. Except perhaps within her own community, she has never been a "public" person. Like most women in her generation, she married and raised a family. Her husband, an Olympic pitcher, coached athletics at a prestigious small college, while she fulfilled her duties as a kindergarten teacher and faculty wife, contributing her talents not only to the college and the hundreds of students whose paths crossed hers over the years, but to her community as well. In short, hers has been a life that many people would characterize as fairly ordinary. In a much larger sense, however, this woman exemplifies the same spirit that has motivated women throughout American history. The vast majority of women who have moved through the decades have done so without the recognition they so richly deserve. And yet, without their contributions to American life and culture, each generation building on the foundations laid by the previous generation—standing on their mothers' shoulders—the history of America would be unrecognizable to our eyes. At the same time, it is the millions of unsung women who created the subtext out of which emerged those public women whose contributions not only helped shape the contours of American life, but sometimes helped to change its destiny.

If you asked a group of people to make a list of ten Americans who have contributed in one way or another to our history, the lists would probably vary markedly from person to person, but no one would have difficulty coming up with ten names. The lists would likely contain the names of presidents, scientists, statesmen, inventors, explorers, athletes, writers, physicians, and every other possible category. And they would probably have one thing in common: it is almost certain that the vast majority, if not all, of the lists would contain the names of famous men. If the same group of people were asked to name ten women who have contributed to American history, they would have much more difficulty and would continue to fall back on those few women who did make it into the history books: Betsy Ross, Florence Nightingale (no, she was not an American), and for reasons not entirely clear, Mary Todd Lincoln. While this may be a slight exaggeration, it is not too far from the truth, and most people would probably have to really think about the question to come up with further examples.

Since the first permanent European settlements in the New World in 1607, women have been prominently involved in all aspects of the growth and development of the nation. Without women, the colonies would have failed. The first published American author was a woman. Washington's army was supported thanks to money raised by women patriots. Women have fought in every single war in which America has been involved. The factory system and American industrialization depended on the labor of women. Women fueled the abolitionist movement, they helped reform the cities, and they flew thousands of missions as pilots during World War II. The amazing thing is that they managed to accomplish so much with so many limitations to their own personal freedom. For most of American history, women were not even allowed to vote, nor were they allowed to participate in affairs outside of the home without the risk of public censure.

This book contains two hundred events, beginning in 1607 and continuing through the early 1990s, in which women were either the primary players or that affected the lives of women in a significant way. The difficulty in putting together such a book lies not in finding two hundred events to include, but in determining which events can be excluded in order to bring the list down to the desired size. There will undoubtedly be many readers who can justifiably point to certain events or women not mentioned and wonder why. In an effort to try and be as broad as possible in including a fair representation of all the areas of life to which women have been contributors, many episodes had to be left out. It is simply a further demonstration of the richness and fullness of women's participation and contribution to American life and culture.

> — *Christine A. Lunardini*
> New York City
> July 4, 1994

1607: The First European Women Arrive at the Jamestown Colony

(Family Life)

In May 1607, the first permanent European colony was established at Jamestown, Virginia. After a near-disastrous first year, in which only 38 of the original 104 male settlers survived, the first two women settlers arrived at Jamestown. A forecast of the immigration pattern that would emerge over the next fifty years, one of the women was Anne Forrest, the wife of a male settler, and the other, Anne Buras, was her servant.

The first permanent English colony in the New World was established at Jamestown, Virginia, in 1607. The Jamestown colony was actually preceded by a short-lived colony at Roanoke Island, North Carolina, settled by 120 men, women, and children in 1590. Inadequate preparation for the harshness of the frontier, without ready access to support and supplies, added to the settlers' inability, or unwillingness, to deal with the Indians, resulted in a complete disintegration of the colony. Moreover, all traces of the settlers disappeared. To this day it is unclear what happened in Roanoke and where the colonists went. The settlement became known as the "Lost Colony," and it took another fifteen years before a second attempt to establish a colony was undertaken. Beyond that, of course, there were several women among the Spanish-speaking colonists who had arrived several decades before the English colonies were established, but they, too, were short-lived residents of the New World.

Women who immigrated to Jamestown, particularly in the early decades, tended to fall into one of three categories. They were either married to colonists, they were daughters of colonists, or they were indentured servants. Women who came to the colonies as indentured servants did so with the intention of getting married as soon as their terms of servitude were completed. Because the ratio of men to women was so skewed in the early decades of colonization, even the lowliest of servant women confidently anticipated the day when they would no longer be servants, but housewives. Moreover, a woman might also anticipate becoming the mistress of one or more servants in her own household. When Anne Buras had worked off her indenture, she married another settler almost immediately. Getting to that point, however, required that she survive the brutal conditions under which the first generation of colonists lived. Like the lost colony of Roanoke, the Jamestown endeavor was ill-planned. So harsh were conditions in the first two years that nearly all the original colonists died from disease or starvation. Fortunately, help arrived just in time, in the form of replenishments of food stores and replenishments of colonists.

It was the assurance of mobility, virtually impossible in their native countries, that prompted so many single women to enter into desperate agreements that would bind them to servitude for as many as seven years in a new, unknown world fraught with risk. Indeed, some women were willing to make the voyage to the colonies without having secured even their short-term futures. Such was the case in 1620, when more than ninety women arrived at Jamestown, having agreed to be auctioned off to prospective husbands. Male colonists who could come up with the asking price of 120 pounds of tobacco (approximately $80) put in their bids for a wife. Almost immediately, all ninety of the "tobacco brides" were spoken for.

1638: Anne Hutchinson Is Expelled from the Massachusetts Bay Colony

(Equal Rights)

After a series of trials conducted by the Massachusetts General Court beginning in 1637, Anne Hutchinson, accused of heresy for criticizing Puritanism, was found guilty and banished from the Massachusetts Bay Colony.

A fundamental tenet of Puritanism was the belief that the way to salvation lay in entering into a "Covenant of Works," and then progressing to a "Covenant of Grace," the outward signs of which would indicate sainthood and ultimate salvation. The Covenant of Grace was the enlightened step forward that Anglican Minister Cotton Mather took to relieve some of the anxiety and oppression of Old Testament damnation. Mather's relative liberalism forced him to leave England and flee to Boston. Some of Mather's flock followed him, including Anne Hutchinson, who had found in Mather's preaching some hope for her own imperfections and for the souls of her two young daughters, who had died within a month of each other. Unlike most of her peers, however, Anne Hutchinson had taken Mather's interpretation of Puritanism to its logical conclusion: an individual's internal acceptance of the state of grace and, therefore, salvation, put that person in direct contact with God. It also made superfluous other encumbrances, including the concept of the Covenant of Works. It was a dangerous personal theology to the Puritans because it flew in the face of Protestantism.

Hutchinson and her husband, William, arrived in Boston in September 1634. Very quickly, William's successful entry into the cloth trade brought the family prestige and enough wealth to purchase land tracts and invest in other businesses. His elevation to Boston selectman and his position as a deputy to the Massachusetts General Court indicated that the family had reached the highest level of colonial society. Anne, in the meantime, with her outgoing personality and nursing skills, became a welcome presence in the community, particularly among the women of Boston. Distressed to discover that most women were still locked into the ideology of the Covenant of Works, Hutchinson began sharing her interpretation of Mather's theology. She soon had a large following that included many of the prominent members of her congregation, including the wealthiest merchants and craftsmen, and even the governor, Henry Vane.

Hutchinson invoked the anger of Mather's fellow minister, John Wilson. Hutchinson did not like Wilson's conservatism and made her feelings clear to all who cared to listen, contrasting his methods with those of Cotton Mather. In the controversy that arose, the entire city of Boston took sides. Before long, it spread to other communities as well. When John Winthrop was elected governor of the colony, he reasserted control over the general court by removing Hutchinson's sympathizers. And when a church synod condemned Hutchinson for numerous errors in her theology, Mather sided with the synod. Although he later came to her assistance during her trial, the damage had already been done. The general court tried Hutchinson in 1637, found her guilty of preaching heresy, and banished her from the colony. In 1638, Hutchinson and her family left Massachusetts, first going to Rhode Island where she believed she could find peace of mind among the more liberal colonists led by Roger Williams, and then finally to New York. In 1643, Hutchinson, her family, and neighbors were the victims of an Indian attack.

The danger posed by Anne Hutchinson lay not only in her interpretation of theology, but in the fact that she was a woman. Her eloquent self-defense before the general court proved her the theological equal of her accusers. But, as Mather noted at her trial, "she is only a woman and many unsound and dangerous principles are held by her." The most dangerous principle held by Hutchinson was the notion of independent thinking, for that threatened the entire structure of colonial society. Violating the Puritan standard of acceptable female behavior, Hutchinson threatened to bring down not only the theological covenantal relationships, but the covenantal relationships that governed gender roles as well.

1650: Anne Bradstreet, Earliest American Poet, Publishes Her First Poem

(Cultural Life)

In 1650, Anne Bradstreet's brother-in-law, the Reverend John Woodbridge, obtained a copy of some of her poetry. Woodbridge was so impressed that, without consulting Bradstreet, he sent them to a London publisher. The poetry collection was published anonymously under the unlikely title, *The Tenth Muse Lately Sprung up in America. Or Severall Poems, Compiled with Great Variety of Wit and Learning, Full of Delight.... By a Gentlewoman in Those Parts.*

A well-born Englishwoman whose father was steward in charge of the vast estate of the Earl of Lincoln, much of Anne Bradstreet's childhood was spent growing up in the cultured surroundings of Tattershall Castle. There, raised in a strict, religious household influenced by her father's belief in Nonconformist doctrine, Anne was tutored privately. That in itself was unusual for a female. But more importantly, Anne had access to the earl's library and the intellectual stimulation it provided for a young mind. When Anne was sixteen, she married Simon Bradstreet. Two years later in 1630, she and her entire family left England for the Massachusetts Bay Colony. Both her father and husband were important members of the new government. Anne, therefore, enjoyed a position of status in the colony.

If Anne Bradstreet was unusual in some ways, she was still the model of a colonial wife and mother. Because she was more visible than the average woman, Bradstreet was expected to conform rigorously to Puritan philosophy. Although the contrast between old and New England initially left her somewhat shocked, she quickly accepted her new life. Despite the demands on her time and attention from eight children and a large household, Bradstreet found time to write poetry and to keep her journals. In the best Puritan tradition, her writings were not for public consumption, but rather shared with her father and her husband, or kept entirely private.

Her first collection of poetry was well-received, particularly because the poems were written by a woman. Yet these poems did not really reflect the inner voice she would develop over time by virtue of her colonial experiences and maturity. *The Tenth Muse* was more a tribute to what she had grown up with and left behind. Her second volume of poetry, published in 1678 six years after her death, contained both revisions of her earlier poetry and the body of her mature work. These poems reflected her New England experiences. Rather than. imitating poets she had read and admired, Bradstreet had found her own inner vision as a poet. The poems, written about her own struggles with Puritanism, her children, her husband, and her life experiences, reflect the strength of her character and the virtues with which she faced life. They provide a portrait of Puritan life at odds with modern notions of Puritanism. In a poem entitled "To My Dear Loving Husband," Bradstreet wrote, "If ever two were one, then surely we. If ever man were lov'd by wife, than thee;…Then while we live, in love lets go persever, That when we live no longer, we may live ever." The best of her poetry is timeless and ageless. Adrienne Rich, a modern American poet, said of Bradstreet: "To have written these, the first good poems in America, while rearing eight children, lying frequently sick, keeping house at the edge of wilderness, was to have managed a poet's range and extension within confines as severe as any American poet has confronted."

Remarkably, Anne Bradstreet was not alone as an author. Other women during the early years of colonialism and nationhood also produced stories, poetry, and essays that have been preserved as part of American culture. It was not unusual for women to publish their works anonymously or to adopt a pseudonym, but it has been estimated that fully one-third of all the novels written in America up to 1820 were written by women authors.

1692: Salem Witch Trials

(Family, Culture, Politics)

In the town of Salem, Massachusetts, in 1692, 115 persons, mostly women, were accused of practicing witchcraft. The term "witch trials" resulted in the execution of twenty women and girls.

Witchcraft accusations were not unheard of in New England. Colonists, after all, had brought with them the same superstitions and beliefs that had been part of their lives in Europe. And occasionally, people—generally women—were put to death because they were found guilty of practicing witchcraft. In 1648, Margaret Jones was executed for intemperate behavior, having a malignant touch, using suspicious medications, and for notorious lying. In 1656, Ann Hibbens was put to death for having a suspiciously crabby nature. In the 1680s, incidents of witch executions increased with the deaths of several women, including a widely known woman named Glover who supposedly caused children to have fits.

But even with this history of witchcraft and accusations, what happened in Salem, Massachusetts, in 1692 was extraordinary. Spurred on by a group of teenage girls who accused countless neighbors, as well as family members in some cases, a witch hysteria gripped the small seacoast town of Salem. There were in fact two Salems: Salem Village, which was a small rural farming community, and Salem Town, where the prosperous merchants and traders lived. The animosity that existed between town and village created ideal conditions for these accusations to get out of hand. The fact that the accusers were teenage girls was not unusual in these situations. Nor was it unusual for the accused to be primarily middle-aged women, as they were in Salem. Moreover, it was common for the accused to have characteristic deviance or peculiarity that could easily be exploited by accusers and readily accepted by irrational judges and juries.

What began as a routine accusation by one young woman quickly escalated until a small coterie of teenagers and young women became the center of an ever-expanding circle of accused "witches." The charges leveled against the accused often amounted to no more than a "look" that an accuser claimed caused her to engage in abnormal behavior. In these instances, the accused were charged with being agents of the devil. Before the year was out, 115 women, men, and children had been accused of witchcraft. Twenty women and girls were executed. The hysteria created was not unlike twentieth-century McCarthyism, with neighbors fearing neighbors, family members keeping watchful eyes on other family members, and everyone afraid to do anything that could be interpreted as "odd." It was not until the accusations extended beyond average citizens and began to include magistrates, ministers, and others in positions of authority that the Salem residents began to regain control of their senses, their lives, and their town.

Finding an explanation for the Salem witch trials has been the focus of the work of a number of historians who have offered a variety of theories. The most plausible explanation has to do with the tensions existing in seventeenth-century New England between young women who were unmarried and powerless, and older women who had families, homes, and a certain amount of power within the community by virtue of their status. By 1692, these young women were faced with a new set of circumstances in colonial New England: a shortage of land and a shortage of available marriageable males, the combination of which made for significantly lower expectations for the younger generation. Whatever else the accusers thought would happen, the witch trials did not rescue them from their insignificant status within the community. Indeed, within twenty years, the courts would reverse the witchcraft convictions, declaring that it was the accusers, after all, who were acting as the devil's agents. Needless to say, the vindication of the accused "witches" did not affect those who had paid the ultimate price for being nothing more than an easy target.

1740: Eliza Lucas Pinckney Begins Managing Her Father's Plantation

(Social Equality, Work)

In 1739, George Lucas, the lieutenant governor of Antigua, who had brought his family to the Carolinas in search of a better climate for his ailing wife, was called back to his post. When he left the Carolinas, responsibility for the plantation fell to his daughter, Elizabeth, better known as Eliza, who took over management of the family's five thousand acres in 1740, at the age of seventeen.

In 1740, at the age of only seventeen, Eliza Lucas Pinckney began managing her father's plantations, located in the southernmost colonies called the Carolinas. A resourceful and innovative young woman, Eliza had received most of her education in England, and brought with her a fairly sophisticated perspective on life. George Lucas had enormous confidence in Eliza and he advised his daughter to try experimenting with the crops, a suggestion she lost no time in pursuing. Once in control, she proceeded to experiment with new crops that proved to be a major contribution to the colonies' economy. Up until then, the only thing the Carolinas exported was rice, which made them vulnerable to both natural forces that harmed that crop and to unfavorable fluctuations in the price of the crop abroad. Pinckney tried a number of alternatives, and found a winner in indigo, a seed used in making blue dye. The seeds became the Carolinas' second most important export.

Pinckney's powerful influence in her own family's affairs and on the life of her community was notable but hardly unique in the thirteen colonies. During these early years, women gained important new—although sometimes only temporary—rights denied to their sisters who remained in Europe. American women had greater rights to own and, as we have seen, administered property. They were sometimes able to represent themselves in court rather than rely on a male relative or guardian, and they were more fairly treated during a divorce. They could conduct business on their own, under certain conditions, and widows were far more likely to inherit land and other property.

The reason for this higher status lay in the frontier nature of colonial society, particularly in the southern colonies, and with the almost obsessive desire of Puritans in the northern colonies to maintain order at all costs. In England, land was scarce, so it was generally willed only to the eldest son. In America, in the early years of colonization, land was plentiful, so that there was often enough to pass on to all the sons. Moreover, it was not uncommon for widows to be left with land or other property of their own. In the Old World, labor was plentiful, so there was fierce competition for available businesses and jobs. In the New World, though, labor was scarce. There was greater opportunity for women to engage in commerce. While it was not an everyday occurrence to find a woman shopkeeper or innkeeper, there were enough throughout the colonies that it was not an oddity either. Women also had opportunities not generally enjoyed in England. For example, there were nearly one hundred women printers or publishers in the first decades of colonization. Printing and publishing were fairly specialized, and women whose husbands made their living in that occupation sometimes had to take over when the husband died, or when he had to leave for extended periods of time. Finally, in the colonies, women were particularly scarce. In England they made up more than half the population, but as late as the mid-1700s they made up only 35 to 40 percent of the people in the thirteen colonies. As in any market, a scarce commodity commands a higher price, and in this case the price for men to attract and keep women was a greater willingness to allow more leeway, although always within prescribed parameters.

In addition to these market factors, colonial women were more likely to come naturally into positions of greater responsibility, and hence greater rights. In contrast to the crowded villages in England and Europe, American farmsteads and plantations were often quite isolated. If a man went away on business or to participate in colonial politics, his wife would remain behind in charge. And in the unsettled conditions of colonial life, many such women found themselves permanently in charge, as widows. Frontier societies could not afford to observe the formalities and maintain the artificial distinctions of settled civilizations, and in the rough and ready conditions of the American frontier American women, like American men, began to be aware of their intrinsic worth and their essential equality.

1769–70: The Daughters of Liberty Support the Nonimportation Agreement

(Political Reform, Family Life, Equal Rights)

When colonial merchants agreed not to import British goods in order to protest the recently imposed Townsend Duties, the Daughters of Liberty, a loosely structured but very effective organization of women patriots, were instrumental in helping to enforce nonimportation. Nonimportation began in the spring of 1769; within a year, the British were forced to repeal almost all of the Townsend Duties.

Just as male patriots put their lives at risk for principles, female patriots rose to the occasion in the years before the Revolutionary War. A loosely organized group called the Daughters of Liberty was instrumental in the success of colonial actions against the British government that required the cooperation of the colonists. In the summer of 1766, the Grenville government in Great Britain fell from power and was replaced with the Townsend government. Charles Townsend, the Chancellor of the Exchequer, considered colonial objections to English-imposed taxes as "so much nonsense." He immediately set about imposing new taxes on imported goods.

The Townsend Duties, as they became known, touched off a wave of hostility in the colonies. Angry merchants agreed to impose another economic boycott against importation of British goods, just as they had done when the British Parliament passed the Stamp Act in 1765. And, as they had before, the Daughters of Liberty improvised to lessen the hardships that would otherwise accompany a shortage of goods. They experimented with tea substitutes, returned to raising sheep and weaving their own cloth from the wool, and relied on homemade goods rather than imported ones. More importantly, the Daughters

of Liberty acted as both teachers of the patriotic message and enforcers, to make sure that other women observed the ban on imports.

When the Revolution began a few years later in 1776, these same women stepped up to do whatever they could to support the Revolution and the Continental Army. Organized in various communities throughout the colonies, calling themselves the Ladies' Association, women helped to finance George Washington's army by going door-to-door and collecting funds. In Philadelphia, Esther Reed and Sarah Bache (the daughter of Benjamin Franklin) raised three hundred thousand continental dollars, which, at Washington's suggestion, they used to buy cloth to make uniforms for the ill-equipped army. Similar efforts were made in other communities, with money going for food, medicine, and clothing. Spinning societies were common in colonial communities, but far from being merely occasions for social gatherings, the societies allowed colonists to replenish supplies of cloth no longer available from England.

While most women in the colonies tried to stay out of harm's way and to avoid disease and deprivation during the Revolution, some women chose to travel with the army and even to fight when the opportunity arose. With little to fall back on once their husbands joined the army, many women elected to go with their husbands. They earned money by cooking and doing laundry and were in no way considered women of loose morals, as the term "camp follower" later came to imply. Indeed, Martha Washington, on more than one occasion, accompanied George.

A number of women picked up weapons in the heat of battle and fought alongside the men. Molly Pitcher, for example, whose real name was Mary Ludwig Hayes, became famous at the Battle of Monmouth when she took over her husband's position after he was felled by a bullet. George Washington himself praised her performance and successfully urged Congress to make her a sergeant and award her half-pay for the remainder of her life. In other instances, women actually enlisted in the army disguised as men. Deborah Samson of Massachusetts joined a regiment towards the end of the war. In May 1782, she enlisted as Robert Shurtleff. Engaged in battles in New York state near West Point and Tarrytown, Samson was wounded. Even then, no one found her out. But a short while later Samson was discovered when she had to be

hospitalized with a fever. Her doctor refused to inform on her and she was discharged, still posing as Robert Shurtleff in October 1783. Eventually, her husband was awarded a pension as the widower of a soldier.

Regardless of their specific contributions to the business of building a democracy, colonial women played a pivotal role. Their contributions in the Revolutionary War and in the years leading up to it were an important part of the ultimate success of the colonists. During the conflict, the sacrifices made by women did not go unnoticed. As one colonial newspaper editorialized, "The industry and frugality of the American ladies must exalt their character in the eyes of the World and serve to show how greatly they are contributing to the salvation of a whole Continent." Once the war ended, the Daughters of Liberty and the Ladies' Associations disbanded, believing that they had served their purpose in helping to establish the new nation. But recognition of these first national women's organizations came in 1875 with the founding of the National Council of the Sons and Daughters of Liberty, an organization whose purpose was to commemorate their service to America.

1773: Phillis Wheatley's Poetry Becomes the First Book by a Black American

(Cultural Life)

In 1773, twenty-year-old Phillis Wheatley, a slave from Boston, traveled with the son of her master to visit the Countess of Huntingdon, who arranged for her writings to be issued as *Poems on Various Subjects, Religious and Moral.* This young woman, who had known English for less than a decade, thus became the first African-American to publish a book.

Phillis Wheatley arrived in America in 1771, a seven-year-old girl, recently torn from her roots in Gambia. She caught the eye of a Boston matron, Susan Wheatley, who was looking for a personal servant, and even though Phillis was young and thin, Susan bought her and took her home.

Phillis got her first name from the ship that brought her to America, and her last name from her adoptive family. Far from treating her like a servant, the Wheatleys quickly began acting as if she was a member of the family, giving her her own room, excusing her from the tasks assigned to the other black servants, and teaching her to read and write. Within two years, Phillis could not only speak English, but could read it and write in it as well.

Phillis used her newfound skill to write poetry, and published her first poem when she was fourteen and had been in America just six years. Her work expressed a maturity and skill so great that many prominent men endorsed her talents. Thomas Jefferson, for example, sought her out, and John Hancock was one of eighteen friends of the family who signed the foreword to her book. She was similarly well-received by London society when she went to England to arrange its publication, and both her friends and her friendship encouraged the Wheatleys to grant her freedom when she returned.

Wheatley returned to America after just five weeks because Susan had fallen ill, and she chose to stay with the family when she was free. When the Revolutionary War broke out, she wrote several pieces supportive of the patriot cause, including a tribute to George Washington in 1776. He was so impressed that he invited her to visit him at his headquarters.

Sadly, from this point onward, Wheatley's life appears to have gone downhill. Susan died soon after Phillis returned from England, the two Wheatley children moved away, and John Wheatley died in 1778. Phillis,

just twenty-five, was now on her own. She married John Peters in the same year that John Wheatley died, but the match was not a good one. Peters was a free man, well-dressed, and intelligent, but he was irresponsible. He got her pregnant and then deserted her three times, and the third time proved fatal. Even as she continued to write and was trying to arrange for her second book to be published, she was living alone in an unheated apartment with her newborn baby. In 1784, at thirty-one, she and her baby both died of cold and malnutrition.

1776: Abigail Adams Admonishes John to "Remember the Ladies"

(Equal Rights)

Writing to her husband, John Adams, a member of the Continental Congress, Abigail Adams expressed reservations regarding the sincerity of some patriots who professed to have a "passion for Liberty." The letter went on to say that she hoped that the Congress would "Remember the Ladies" as it deliberated on the nature of the new country, and not continue to put "unlimited power into the hands of the Husbands."

Abigail Adams was every bit her husband's equal in the confines of their marriage. The wife of John Adams, the second president of the

United States, Abigail Adams became as astute an observer of the political system born out of the Revolutionary War as any of her husband's col-

---

leagues. Although she never pushed the boundaries of acceptable public behavior for women of her time, her determination to do what had to be done in order to keep her home and family secure and prosperous during the extended periods of John Adams' absences, did indeed help to shift those boundaries.

Between 1774 and 1784, John Adams was rarely in residence at the family home because of the ongoing colonial crises that led to independence and nationhood. To Abigail fell the task of raising four small children and maintaining two homes. She did so willingly, first because the couple loved each other wholly and completely from courtship to death, and second because Abigail possessed the strength of character, intelligence, and resourcefulness that made her equal to the task. It was not her nature to complain. Instead, she resolved to become as good an overseer of family life as her husband would have been, had he not been called away so often. John Adams grew to depend more and more on her expertise in running their family affairs and was proud of her managerial skill. Abigail gained a well-deserved reputation, buying farm stock, hiring help, buying pieces of land, paying bills, raising children, and living economically and prudently.

Abigail's grandson, Charles Francis Adams, credited his grandmother with saving the family from the financial ruin that overtook many of John's contemporaries who also gave themselves over to public service.

Much of what is known about Abigail and John Adams' relationship came from letters written by Abigail over the course of her life. Her letter-writing flourished in the ten years when John was away from home. In her letters, Abigail combined the personal and the political. They were filled with her observations on the status of women in the eighteenth century. Her letters were not, of course, confined to John. Children, grandchildren, relatives, and friends rounded out her extensive list of correspondents. The portrait that emerges of Abigail shows a woman who had a strong sense of what was morally and ethically acceptable and who was also comfortable with certain limitations. For example, she had no reservations about making known her view that slavery had an evil effect on both character and society. When a young African-American servant boy requested to learn to read and write, Abigail sent him to the local school. Parents of other children in the school who registered complaints were told in no uncertain terms that the youngster's color should in no way limit his opportunity.

Abigail believed as strongly in equal education for girls as she did in equal education for African-Americans. She wrote often about her belief that girls should be afforded the same education as boys. She was critical of the legal and social status ascribed to women. This was clearly part of her admonition to John to "Remember the Ladies, and be more generous and favourable to them than your ancestors. Do not put such unlimited power into the hands of the Husbands. Remember, all men would be tyrants if they could." At the same time, it was not a plea to include women in public life, but rather to redistribute power within the family. "Emancipating all nations, you insist upon retaining absolute power over Wives." She went on to say that "If particular care and attention is not paid to the Ladies, we are determined to foment a Rebellion, and will not hold ourselves bound by any Laws in which we have no voice, or Representation."

Abigail Adams undoubtedly thought it humorous to use the same rhetoric that the Americans used in complaining to the English government, at least to one of the Founding Fathers. But her concerns about the rights of women within the family were serious, and reflected the concerns of many women in the revolutionary era.

1783: New Jersey Women Vote Under the Terms of a State Statute

(Equal Rights)

A statute passed by the New Jersey legislature in 1783, authorized voting rights to "all inhabitants of this state, of full age, who are worth fifty pounds proclamation money." Under the terms of the statute, women in New Jersey exercised their right to vote.

Despite the enormous contributions to the Revolutionary War effort made by the women of the colonies, little in the way of rights or privileges accrued to them that they had not previously held. While the Declaration of Independence and the Constitution of the United States are both viewed as seminal documents in American history, for women they were not. Several oppressed groups sought recognition in the Constitution while it was being written by the Founding Fathers. African-Americans, Native Americans, nonproperty holders, and artisans, all of whom were excluded from participation in the public sphere, including suffrage, had all participated in the Revolution and sought inclusion in the new nation. At bottom, all hoped that the rhetoric used by the colonists against the British would give the framers of the Constitution pause when dealing with minority groups at home.

Women, too, sought their just reward for responding to the political crisis as they did. While husbands and fathers were away fighting the British, women had to take over the tasks of keeping households, estates, and businesses as intact as possible. These new responsibilities were, of course, in addition to the multitude of daily tasks that traditionally fell to women. While women felt themselves inadequate to the responsibilities thrust upon them in the beginning, they gradually became competent managers. And, while it was expected that women would revert to their former roles once the war ended, women wanted recognition for the invaluable service they had rendered. Many of them were outspoken in their expectations. Abigail Adams had warned her husband John not to forget the ladies. And Mary Willing Byrd of Virginia voiced the discontent of many women when she noted that, despite all she had done, despite the fact that she was a model citizen, despite her patriotism, she "paid [her] taxes and have not been Personally or Virtually represented. My property is taken from me and I have no redress."

Nevertheless, the Constitution made no mention of women. Indians were granted a special role, slaves were designated as "three-fifths a person," and virtually all adult white males were guaranteed suffrage. But women were excluded. They were also excluded in state constitutions, with one notable exception. New Jersey enacted a statute that made it legal for women to vote in 1783. In 1787, there is evidence that women voted, and the election law of 1790 in New Jersey made clear reference to voters as "he or she." In October 1797, women voted in large numbers for a Federalist candidate in a hotly contested election. But repeated attempts were made to overturn the statute allowing women to vote, and in 1806, a raucous election in which people voted more than once, became the catalyst for the change that prohibited women from voting. The committee charged with investigating voter fraud in the 1806 election enacted a new statute in 1807, aimed at preventing "undesirables" from voting. Women were included in this category, and thereafter suffrage in New Jersey was limited to adult white males of property.

1790: Judith Sargent Stevens Murray Argues for Equal Education for Women

(Equal Rights, Education)

In 1790, two years before Mary Wollstonecraft published her book on women's rights, Judith Sargent Stevens Murray argued in *Massachusetts Magazine* that women were just as capable of rational thought as men (and perhaps more so).

The late eighteenth century was a time of great intellectual ferment in America just as in Europe, a time known as the Enlightenment. Part of that ferment was a reevaluation of the place and potential of women, a critical assessment of the roles and responsibilities that had traditionally been assigned to them. One example of this trend was a debate held by Yale students on the topic of "Whether women ought to be admitted into the magistracy and government of empires and republics." Another was the essay by Judith Sargent Stevens Murray.

Murray demonstrated a strong intellectual bent from early childhood. As a result, she was allowed to share lessons with her brother Winthrop, who was studying with a local minister in preparation for entering Harvard. Schooled only by the books her brother used for Harvard, Murray began writing to fill the days while her husband, a ship's captain, was at sea. She began publishing under the pseudonym "Constantia" in 1784. Her first published essay was entitled "Desultory Thoughts upon the Utility of Encouraging a Degree of Self-Complacency, Especially in Female Bosoms" and appeared in the *Gentlemen and Ladies Town and Country Magazine*. The essay argued, among other things, that instilling a healthy degree of self-respect in women would prevent them from rushing into marriage as a means of avoiding spinsterhood.

Her husband died in 1786 while she was still childless, but she married an itinerant preacher, John Murray, the founder of the Universalist Church in America, four years later. Despite the birth of two children in 1789 and 1791 she continued her writing career, producing essays, poems, and even plays. Murray read Mary Wollstonecraft's *A Vindication of the Rights of Women*, published in America in 1792, and although she did not agree with Wollstonecraft's radical politics, she found a kindred soul in the Englishwoman's plea for equal education for women.

It was during this period that she issued her famous challenge concerning women. "Suffer me to ask, in what" she wrote in *Massachusetts Magazine*, "the minds of females are so notoriously deficient?" She went on to inquire whether "the judgment of a male of two years old is more sage than that of a female's of the same age?" and observed "but from that period what partiality! How is the one exalted and the other depressed...The one is taught to aspire, and the other is early confined and limited." Without stating it directly, she posed the central issue of the debate about "nature versus nurture" that has been a cornerstone of the women's movement ever since.

Needing money, Murray, in 1798, published a three volume set of essays entitled *The Gleaner* under a subscription plan that included George Washington. Seven hundred and fifty people subscribed to the essays, which some critics compared to the essays of Noah Webster. When her husband suffered a stroke in 1809, Murray turned her attention to publishing his letters and sermons, and saw to the publication of his autobiography in 1816, a year after his death. Then, widowed, she moved from the vibrant cultural center of Boston where she had lived all her life to the small town of Natchez, Mississippi, to live with her daughter. Four years later, at the age of sixty-nine, she died.

1792: Mary Wollstonecraft's *A Vindication of the Rights of Women* Is First Published in America

(Equal Rights)

In 1792, Englishwoman Mary Wollstonecraft published her controversial book, *A Vindication of the Rights of Women*, in America.

America was not the only country affected by the revolutionary tides of the late eighteenth century. Across the Atlantic in both England and France radical thinkers were challenging the old orthodoxies in the name of equality and individual rights. The Englishwoman Mary Wollstonecraft was one of the first to apply these concepts to women, and her book was widely read when it was published in America.

The daughter of an abusive, alcoholic father, Mary Wollstonecraft spent her early adulthood as a governess. Unable to endure the restrictions of this position, she left to become a writer, and came to know many of the leading liberals of the age. Inspired by the French Revolution's "Declaration of the Rights of Man," and a Frenchwoman's draft of a comparable document for women, Wollstonecraft wrote a tract entitled *A Vindication of the Rights of Women*. Its revolutionary contribution was to apply to women the same standards that reformers were championing for men. She asked if men were to "contend for their freedom and to be allowed to judge for themselves respecting their own happiness, be it not inconsistent and unjust to subjugate women?" To counter the argument that women's subordination was natural and inevitable, Wollstonecraft insisted on the importance of education in shaping character. The inequities in the educational system made women weak and dependent, she argued, and it should be changed to make them strong and independent. Wollstonecraft rejected the literal language used in the Declaration of Independence and similar documents of the day, regarding the "rights of man." Though philosophers might argue that such language was merely figurative, Wollstonecraft argued that its presence denied women equal access or participation in democracy.

Wollstonecraft's life after publishing the essay was as unhappy as her life before. She fell desperately in love with a man who deserted her when she became pregnant. She later became lover to the radical philosopher Godwin, and married him when she became pregnant again. She then died in childbirth, but not before she saw the degeneration of the glorious French Revolution into bloody factionalism. Her daughter, Mary, grew up to marry the poet Percy Bysshe Shelley and write the classic *Frankenstein*, but she turned her back on her mother's activism.

Wollstonecraft's critics pointed to her unorthodox life as proof that her beliefs were dangerous. Nevertheless, Mary Wollstonecraft's work lived on, and lives on, serving as the wellspring for virtually all subsequent feminist writing. *Vindication* inspired the most influential American feminist of the next generation, Fanny Wright, and was read by progressive thinkers throughout the nineteenth century. Indeed, her basic points—the equal applicability to women of fundamental human rights and the essential malleability of human character to social conditioning—lie at the roots of feminist positions even today.

1818: Emma Willard Asks for Taxpayer Support to Educate Females

(Equal Rights, Education)

Educator Emma Willard, the first important woman educator in America, made an appeal to the New York state legislature in 1818, asking that taxes be allocated for the education of young women. This was followed in 1819 by a written proposal, *An Address to the Public:....Proposing a Plan for Improving Female Education*, in which Willard once again argued for taxpayer support in funding female education.

L ike many notable American women, Emma Willard, the founder of the Troy Female Seminary, might never have become an influential public figure in education had not economic necessity forced her to supplement her family's income. When her husband John was confronted with severe economic problems, Willard quit her job as a teacher at a small female academy and opened her own school, the Middlebury (Conn.) Female Seminary. While the plan originally was to realize more income, Willard very quickly became convinced that she could make an important difference in the lives of young women, as well as an important change in education "by the introduction of a grade of schools for women higher than any heretofore known." Willard, never one to let convention determine her life, had always believed that women were far more capable than society gave them credit for. When she was seventeen, she taught herself geometry—a subject that male educators believed to be beyond the capacity of women to grasp.

The major advantage enjoyed by schools for young men, in Willard's view, was the funding. In her *Plan for Improving Female Education,* Willard suggested that the state fund education for young women. Connecticut was not receptive to the idea, and several of her students suggested that Willard might reach more sympathetic ears in New York state. Committed now to her strategy, the Willards moved the school to Waterford, New York, and submitted to the governor *An Address to the Public: Particularly to the Members of the Legislature of New York, Proposing a Plan for Improving Female Education.* The Willards then lobbied the legislature, which was not receptive to the idea. The necessary funding failed to materialize. Publication of her proposal garnered her far-reaching support, including that of former president Thomas Jefferson. Finally, in 1821, Willard agreed to move her school to Troy, New York, when the Common Council offered to provide $4,000 to fund the school.

The Troy Female Seminary, opened in September 1821, offered a full course of subjects comparable in rigor to curriculum found in the best men's schools. Classes in mathematics and science were quickly added as well, something that no other women's schools at the time offered. The school very quickly became successful and self-supporting, and Willard, anxious to return to Connecticut to continue spreading her message, turned it over in 1838 to her son and daughter-in-law. Many of those who

Willard had educated at the Troy school were already helping to promote Willard's educational philosophy. Having trained a new generation of teachers, Willard's students were her best advocates. And even those who had not been taught directly by Willard knew what she had accomplished and followed her example in their own efforts to improve female education. When Mary Lyon, the founder of Mount Holyoke College, wanted to establish a school in Massachusetts, she sought out Willard's advice. Ultimately, Mount Holyoke College was established in South Hadley, Massachusetts, because the town of South Hadley was willing to make an investment in women's education.

1826: The American Society for the Promotion of Temperance Is Founded

(Social Reform)

In 1826, a strong grassroots movement to curtail the use of alcohol, supported primarily by women, resulted in the formation of the first anti-alcohol organization, the American Society for the Promotion of Temperance.

During the early nineteenth century, per capita consumption of alcoholic beverages reached alarming proportions, alarming at least to reformers who saw alcohol as the root of diverse evils.These reformers called for laws prohibiting the manufacture and sale of all alcohol.

Alcohol consumption was by no means a recent phenomenon in the still-new nation. Ale and rum were, after all, key commodities in colonial trade with England. Ale was considered an important part of the average diet, and not only for adults. Children, too, grew up drinking ale on a daily basis. Alcohol was regularly administered medicinally, especially since it was the medicine most often available. By 1810, annual alcohol consumption per adult was approximately seven gallons, a figure that rose to ten gallons by 1820. Such a high consumption of alcohol led to problems other than mere drunkenness on the part of the imbiber. At risk especially was the sanctity of the home. With the overwhelming majority of alcohol abusers being men, and with virtually no legal protection—either through divorce or prohibition—women and children often bore the brunt of excessive alcohol consumption. It seemed a natural consequence, then, for women to become the primary agents for change and reform.

In 1826, the American Society for the Promotion of Temperance was founded, and immediately attracted scores of volunteers, mostly women, motivated either by the practical desire to preserve family unity or by a moral desire to eliminate a socially unacceptable vice. The reasons women joined the crusade against alcohol, moreover, were often related to class. Middle-class men were usually less likely to resort to physical abuse than were working class men. So the moralists tended to come from the ranks of the middle class, while the practical reformers more often than not emerged from the working class. All had the same goal and in 1833, the first national temperance convention was held in Philadelphia. The agitation gradually produced results. In 1834, Congress passed a law forbidding the sale of alcoholic spirits to Indians. Two years later, several groups banded together into the American Temperance Union, and in 1851 they scored an even bigger success when Maine became the first state to enact prohibition. About a dozen states followed, and more enacted "local option" laws giving municipalities the option of prohibiting the sale of alcohol locally.

In addition to these legal victories, alcohol's opponents gradually changed Americans' personal mores. They published newspapers and pamphlets and even organized a "Cold Water Army" of children, complete with uniforms and marching songs. Revival-like "Washington Society" meetings were held in which former drunkards described their living hell, and inspired legions of listeners to swear off drinking. Although recent German and Irish immigrants resisted the moralizing of puritanical Yankees, the incessant pressure did persuade millions of drinkers to moderate or even stop, and drunkenness gradually changed from an unquestioned norm to a sign of weakness and even degeneracy. The early temperance activity formed the foundation for a later groundswell of support for the national legislation against alcohol that would occur in the latter part of the nineteenth century.

1829: Fanny Wright Becomes the First Female Public Speaker in America

(Equal Rights)

A remarkable figure already known for her writings and her reform efforts, Frances Wright became the first woman in America to take to the lectern to speak out on public affairs. Her speaking tour in 1829 attracted thousands of men and women who wanted to hear her thoughts on a variety of issues from equal education for girls to birth control.

Fanny Wright grew up as an orphaned Scottish heiress, but instead of settling into comfortable indolence, she threw herself into a life of learning and action that blazed the trails that women would follow over the next century. She began by studying Greek as a girl, and published solid scholarship as a teenager. In 1818 she traveled to America, accompanied only by her younger sister Camilla, to see a play produced that she had written.

Out of their travels came the first source of her fame, a book entitled *Views of Society and Manners in America*. Published in 1821, more than a decade before the similar travelogues of Alexis de Tocqueville (*Democracy in America*) and Frances Trollope (*Domestic Manners of the Americans*), it was widely read in Europe and established the young woman's reputation as a promising *savant*. Lafayette invited her and Camilla to join him on his 1824 tour in the United States, among the high points of which were meetings with former presidents Thomas Jefferson and James Madison.

The tour also introduced her to slavery, which began her lifelong commitment to abolitionism. In 1825 she penned *A Plan for the Gradual Abolition of Slavery in the United States without Danger of Loss to the Citizens of the South*. Wright's plan predated other abolitionists' similar suggestions. The next year she took more concrete action, buying 640 acres of wilderness near Memphis, which she called "Nashoba," in order to found a self-help colony in which slaves could learn the skills and attitudes they would need in order to be free. After leading the initial effort of clearing the site, Fanny became ill and had to return to Europe in 1827. While she was away a huge scandal blew up involving the Scottish foreman of the property and the women under his charge. The colony failed as a business, but Wright made good on her promise to the former slaves there, and in 1830, she helped the remaining thirty colonists to emigrate to Haiti, paying the expenses out of her own pocket. More importantly for Wright, the conduct of her foreman made Nashoba, and Wright herself, synonymous with scandal.

Changing direction, Wright embarked on a career of publishing and lecturing. She joined with Robert Owen in editing the *Free Enquirer* and began her lecturing with a tour in 1828–29. She decried the second class status of women, called for equal education for girls, equal property rights for women, fairer divorce laws, and accessible birth control.

Wright's public lectures, although delivered to packed audiences, nevertheless made her a target of criticism and scandalous gossip. Her demeanor on stage belied her groundbreaking role as the first female public lecturer. Tall and imposing, Wright was both eloquent and effective as a speaker. More often than not, she dressed in white and carried a copy of the Declaration of Independence, to which she frequently referred. Public speaking was still considered an unnatural activity for a woman to undertake. Ministers denounced her from their pulpits, and the press characterized her as a "female monster whom all decent people ought to avoid." In 1829, she founded the Workingmen's Association in New York City, and in the 1830s, she became a prominent supporter of Jacksonian democracy. She married in 1831 and bore two children, still managing to write a book calling for world government in 1838. Divorced in 1852, Wright died some months later after a fall on the ice.

1829: Anne Royall, Publisher and Writer, Is Convicted of Slander

(Cultural Life, Work)

In 1829, Anne Royall, often called the "Grandmother of Muckrakers," was convicted in a Maryland court for "publicly abusing" a group of Presbyterians who objected to her characterization of them.

While Anne Royall was not the first American woman to publish a newspaper, she was certainly one of the most outspoken and sharp-tongued. Royall wrote extensively about travel, recording her observations as she visited almost every important city in the nation in the 1820s. By then, she was well into her fifties, a widow whose husband left her penniless when he died in 1813, and whose stepchildren went to court to insure that she would receive no part of her late husband's estate. Under the circumstances, a lesser person might have been defeated. Royall, however, chose instead to find a way to support herself. Her travel books sold well, but her observations of life in America, often tinged with vitriol, made people uneasy. Between her travels throughout the country, Royall would return to Washington, partially to press for a pension due her late husband, who had been a Revolutionary War veteran, but partially because she had developed friendships over the years with influential government officials.

It was on a trip back to Washington that Royall was accused by her Presbyterian neighbors of slandering them. Royall was appalled at minister Ezra Stiles Ely, a fundamentalist with political ambitions, and his cronies, who she characterized as being "morticians…hoping to preside at the death of the Constitution." Ely had her charged with being a "common scold," a crime that only a woman could commit and that involved speaking one's mind. Defined in *Jacob's Law Dictionary*, scolds "in a legal sense, are troublesome and angry women." So, Anne Royall was convicted by a Maryland jury, where Ely brought the charges, but because of her advanced age, the proscribed punishment—a public dunking—was changed to a ten dollar fine. The fine was paid for her by Secretary of War John Eaton, a friend who had testified on her behalf.

If the Reverend Ely thought that her conviction would stop Royall, he could not have been more mistaken. Deterred not in the least by her brush with the law, Royall began publication of a weekly newspaper, called *Paul's Pry* in 1831. The newspaper reflected Royall's penchant for local Washington gossip, and was noted for its acerbic editorials. In both *Paul's Pry* and *The Huntress,* its successor, Royall continued to lampoon Washingtonians both in and out of government who, in her view, needed to be skewered. She became something of a fixture in the halls of Congress, a wiry and energetic figure, dressed in green, searching out both subjects and customers. Not at all afraid to go where others might hesitate, and not one to let a friendship prevent her from pursuing news, Royall allegedly came across John Quincy Adams swimming in the Potomac, and asked him to sit for an interview with her. When Adams declined, Royall sat down on top of his clothing, piled on the shore, and refused to leave until he agreed to the interview. In general, politicians

learned to steer clear of Royall, who had a knack for ferreting out graft and corruption. While she was not terribly concerned with making sure all her facts were accurate, her newspapers gained a reputation as being watchdogs of honesty and morality in government.

Royall continued as a Washington and publishing fixture until the age of eighty-five. She did not mellow with age, she did not lose her fiery indignation at things she considered wrong, and she did not stop championing people and causes that she felt were unfairly attacked. She campaigned for tolerance for Catholics when strong anti-Catholic feelings swept the country, and she defended Masons against attacks by anti-Masons. Indeed, in her usual fashion, she berated one anti-Mason so doggedly that he actually threw her down a flight of stairs, causing her to break a leg. If her detractors and enemies were many, Royall also managed to accumulate admirers, however reluctant, who were impressed with her sincerity, tenacity, and refusal to avoid printing stories that she believed the public had a right to know. Her refusal to succumb to pressure established Royall as one of the earliest defenders of First Amendment rights.

1830: The First Book Advocating Birth Control Is Published in the United States

(Family Life)

In 1830, Robert Dale Owen published *Moral Physiology*, the first birth control essay published in America, in which he advocated fewer children and better education. Owen also argued that women had the right to decide whether or not they wished to bear children.

In 1800, there were 7 children per woman in the United States. In 1900 there were only 3.5, and by 1940 just slightly over 2. This demographic trend played a vital role in women's history, for it represents the gradual liberation of women from the tyranny of nature, the certainty that unless they practiced sexual abstinence, contraception, or abortion, they would spend most of their middle years pregnant, nursing, and/or rearing children. Abstinence (and natural infertility) have freed some women from this burden throughout history, but the mass emancipation of the last century depended in large measure on the spread of knowledge about how to avoid pregnancy.

In 1830, Robert Owen published his book entitled *Moral Physiology*, offering rudimentary birth control advice. Owen's book was not the first such work ever written, but it was the first to be published in America, and it was followed shortly by several others that gradually changed the mores of American couples and the character of American families. Just two years later, Charles Knowlton advocated even more effective contraceptives in his *Fruits of Philosophy*, and in 1839, William Greenfield translated Jean Du Bois' *Marriage Physiologically Discussed* from the French, which covered five different methods of contraception, including condoms and chemically treated sponges. More books explaining these and other methods followed in the 1850s, so by the Civil War information on contraception and family planning was available widely.

The effects of this knowledge were profound. Behind the sheer statistics of children per woman lies a fundamental shift in the condition of women and the nature of the family. As the size of families shrank, the demands on women were correspondingly diminished. A woman who bore one child per year from the age of twenty until her early thirties could do little with her life beyond being a mother (assuming, of course, that she survived all those childbirths, a large assumption in itself). A woman who delayed pregnancy for several years after marriage had a chance to gain experience and stature in an adult role other than mother, and if she limited her reproduction to just one to three children, theoretically she would have the opportunity to return to that other adult role or to establish another as the children grew to independence.

Contraception did not only change the situation of women, however. It also radically altered the experience and status of children. As family size dropped, the value of the children who were produced increased. Couples could delay parenthood until they felt ready, and once they chose it they could focus more of their affection, energy, and material resources on each individual child. Contraception thus led to the modern attitudes toward children, as well as the modern status of women.

1832: Fanny Kemble, the Brilliant English Actress, Makes Her American Debut in New York

(Entertainment)

On September 18, 1832, Fanny Kemble, a world-famous English actress, made her American debut at the Park Theatre in New York City in the role of the tempestuous Bianca, in a production of *Fazio*, for which she won accolades from the critics.

Fanny Kemble came from an illustrious acting family in England. Her father was part owner of Covent Garden Theatre; her deceased uncle, John Kemble, was known as "Glorious John," in his heyday as an actor; and her aunt, Sarah Siddons, known as the "tragic Muse," had already gained renown as the greatest actress the world had ever seen, according to more than one critic. A reversal of fortune brought Kemble's father face-to-face with the prospect of selling Covent Garden in 1829. In a last ditch effort, he staged a one-night family performance of *Romeo and Juliet,* with Fanny as Juliet. The theatre was saved for the moment, and the young actress became a literal overnight sensation, so moving was her performance. Nevertheless, within another three years, the family lost Covent Garden and decided to make an American tour.

Fanny's American debut took place in New York on September 18, 1832. Critics and audiences loved her. Indeed, she was the main reason for the tour's dramatic impact. The troupe drew crowds of Americans who had never had the slightest desire to go to the theatre before. She united youth, passion, intelligence, and charm, and she became the standard by which actresses would be measured for decades to come. Critics could point to flaws in her performances, but the audiences continued to love her, and she inspired the first famous native born actress, Cora Ogden. She introduced Shakespeare to the masses, and to them she remained the one true Juliet.

Her next move seemed a page out of a contemporary romance: she turned her back on the adulation and fame to marry a southern gentleman, Pierce Butler. The marriage was much less than Kemble hoped for. For one thing, Butler's family treated her with disdain because of her profession, holding the narrow view that acting placed her just slightly above the status of a prostitute. Their attitude was doubly shocking because the Kembles had always been treated like royalty in their native England. Kemble's vain hope for happiness turned sour when her husband revealed himself to be a self-centered philanderer. Moreover, Kemble's intimate view of slavery, acquired during the time they spent at Butler's plantation in Georgia, quickly convinced her of the immorality of the system.

Kemble and Butler spent long periods apart, especially after Fanny discovered his infidelity, even though Butler insisted that their two daughters had to remain in Georgia. Kemble returned to the stage for a brief time, and then considered returning to her husband and daughters. Before that could be accomplished, Butler filed for a divorce, and Kemble soon found herself at the center of a squalid divorce in which she was forced to endure humiliation and the loss of all property in order to keep the right just to see her own children. If her bitter experience had any redeeming feature, it was that her fame drew a glaring light on the injustice of a system that gave all rights in such cases to the husband.

Besides acting, Kemble turned to writing, with what would prove to have consequential results. Her views on slavery kept her out of the South, but they also caused her to publish an influential volume entitled *Journal of a Resident on a Georgia Plantation* in 1863. *Journal* was Kemble's indictment of slavery and it caused an immediate sensation both in America and in Europe. It also caused English sympathizers to rethink their feelings for the Confederacy, and ultimately to withhold support for the South.

In 1867, Kemble moved to a small farm in Pennsylvania, near her daughter, Sally Wister. Winner of the highest rewards her profession had to offer, Fanny Kemble inspired not just a generation of American actresses, but all women who aspired to greatness in whatever field in which they cultivated their talents.

1833: Oberlin Is Founded as America's First Coeducational College

(Education)

In 1833, a new college in Oberlin, Ohio, was chartered as the first institution of higher learning to admit not only men *and* women, but also both blacks and whites as students.

Oberlin was started in response to the suppression of abolitionist activity at the Lane Theology Seminary in Cincinnati. Following the lead of

Theodore Weld, most of the students withdrew and moved to Oberlin, Ohio, where Oberlin College had been chartered as the first college that would admit women and blacks, as well as white males. The college played an important role as a liberal center throughout the nineteenth century, and continues to offer a progressive educational environment even today.

The position of women in the college was not, however, fully equal. Most remained in the "Female Department" where they followed the "Ladies Course" designed to prepare them for educated motherhood. The first female to finish the "Full Course" graduated in 1841, and by 1857, 279 of the 299 women who had attended the college had opted for the "Ladies" literary program. Nevertheless, among the prominent early female graduates of the college were the theologian Antoinette Brown Blackwell, the physician Emeline Horton Cleveland, the feminist Lucy Stone, and Anna Julia Cooper.

The last named graduate was doubly special because she was not only a female graduate, but was a black female graduate. Blacks made up about 5 percent of the student body, and black women a minority of that. Of the 140 who attended between 1835 and 1865, 83 took a preparatory program, 56 opted for the literary course, and only one, Mary Jane Patterson, earned a full bachelor's degree.

Almost all of the black women came from wealthy families of freemen. Interestingly, as many came from the South as from the North. Among their white classmates the regional distribution was more heavily weighted toward the North, although a number were the daughters of slaveowners. Despite the presence of these plantation daughters, the overall level of wealth among the whites was somewhat higher than among the blacks, reflecting the greater difficulties confronting blacks attempting to maintain a middle- or upper-class existence.

In 1846, Oberlin invited the feminist lecturer Abby Kelly Foster to speak, beginning a long tradition of support for feminist causes. Perhaps its most important contribution, though, was simply admitting women. When it opened its doors, only one institution in the world offered women a college degree, in Brazil. Following its lead, in 1852 Antioch College welcomed women as students, and went it one better by accepting them as faculty as well. In Iowa, first Grinnell and later the state university followed in its footsteps. By proving that women could not only survive but thrive in the halls of learning, Oberlin helped open the doors to women's higher education.

1833: Prudence Crandall Opens a School for African-American Girls

(Education, Social Reform)

Prudence Crandall, a young Quaker from Canterbury, Connecticut, opened the Canterbury Female Boarding School for "young ladies and little misses of color," in April 1833.

Prudence Crandall never intended to become a champion of civil rights for young African-American girls and women seeking to acquire a teacher's education. The Canterbury Female Boarding School, opened by her originally in 1831, was nothing more controversial than a school for middle-class girls from well-to-do families in the Connecticut area. She enjoyed the support of the townspeople, who considered themselves liberal advocates of equal education for both sexes. All of that changed when Sarah Harris, the seventeen-year-old daughter of a respectable local African-American farmer applied for admission to the school. Harris had already finished her primary education and wanted nothing more than to become a teacher and teach other African-American children.

Reaction was swift and unambiguous. Parents threatened to immediately withdraw their daughters from the school if Harris was allowed to remain. The school's financial supporters were also quick to raise objections. A lesser person might have folded under the pressure, particularly since she was economically dependent on a thriving school, but Crandall did not. Although she was a Quaker, and supported abolitionism in a general sort of way, she had never really been committed to the cause. Faced with the racism of her "liberal" neighbors, however, Crandall found her own thoughts and beliefs on the subject quickly crystallizing. She had had an opportunity to read a copy of William Lloyd Garrison's pro-abolition newspaper, the *Liberator*, and wrote to him, stating her intention of doing something worthwhile for African Americans, if possible. She also sought out well-to-do African-American families from Connecticut, New York, and

Massachusetts, soliciting them to support her cause. Garrison and others encouraged her in her plan to close the original school and reopen it as a school for, as she characterized them, "young ladies and little misses of color." Garrison assured Crandall he would find appropriate students for her.

In April 1833, the new Canterbury School opened as a teacher-training school for African-American girls. The now-furious citizens of Canterbury mobilized to close it down as quickly as possible. Merchants refused to sell supplies to Crandall, threatened the students with prosecution as paupers and vagrants, and refused to allow them to attend the Congregational church. When that didn't work, townspeople secured passage of a state "black law," which forbade the establishment of any school that taught African American students from out of state, and that also prohibited teaching any student not a resident of a town in the state. Crandall was arrested and taken to the local jail.

Crandall's abolitionist supporters were not silent during this controversy. Almost overnight, Crandall and her Canterbury School had become a *cause célèbre* throughout the country. William Lloyd Garrison publicized the case in the pages of the *Liberator*, and abolitionist Arthur Tappan supplied

money for publicity and for Crandall's legal defense. Since the Garrison abolitionists had Crandall's confidence, she did not object when they suggested she spend a night in jail in the very cell that had been previously occupied by a murderer. Such publicity was too good for the cause not to exploit.

Crandall went through two trials, the first of which ended in a hung jury. In the second trial, she was convicted. A higher court overturned the conviction, but the reprieve for the school was short-lived. The town turned quite vicious, poisoning the well water at the school, breaking windows, and terrorizing Crandall and her students. In September 1834, Crandall gave up the fight, closed her school, and moved out of state with her husband. She spent the remainder of her life working for the causes of abolition and women's rights She never returned to Connecticut, but four years before her death, in 1890, the state legislature voted to award her a small pension as an apology for her suffering. Although Crandall's ordeal lasted less than two years, it served to help bring abolition to the forefront of America's consciousness. The Crandall case was the first one in which national attention was drawn to the still emerging abolitionist cause.

1833: The Female Anti-Slavery Society of Philadelphia Is Founded

(Social Reform)

Following the national convention of the American Anti-Slavery Society (AASS), an all-male organization, Lucretia Mott organized the Philadelphia Female Anti-Slavery Society in 1833.

For abolitionism, 1833 was a watershed year. In England, the British Anti-Slavery Society won a long campaign when Parliament outlawed slavery in the British Empire. Its success inspired American abolitionists to found the American Anti-Slavery Society in Philadelphia in 1833. That same year, popular author Lydia Maria Francis Child published *An Appeal in Favor of that Class of Americans Called Africans*. And one year earlier, just after William Lloyd Garrison formed the New England Anti-Slavery Society, a group of African-American women formed the Female Anti-Slavery Society, followed a short time later by Maria Weston Chapman's more aristocratic Boston Female Anti-Slavery Society. It was in this climate of ferment that reform-minded women in Philadelphia formed their own organization to advance the cause of abolitionism.

Since the American Anti-Slavery Society was restricted to males, female abolitionists, notably Lucretia Mott, met after the convention to form the Female Anti-Slavery Society. Drawing on the themes and methods of evangelical religion, the women's society undertook a variety of activities to mobilize support against the slave system. It helped to gather hundreds of thousands of signatures on petitions calling upon Congress to abolish slavery, immediately and unconditionally, in the District of Columbia, where it had direct jurisdiction. The original society quickly spawned numerous branches. By 1837, when there were 1,006 anti-slavery groups, over half of their 150,000 total membership were women. And in that same year women gathered in New York for their first national antislavery convention.

This early abolitionist movement

by women had a number of important impacts. First and foremost, of course, was its contribution to abolition. Women played a critical role in the mobilization of public opinion in the 1830s that was to make slavery, or rather the abolition of slavery, the foremost public issue in the 1840s and 1850s. But the involvement of women in the abolitionist movement had other effects beyond that immediate objective. Abolitionism was the first overtly political movement in which American women participated, and their experiences in it formed an enduring legacy. On a personal level, many of the women who would become leaders of the women's movement met at abolitionist functions. In fact, the seminal women's rights convention at Seneca Falls in 1848 grew out of connections that were made at the international antislavery convention held in London in 1840.

Perhaps most importantly, on an institutional level, female abolitionists gained experience that they and other women would later draw on in mobilizing for other causes, including, of course, their own rights. The antislavery societies were where many women learned the basic procedures of political mobilization: drawing up a constitution and bylaws, electing officers, speaking before groups, taking votes, organizing committees, and planning collective actions. Similarly, in speaking out against slavery, they learned to speak out, period. The lesson was not forgotten when they confronted other injustices and their own grievances. Finally, their outrage against slavery made them conscious of other outrages—of the brutality of war, the debilitation of poverty, and the injustice of their own position in society. In all these ways, women's fight for the rights of African Americans gave birth to their fight for rights of their own.

1833: The First National Temperance Convention Is Held

(Social Reform)

In 1833, the national campaign against alcohol began when advocates of temperance met in Philadelphia to design a plan of action.

Delegates from all over the country attended the first national temperance convention in 1833. They included not just preachers and moral reformers but also doctors and businessmen. The former focused on drunkenness as the source of immorality, while the latter regarded drink as a practical problem, a threat to individual health, occupational safety, and public order. Opposed to all drinking, the more radical of them called for laws prohibiting the manufacture and sale of all alcohol.

The agitation gradually produced results. In 1834, Congress passed a law forbidding the sale of alcoholic spirits to Indians. Two years later, several groups banded together into the American Temperance Union, and in 1851 they scored an even bigger success when Maine became the first state to enact prohibition. About a dozen states followed, and more enacted "local option" laws giving municipalities the option of prohibiting the sale of alcohol locally.

In addition to these legal victories, alcohol's opponents gradually changed Americans' personal mores. They published newspapers and pamphlets and even organized a "Cold Water Army" of children, complete with uniforms and marching songs. Revival-like "Washington Society" meetings were held in which former drunkards described their living hell, and inspired legions of listeners to swear off drinking. Although recent German and Irish immigrants resisted the moralizing of puritanical Yankees, the incessant pressure did persuade millions of drinkers to moderate or even stop, and drunkenness gradually changed from an unquestioned norm to a sign of weakness and even degeneracy.

The relationship between women and temperance may not be obvious to the modern reader, but at the time it seemed completely natural. On the practical level, drunkenness, or at least the kind of public drunkenness that aroused the reformers' ire, was unquestionably a problem of men, and just as surely women were disproportionately the object of the resulting array of alcoholic abuse and neglect. On the moral level, women were assumed to be the more moral sex, and they took this role seriously. As they emerged into public life over the course of the nineteenth century, women played an increasingly prominent role in the temperance movement, and so it was no coincidence that the Eighteenth Amendment enacting prohibition was passed in 1918, just one year before the Nineteenth Amendment enfranchising women.

1833: Lydia Maria Child Publishes the First Antislavery Book in the United States

(Social Reform)

Successful author Lydia Maria Child published an antislavery book in 1833, entitled *Appeal in Favor of That Class of Americans Called Africans*. In her book, Child described the evils of slavery and called for racial equality.

When Lydia Maria Child published her antislavery book in 1833, she was subjected to ostracism, ridicule, and a loss of income. Until she became involved in the abolitionist movement, Child's writings had all been popular, superficial, and generally undemanding. She began her writing career in 1824, with the publication of *Hobomok*, a fictional account of New England history centering on the relationship between an Indian and a white woman. Its success earned her access to the collection at the prestigious Boston Athenaeum library. Other books followed, including *The Rebels, or Boston before the Revolution* (1825); *The Frugal Housewife* (1829), an advice-to-housewives book; *The Mother's Book;* and *The Little Girl's Own Book* (1831). She also published the first children's magazine in America, a bimonthly entitled *Juvenile Miscellany.* The income from her writing was enough to support both her and her husband, who devoted his time to various reform causes.

Child had not been particularly interested in reform until her husband persuaded her to attend an abolitionist meeting where William Lloyd Garrison was the main speaker. Garrison, she said later, "got hold of the strings of my conscience." After that, Child devoted most of her energies to the abolition cause. When *Appeal…*was published, it created enormous controversy, denouncing, as it did, laws against miscegenation and the unequal treatment accorded to African Americans. It was Child's book that drew people like William Ellery Channing, Wendall Phillips, and Charles Sumner to the abolitionist movement. But while some applauded and were moved by her treatise, most Bostonians thought that Child had gone beyond the bounds of acceptable opinion. She was no longer welcome in society circles, the Athenaeum revoked her privileges, and *Juvenile Miscellany* suddenly failed to sell.

Despite the treatment accorded her by so-called proper Bostonians, Child continued both to work for abolition and to write on a variety of issues, both serious and more lighthearted. Her friendship with Garrison led to her appointment to the executive committee of the American Anti-Slavery Society in 1840, and for three years she edited the *National Anti-Slavery Standard.* But she also returned to less political writing, and gradually her books began to find renewed acceptance with the reading public.

Lydia Maria Child lived to the age of seventy-eight, and continued writing almost up to day she died. She was one of America's premier writers. Of all the books, essays, and pamphlets she wrote, those that maintained historical significance were her antislavery book and several subsequent pamphlets on such topics as the Fugitive Slave Law.

1834: Lowell Mill Girls Go on Strike

(Work)

On February 20, 1834, women workers from the Lowell Mills went on strike to protest proposed wage cuts of up to 15 percent.

The Lowell Mills, in Lowell, Massachusetts, were the first mills that hired women in large numbers. Beginning in the early 1830s, the Lowell Mills had begun recruiting young women from rural New England farms to work in the mills. Lowell succeeded in attracting the farm girls because they provided a protected environment, a deal maker for parents who would otherwise never allow their unmarried daughters to live away from home. Lowell girls slept in supervised boarding houses, ate family-style meals together in a common cafeteria, observed strict dress codes, were provided with educational and recreational programs including a library and lecture series within the mill complex, and in all ways were expected to behave with the same decorum that they would if they were at home. Moreover, they were paid their wages in cash and had the services of a bank to encourage saving. The Lowell girls, as a consequence, developed a remarkable esprit de corps that made them excellent workers.

That same esprit de corps, however, worked against the mill owners when the Lowell mill system began to unravel because of increased competition. In order to meet the competition and retain their profit margins, mill owners began cutting wages and increasing production expectations. The first strike took place on February 20, 1834, when the company announced intended wage cuts of up to 15 percent in certain departments. Workers from the affected departments held several meetings, and decided to go on strike and make a run on the company bank as well. The strike organizer was promptly fired by the mill agent, but when she left she took with her eight hundred coworkers, leading them in a procession around the town. The strikers issued what they called the "Lowell Proclamation," which stated that they would not return to work until wages were restored.

The first Lowell strike did not succeed in the sense that wages were not restored. On the other hand, the strikers obviously had no intention of remaining off the job for more than a few hours, since they walked out on Saturday and returned to work first thing Monday morning. The wage cuts took place as scheduled about three weeks later, with no further protest. In another sense, however, the Lowell strike should have been instructive for both mill owners and labor organizers. The former because a few years later, in 1836, the Lowell girls again went on strike, and again met with no real success. But in 1846 they struck again and in that strike, they did succeed in achieving their somewhat limited goals. Each time they struck, the workers were more and more sophisticated about what they were doing and what they wanted. Eventually, they were in the forefront of women who fought for a ten-hour work day, which was finally secured in 1874. Labor leaders should have found Lowell more instructive because the Lowell women proved time and again that women could be as organized and persistent in achieving labor reforms as any group of male workers.

1834: The American Female Moral Reform Society Is Founded

(Social Reform)

In May 1834, a small group of women meeting in the Third Presbyterian Church in New York founded one of the earliest and most ambitious of the women's reform movements: the New York (later American) Female Moral Reform Society.

The goal of the women who founded the American Female Moral Reform Society was as simple as it was ambitious: to rid society of prostitution, promiscuity, and all other forms of male-inspired licentiousness. Women throughout New York and New England heard their call, and within ten short years the organization had over four hundred chapters.

While the ultimate objective of the society was the thoroughgoing reform of America's sexual mores, its particular focus was on prostitution. To some extent, the upright matrons saw the prostitutes as the problem, mixing middle-class scorn of the "working girls" with attempts to provide support and haven in order to help them regain the path of righteousness. But on the whole they looked on the prostitutes as symptoms rather than causes of the problem, as victims rather than seducers of men. It was the task of American women, led by the women of the society, to protect America's homes and families from the "predatory nature of the American male," who was "bold," "reckless," and "drenched in sin."

The society undertook a range of activities to promote its goals. Beyond organizing the auxiliary chapters, the society published a newspaper entitled the *Advocate,* which lasted into the 1850s and both facilitated communications among the group's members and spread its message to the larger society beyond. The society also sought to reform prostitutes by creating a "House of Reception" where they could go to be rehabilitated. But their most energetic efforts went into direct action to discourage the patrons of sin. Members took up prominent positions in front of brothels, and wrote down the names of men who ventured in. The *Advocate* published their names, along with those submitted by readers, and others supplied by members who actually infiltrated the dens of iniquity by taking employment as domestics.

The impact of the society was mixed. It certainly did not succeed in what it saw as its primary mission, the elimination of prostitution. Ironically, though, it seems to have contributed more to a shift in the mores of mainstream society, for illegitimacy rates fell significantly during the time it was active. And the society certainly contributed to, as well as reflected, the cultural trend that portrayed women as the morally superior sex, as the natural guardians of the virtues and values necessary for the health and prosperity of the home and family. While the women of the society vehemently rejected explicitly feminist views, they did oppose "the tyranny exercised in the home department, where lordly man…rules his trembling subjects with a rod of iron, conscious of entire impunity and exalting in his fancied superiority." Thus, their moralistic understanding of men and women led them in the direction of social, and ultimately political, emancipation, just as their experience in organization and agitation for the benefit of others gave them tools that later women would use to gain improvements for their own situations.

1837: Mount Holyoke Seminary, the First Women's College, Is Founded by Mary Lyon

(Education, Equal Rights, Cultural Life)

Educator Mary Lyon, seeking to establish an endowed institution of higher learning for women, raised funds and obtained a charter to open Mount Holyoke Female Seminary in 1836. The following year, the first class of eighty students arrived at the newly opened campus in South Hadley, Massachusetts.

In the summer of 1833, Mary Lyon traveled throughout the northeast and as far as Detroit, visiting schools and academies for young girls, as well as touching base with some notable educators, including Emma Willard. A long-time believer in higher education for women, Lyon came back to her Buckland, Massachusetts, home convinced that the time was right to proceed. Unlike many of the academies established for young women in the 1820s and 1830s, Lyon was determined that her school would maintain high academic standards. Many of the existing female academies were criticized because they offered a curriculum lacking real substance. Lyon also sought to establish an endowed institution that would continue to operate independent of any one person.

From her teaching position at Ipswich Academy in Ipswich, Massachusetts, Lyon began the task of raising money for her school. Her goal was to prepare young women for the larger social roles that would be demanded of them. She refused to be deterred by the multitude of arguments against educating women that she heard over and over. Education was wasted on women, her critics believed. And conversely, educated women would abandon the home and domestic life. These and other protests failed to move the determined Lyon. Three Massachusetts communities vied to have the school built in their town: South Deerfield, Sunderland, and South Hadley. Her choice of South

Hadley as the site of her school was made primarily because the town offered $8,000 in support of the project. In 1836 Lyon obtained a charter and appointed a committee of advisors. A four-story, red brick, Georgian edifice that served as both academic building and residence, was ready the following year when the first class of eighty students arrived in South Hadley.

Mount Holyoke Female Seminary was the first institution of higher learning to offer a complete education for young women. The curriculum offered was similar to those found at men's colleges, with courses ranging from Greek and Latin to human anatomy. The few full-time teachers were supplemented with professors from nearby schools and colleges who agreed to lecture at the seminary. Over time, the seminary evolved into a four-year institution. In addition to the standard academic courses, Mount Holyoke women were also expected to contribute to the upkeep of the school, partially as preparation for fu-

ture domesticity and partly to help defer the cost of hiring help to perform such tasks. Finally, and in Lyon's view most importantly, Mount Holyoke placed significant emphasis on piety. The 1839 catalogue noted that a Mount Holyoke graduate was expected to be "a handmaid to the Gospel, and an efficient auxiliary in the great task of renovating the world."

Mary Lyon's expectations seemed borne out in succeeding decades as Mount Holyoke trained and supported hundreds of missionaries and teachers. Although Mount Holyoke did not become a full-fledged college until 1888, its reputation was well-established long before that. Inspired by Mary Lyon's success, several other women's colleges were founded, including Barnard College, Radcliffe, Vassar, Smith, Wellesley, and Bryn Mawr. Collectively they became known as the Seven Sisters and were considered female counterparts to the male Ivy League colleges.

1837: Angelina and Sarah Grimké Lecture Mixed-Sex Audiences on Abolitionism

(Equal Rights, Social Reform)

Angelina and Sarah Grimké, daughters of a wealthy South Carolina plantation family, began lecturing to audiences of men and women on the subject of abolitionism in 1837. Their first such lectures caused a sensation, since it was not the custom for women to address mixed audiences.

The Grimké sisters of Charleston, South Carolina, led a life so far removed from their genteel southern background of wealth and tradition that after they left the South in 1829, neither one could ever return, even for a visit. Sarah, the older of the two, and her sister Angelina, thirteen years her junior, grew up despising their family's connection to slavery. The Grimkés were plantation owners, and the sisters and their twelve siblings grew up witnessing on a daily basis the cruelty of slavery. When Sarah taught Sunday school in Charleston, she used the occasion to teach her young charges that preventing slaves from learning to read and write was wrong. She traveled north for the first time in 1819, in order to accompany her father to

Philadelphia where he sought medical help for an illness. Sarah was encouraged to find other white people who agreed with her feelings about slavery, and was especially impressed with the Quakers she met. Two years later, after her father died, Sarah moved permanently to Philadelphia, took up Quakerism, and hoped to become a Quaker minister. Angelina, who had an equally dim view of the slave system, as her diary later revealed, joined Sarah in 1829. Both sisters were avid readers of William Lloyd Garrison's abolitionist newspaper, the *Liberator*. In 1835, a letter that Angelina wrote to Garrison was printed in the *Liberator*. Thereafter, the sisters' names were associated with the abolitionist movement.

The Grimkés were unique among abolitionists. They could personally testify about the cruelty of slavery, something that no other abolitionist could do since no southern white males had joined the abolitionist movement. Thus, despite the fact that they were women, the Grimkés held a special place in the movement and they were encouraged to speak out on behalf of abolitionism. Angelina left Philadelphia to work with the American Anti-Slavery Society in New York. Sarah, who still harbored some hopes of becoming a Quaker minister despite earlier rejection because of her poor performance as a preacher, remained in Philadelphia a little longer. When, in 1836, she attempted to address a Quaker gathering on abolitionism, she was prohibited. The pacifist Quakers believed that abolitionism was too incendiary a topic for their comfort. Sarah left Philadelphia and joined Angelina in New York.

The Grimkés became well-known because of several pamphlets they wrote on slavery. In 1836, a pamphlet entitled *An Appeal to Christian Women of the South* was published by the American Anti-Slavery Society. Although it was intended to be read by southern women, the pamphlet was actually more well-known in the North. Southern postmasters took the liberty of destroying copies of the pamphlet that made their way into the postal system. Angelina was warned that she was no longer welcome in the South.

Initially, the Grimkés spoke to small groups of women in private homes. Gradually, as their fame as speakers spread, the small audiences grew to overflowing, and finally led to public lectures attended by both men and women. It was the latter that caused an outpouring of criticism from both public and private sources. In July 1837, the ministerial association of Massachusetts issued a pastoral letter accusing the Grimkés of behavior unbecoming to women. Angelina realized that this criticism placed them in the middle of a conflict that was not about abolition, but rather about their rights as "moral, intelligent, and responsible" women. While some abolitionists hoped that the Grimkés would not let what they considered a secondary issue deter them from speaking, the Grimkés believed they had little choice but to assert their rights as women. Garrison encouraged them to face the issue head on. Angelina wrote a series of letters to the *Liberator* in which she defended her right to speak out, and declared that women ought to have a say in all laws that affected them. Sarah wrote a pamphlet entitled

Letters on the Equality of the Sexes and the Condition of Woman. Angelina also became the first woman to testify before a committee of the Massachusetts legislature.

In May 1838, Angelina Grimké and Theodore Weld, a noted abolitionist minister, were married in Philadelphia. Several African-American guests of the wedding party attended the ceremony. Philadelphians were outraged over the integrated ceremony. Two days later, Angelina Weld delivered a passionate abolitionist speech to an overflow crowd at a Philadelphia anti-slavery convention. An angry crowd worked itself up outside, while Angelina spoke inside. Riotous crowds later burned the building down to the ground, and for good measure set fire to the Shelter for Colored Orphans. The response disheartened the Grimké sisters and their public speaking careers were markedly diminished after that. Both continued to write about and speak on behalf of abolition and women's rights, but neither attracted—nor wished to attract—the audiences they had in their early years of public speaking. The births of Angelina's three children were not easy on her, and her good health never returned. Sarah Grimké and Theodore Weld published a remarkable book entitled *American Slavery as It Is: Testimony of a Thousand Witnesses* in 1838. The volume was a collection of newspaper articles and editorials published in the South that provided poignant, if unwitting, testimony about slavery. But by 1839, the Welds and Sarah Grimké had moved to a rural farm and thereafter remained largely out of the public eye. In their eighties, the Grimké sisters were still willing to demonstrate their commitment to their causes, however. They were among a group of women who tested the Fifteenth Amendment by attempting to vote in the election of 1870.

1839: Margaret Fuller Initiates "Conversations" with Prominent Boston Women

(Cultural Life, Equal Rights)

Margaret Fuller, who by many accounts possessed the nineteenth century's most brilliant mind, began holding seminars, referred to as "conversations," on topics so fascinating that Boston's most illustrious women paid to attend the weekly gatherings. The seminars, which quickly became famous for their intellectual exchanges, attracted Boston luminaries including Lydia Maria Child, Sophia Peabody, Mrs. Ralph Waldo Emerson, Mrs. Nathaniel Hawthorne, and Mrs. Horace Mann. In this manner, Fuller supported herself for several years.

Margaret Fuller, for a brief moment in time, was at the center of the philosophical movement created and encouraged by nineteenth-century New England's leading intellectuals. For Fuller, the idea of Transcendentalism especially fit in with her long-held belief that women were as much intellectual creatures as men, and therefore ought not to be resigned automatically to a life of domesticity. The Transcendentalists proposed to cultivate the intuitive moral and intellectual powers of the human mind, a philosophy that required honest intellectual discourse. Conversation was the milieu of the Transcendentalists.

Fuller's own background was as exceptional as the life she led as an adult. At an age when most children were learning the alphabet, Fuller was reading Greek and Latin, having been educated by her father in the classics. When her father died in 1835, Fuller became head of the family. For the next three years, she taught school in Cambridge and in Providence, Rhode Island, translated and published Johann Eckermann's *Conversations with Goethe*, and wrote her first important piece of criticism, published two years later in the first issue of the *Dial*. More than anyone else, Fuller knew that she was wasting her abilities teaching young women, as noble a profession as that might be for others, and in 1838 she returned to Boston, seeking to expand her opportunities. Shortly thereafter, she began her weekly conversations.

Fuller was probably the first woman to ignore the bans on women engaging in paid public speaking. In addition to encouraging her female audience to cultivate their own growth and freedom, Fuller's conversations covered a broad range of topics, including mythology, art, ethics, education, health, science, and the lives and minds of great men. By 1841, Fuller's seminars had attracted so much attention that she began to invite men as well as women. Most of the Transcendentalist community came to Fuller's parlor at one time or another. But with so many individualists attempting to capture the audience, the conversations lost their focus, and the experiment ended rather abruptly.

In 1840, Fuller teamed up with Ralph Waldo Emerson in publishing a quarterly journal of Transcendentalism, called the *Dial.* Fuller edited the quarterly for two years. In that time, the *Dial* became one of the most respected intellectual journals of its day. Fuller herself was a frequent contributor, and set a standard for deliberative,

careful criticism, perhaps her most valuable contribution to American literature. In 1843, Fuller wrote an article for the *Dial* entitled "The Great Lawsuit. Man *versus* Men, Woman *versus* Women," which she later expanded and published in book form in 1845, under the title *Woman in the Nineteenth Century.* It immediately became a classic of nineteenth-century feminism, and influenced directly the Seneca Falls women's rights convention in 1848. By then, Fuller had already left America for Europe, where she traveled extensively, meeting and interviewing the great literary and artistic minds of the Continent. She met William Wordsworth, the Carlyles, Joanna Baillie, and the Italian expatriate, Giuseppe Mazzini. She interviewed George Sand, spoke with Frédéric Chopin, Pierre-Jean de Béranger, and Lamennais, and became close friends with Robert and Elizabeth Barrett Browning. As she traveled throughout Europe, Fuller became more and more taken with political ferment. In Italy, Giovanni Angelo, Marchese d'Ossoli, ten years younger than Fuller, brought her more fully into the Italian revolution. Fuller married Ossoli in 1849, shortly before the birth of their son. During this period, she corresponded regularly for the *New York Tribune,* reporting on events in Europe. She wrote to both family and friends, assuring them all that she was happier than she had ever been. Political events forced the Ossolis to leave Rome, and for a time they settled in Florence, where Fuller began working on what she believed would be her most ambitious project to date—an account of the revolution. It soon became clear that she would have difficulty publishing her book in Italy, and that, along with police surveillance, persuaded Fuller that they should leave for America. Fuller was ambivalent about returning, however, because, as she told several friends, she had inexplicable bad feelings about leaving Italy. Her foreboding

was borne out. As their ship approached New York harbor, it ran aground and sank off of Fire Island, a few hundred feet from the shore. All three drowned.

Fuller was too young and too early into her life work to know how far she might have gone, had she lived out a full lifetime. Her book on women's rights, her interviews with notable intellectuals of the day, and her literary criticism all suggest that she was only beginning to fulfill her promise. Her advice to other women was the example she set for herself: "Very early," she had written once, "I knew that the only object in life was to grow."

1840: The Abolitionist Movement Divides over Women's Rights

(Equal Rights, Social Reform)

The abolitionist movement, racked for years over the increasingly controversial role played by women in the movement, finally split in 1840 when Arthur and Lewis Tappan left the American Anti-Slavery Society, taking with them the conservative abolitionists who opposed William Lloyd Garrison's inclusion of women's rights as a legitimate concern of abolitionists.

From 1831, when William Lloyd Garrison organized the New England Anti-Slavery Society and began publishing the *Liberator*, women had been welcomed into the movement. Willing to form auxiliary organizations in order not to divert attention away from abolitionism by those who objected to women in the public sphere, female abolitionists like Lucretia Mott, Lydia Maria Child, and the Grimké sisters, nevertheless played a crucial role. The Grimkés publicized the slave system as no other speakers could, because they were the daughters of a plantation owner and they were willing to risk the opprobrium of public indignation.

The fact that their presence produced reactions that ranged from discomfort to outrage was not lost on women who were lobbying to rid the nation of a system that enslaved people. Many women did question their own status in society, making the obvious comparisons between slaves and the female sex that was prohibited from participating in the full benefits of citizenship. When writer Lydia Maria Child published a pamphlet entitled *Appeal in Favor of That Class of Americans Called Africans*, she was ridiculed and ostracized, and her book sales, which had been robust enough to support her, fell off dramatically. Incidents like that experienced by Child led women in the abolitionist movement to raise fundamental questions about their own rights. At a national women's antislavery conference in 1837, delegates spent a good deal of time discussing the issue, finally passing a resolution that said, "The time has come for woman to move in that sphere which providence has assigned her, and no longer remain satisfied in the circumscribed limits which corrupt custom and a perverted application of Scripture have encircled her."

Garrison and other radical abolitionists fully supported this position. But the more conservative abolitionists were disturbed by this turn of events. When the American Anti-Slavery Society had proposed a year earlier that women be hired as antislavery agents, criticism came from a number of quarters, including the clergy who objected to women who assumed "the place and tone of man as public reformer." By the late 1830s, the controversy had caused abolitionists to divide into factions. The still-dominant New England branch of the movement broke into two opposing camps in 1839. The following year, both the Boston Female Anti-Slavery Society and the American Anti-Slavery Society split into factions. Garrison, certain that the conservatives would attempt to push women into the background by bringing the issue up for a vote at the national convention, made sure that the Garrisonians had the majority. In 1840, the American delegates to the World Anti-Slavery Conference in London arrived in England only to discover that the women delegates would not be seated.

After 1840, after the conservatives had walked away from the American Anti-Slavery Society, leaving it in the hands of the Garrisonians, the abolitionist movement proceeded along two separate tracks. Less cohesive than their radical counterparts, the conservatives moved along more diffuse paths. The Tappan brothers, Albert and Lewis, formed their own antislavery society, while James Birney became the Liberty Party candidate for president in the 1840 election. Women's rights continued to be a legitimate issue for the Garrisonians.

1840: Georgia Female College Grants the First Full Bachelor's Degrees to Women

(Education)

In 1840, the Georgia Female College graduated its first students, who thus became the first women to earn full bachelor's degrees from an American college.

The Georgia Female College was founded in 1836, although financial difficulties kept it from full operations until 1839. Located in Macon, Georgia, in the heart of the old South, it was a remarkably liberal institution, the first in the country to offer young women the same curriculum as other institutions offered to young men. Housed in one large building set on a four-acre lot, the students could take a year's preparatory course if they needed it, and then standard courses in mathematics, science, Latin, and French. Its enrollment, which in the nineteenth century fluctuated between

150 and 300 women, approximated that of the University of Georgia's men.

The college was supported by the Methodist Church, so in 1843 it changed its name to Wesleyan Female College. The "Female" was dropped in 1919, at which time it was formally accredited as a four-year liberal arts college, but the school has remained all female.

Over the years, the institution's fortunes have fluctuated in response to larger social tides. It managed to stay open all but two weeks during the Civil War, but during Reconstruction its student body remained at a low of 150 students or so. A large donation in 1880 enabled the original building to be remodeled, but the depression of 1893 pushed enrollments, and its financial outlook, down again. Its finances improved steadily in the early twentieth century, climaxing with the creation of a large, beautiful new suburban campus in 1928. The next year, the stock market crashed, and so did the college's finances. Saddled with a million dollar mortgage and a student body half the size of the six hundred needed to support it, the college slid into bankruptcy.

After the Second World War, the college's finances and fortunes improved, so that by 1950 the debt had been paid and enrollments had reached seven hundred. A fire in 1963 destroyed the old campus, however, and the decline of interest in single-sex schools in the 1960s brought enrollments down once again. The 1980s brought renewed interest in women's colleges, though, and so that crisis passed. Today, the college continues to offer young women a liberal education in the heart of Dixie.

Graduates of the college formed the world's first alumnae organization in 1859. Probably the most famous of their number was Soong Ch'ing-ling, a 1913 graduate who went on to marry Sun Yat-sen, the leader of the 1911 Chinese revolution. Both her sisters studied at the college as well, and Mei-ling, who went on to graduate from Wellesley College in Massachusetts, eventually married Chiang Kai-shek.

1840: Lucretia Mott Is Denied a Seat at the World Anti-Slavery Conference

(Equal Rights)

In 1840, Lucretia Mott and several other women chosen as delegates to the World Anti-Slavery Conference in London were denied seats at the conference on the basis of their sex.

L ucretia Mott, a devout Quaker and long-time advocate of abolitionism, had devoted several years to the abolitionist cause when, in 1840, she was chosen to attend the World's Anti-Slavery Conference to be held in London. Mott had befriended William Lloyd Garrison in 1831 when Garrison was just beginning publication of the *Liberator*. She attended the organizational meeting of the American Anti-Slavery Society (AASS) in Philadelphia in 1833, and formed the auxiliary Philadelphia Female Anti-Slavery Society when the AASS excluded women. The AASS dropped its restrictions against women members fairly quickly, however, and Mott became an active member of both the national organization and the Pennsylvania branch as an executive committee member. She remained steadfast in her commitment to Garrisonian, or immediate, abolition, even when the more conservative members of her church condemned the radicals in favor of a more gradual approach to emancipation. Mott was instrumental in organizing the Anti-Slavery Convention of American Women held in Philadelphia in 1838. When riotous anti-abolitionists wreaked havoc at the convention, Mott counseled the women delegates to remain calm. The mobs later burned down the convention hall and the Shelter for Colored Orphans, and marched off in search of the Mott home. Fortunately, they were distracted and never made it there.

When Mott arrived in England with her husband, ready to take her seat at the World's Anti-Slavery Conference, she was distressed to learn that she and the other women delegates would not be allowed to be seated. The conference was controlled by the more conservative American and Foreign Anti-Slavery Society and its British counterpart, the British and Foreign Anti-Slavery Society, both of which objected to women in the public arena. The male abolitionists that accompanied Mott and the other women tried to persuade the convention organizers to seat them, but the best that could be accomplished was an assignment to sit in the gallery without any opportunity to participate except as a viewer.

Another woman delegate refused a seat at the convention, Elizabeth Cady Stanton, made it her business to meet Lucretia Mott as they both sat out the meetings in the gallery. The irony struck both of them that the conven-

tion, which billed itself as a world convention, could begin its proceedings by denying representation to half of the human population. Mott and Stanton concluded that they had an obligation to promote women's rights when they returned to the United States. Both Mott and Stanton continued to campaign against slavery on their return to America, but both had undergone a critical transformation. Neither one would advocate other issues without also placing the rights of women in the forefront. Although it would take another eight years before the two could find the time and opportunity to organize a women's rights convention, the historic meeting at Seneca Falls in 1848 marked the start of a concentrated feminist movement that would ultimately affect the lives of all American women.

1843: Dorothea Dix Exposes the Harsh Treatment Accorded the Mentally Ill in Massachusetts Hospitals

(Social Reform)

In January 1843, Dorothea Dix testified before the Massachusetts state legislature, providing them with information she had gathered over the course of two years about the inhuman conditions under which the state's mentally ill patients were confined.

"I come to place before the Legislature of Massachusetts the condition of the miserable, the desolate, the outcast." So began the testimony of Dorothea Dix before the state legislature that would eventually lead to reform of the system providing care to the mentally ill. Dix's appearance before the legislature was noteworthy not only because of the scandalous conditions that she revealed, but because it was still considered unseemly for a woman to address a mixed audience in public.

With the support of social reformers like William Ellery Channing and Samuel Gridley Howe, Dix had begun her investigation after a chance encounter at the East Cambridge jail in March 1841. At that time, Dix, a teacher with no ambitions for becoming a social reformer, filled a friend's request to visit the jail in order to teach a Sunday school class for women. She was astounded to discover that among those incarcerated with the drunks, vagrants, and criminals, were people whose only crime was mental illness. The conditions there galvanized Dix to complain to the local authorities. Gaining a reputation as a meddlesome troublemaker did not deter her, and with newspaper publicity provided by Howe, some improvements were made. For the East Cambridge jail, the incident was finished. For Dorothea Dix, a life's work was begun.

Her efforts in Massachusetts resulted in reforms to the system so that the mentally ill who could not afford private care were not consigned to lives of degradation and animal-like incarceration. After achieving success there, Dix moved further afield, conducting similar studies in New York, Rhode Island, New Jersey, Pennsylvania, Kentucky, Maryland, Ohio, Illinois, Mississippi, Alabama, Tennessee, North Carolina, and other states. In each, she prepared similar reports to the one she presented in Massachusetts. Single-handedly, Dix succeeded in persuading nearly all the legislatures to appropriate funds for new facilities and for extended care.

By then, Dix's name had become a household word. Other reformers sought her assistance with their own causes, but Dix generally refrained from getting involved with them regardless of her favorable attitude toward them. She sympathized with women's rights, abolition, temperance, peace, and public education, but feared that spreading herself too thin would cause her to lose her focus on the mentally ill. Because of her extensive knowledge of the penal system, however, she did agree to write a treatise entitled *Remarks on Prisons and Prison Discipline in the United States*, published in 1845. Many of Dix's observations and recommendations re-

garding reform of the prison system were later adopted by prison reformers, including her recommendations that prisoners not all be incarcerated together regardless of their crime, and that prisoners be given the opportunity to acquire some education.

For the next several years, Dix traveled back and forth between various states and Washington, D.C., where she lobbied constantly for passage of a bill that would allocate several million acres of federal lands for the care and treatment of the mentally ill. Although the bill eventually passed both houses of congress, it was vetoed by the president. Disheartened, Dix left for Europe, both to get away from the frustration of politics and to regain her strength after so many years of nonstop work. In Europe, she continued her investigations in a number of countries, with some positive results. At one point, she enlisted the assistance of Pope Pius IX in order to secure reforms in Rome hospitals.

Dix was back in the United States when the Civil War broke out. Her fame and expertise made her a logical choice to become superintendent of army nurses. But her investigative prowess and reform zeal did not necessarily translate themselves into qualities required of a good administrator. Nevertheless, she did set up and staff infirmaries, oversaw sewing societies, stockpiled medical supplies, and made periodic calls for voluntary contributions of needed goods. Her conflicts with the Medical Bureau and the U.S. Sanitary Commission ultimately led to the appointment of a cosuperintendent.

Dorothea Dix remained on the job until 1866, then returned to her prewar task of traveling throughout the country visiting mental facilities and recommending reforms where needed. Her contributions to the field of mental health were invaluable. When she began in 1841, there were 13 mental hospitals in the United States. When she died in 1885, there were 123. She was directly responsible for the founding of 32 state mental facilities, and indirectly responsible for many more than that throughout the country and the world. Dix helped to pave the way for progressive treatment of the mentally ill, including psychiatric diagnoses.

1843: Oliver Wendell Holmes Publishes *The Contagiousness of Puerperal Fever*

(Medicine, Family Life)

Puerperal, or childbed, fever, has been the scourge of women since time immemorial, accounting for the great majority of deaths of mature women before menopause. In 1843, the poet and physician Oliver Wendell Holmes brought to Americans' attention the growing evidence that, far from alleviating this disease, doctors and hospitals were actually responsible for spreading it.

As early as the fifth century B.C.E., the founder of Western medicine, Hippocrates, observed that "if a woman in childbed has erysipelas of the womb she will usually die." William Harvey described puerperal fever's symptoms in 1651, but the critical advance in knowledge came in 1773, when Charles White of Manchester, England, linked the disease with "surgical" fever, and advised postural drainage of the womb, and insisted on cleanliness during deliveries and isolation of infected patients. His work was seconded in 1795 by Alexander Gordon, who noted that the disease only struck women whose midwife or doctor had recently been in contact with another infected patient. Further support came in 1789, when Jean Louis Baudelocque observed that the fever was more likely to develop if hands or instruments had been introduced into the birth canal.

Despite this growing scientific evidence, when Oliver Wendell Holmes, a physician and a poet, and the father of U.S. Supreme Court Justice Oliver Wendell Holmes, attempted to bring this life-saving knowledge to the attention of American doctors, they greeted his news with disdain. The publication of Holmes' *The Contagiousness of Puerperal Fever* in 1845, dismissed by most physicians as nonsense, did have some supporters. But the medical profession in general required more than the publication of Holmes' book before they would accept the obvious. Four years later, I. P. Semmelweis demonstrated conclusively that the women attended by doctors and medical students who dissected cadavers contracted the disease far more frequently than women attended by midwives alone. Even then, most of his colleagues refused to heed Semmelweis' advice to wash their hands in antiseptic solution before helping in childbirth, and he suffered greatly under sustained criticism. Nevertheless, more and more doctors paid attention to the evidence, and the profession gradually, if grudgingly, began to take the precautions necessary to bring the disease under control.

In 1855, a second edition of Holmes's book came out, and by this time it was greeted with respect rather than rejection. Doctors began to clean their hands before childbirth and surgery, and infected patients were carefully isolated to prevent the disease's spread. Once a woman became infected there was little doctors could do to save her until the introduction of sulfonamides in the twentieth century, but these measures of hygiene led to a dramatic decrease in the incidence of the disease long before modern medicine found a cure. It is unfortunate that so many women had to die before these simple measures of cleanliness came to be habitual and required practice among medical personnel.

1844: The Lowell Female Labor Reform Association Is Organized

(Work)

In an effort to counteract deteriorating work conditions and decreasing wages, Lowell Mill employee Sarah Bagley founded the Lowell Female Labor Reform Association in December 1844.

Sarah Bagley's efforts to organize an effective union was not the first labor action involving working women. As early as 1824, female textile mill workers in Pawtucket, Rhode Island, joined their male counterparts in America's first strike, initiated to halt wage cuts. In 1825, the United Tailoresses of New York City waged an all-woman strike for higher wages. These incidences are the first recorded instances of American women joining in modern-style factory labor actions. Despite traditional beliefs held by male union leaders that women would not support strike actions, early union activity, including strikes, found women participating on a large scale. Women shoemakers in Saugus, Massachusetts, successfully struck for higher wages in 1833, and inspired a similar strike in nearby Lynn, Massachusetts. Women shoemakers in Philadelphia struck for months in 1836, and women textile workers in Pennsylvania went without wages for several months in favor of maintaining their strike against a cotton mill.

While the Lowell Mills strike of 1834 did not succeed, it did establish Sarah Bagley as a union force to be reckoned with. The mills in Lowell had long had a reputation as model factories. Almost all the workers were young women from rural areas in Massachusetts and neighboring states. Sarah Bagley left her home in Meredith, New Hampshire, in 1836 to work for the Hamilton Company in Lowell. Women workers were housed in company-owned and -operated dormitories, and lived according to rigid rules designed to ensure that their behavior was proper, for it was only in these circumstances that middle-class families would allow their unmarried daughters to live away from home. Their ultimate discontent was not with this regimen—in fact, the women enforced it more severely than did the owners—but instead with the grueling, twelve-hour days and an attempt by the owners to cut their pay. In October 1836, the "girls" working at the Hamilton Manufacturing Company, including Sarah Bagley, walked off their jobs, demanding higher wages and a ten-hour day.

When the strike did not bring success, discontent among the workers festered. They formed a loose organization in 1836, and in 1844 Bagley transformed it into the large and vigorous Lowell Female Labor Reform Association. Its several hundred members collected more than two thousand signatures on a petition for the ten-hour day. Bagley led a five-member delegation to testify before the Massachusetts legislature regarding working conditions, thereby joining the handful of women who dared to speak in public before a "promiscuous" group. When their efforts met with defeat, Bagley found a way to re-taliate. She campaigned against a local legislator who had opposed them, and forced him out of office. The legislator secured his own revenge when he was able to link Bagley with corruption by a male union member that had been uncovered. Bagley was convinced that, for the good of the union, she had to resign and leave the mill, even though she was innocent of any wrongdoing.

These early struggles for improved conditions failed in their immediate objectives, but they showed the potential of collective action. In fact, so prominent were the young women from the dormitories in leading the labor agitation that new construction of these facilities was forbidden in Lowell, and all newly hired women had to seek lodging in privately run tenements or as boarders with families. Thus, the potent combination of working and living together was ended, which, along with the arrival of Irish immigrant labor in the late 1840s, brought to a close this first episode of female labor organizing.

1848: Maria Mitchell Is Elected to the American Academy of Arts and Sciences

(Equal Rights, Science, Education)

On October 1, 1847, self-taught astronomer Maria Mitchell was working with her father at their Nantucket home gathering data for the U.S. Coastal Survey. Using a two-inch Dollard telescope, Mitchell spotted what she believed to be a new comet streaking across the sky. Her discovery was confirmed, the comet was named after her, and the following year Mitchell became the first woman to be elected to the American Academy of Arts and Sciences. For nearly a century, until 1943, she remained the only woman member.

Maria Mitchell once said that she was born of "average ability but of extraordinary persistence." If that was so, her persistence helped to develop a remarkable scholar whose powers of observation and love of learning left an indelible mark on the scientific world, as well as the generation of women students who studied with her at Vassar. The road to Vassar was an unlikely one for Mitchell. Her father, William Mitchell, a man of little formal schooling but far-ranging intellectual curiosity, provided for his daughter the best of examples. He became interested in astronomy because knowledge of the skies was so important to the whaling industry in Nantucket. Maria helped him when she was a child, but after attending school, she herself took a job as a librarian. While the library was closed, she exhausted its resources, studying texts on navigation, reading French and German scientists (after teaching herself those languages), and volumes on astronomy. In addition, she attended the lectures sponsored by the Athenium, featuring speakers such as Ralph Waldo Emerson, William Ellery Channing, Theodore Parker, and Lucy Stone. Her self-education, therefore, was formidable. But science remained her first love.

After Mitchell discovered her comet, her reputation as a first-rate astronomer was established. In addition to her election to the American Academy of Arts and Sciences, Mitchell received a gold medal from the King of Denmark. In his survey entitled *The Recent Progress of Astronomy: Especially in the United States*, Elias Loomis devoted an entire chapter to "Miss Mitchell's Comet." She was elected to the American Association for the Advancement of Science by none other than famed Harvard anthropologist Louis Agassiz.

Uncomfortable with her sudden renown, Mitchell continued to work at the library until 1861. Shortly thereafter, Matthew Vassar, the founder of Vassar College, invited her to become a member of the faculty. Vassar considered Mitchell, with her status and reputation, to be essential to his first faculty. He offered to build an observatory and a twelve-inch telescope, the third largest in the country, if she would accept the invitation. After some hesitation, Mitchell accepted. For the next twenty years, Mitchell worked closely with some of the brightest young women in the country, imparting her philosophy: accept nothing as given beyond the first mathematical formulae, question everything, and learn from observation.

Mitchell's influence extended beyond the groves of academe. In 1875, she founded the Association for the Advancement of Women, which met annually to discuss the work and problems of women in the professions. She gave numerous lectures pleading for recognition of women scientists. In 1869, in recognition of her own professional contributions, she was the first woman elected to the American Philosophical Society. Although women remained a small minority in the sciences for many years, Mitchell helped to open doors for the first time.

1848: The Seneca Falls Convention

(Equal Rights)

Abolitionists Elizabeth Cady Stanton and Lucretia Mott, disturbed at the manner in which women in the abolition movement were treated by some males, had long discussed the need for a women's rights convention. They, together with Jane Hunt, Mary McClintock, and Martha Wright, issued a call to women to meet at the Wesleyan Methodist Church in Seneca Falls, New York, on July 19, 1848, the first political gathering called specifically to address the rights of women.

When Lucretia Mott, one of the moving forces in the American abolitionist movement, and Elizabeth Cady Stanton found themselves denied seating at a world abolition convention in London in 1840, the irony of their position as women seeking to gain freedom for African Americans could not be ignored. Together they discussed the necessity for organizing a women's rights convention. It took nearly eight years before the idea came to fruition, but in 1848, when Stanton was then living with her husband and family in Seneca Falls, New York, she learned that Mott was visiting in nearby Waterloo, New York. Stanton went to Waterloo to meet with Mott and learned that the fifty-five-year-old Quaker was ready to proceed with the women's rights convention. The convention, held on July 19, 1848, in Seneca Falls, New York, was attended by 240 women. Since neither Stanton nor Mott wanted to preside over the meeting, James Mott agreed to chair the meeting. The first session was followed some two weeks later when the convention was reconvened at the Rochester Community Church.

The seminal document to come out of the convention was the "Declaration of Sentiments," modeled after the Declaration of Independence, written by Stanton. The Declaration of Sentiments began by stating, "We hold these truths to be self evident, that all men and women are created equal." There followed eighteen legal grievances that women had to submit to, which the convention considered one by one. Women, it was noted, could not legally keep their own wages, their children, even themselves. They had very limited educational and economic opportunity, and they had to endure a double standard in morals. Moreover, women were not allowed to vote. After discussion of each issue, a series of twelve resolutions were put before the convention and voted upon. All twelve resolutions were unanimously adopted, with the exception of the suffrage resolution. Conventioneers, including Stanton and Mott, were divided over the suffrage issue, partially because many women feared that a demand for woman suffrage at that moment in history was simply too radical. In the end, even that resolution received a majority vote at the Rochester session of the convention. The Declaration of Sentiments, the first formal statement of women's rights, was signed by sixty-eight women and thirty-two men.

The convention itself and the women who organized and attended it were ridiculed by public and press alike. Very few newspapers took the women seriously. The major exception was Horace Greeley's *New York Tribune*, which reported on and treated the issues with the seriousness and respect they deserved. It took some years before the newly launched women's movement gained the support of a majority of women and it took longer before people generally began to take it seriously, whether or not they agreed with the goals of the movement. But the issues discussed at the first women's rights convention remained the issues with which women continued to be concerned. Indeed, in some instances, they are still viable. It is ironic that the one issue—suffrage—that divided the convention initially, quickly became, in the eyes of most women, the key to obtaining ultimate equality. Suffrage remained the key issue for the next seventy years, until the Nineteenth Amendment was ratified in 1920.

1849: Elizabeth Blackwell Becomes the First Modern Woman to Graduate from Medical School

(Work, Education, Professionalization, Equal Rights)

Intent on becoming a doctor, Elizabeth Blackwell applied to school after school and was rejected by every one because she was a woman. Finally, Geneva Medical College in New York accepted Blackwell. After successfully completing the proscribed program, Elizabeth Blackwell, graduating at the head of her class, became the first woman in modern times to earn a medical degree.

When Elizabeth Blackwell applied to medical schools in the mid-nineteenth century, and was consistently rejected because of her sex, she considered it a test of her moral character and refused to give up. At the age of twenty-six, she was no stranger to personal hardship. Her father died suddenly in 1837, leaving Elizabeth, her mother, and eight brothers and sisters almost penniless. Both parents had imbued their children with what was then an unusual belief in women's rights. When Samuel died, the four older children, Elizabeth among them, had to help pull the family through the crisis by going to work. Strong-willed and determined, Mrs. Blackwell and her four oldest daughters immediately established a school where, for the next several years, all of them taught and thus helped to support the family.

Out of this experience, Elizabeth brought three convictions: first, she could take care of herself; second, marriage was not her destiny; and third, she would find a way to channel her ambition into a fulfilling life. A medical career seemed eminently suited to fit all three convictions. The fact that there was absolutely no precedent for a woman entering medical school did not deter her. When finally Blackwell was accepted by Geneva College, she was overjoyed. To her chagrin, once she arrived on campus, she discovered that the only reason she was accepted was that the faculty and students believed that her application was a hoax perpetrated by a rival medical school. She was accepted as a joke. Always polite to the faculty and her fellow students, and deferential to her professors, Blackwell nevertheless had to endure isolation, loneliness, and hostility. The townspeople of Geneva, who characterized her behavior as immoral, ostracized Blackwell. When she graduated, she did so at the head of her class, having won over most of her peers and professors with her dedication and talent.

Blackwell's younger sister, Emily, followed in Elizabeth's footsteps. By then, Elizabeth had opened up the New York Infirmary for Women and Children, staffed entirely by women professionals. Blackwell did not rest with founding her own hospital. She was also one of the earliest advocates of personal hygiene for physicians as a way to reduce infectious disease from developing and spreading in the patient populations of hospitals. Blackwell was also one of the earliest—if not *the* earliest—proponent of preventative medicine, urging regular medical care and early treatment of health problems. And, determined that other women would find an easier career path into medicine, she established a women's medical college, affiliated with the New York Infirmary. To eliminate any possible charge of unprofessionalism, Blackwell insisted on a strict set of requirements, including entrance exams (unheard of at that time), a rigorous curriculum, and graduate examinations to be administered not by the medical school faculty, but by a board of independent physicians.

Although Elizabeth Blackwell was the first woman to earn a medical degree, her women's medical school was not the first established in the United States. In 1850, the Woman's Medical College of Pennsylvania opened its doors to eight students. The college succeeded, despite the efforts to derail its progress, and in 1969, it began accepting male medical students as well as female students. Shortly thereafter, its name was changed to the Medical College of Pennsylvania.

In New England, the New England Female Medical College, established in 1848, was not really a medical college but rather a school for midwives. Its founding father, Samuel Gregory, believed that male doctors had no place in the delivery room. When Dr. Marie Zakrezewska left Blackwell's New York Infirmary, she initially joined the staff of the New England Female Medical College. Her desire to upgrade and employ higher standards met with resistance from Gregory. Ultimately, the management and the Board of Directors split over the controversy. Zakrezewska left with most of the Board of Lady Managers to open the New England Hospital for Women and Children in Boston. The New England Female Medical College closed.

The groundbreaking work done by Elizabeth Blackwell and other women physicians in the mid- to late nineteenth century was beneficial to women who wanted to enter the medical profession as doctors, as nurses, or as health care workers. It was also beneficial to the health and well-being of thousands of women and children who sought professional help.

1850s: Amelia Bloomer Introduces Bloomers

(Cultural Life, Equal Rights)

Amelia Jenks Bloomer, publisher and editor of a women's rights newspaper called the *Lily*, publicized a new style of women's clothing, introduced by actress Fannie Kemble and adopted by several notable feminists, including Elizabeth Cady Stanton and Susan B. Anthony.

Throughout most of history, and certainly in America up to the early twentieth century, women's clothing has always been cumbersome and restrictive. In the mid-nineteenth century, with the first full-fledged feminist movement taking shape, women began to challenge the accepted clothing norms. As a substantial middle class emerged in America, women's clothing became more and more a measure of success rather than functional attire, with increasingly elaborate petticoats, hoops, bonnets, and bustles. Clothing consisted of constrictive corsets with series of laces to cinch in waists, hips, and breasts; layers and layers of heavy petticoats; and dresses often made with as much as twenty yards of fabric that added yet more weight. The image of Scarlett O'Hara holding onto the bed-post for stability while Mammie pulls at the laces of her corset in order to give Scarlett her twenty-inch waist may have been somewhat of an exaggeration for most American women, but it wasn't too far off. Critics of the trends in women's clothing, even very early critics, were not reticent about placing the blame for nonfunctional clothing on male shoulders. In 1787, Dr. Benjamin Rush, a signer of the Declaration of Independence, ascribed the invention of "ridiculous and expensive fashions in female dress entirely to the gentlemen, in order to divert the ladies from improving their minds...[and] to secure more arbitrary and unlimited authority over them."

While feminists could embrace Dr. Rush's sentiments, their own experiences were more than enough to convince them that their clothing helped to limit not only their mobility but their ability to participate fully in all aspects of life. Moreover, the numerous physicians who were concerned over the potential health problems related to wearing severely laced corsets added more ammunition to feminists' desires to wear more appropriate clothing. To be sure, the doctors who fretted over women's health were mostly concerned with interference with reproductive ability, rather than interference with lifestyle choices.

One of the first women to adopt the freer dress style was British-born actress Fanny Kemble. Kemble, the daughter of a respected British acting family, toured widely in both England and America before marrying an American plantation owner, Pierce Butler. A feminist, Kemble began appearing publicly wearing loose-fitting pants under a skirt. When critics blasted Kemble for wearing such outlandish clothing, editor Amelia Bloomer came to her defense in the pages of the *Lily*. Very quickly, other feminists adopted the new style, including Elizabeth Cady Stanton and Susan B. Anthony. When Stanton began wearing the new "American Cos-

tume," as it also became known, Bloomer once again wrote it up in the pages of the *Lily*. The story was picked up by newspapers throughout the country, most of which referred to the style as "bloomers," because of Amelia Bloomers staunch defense of it.

Not all feminists were as enamored of bloomers as were Stanton and Anthony. In the end, Stanton and others agreed to forego wearing bloomers because they did not want the public or their critics to reduce the feminist cause to nothing more than a dispute over clothing, even though they continued to believe that women's dress was a serious issue.

Nearly a century later, another independent actress, Katharine Hepburn, would once again raise eyebrows with her insistence upon wearing stylish slacks almost exclusively and in total disregard for what polite society thought was appropriate. This time, however, Hepburn's popularity, intelligence, and classy style helped to foment a wide-spread revolution in women's clothing. Thereafter, women in slacks became more and more a common sight.

1850: Philadelphia Quakers Found the Woman's Medical College of Pennsylvania

(Equal Rights, Medicine)

In September 1850, a group of Philadelphia Quakers founded the Woman's Medical College of Pennsylvania, then called the Female Medical College of Pennsylvania, in a rented building on Arch Street.

Several years after Elizabeth Blackwell had searched so long to find a medical school that would accept her, a group of Philadelphia Quakers opened a woman's medical school in that city. Although the Woman's Medical College was not a direct response to Blackwell's experience, the founders were influenced nevertheless by the difficulty that women had in gaining access to medical schools.

The first class to enroll at the Woman's Medical College consisted of eight students, five of whom were Pennsylvania residents. The other three came from New York, Massachusetts, and London. Several of the entering women had already had experience in medicine, having mostly taught themselves because of their inability to gain entrance to male medical schools. Hannah Longshore, whose husband Joseph Longshore was a physician and one of the founders of the medical school, and who also taught at the school, had been encouraged by her husband to enroll. Hannah's sister-in-law, Anna Longshore, also enrolled. Another student, Ann Preston, also had prior training. Preston had apprenticed herself to a local doctor and taught local Philadelphia women about health in private classes.

Because of their prior experiences, both Preston and Longshore were able to accelerate their course of study, graduating in 1851. The graduation ceremonies were almost disrupted by male medical students from a nearby school. Longshore, a mother of two children, eventually accepted an internship at the New England Female Medical College, while Preston returned to Woman's Medical College in 1853 as a member of the faculty. The college continued to come under attack from the male medical community, not only from medical students like those who had tried to disrupt the graduating ceremonies, but from doctors as well who could not accept the idea of a woman's medical school or of women in medicine. Although the school closed very briefly during the Civil War, it reopened and has remained a vibrant institution since then. In 1969, when the school began accepting male students, it changed its name once again, to the Medical College of Pennsylvania.

1850: Harriet Tubman First Leads Slaves to Freedom

(Social Reform)

In 1850, Harriet Tubman, herself a recently escaped slave, traveled into the slave state of Maryland to lead her sister's family to join her in her new-found freedom.

Harriet Tubman fled from Maryland to Philadelphia in 1849 to gain her freedom. But instead of contenting herself with enjoying her personal accomplishment, or satisfying her conscience with verbal attacks on the slave system, she turned around and went back into slave states to lead her friends and family to freedom. She did this not once, not twice, but a total of nineteen times. Then, when the country went to war in order to abolish slavery once and for all, she drew upon her prewar experiences to serve with distinction as a spy and a scout.

Born into slavery on the eastern shore of Maryland, Harriet Tubman took her first name from her mother and her last name from her first husband, John Tubman, a free black whom she married in 1844 when she was twenty-four. Five years later, she heard rumors that she was to be sold and moved further south, and it was then that she decided to escape.

For the next fifteen years, she led a

life that combined high moral purpose and high adventure. At first glance, she appeared to be an unlikely candidate for this life. Besides being black and a woman, she suffered from unpredictable headaches and blackout spells after a blow to the head from an overseer that she had suffered when she was thirteen. Furthermore, she was naturally shy, had "no pretensions," was "ordinary" in her appearance, and was illiterate and unable to read signs or maps. But balanced against these liabilities were some remarkable strengths. She navigated by memorizing landmarks and cultivating an uncanny sense of direction. She communicated through coded messages contained in songs and quotes from the Bible. Her quick wits enabled her to avoid discovery time and again, the most famous perhaps being when she bought tickets on a southbound train in order to make a man who was following think she was a trusted slave escorting others back to their plantation. Most important of all, of course, were her raw courage and dedication. These strengths far outweighed her limitations, enabling her to help over three hundred slaves escape to freedom and earning her the high honor of a bounty of $40,000 offered for her head.

Tubman's public life did not come to an end with the end of the Civil War. After ten years as a secret agent and five years as a military spy, she turned her attention to caring for indigent former slaves and, increasingly, to women's issues. She attended the frequent meetings in the Seneca Falls area of New York, near to where her farm was, and spoke to the National American Woman Suffrage Association in 1896. The next year the organization honored her with a reception. In the same year, the country finally awarded her a much needed pension, in recognition of her service as "commander of several men as scouts during the late War of Rebellion." But her full contribution to the cause of freedom was best summed up by Booker T. Washington. "Excepting John Brown," he said, "I know of no one who has willingly encountered more perils and hardships to serve our people."

1851: Sojourner Truth Addresses a Women's Rights Convention in Akron, Ohio

(Social Reform)

Over the protests of participants, presiding officers of a women's rights convention in Akron, Ohio, in 1851, allowed African-American preacher Sojourner Truth to address the audience. The speech she gave proved to be Truth's most famous and enduring one.

Born a slave with the name Isabella Baumfree, this African-American woman became a preacher and changed her name to Sojourner Truth in 1843, at the age of forty-six. For the next forty years, she fought against slavery and segregation, and for women's rights.

This resolute crusader was born into slavery in Ulster County, New York, in 1797. At the age of nine, she was sold for the first time, along with a flock of sheep. Ultimately, she was sold to the Dumont family and remained there for twenty years. The Dumonts were relatively benign, as slave owners went, but the children she bore that survived were eventually sold away from her. In 1827, Truth ran away from the Dumont's.

A Quaker family, the Van Wageners, took Truth in and supported her petition to get her son Peter back from the Alabama plantation owner who had bought him from the Dumonts illegally under New York law. Peter was returned to her, and Isabella Van Wagener (the name she adopted) and her son left for New York City in 1829. In 1843, she changed her name to Sojourner Truth and began a forty-year career as a public speaker. Her new name accurately foretold how she would spend the rest of her life, as a restless spirit dedicated to exposing falsehoods and hypocrisy.

Truth's first crusade was the struggle against slavery. But even at this point, when abolition was still a dream held by a few, she insisted on the importance of emancipating black women not only from their status as slaves, but also from their unequal status as women. Tall and majestic in appearance, she repeatedly took the podium at abolitionist meetings to argue that, for all the concern about the rights of black men, there seemed to be little interest in the rights of black women. If women were emancipated without reform of women's status, they would simply be exchanging white masters for black ones. Her words stood as a double challenge: to abolitionists who ignored women's rights and to feminists who overlooked black women. In 1851, Truth attended her second women's rights convention, and asked to be allowed to speak to the audience. Although many of the delegates raised objections, and the presiding officers were a little leery, they nevertheless agreed to let the imposing speaker address the convention. Her demeanor, her words, and her delivery mesmerized the audience and moved them to tears and "roars of applause." "That man over there says women need to be helped into carriages, and lifted over ditches, and to have the best place everywhere. Nobody ever helps me into carriages or over puddles, or gives me the best place—and ain't I a woman?...I have borne thirteen chil-

dren and seen most of 'em sold into slavery, and when I cried out with my mother's grief, none but Jesus heard me—and ain't I a woman?"

After the Civil War, Sojourner Truth protested the exclusion of women from the Fourteenth Amendment, which secured the vote for black men only. Like other women's rights activists, Truth tested the amendment by attempting to vote in the presidential election of 1872. While her protests proved fruitless (as did those of white suffragists like Susan B. Anthony and Elizabeth Cady Stanton), she was able to take concrete steps to act on her concerns when she was appointed by the Freedmen's Bureau to train black women for employment. Here was a practical measure she could do to help former slave women avoid the pitfalls she had foreseen. While she lamented that many freed men let their wives work and then took the paycheck for themselves, at least some black women gained the basis for self-sufficiency.

Truth continued her crusades even as she approached eighty years old. Living in Washington, D.C., she repeatedly boarded segregated street cars and sat in the white section, only to be expelled forcibly by the conductors. Each time, she made sure that everyone watching, especially the whites, would see the violence and in-humanity that segregation entailed.

Despite her desire to see freedom for African Americans and equal rights for women, Truth never advocated violence, as did famed abolitionist Frederick Douglass. The two dis-agreed on the issue, and Truth did not hesitate to call for Douglass to account for his views. She also disagreed with Douglass and others who argued that women were jeopardizing progress for African Americans by insisting on their own rights. Truth did not believe that the "Negro's Hour" needed to be secured at the expense of women's rights. In the post–Civil War years until her death in 1883, Truth became more and more an advocate for women's rights. More than a thousand people attended her funeral, where she was memorialized by Lucy Stone as a "ter-rible force, moving friend and foe alike."

1852: Harriet Beecher Stowe Writes *Uncle Tom's Cabin*

(Social Reform, Cultural Life)

In 1852, Harriet Beecher Stowe wrote the most famous and widely read antislavery novel in American history. The publication of *Uncle Tom's Cabin* gave the public some of the most enduring characters in American fiction, including Tom, little Eva, Topsy, and the aristocratic St. Clair.

Harriet Beecher Stowe, a member of two of the most illustrious abolitionist families in the nineteenth century—the Beechers and the Wards—and a sister of Catharine Beecher, a noted educator, wrote *Uncle Tom's Cabin* in response to the passage of the Fugitive Slave Act of 1850. The Fugitive Slave Act was part of the Compromise of 1850, an effort to stave off conflict between the free and slave states. In exchange for con-cessions against slavery, such as pro-hibiting slave trade in the District of Columbia, the government agreed to make it easier for slave owners to re-trieve runaway slaves from free states. It was a tacit acknowledgment that the government considered slaves to be the "property" of their owners, and therefore subject to the same rights of possession practices generally observed. Such an admission did not sit well with abolitionists and others opposed to the slave system. With her brothers, Edward and Henry Ward, denouncing the Slave Act from their pulpits, Harriet felt moved to take action in her own way. A long-time writer who had previously written and sold pieces of a much lighter weight, and compelled, as she often noted, by divine intervention, Stowe began writing in the spring of 1851. Over the next forty weeks, the book was serialized in an abolitionist newspaper. Even so, when the novel was published in book form, thousands of people were eagerly waiting to purchase copies. Indeed, the book did so well that in the first four months of publication, book sales netted its author $10,000 in royalties.

In addition to its condemnation of the slave system, *Uncle Tom's Cabin* made a strong case for the inevitable harm that slavery caused to the mainstream American family structure. Through the voices that Beecher provided for her characters, slave and free, young and old, northern and southern, she intended to draw a portrait of slavery with all its complexities.

That she was able to reach a significant audience there is no doubt. *Uncle Tom's Cabin* has been called one of the antislavery movement's most influential weapons. Whether apocryphal or real, no less than Abraham Lincoln himself, on meeting Harriet Beecher Stowe, asked if she was "the little woman who made this great war." The poet Henry Wadsworth Longfellow wrote in his journal, somewhat enviously, "How she is shaking the world with her Uncle Tom's Cabin!...At one step she has reached the top of the staircase up which the rest of us climb on our knees year after year." Southerners, recognizing the threat to their entire social and economic structure supported by slavery, were zealous in their attacks upon both Stowe and the book. Characterized as "sexually driven" and a "nigger lover," Southerners castigated Stowe, banned her novel throughout the South, and produced some thirty novels holding slavery in a positive light.

Stowe responded to the criticism by writing a sequel, called *The Key to Uncle Tom's Cabin*, in 1853. But the second novel never even approached the first in popularity, sales, or emotional response. In England, it was referred to as "the *Iliad* of the blacks." Altogether, *Uncle Tom's Cabin* was printed in twenty languages throughout the world, and has gone through forty editions. Houghton Mifflin acquired the rights to it in 1862, and since then it has never allowed the book to go out of publication.

1852: Emily Dickinson's First Poem Is Published

(Cultural Life)

Emily Dickinson's first poem was published in 1852. The poem was published without her knowledge or permission, and assigned the title *"The Valentine."*

Emily Dickinson wrote nearly 1,800 poems, but only six were published in her lifetime. Posthumously, she has been acknowledged, along with Walt Whitman, as one of the nineteenth century's two foremost American poets, and, by some accounts, one of—if not *the*—finest American poet. She was born and died in Amherst, Massachusetts, a contemporary of the poets of the American Renaissance (1830s–1850s) and the Transcendentalists (Margaret Fuller, Ralph Waldo Emerson), but remained unknown to any of them. She left Amherst infrequently and usually for not more than a day or two at a time. As she grew older, Dickinson also grew more and more reclusive, sometimes remaining in her upstairs bedroom when friends came to call. It was not until after her death that her poetry was discovered and published.

Dickinson has always been something of an enigma to admirers of her poetry and to her biographers. She graduated from Amherst Academy in 1847 and attended nearby Mount Holyoke Seminary for one year. Mary Lyon's efforts to convert Dickinson to the Congregational Church persuaded the young woman that Mount Holyoke was not for her, and she returned to her father's home in Amherst. For Dickinson, who read and re-read Ralph Waldo Emerson's essays, the Transcendentalists' optimistic affirmation of the immediate and benevolent presence of God in the human soul and in nature was far more appealing.

The contours of Dickinson's external life remained always simple and unencumbered. She lived in the family home. In her early years, she had suitors from her father's law office and from nearby Amherst College, whom she ultimately discouraged. Much of her poetry written in the 1850s suggests that she loved at least one man passionately, but his identity has never been conclusively determined. Much later, she developed a close relationship with Judge Otis P. Lord, a widowed friend of her father. But the truth was that Dickinson purposely chose to remain unburdened by relationships because she was much more passionate about the life of the mind.

Dickinson was totally confident that her poetry would be recognized after her death. Perhaps for this reason, and fearing that she might be misunderstood in the present, she chose not to publish her work. When the neatly tied packets of her poetry were uncovered after her death in 1886, it was clear how confident she had been of their worth. Each packet was carefully tied and dated. Dickinson's sister Lavinia and her niece and grandniece made sure that all 1,800 poems were ultimately published.

Literary critics have attested to the depth and complexity of Dickinson's poetry. Her unusual life inspired others to memorialize her. Susan Glaspell, the founder of the Provincetown Players, wrote a Pulitzer Prize–winning play entitled *Alison's House* in 1931 about Dickinson's life. In 1940, dancer-choreographer Martha Graham composed a dance recital, *Letter to the World,* and in 1976, actress Julie Harris performed a one-woman show on Broadway entitled *The Belle of Amherst,* both about Dickinson.

After her death, among the many scraps of paper found in her possession in addition to her poetry, was one which said simply, "Area—no test of depth." It is perhaps the best indication of how fully immersed Dickinson was in her inner life and how limitless the boundaries of that life were. The last several years of her life were spent entirely in her home and garden, yet, while her physical world grew more and more restricted, her inner world seemed to have expanded exponentially.

1853: Antoinette Blackwell Becomes the First Ordained Woman Minister in America

(Professions, Religion)

On September 15, 1853, Antoinette Blackwell was ordained minister of the South Butler, New York, Congregational Church. Blackwell was the first American woman to be ordained by a Protestant denomination.

From the time she was a young child, Antoinette Brown Blackwell wanted to preach. Even though the Congregational Church in her community of Henrietta, New York, voted to make her a full church member at the age of nine in recognition of her precocious talent, the idea of a woman entering the ministry was never seriously entertained by anyone but herself. Her parents, progressive for the day, allowed Blackwell to enroll at Oberlin College in Ohio in 1846. She had saved money to attend Oberlin by teaching, and her father financed the remainder. When she finished a nondegree course in literature in 1847, Blackwell announced her desire to earn a theology degree. The Oberlin officials were in a bind. The college advocated accepting men and women openly without restrictions. They really could not deny allowing a student to enter a particular field of study. But the three years that Blackwell spent in the theology department were filled with constant reminders to her—from both the faculty and her fellow students—that the Bible did not approve of women being heard in church. When she graduated in 1850, she was neither awarded a degree in theology nor licensed as a minister. Refusing to give up her aspiration, Blackwell traveled for the next two years, giving sermons where invited. Finally, the Congregational Church in South Butler, New York, invited her to become pastor of their congregation.

Within a year of accepting the position in South Butler, Blackwell asked to be released from her commitment.

The years of constantly battling the establishment against doing something that she believed she had a God-given right to do had led Blackwell to adopt a progressively more liberal interpretation of theology than that espoused by the Congregational Church. She was too much at odds with such Calvinist tenets as infant damnation, to continue preaching in good faith. She turned instead to the more optimistic Unitarian Church.

While she was still in South Butler, Blackwell met her future husband, Charles Samuel Blackwell, whose brother Henry was about to marry Antoinette's former Oberlin classmate, the feminist and abolitionist Lucy Stone Blackwell. Much of their married life was spent in New Jersey, and the couple eventually had seven children. But Blackwell remained active throughout her life. In 1869, she published *Studies in General Science*, integrating her belief in women's rights with scientific knowledge. Several years later, in 1875, she followed up with a rebuttal of sorts to Darwin's *Origin of the Species*, with *The Sexes Throughout Nature*. Blackwell was one of a few women elected to membership in the American Association for the Advancement of Science in 1881. Ultimately Blackwell published three more volumes in her life: *The Philosophy of Individuality* (1893), *The Making of the Universe* (1914), and *The Social Side of Mind and Action* (1915). She also continued to preach occasionally, ordained two other women preachers, and worked on behalf of the ideals first espoused at the women's rights convention at Seneca Falls, New York. In 1920, she was the sole surviving woman who had attended the convention. It was her profoundest pleasure to go to the polls in 1920 to cast her vote for president of the United States.

Despite Blackwell's odyssey to become an ordained minister, the ministry remained one of the professions most difficult to open up. Pioneers such as herself, Olympia Brown, the first Universalist minister, and Anna Howard Shaw, who was both a minister and a physician, could not clear paths that others would more easily follow. The ministry remained predominantly closed to women until well into the twentieth century.

1859: The American Medical Association Announces Its Opposition to Abortion

(Family Life)

Prodded by Dr. Horatio Storer, the American Medical Association (AMA), the leading organization of American doctors, declared its opposition to the practice of abortion in 1859.

Before the 1820s, American women resorted to abortion as a means of birth control without feeling that they had committed an immoral act. Until the 1820s, abortion was neither an epidemic nor a rarity. But over the next three decades, abortion became more and more frequent, until, as Dr. Horatio Storer, the leading contemporary medical authority commented, that what had been "a rare and secret occurrence, has become frequent and bold." As an opponent of abortion, it served Storer's purpose to create the fiction that the practice had been both rare and secret. With an eye toward removing abortion as an option open to women, the anti-abortionists began to paint a picture of rampant wantonness on the part of women in electing to terminate pregnancies. Women of all classes resorted to it, contemporary observers noted, pointing out how frequently it was used by married women. Morse Stewart, for example, observed that "among married persons so extensive has this practice become, that people of high repute not only commit this crime, but do not even shun to speak boastingly among their intimates, of the deed and the means of accomplishing it." The rhetoric of the anti-abortionists elevated the act to the status of a "crime," an increasingly common characterization as they attempted to solicit support for restrictions.

The American Medical Association's opposition to abortion played a critical role in redefining the legal status of abortion in America over the next two decades. Between 1860 and

1880, over forty states and territories passed laws against the practice, and the main impetus came not from clergy but from doctors. Catholic bishops did not make a general statement of opposition to abortion until 1869, and most Protestant denominations did not take a position until after 1870.

This did not mean, though, that the opposition to abortion was based on scientific or humanitarian reasons. While scientists and doctors were certainly aware that abortion posed risks to the woman involved, they did not advance these reasons as their primary objections to the practice. Instead, they emphasized moral and social objections. A report by the AMA's Committee on Criminal Abortion in 1871, for example, denounced abortion as a violation of the laws of God and nature, quoting the Bible and concluding that a woman resorting to abortion "becomes unmindful of the course marked out for her by Providence" and "overlooks the duties imposed on her by the marriage contract." To the extent that doctors opposed to abortion considered the risks to the woman at all, it was to pose risks as the "penalties to their transgressions" imposed by "natural laws."

The AMA opposed abortion so vehemently for two reasons. The first pertained to doctors' professionalization of their discipline. Prior to the professionalization of medicine, midwives were often an integral part of pregnancy experiences, whether the pregnancy ended in the birth of a child, or was terminated at the request of the mother. Women often relied on local midwives for medical care. Regulating health care in all its aspects, including abortion, was one way to eliminate unlicensed practitioners. The second reason had little to do with medicine and everything to do with social control. They opposed it for the same reason that so many married women resorted to it. It was the only form of family limitation entirely under the woman's control.

1863: The National Women's Loyal League Supports Emancipation

(Social Reform)

In May 1863, Elizabeth Cady Stanton and Susan B. Anthony organized the National Women's Loyal League. Several hundred women, eager to demonstrate their support of Union war efforts and of emancipation, answered Stanton's and Anthony's call to meet in New York on May 14, 1863. Stanton was elected president.

B oth Elizabeth Cady Stanton and Susan B. Anthony had long been involved in abolition and women's rights prior to the outbreak of the Civil War. While they never denied the importance of women's rights, they, like all other women, were willing to suspend activities until the war was successfully concluded. As early as 1861, Stanton began advocating emancipation for slaves, but when President Abraham Lincoln delivered his Emancipation Proclamation to take effect on January 1, 1863, Stanton and other abolitionists were somewhat disappointed. The Emancipation Proclamation really only affected slaves in the Confederate states, where there was precious little anyone could do to enforce the edict until the Confederacy was defeated. Slaves residing in the so-called border states were not affected

by the Emancipation Proclamation.

Despite this disappointment, Stanton sought ways in which women could express their support for the aims of the Union and for full emancipation. Public affirmations of any kind by women were still unusual, but Stanton and Anthony wanted to do more than knit garments to support the war effort. By then a resident of New York City, Stanton, with Anthony, issued a call for women to meet on May 14 to join an organization that would take a more active role. Several hundred women responded.

At the initial meeting, the members adopted several resolutions. Some members wanted resolutions that would have confined the Loyal League only to those issues that addressed Lincoln's conduct of the war, hoping to circumvent the possibility of either women's rights or abolition becoming the domain of the league. The conservative faction was voted down, however, and the most significant resolution was to mount a petition campaign urging Congress to vote for immediate emancipation of all slaves in the Union. It also passed a resolution supporting the government so long as it continued to wage a war for freedom. Finally, the members voted to attempt to collect one million signatures in support of passage of the Thirteenth Amendment, which would abolish slavery.

The Loyal League remained in existence for a little over one year, disbanding in August 1864. At its height, the Loyal League counted nearly five thousand women as members. Operating on a shoe-string budget, volunteers fanned out seeking signatures to their petition, eventually collecting almost four hundred thousand names. Their ability to collect signatures was only slightly hampered by collecting one penny for each signature, as a means of financing their organization. In its short lifetime, the Loyal League was an invaluable educational experience for thousands of women who, after the Civil War, would turn their energies to other reform causes.

1867: The Grange Movement Accepts Women as Equal Members

(Family Life, Cultural Life)

Disturbed by the bleak isolation of farmers on the Great Plains, Oliver Hudson Kelly founded a secret society in 1867, the Grange, dedicated to bringing farmers together for social and cultural activities. From the beginning, the organization admitted women on an equal basis.

As an inspector for the U.S. Department of Agriculture, Oliver Hudson Kelly, a Minnesota farmer, traveled extensively through the post–Civil War South and West, and saw firsthand how isolated and impoverished the lives of farmers and their families had become. In the wide-open spaces of the Great Plains, the nearest neighbor was often miles away, the nearest town dozens of miles away. In these circumstances, even prosperous farmers lived meager lives.

Farmwives lived in even greater bleakness. The men at least occasionally traveled to town to conduct business. While there, they would meet friends to exchange news and discuss politics. Women, in contrast, were not expected to participate in business or politics, so there was no pressing reason for them to leave the house and children. In fact, their presence at home was necessary while the husband was away, and few would venture to travel alone. As a consequence, they spent months, or even years, in the same small area, bereft of new faces, friends, ideas, or entertainment.

Kelley believed that the farmers had to unite and promote their interests collectively. Through Kelley's efforts, the Order of the Patrons of Husbandry was charted in Washington, D.C., on December 4, 1867, as a fraternal organization. Better known as the Grange movement for the local unit of organization, it offered a framework in which farmers and farmwives could organize regular gatherings for educational programs, discussions, debates, picnics, and dances. Although the society's constitution forebade involvement in politics, once the meetings were over the members would stay and discuss current affairs. The movement never abandoned its cultural and intellectual goal, but it also served as an important outlet for economic discontents and as a collective voice in local, state, and eventually national politics.

For women, the Grange proved to be particularly valuable. Under the terms of establishing a Grange branch, four women and nine men had to apply for membership, so women's role in the Grange was institutionalized from the start. Women had full voting rights, they could hold any Grange office, and there were special posts designated to manage female affairs. Most often, the Grange lectures were arranged by women in both New England and in the Midwest. In the southern Grange branches, women were not afforded the opportunity to participate in political affairs. The Grange charter did not cease to exist in the South; rather it was the weight of cultural bias that relegated women to a peripheral role in that region.

Grange women took to politics quite readily. Grange women were able to persuade many male members to support woman suffrage. By the mid 1870s, there were 750,000 Grange members in 25,000 chapters around the country. Some of the most outspoken agrarian radicals came out of the Grange movement, including Mary Lease, who ran for the U.S. Senate in 1893. But the majority of Grange women were not outspoken lecturers. They were dedicated members who worked tirelessly for the agrarian crusade, and who brought to it their own talents and interests, from advocating equal education for girls to equal rights for women.

1869: The Knights of Labor Is Founded and Includes Women Workers

(Work, Equal Rights)

Inspired by the dream of uniting all workers in one massive organization, the Philadelphia tailor Uriah S. Stephens founded the Knights of Labor "to secure to the toilers a proper share of the wealth that they create." From the beginning, the organization accepted women as members, and some rose to positions of national leadership.

At the same time that Oliver Hudson Kelly was organizing American farmers into the vast network of Granges, Uriah Stephens began drawing American workers into what he hoped would be an embracing organization of laborers. If the Grange movement faced daunting obstacles in the great distances, economic disparities, and traditional individualism that kept American farmers apart, the Knights of Labor faced the equally daunting obstacles in ethnic differences, different levels of skills, and different ambitions and goals. In the case of the labor organizers, these difficulties were on top of the inevitable opposition of employers and hostility of government.

The Knights succeeded in bringing together immigrants and natives, skilled artisans and day laborers, men and women, because they espoused a moderate and practical course of action. In contrast to craft unions, they advocated arbitration over strikes and political agitation over physical violence. The Knights created cooperative stores, which they hoped would provide better merchandise while charging less than stores run for profit. Their job-related platform included an eight-hour workday and an end to child labor. Their organization was based on local assemblies that included all of the workers in a shop or neighborhood; their program addressed common problems and offered collective solutions.

Ironically, the high point of the Knights' fortunes followed a series of strikes that local assemblies called against the wishes of the national leaders. Their success brought a rise in membership from five hundred thousand in 1885 to seven hundred thousand in 1886. But the sudden rise was followed by just as sudden a decline.

Further strikes failed miserably, and by 1890 membership had fallen to one hundred thousand. By the end of the decade, the Knights of Labor had disappeared completely.

The failure of the Knights of Labor had particular importance for women, because their successors were the craft unions of the American Federation of Labor (AFL). Focusing on the interests of skilled workers only, they slighted women doubly, both because they tended to be unskilled and because they were women. To the extent that they were unskilled, the AFL ignored their needs. To the extent that they competed with skilled men, the AFL opposed them, since they depressed the wage scales. "Organized labor" agitated for restrictions on female (and child) labor on the basis of decency, but the root of its opposition was economic competition. What the history of American women in the workplace would have been had labor organized along the embracing lines of the Knights of Labor rather than the exclusionary basis of the AFL must remain an open question.

1869: Suffragists Organize

(Equal Rights)

In May 1869, Elizabeth Cady Stanton and Susan B. Anthony organized the National Woman Suffrage Association in New York City. The following November, Lucy Stone, of the New England Woman Suffrage Association, founded the American Woman Suffrage Association.

Eighteen years after the historic women's rights convention in Seneca Falls, New York, suffragists founded the first national suffrage organization. The American Equal Rights Association, founded in 1866, was intended to reconcile the American women's movement that had run on two increasingly divergent paths ever since the World Anti-Slavery Conference in London in 1840, when women delegates from the United States had been refused seats. The new organization hoped to bring together the anti-slavery movement and the women's rights movement to work simultaneously for legal rights for both former slaves and women. The slate of officers included Lucretia Mott, president; Susan B. Anthony, secretary; and Elizabeth Cady Stanton, vice president. Their combined credentials seemed to insure that the organization would remain on track with its dual goals. But die-hard abolitionists, mostly men, had other agendas. Wendall Phillips and Frederick Douglass were among the biggest critics of pursuing women's rights at what they considered a crucial time. The feminists argued that women had deferred their suffrage quest long enough when they suspended virtually all women's rights activity for the duration of the war. The final straw for feminists came when abolitionists insisted that the reform agenda, in the words of Wendall Phillips, had to be "Negro suffrage, then temperance, then the eight-hour movement, then woman suffrage." And, they were outraged when the Fifteenth Amendment did not include women's rights to vote and received no support for inclusion from abolitionists within the American Equal Rights Association.

In May 1869, at the New York Women's Bureau, Susan B. Anthony and Elizabeth Cady Stanton organized the National Woman's Suffrage Association (NWSA), with 118 women signing up on the spot. Among the initial joiners were Lucretia Mott, Martha Wright, and Paulina Wright Davis, all noted feminists and former members of the American Equal Rights Association. From the start, the NWSA excluded men from leadership positions and elected offices, and emphasized the necessity to secure an amendment to the U.S. Constitution that would guarantee women the right to vote. Stanton was elected the first president of NWSA, and Anthony served first on the executive committee and then as vice president. Eventually, Anthony would become president of the organization. Stanton, as president, did not mask her own radical feminist views, and NWSA tended to reflect her position. Cross-country lecture tours, discussions, and rallies helped to ignite the still-fledgling women's rights movement and NWSA chapters sprang up, especially in the east and midwest.

In the meantime, a second organization, the American Woman Suffrage Association (AWSA), was founded in Cleveland, Ohio, in November 1869, by Lucy Stone. Stone, whose abolitionist roots ran deeper than her feminist roots, disagreed with what she perceived as the radicalism of Stanton and Anthony. AWSA expressed a willingness to defer woman suffrage, and it also prominently featured male office holders. The first AWSA president was Henry Ward Beecher. AWSA also undertook a nationwide lecture tour in an effort to build a national audience. Almost from the start, NWSA far outstripped AWSA in its ability to attract members and money. Although AWSA also advocated a national suffrage amendment, its advocacy was somewhat diluted by the fact that the organization concentrated instead on campaigning state-by-state in an effort to change individual state constitutions.

With the establishment of the two major suffrage organizations of the nineteenth century, the women's movement itself had identified the two strains that would continue to separate women well into the twentieth century, despite apparent reconciliations from time to time. Feminists argued that as long as half the population was denied its rights, all other issues had to be secondary. The moderates, on the other hand, viewed women's rights as conditional, depending on other issues in consideration at any given time.

1872: Victoria Woodhull Runs for President of the United States

(Equal Rights, Political Reform)

Victoria Woodhull, whose notoriety made her a household name long before she entered politics, announced in 1870 that she would run for president in the election of 1872. Although she held no real expectations of success, her campaign allowed her to focus on a number of women's issues. Running on a ticket with noted, but nonconsenting, abolitionist Frederick Douglass, Woodhull's campaign ended in a scandal that rocked the nation.

Victoria Woodhull was surely one of the most colorful women in American history. From her early childhood and teen years spent traveling the country with a family medicine show, to years spent drifting from town to town with her young daughter Zula Maud and her sister Tennessee, to her later years as a successful Wall Street broker and psychic to Cornelius Vanderbilt, Victoria and her family, as one historian described them, were like "characters released from a raucous novel." Victoria had a penchant for finding unlikely mentors who influenced the direction of her life. After a short-lived first marriage, she married Civil War veteran Colonel James Harvey Blood. It was Blood who introduced Victoria to several reform causes that surrounded her belief in spiritualism. When she decided to move to New York in 1868, she claimed it was because the spirit of Demosthenes had spoken to her and urged her to go. It was there that she and Tennessee met Cornelius Vanderbilt, a recent widower who wanted to contact the spirit of his dead wife. The sisters accommodated him, and in return, he helped them to launch their first real estate venture. After experiencing success there, the sisters opened brokerage offices in the heart of the Wall Street district, and again were highly successful. Undoubtedly, Vanderbilt's advice helped them to do well for their clients. But both Victoria and Tennessee were intelligent women and learned quickly. The "Bewitching Brokers," as they were called, both admiringly and derisively, charmed and outraged Wall Street with their success.

Another mentor, Stephen Paul Andrews, a sometimes philosopher, linguist, and abolitionist, encouraged Woodhull's long-growing suspicion that marriage ties were simply a way to keep women in bondage. Intent now on publicizing the cause of women's rights, Woodhull announced that she would run for president in 1872. Six weeks later, the first issue of *Woodhull and Claflin's Weekly* was published, outlining Woodhull's program, which included free love, shorter skirts, legalized prostitution, and reforms in taxation, housing, and diet. The *Weekly* became an early example of muckraking journalism, with its exposés of Wall Street fraud. It was also the first place where Karl Marx's *Communist Manifesto* was published in America.

Having no connection with any suffrage group, she nevertheless urged Congress to legalize woman suffrage under the Fourteenth Amendment. Suffragists were divided over the flamboyant Woodhull. On the one hand, they feared that supporting her candidacy would make a mockery out of women's rights issues. On the other hand, she had dared to do what many feminists were fighting for—demanding her right to participate fully in the political process.

About a year before the election, Canning Woodhull, her first husband, reappeared and moved in with Woodhull and Blood. This sparked charges that Woodhull had never really divorced her first husband and that she was guilty of bigamy. Woodhull fired back at the scandalmongers for being hypocritical in not assailing the liaison between the Reverend Henry Ward Beecher and Elizabeth Tilton, the wife of editor Theodore Tilton, both of whom were Beecher's parishioners. Within the Beecher family, Harriet Beecher Stowe, a critic of Woodhull, took up her brother's cause, while Isobel Beecher, another sister, remained fast friends with Woodhull. It was a messy situation all around. Even so, Woodhull found it difficult to publicize the Beecher-Tilton scandal, until she was finally forced to revive her by-now defunct *Woodhull and Claflin's Weekly* for one special issue. When she did, moral crusader Anthony Comstock had her arrested for disseminating obscene material through the mail.

Woodhull's presidential campaign was over. She was eventually acquitted, under first amendment guarantees. Henry Ward Beecher was also acquitted in a subsequent trial. Ultimately, Woodhull and her sister left

America for England, where they lectured, both married, and lived reasonably respectable lives. Woodhull's antics may have caused consternation, outrage, shock, and anger among those who witnessed or read about her many escapades and endeavors. But she also made women think about their own status, whether or not they agreed with her. She pushed the accepted boundaries and forced men to acknowledge that they did not consider women included or protected in the rights and privileges to which citizens were entitled under the terms of the Constitution, either in the Four-

teenth or Fifteenth Amendments. Other feminists decided to test the waters themselves, perhaps because of Woodhull, including Susan B. Anthony. Anthony showed up in Rochester on election day in 1872 and cast her vote for president. She was immediately arrested. Finally, Woodhull, by virtue of her own flamboyance, made mainstream feminists look reasonable and moderate by contrast. In the wake of—though certainly not because of—the Woodhull campaign, feminists were more determined than ever to resolve their own differences and work together to achieve their goals.

1873: The "Women's Uprising"

(Social Reform)

In the winter of 1873–74, the women of Hillsboro, Ohio, and neighboring towns, undertook a series of spontaneous demonstrations intended to drive men from drinking and close down saloons.

The "women's uprising" began one morning when a group of eighty Hillsboro women met to discuss a temperance meeting that had been held the night before. Not content to talk and pray in church, they marched two-by-two downtown intending to sing and pray in the bars and saloons

until the owners agreed to close them down. They returned morning after morning, embarrassing their sons, fathers, and brothers into signing temperance pledges, and inducing one saloon keeper after another to empty his casks into the street.

Despite the fact that the movement

had no organization or conspicuous leaders, it spread rapidly. First women in neighboring towns in Ohio and, by the next year, women all over the Northeast embarked on similar crusades. Over sixty thousand women participated in the movement, and their efforts succeeded in closing down over one thousand saloons and bars. The campaign sent a shock-wave through the nation, and led to more organized and more persistent efforts that led ultimately to the grand, if futile, experiment of national prohibition in the 1920s.

Why did the women of Hillsboro and their sisters throughout the country erupt with such energy and such passion in the winter of 1873? For one thing, the country was in the midst of a depression, and the women knew that saloonkeepers were pressuring the Ohio legislature to relax the liquor laws. For another, temperance was one issue that women of diverse political inclinations could agree on. Staunch suffragettes and conservative churchgoers agreed in their assessment of drinking as a particularly noxious male activity that threatened the home and family with violence, financial ruin, desertion, and immorality. Accepting their culturally assigned role as the protectors of children and the community, late nineteenth century American women, building on pre–Civil War efforts to curb drinking, found a common rallying point in the fight against demon alcohol.

The effects of this campaign carried far beyond the eventual achievement of prohibition, however. As Frances Willard, leader of the Women's Christian Temperance Union, noted, "Perhaps the most significant outcome of this movement was the knowledge of their own power gained by the conservative women of the Churches." The temperance movement acted as a focal point for women's discontent, and it served as a proving ground for their exercise of power.

1873: Remington Begins Manufacture of the Typewriter

(Work)

In 1873, Christopher Latham Sholes and his associates licensed their invention, a typewriter, to E. Remington and Sons, who immediately began its commercial manufacture. Within ten years the machine had revolutionized office record keeping and business communication, and opened up a new type of employment to women.

Before the Civil War, most businesses were small individual proprietorships employing a few dozen workers at most and needing only a handful of office employees to help the owner. During the 1870s and 1880s, though, the scale of business burgeoned, with corporations and trusts coming to control tens of thousands of workers scattered across the country, and eventually around the world. By 1904, just 1 percent of American corporations controlled a full third of all manufacturing, and by this time the total value of manufacturing output had increased over ten times since 1860, while the labor force used to produce it had risen five times. To control the operations of these large and scattered operations, big businesses organized themselves along military lines. They created a carefully designed hierarchy of control, functional divisions within the organization, and corps of middle managers who both mediated between top management and labor and coordinated the activities of separate branches of the organization.

Both a prerequisite and result of this growth of bureaucracy was a concomitant growth in paperwork. Consequently, when Remington began selling Sholes' invention it found a ready market. By 1886, the company was making 1,500 per month, and a year later a business journal noted that "five years ago the typewriter was simply a mechanical curiosity. Today its monotonous click can be heard in almost every well-regulated business establishment in the country. A great revolution is taking place, and the typewriter is at the bottom of it."

Although the business journal probably had a revolution in business procedures in mind, the impact of the typewriter, coupled with the growing scale and bureaucratization of enterprise, was revolutionizing the status of its operators as well. Before the Civil War, a clerk in a business was usually a young man at the bottom of the corporate ladder, for what better way was there to learn the business than to keep its records and transcribe its correspondence. With the rise of the typewriter, though, transcribing documents became a task requiring special manual training, and hence conducted by specialists who were no longer managers in training, but a new form of skilled worker.

As the status of the clerk changed, so too did the characteristics of the stenographer, file clerk, and typist who replaced him. Remarkably quickly, in fact, all three jobs came to be seen as women's work, new specialties open to literate, native born whites with a basic education. As early as 1875, Remington advertised its new product as an ideal Christmas present since "no invention has opened for women so broad and easy an avenue to profitable and suitable employment as the 'Type-Writer.' " In 1881, when the New York Young Women's Christian Association (YWCA) offered typing training for women, its classes quickly filled up. If the work was repetitive and limited in its prospects, in the late nineteenth century it was one of the few occupations available for literate women other than teaching.

1873: Congress Passes the Comstock Law

(Family Life)

In 1873, the United States Congress passed an "Act for the Suppression of Trade in, and Circulation of, Obscene Literature and Articles of Immoral Use." Passed at the urging of Anthony Comstock, the head of the New York Society for the Suppression of Vice, the law quickly became known as the "Comstock Law."

The Comstock Law, passed by Congress in 1873, was the culmination of a crusade conducted by middle-class reformers who feared that easy access to certain types of materials or devices would lead to immoral, if not criminal, behavior. The chief proponent of the law was Anthony Comstock, the moral reformer who headed the New York Society for the Suppression of Vice. Comstock had long fought for the suppression of materials that he considered illicit and obscene. Included in the list of outlawed materials was any type of literature dealing with birth control or abortion. The law, as it was enacted, made little distinction between drugs used for abortion and materials used for contraception. Everything was considered pornographic material, and the penalty for those found guilty of violating the law was harsh. Persons convicted in a court of law were subject to imprisonment "at hard labor" for not less than six months, nor more than five years for *each* offense. A convicted person could also be fined between $100 and $2,000, and be liable for court costs as well.

Up until 1873, peddlers of contraceptive devices, rudimentary though they were, were allowed to advertise and did so widely, providing some recourse to women who sought to limit their pregnancies. The prevalence of advertisements throughout the country indicates a strong interest on the part of consumers for information regarding birth control. But the federal law prohibited that after 1873. In addition, many states passed supportive laws. Following passage of the Comstock Law, Anthony Comstock was appointed a special postal agent. Thereafter, he took it upon himself to enforce zealously the new law.

The widespread support for such legislation came from a variety of sources. First of all, most of the medical profession objected to contraceptives. The commonly held belief was that contraceptives were a violation of nature's laws, that they encouraged immorality, that they were harmful to the health of women, and that they might constitute a threat to motherhood itself. Very few physicians supported the use of contraceptives. Those that did cited the advantages to the poor to limit family size, or the benefit of improved health and happier marriages. Physicians who took a broader view of the benefits of contraceptive use were too few in number to influence policymakers.

With immigration on the increase following the Civil War, many people were also fearful that efforts on the part of native-born, middle-class white

Americans to limit family size would lead to "race suicide." In addition, middle-class women themselves had their own reasons for supporting the Comstock Law. Although many of them did want to limit family size, or at least space out their pregnancies, they were willing to forego contraceptives in order to end promiscuity.

After 1873, it became extremely difficult for women to obtain either contraceptives or information about contraceptives. Similarly, abortion was outlawed by every state but one by 1899. Moreover, the law made distri-bution of contraceptive information extremely difficult for those who were inclined to help. With such wide-spread support for the Comstock Law, and with the antivice societies remain-ing alert to infractions, violators of the law were usually quickly appre-hended. It was not until 1936 that the Supreme Court ruled that revision of the Comstock Law of 1873 was in or-der, but it took another thirty-five years until the prohibitions against birth control and contraceptives were written out of the law in 1971.

1874: Frances Willard Joins the Women's Christian Temperance Union

(Social Reform)

In order to capitalize on a temperance movement reinvigorated by the actions of the "women's uprisings" in 1873, the Women's Christian Temperance Union (WCTU) was founded.'The following summer in 1874, a group of Chicago women organiz-ing a local WCTU branch asked educator Frances Willard to be their leader. At a statewide convention in Bloomington, Illinois, in October 1874, Willard was elected secretary of the state WCTU.

The Women's Christian Temperance Union was founded to continue the work begun by the spontaneous protests of the "women's uprisings." In the process, it pioneered new forms of social mobilization designed exclusively by and for women. From the beginning, membership was barred to men, and under the tutelage of its able leader, Frances Willard, the WCTU eventually broadened its focus to include other types of reform and evolved an organizational style that was self-consciously female.

Willard joined the WCTU in 1874 when the organization was barely a year old. A brilliant educator, Willard had recently resigned from a position as dean of women and professor of English at Northwestern University because of professional and personal disagreements with Northwestern's new president, Charles Fowler. Her resignation from Northwestern left Willard at loose ends, since she had pursued her teaching career with the belief that she was embarking on a lifelong journey to help young women achieve new heights of self-reliance through education. Her invitation to join the WCTU came at a fortuitous juncture in her life, and she quickly threw herself into the cause. But it was clear to those who worked with her that temperance was only a vehicle to promote women's rights through reform in a number of fields. Her credo was "womanliness first—afterwards what you will," and those words summed up her approach to her new position.

Not everyone in the WCTU wanted to broaden the organization's focus. More conservative, less feminist members feared that trailing "our skirts through the mire of politics" would hurt the cause. So Willard's initial attempts to move the organization beyond temperance did not succeed. Over the next several years, Willard continued to move the organization in the direction she envisioned. This became more feasible when she was elected president of the Illinois WCTU in 1878. She began a campaign to secure signatures for a mammoth petition to the Illinois legislature. While the legislature voted down the first attempt to change the law in Illinois, Willard succeeded in demonstrating how widespread the support for such legislation had become. Thereafter, the Illinois campaign became the model for similar campaigns in other states. In 1879, Willard was elected president of the national WCTU, a position she would hold for twenty years.

Her first and foremost focus had, by definition, to be the fight against alcohol, but that was just one item on her agenda. She promoted suffrage by advocating the "Home Protection Ballot," which would give "the mothers and daughters of America" a voice in whether "the door of the rum shop is opened or shut beside their homes." She saw the WCTU itself as a model of female organization, contrasting its meetings with "any held by men: Its manner is not that of the street, the court, the mart, or office; it is the manner of the home."

But Willard's true genius was her restraint in promoting her broader agenda. Rather than pushing the organization to adopt her views, she encouraged it instead to adopt a "Do-Everything" policy. This policy, formally adopted in 1882, meant that local chapters could do anything and everything they wanted. Conservative groups could focus exclusively on the struggle against alcohol, while liberal ones could use the organization as the basis for promoting a broad range of reforms. By 1889, for example, the Chicago branch had organized "two day nurseries, two Sunday schools, an industrial school, a mission that shel-tered 4,000 homeless or destitute women in a twelve-month period, a free medical dispensary that treated over 1,600 patients a year, a lodging house for men that had to date provided temporary housing for over 50,000 men in total, and a low-price restaurant."

Even more significant than the ecumenical policy was the breadth of its membership. While upper-middle-class, white, Protestant women dominated its leadership, the WCTU included both middle- and working-class women in its ranks, and they came from cities, towns, and farms alike. For long after the issues of the day had been decided, the immediate battles had been won or lost, the organization itself had withered away, its social ideals and its organizational principals lived on through the women who had lived them. Although Frances Willard died in 1898, her programs helped to propel the WCTU along for the additional twenty years it would take to secure a prohibition amendment to the U.S. Constitution.

1874: Mary Ewing Outerbridge Brings Tennis to the United States

(Recreation)

On a vacation trip to Bermuda in 1874, socialite Mary Ewing Outerbridge was taught the game of lawn tennis. She so enjoyed the game that, on her return to America, she taught it to her friends and thereby introduced tennis to this country.

The game of tennis originated in England as an outdoor form of "Royal Tennis." As early as 1793, references to tennis could be found in English magazines. British colonial officials and their wives brought it to their posts, which is how the game came to Bermuda, and it was here that Mary Ewing Outerbridge came to first play the game. She was apparently so taken with it that she bought rackets, balls, and nets and brought them back with her when she returned to her home on Staten Island, New York. Some of the people she taught were equally taken with the game, and it rapidly gained popularity with the new leisure class growing up in industrial America.

One of the new enthusiasts was Outerbridge's brother, who was also a director of the Staten Island Cricket and Baseball Club. Within months of her return, the club had erected the first court on American soil. The U.S. National Lawn Tennis Association, later to become the U.S. Tennis Association, was formed in 1884, and it held the first national championships, men's singles and doubles, that year. The association added the first women's event, women's singles, just three years later, and women's doubles just three years after that, in 1890.

The growth of tennis, and the growth of women in tennis, reflected the social changes that were taking place in America in the "Gilded Age" of the late nineteenth century. The inhabitants of emerging urban industrial society embraced sports both for the physical fitness brought by participation in amateur events and for the entertainment value of professional matches. At the high end of society, the burgeoning upper and upper middle classes had considerable leisure time and the wealth to enjoy it. They created exclusive athletic clubs in which they played their own games, like tennis and golf, which remained amateur far longer than baseball and football.

Well-to-do women avidly participated in these new sports because they, above all, were the beneficiaries of the new leisure time. While some rebelled against the artificial lifestyle their wealth imposed, most resigned themselves to their fate gracefully, demanding only that they be able to enjoy equally the fruits of their husbands' labors (or that of their husbands' employees' labors). The men accepted women playing their sports both because they did not compete directly and because it was, after all, only sports. The days of the million dollar contracts were far in the future, and by the time even elite sports were professionalized, it was too late to turn the clock back on women's participation.

When Mary Ewing Outerbridge brought lawn tennis back to America, she probably never dreamed that the sport would one day achieve such popularity. She might, though, have very much appreciated the irony that such an elite, upper-class sport would someday bring to those who mastered the game, regardless of background, the same wealth and social standing that enabled the game's first admirers to take it up. Outerbridge might also have enjoyed knowing that tennis became the first competitive professional sport in which women participated where they were finally able to break the prize money barrier and play for purses that rivaled those offered in men's tennis.

1874: The U.S. Supreme Court Rules in the Case of *Minor v. Happersett*

(Equal Rights)

In 1872, Virginia Minor, an officer in the National Woman Suffrage Association, brought suit against Reese Happersett, the registrar of voters in St. Louis, Missouri, for refusing to place Minor's name on the eligible voters list because she was not a man. The case went to the U.S. Supreme Court, which handed down its decision in 1874.

The Fifteenth Amendment, both in its wording and in its passage by Congress and ratification by the requisite number of states in 1870, was a source of discontent for feminists since its inception. Women had wanted the amendment to insure voting rights not only for former male slaves, but for women of all colors as well. Politicians had no interest in allowing women to vote and abolitionists, including many women, were inclined to let the woman issue slide for fear of jeopardizing voting privileges for the former male slaves. But ratification of the amendment spurred feminists to challenge the intent to exclude women.

In the first election after ratification, that of 1872, a number of women attempted to force the issue by voting, or trying to vote. Influenced by the National Woman Suffrage Association, an extraordinary example of civil disobedience occurred, in which hundreds of women across the country broke the law by attempting to vote. The actions resulted in many court cases, including the trial of Susan B. Anthony. Anthony had led a small delegation of women to the polls in Rochester, New York, determined to test the validity of their contention that women, as citizens, were entitled to vote under the Fifteenth Amendment. Anthony was convicted at a trial without a jury, by a judge whose opinion had been written before the trial started.

In St. Louis, Missouri, another officer of the National Woman Suffrage Association, Virginia Minor, also attempted to register to vote. When Reese Happersett, the registrar of voters, refused to register her, Minor brought suit against him, asking for $10,000 in damages. Minor contended that, while states could regulate suffrage, the Constitution "nowhere gives them the power to prevent." Her husband, Francis Minor, an attorney, acted as his wife's lawyer to press the suit. Not surprisingly, Minor lost her case in both the St. Louis Circuit Court and the Missouri Court of Appeals. But the Minors pressed on, bringing the case to the Supreme Court. In 1874, Chief Justice Morrison R. Waite handed down the unanimous opinion of the court denying Minor's appeal, stating that "the Constitution of the United States does not confer the right of suffrage upon anyone," because suffrage was not coexistent with citizenship.

With the court's decision, hopes for a judicial solution to the woman suffrage question were dashed. Suffragists turned full force toward the alter- natives, campaigning state-by-state to change individual state constitutions and seeking a federal woman suffrage amendment to the Constitution.

1878: A Woman Suffrage Amendment Is First Submitted to Congress

(Equal Rights)

On January 10, 1878, what would become, over forty-five years later, the Nineteenth Amendment to the U.S. Constitution, was introduced for the first time in the U.S. Senate by Senator Arlen A. Sargent of California.

In 1875, still smarting over the passage of a constitutional amendment that gave voting rights to African- American males without including women, Susan B. Anthony penned the lines of a woman suffrage amendment modeled on the Fifteenth Amendment. Just two sentences long, the woman suffrage amendment was simple and to the point: "The right of citizens of the United States to vote shall not be denied or abridged by the United States or by any State on account of sex. Congress shall have the power, by appropriate legislation, to enforce the provisions of this article." Three years later, Anthony and Eliza- beth Cady Stanton were able to persuade Senator Arlen A. Sargent of California to introduce the legislation in the Senate. For a time, the amendment was referred to as the Sargent Amend- ment, and it was reintroduced in each succeeding congress until its final passage forty-five years later.

When Sargent introduced the legislation for the first time, it was less than favorably received. Some members of congress were openly derisive, others were supportive, indifferent, or even amused. But no one believed then, and for many years after, that the legislation would ever either be favorably reported out of committee or find sufficient support for passage by the full House and Senate. Over the course of the next several decades, the amendment would be reported out of committee twelve times by the Senate and ten times by the House. Between 1887 and 1919, the amendment was brought to a vote before the Senate or the House a total of eight times, with the last five of those votes taking place between January 1918 and June 1919. Clearly, most of the congressional support for a woman suffrage amendment did not come about until the last three years before its passage. In the final two votes, the House passed what had become known as the Susan B. Anthony Amendment, on May 21, 1919, by a vote of 304 in favor to 89 opposed. On June 4, 1919, the Senate passed the Anthony Amendment by a vote of 56 in favor to 25 opposed. Within a year, the Anthony Amendment officially became the law of the land as the Nineteenth Amendment to the Constitution. The wording of the amendment remained as Susan B. Anthony had composed it forty-five years earlier.

1879: Mary Baker Eddy Founds the Christian Science Movement

(Religion, Cultural Life)

Four years after the publication of her book *Science and Health with Key to the Scriptures* (1875), in which she explained the central idea of Christian Science—the power of the mind over matter—Mary Baker Eddy formally founded the First Church of Christ, Scientist, in Massachusetts.

The idea that Mary Baker Eddy would become a charismatic, powerful religious leader would probably have raised a few eyebrows among those who knew her as a sickly, frail child. Born in New Hampshire in 1821, Mary Baker was the youngest of six children. Much of her childhood was spent struggling with emotional problems compounded by a chronic and painful back disorder. Her schooling, therefore, was intermittent, supplemented primarily by tutoring from her older brother, a Dartmouth College student. As a consequence, she probably had a better than average education for young women at that time. With no prospects for using her education, she married a family friend, George Glover, at the age of twenty-two. Within six months George was dead and Mary was left widowed and pregnant. The experience caused a complete emotional collapse that left Mary incapable of caring for her infant son, who was raised in a foster home. For several years, Mary's emotional state of mind remained static. She was treated with morphine and other addictive drugs that created a dependency against which she struggled for the remainder of her life. Gradually, she was able to emerge from her emotional collapse and became well enough to engage in sporadic teaching and writing. Relapses occurred when her mother died, when her father remarried, and because of another depression that settled over her.

Surprisingly, in 1853, Mary wed for a second time, to a dentist named Daniel Patterson. The marriage was never a happy one, for Patterson traveled extensively. During the Civil War.

Patterson was taken prisoner and Mary Baker Glover Patterson realized, perhaps for the first time, that she would have to take her own life in hand and try to make her own way.

Shortly after the war ended, Mary had a chance meeting with Phineas Quimby, a self-styled "doctor" who practiced hypnosis. Quimby firmly believed that mental attitude could both cause and cure disease. With the new realization that she had to take responsibility for herself, Quimby's message reached Mary as nothing had before. It also helped her to extricate herself from her unhappy marriage to Patterson after he returned home from the war. Devoted now to learning all she could about Quimby's philosophy, neither his death nor her divorce struck the emotional blow that either one might have in earlier years. She was able to attract students willing to pay a very high fee to learn about what was now Mary Baker's philosophy. She also began working on the book that would help to establish both herself and her church, *Science and Health*.

With the full flowering of her charisma and magnetic personality, Baker attracted hundreds of disciples, one of whom became her third husband. Asa Eddy supported his wife wholeheartedly and encouraged her to formalize her religious/philosophical movement. In 1879, Mary Baker Eddy formally founded the First Church of Christ, Scientist, and two years later obtained a charter from the state of Massachusetts that allowed her Massachusetts Metaphysical College to grant degrees. A short time later, her husband died. In another surprising turn, Mary Baker Eddy reverted back to her old life of isolation and morphine addiction by 1887.

Nevertheless, the Christian Science religion continued to grow and prosper, though not without some travail. A series of lawsuits plagued Mary Baker Eddy, brought against her and against the Christian Science church. Partially in an effort to offset negative publicity resulting from the lawsuits, the church began publishing its own newspaper. The *Christian Science Monitor*, which began as a vehicle for putting Christian Science in a good light, eventually became an influential newspaper that went far beyond its church mission and attracted independent readers with no church connection, through good reporting and intellectually stimulating editing.

Christian Science today continues to flourish. Mary Baker Eddy remains the only woman to have founded a major religion.

1879: The First Woman Practices before the U.S. Supreme Court

(Equal Rights, Work)

In 1876, lawyer Belva Lockwood petitioned the U.S. Supreme Court for permission to plead a case. When she was denied on the grounds of custom, Lockwood immediately appealed to Congress. In 1879, Congress passed a bill enabling female lawyers to practice before the highest courts in the land.

When Belva Lockwood was widowed for the first time in 1853, she moved with her young daughter to Washington, D.C., in hopes of finding suitable employment to support the two of them. A teacher in her native New York, Lockwood opened a coeducational school in Washington, a novel concept at the time, particularly among private schools. In 1868, she married for a second time, and her husband, Ezekial Lockwood, took over the administration of the school. For the first time, Lockwood was free to pursue other interests, one of which was to study law. Lockwood's interest in the law was partially founded on her interest in promoting women's rights.

Finding a law school that would accept her proved no easy task. Columbian College (later George Washington University) law school turned down her application, citing the standard response for many universities to which women applied, that her presence in class would be too distracting to the male students. She was turned down by Georgetown University and Howard University as well. Finally, however, the newly formed National University Law School accepted her application in 1871. She completed the required course work in good standing in May 1873. The school, however, would not award her a diploma immediately. Lockwood was forced to take proactive steps to get what she had earned. Appealing to the law school's ex-officio president, Ulysses S. Grant, Lockwood demanded

that she be given her diploma. Grant, sympathetic to her situation, interceded on her behalf and Lockwood finally received her law degree in September 1873. Immediately, she was admitted to the bar of the District of Columbia, which, two years earlier, had changed judicial rules in order to allow women to practice law.

Because the District of Columbia has no state courts, anyone practicing in the district, by necessity, must have access to the federal court system. When one of Lockwood's cases came before the federal court of claims, she was denied the right to plead her case on the grounds of sex. In 1876, she petitioned the U.S. Supreme Court. The Supreme Court rejected her petition, despite Lockwood's irrefutable logic that if a woman was entitled to practice law, she had to be entitled to pursue legal matters through the highest courts in the land.

In the midst of this controversy, Lockwood's elderly husband died in 1877. Once again, Lockwood was a widow with a compelling need to earn a living, in addition to her right to pursue a fulfilling and meaningful livelihood. Once again, she fought on her own behalf, lobbying members of Congress to change the laws that made it impossible for women to practice law fully and without hindrance in the courts system. Seeking the assistance of prosuffrage Senators, including Arlen Sargent of California and George Hoar of Massachusetts, Lockwood succeeded in securing passage of legislation in 1879 that permitted women lawyers to practice before the Supreme Court. On March 3 of that year, she became the first woman to do so. Once she had pleaded a case before the Supreme Court, the court of claims and every other federal court had to follow suit. Lockwood's legislation brought an end to discrimination based on sex in the federal courts and set standards for state courts as well. To her great credit, her belief in equality led her a year later to sponsor Samuel R. Lowry, the first African-American lawyer to practice before the Supreme Court.

1881: Clara Barton Founds the American Red Cross

(Social Reform)

In May 1881, Clara Barton and several associates organized the American Association of the Red Cross. In addition to a Board of Consultation, the head of which was the President of the United States, Clara Barton was named president of the association.

Clara Barton was remembered by hundreds of soldiers during the Civil War as the "Angel of the Battlefield," and memorialized thereafter by generations of school children as a selfless heroine who tended wounded soldiers and eventually founded the American Red Cross. While true, such a sketchy outline does not begin to illustrate the enormity of Barton's accomplishments, nor how they benefited Americans both in war and in peace.

Barton was a former teacher working in the U.S. Patent Office in 1860 when the Civil War began. Possibly the first female employee of the federal government, Barton left teaching when she was passed over in favor of a man to become head of a New Jersey public school that she had started. Working for the federal government had similar drawbacks. But Barton's organizational skills were much in demand by her superiors. When the war began, she was shocked to learn how ill-equipped the government was to properly supply its troops and to deal with casualties. On her own initiative, Barton advertised in newspapers for donations in the form of medical supplies and food. She quit her government job and used her home as a storehouse, enlisting the assistance of friends to distribute the supplies to the battlefields in Maryland and Virginia. While she did some battlefield nursing, her forte was in producing the supplies necessary for the military doctors to help the wounded. Considered a nuisance at first, doctors quickly came to appreciate Barton's resourcefulness and dedication. Once the Quartermaster Corp and the Sanitary Commission were organized, Barton became less active. As the war progressed, however, she recognized another need that had to be filled. In 1865, Barton opened an agency to locate missing soldiers. She set up a clearinghouse to track down soldiers whose families had lost contact with them. The funding for this operation came from both donations and Barton's own resources, which she gladly spent.

Traveling abroad in 1869 to recuperate from her Civil War work, Barton heard of the International Committee of the Red Cross for the first time. Formed in Switzerland in 1863 by Swiss banker Jean Henri Dunant, under the auspices of the Geneva convention, the Red Cross was formalized when eleven nations ratified the Geneva Treaty in 1864. Under the terms of the convention, Red Cross personnel in present and future wars would be allowed to enter the battlefield as neutrals under a white flag with a red cross in order to provide relief. Barton was astonished to learn that the U.S. government refused to ratify the Geneva Treaty, and thus began a campaign that would take more than a decade to persuade the United States to support the organization.

Barton conducted her Red Cross campaign with the same skill that she had used to organize during the Civil War. She toured the country giving speeches, meeting with public officials and private citizens, and granting interviews in order to acquaint people with the Red Cross. She also lobbied politicians in Washington and sought support from presidential administrations. In 1881, she formed the American Red Cross, and was appointed its first president. The following year, the Senate finally ratified the Geneva Treaty. Barton remained president of the American Red Cross until 1904. In that time her agency dealt with twenty-one disasters, ranging from floods and hurricanes, to famines and a yellow fever epidemic. Refusing to accept government subsidies, probably because of her experiences with government bureaucracies when she was a teacher and at the Patent Office, Barton was forced to be frugal. She determined when a request for assistance merited Red Cross action, and she oversaw the relief efforts. Under her direction, Red Cross volunteers entered a disaster area; distributed relief in the form of food, clothing, temporary housing, medical supplies, and whatever else was immediately needed; and evacuated the area as soon as other relief agencies could take over.

Perhaps because she had worked so long, organizing so many different types of relief agencies for nearly half a century, Barton found it difficult to relinquish control to other people. When the government issued a federal charter to the Red Cross in 1900, many believed that the opportunity for necessary reorganization was at hand. But Barton continued to cling to the old methods that were quickly becoming outdated in a modern world. Finally in 1904, she retired from the organization that she had founded and nurtured, and through which she had brought relief to thousands of Americans and foreigners alike. The difficulty of her last few years as president does not diminish her accomplishments. The American Red Cross continues to act as a first response agency whenever disasters occur, whether man-made or natural.

1882: The Association of Collegiate Alumnae Is Founded

(Professionalization, Education, Work)

In 1881, a group of seventeen young women representing eight colleges and universities discussed plans to organize an alumnae association for women college graduates. On January 14, 1882, sixty-five of their fellow graduates attended the first meeting of the Association of Collegiate Alumnae (ACA).

In the decades after the Civil War, higher education for women became more and more a serious proposition. With a number of state universities accepting women students, and the founding of the prestigious seven sisters colleges of Mount Holyoke, Wellesley, Smith, Vassar, Radcliffe, Bryn Mawr, and Barnard, more opportunities for education existed for women than ever previously. But although the curriculum at these colleges and universities often mirrored the coursework undertaken in male colleges, very few schools believed that they were training women for anything other than their role as wives and mothers. One notable exception was Bryn Mawr, where its president, Carey Thomas, believed that her students should be trained to take their place in the professions. The fact that very few professions accepted women into their ranks did not deter Thomas, but it did create a sense of purposelessness among women college graduates, especially among the first generation of graduates.

To counteract this feeling, Marian Talbot, Emily Fairbanks Talbot, Ellen Richards, and Alice Hayes called together seventeen of their colleagues in 1881 for the purpose of organizing a network of women graduates. The first meeting of the Association of Collegiate Alumnae drew sixty-five women from Boston University, the University of Michigan, the University of Wisconsin, Cornell, Smith, Vassar, Oberlin, and Wellesley. When most American women did not even know a single college graduate, the ACA provided graduates with a network of others like themselves who had been the pioneers in women's education. Other regional groups quickly formed as well, including the Western Association of Collegiate Alumnae (1883) and the Southern Association of College Women (1903). In 1921, all of the regional groups united as the American Association of University Women (AAUW).

From the beginning, the AAUW has been a leader in efforts to improve conditions for women students and faculty in colleges and universities throughout the country. Shrewd administrators used AAUW leverage to increase their funding for facilities, to increase salaries for female instructors, and to encourage the promotion of women beyond the instructor level. It has also taken the lead in promoting higher education for women. It has maintained a vigorous scholarship and fellowship program to assist promising undergraduate and graduate students, and has the strongest lobbying presence on behalf of not only education, but other issues that affect women directly.

Besides providing a network of support, one of the AAUW's most valuable contributions has been the constant stream of research on issues related to women that has been an integral part of its program and that has contributed to changes in education on all levels. Most recently, an AAUW study investigating why female students fall behind male students by the time they reach junior high school has provided educators with startling insights into the differences between female and male school experiences, even at the very beginning of formal schooling.

From its modest beginning of 65 members, the AAUW now has more than 150,000 members and 2,000 local chapters. Virtually every college and university now has representation in the AAUW.

1883: *Ladies Home Journal* Begins Publication

(Cultural Life, Recreation)

For several years, Cyrus Curtis, the publisher of a farming journal, included a women's supplement in his magazine. The supplement, edited by his wife, Louisa Knapp Curtis, became more popular than the farm journal itself. In 1883, Curtis dropped the farming journal, expanded the women's supplement, calling it the *Ladies Home Journal*, and published it monthly with Louisa Knapp Curtis as the editor.

When Cyrus Curtis began including a women's supplement in his farming magazine in order to broaden the appeal of the publication, he never imagined that the supplement itself would soon be the major selling point. Prior to Curtis' publication, the most popular women's magazine was *Godey's Ladies Book*, begun in 1828 as the *Ladies Magazine*. When Louis Godey bought the magazine in 1837, he added his name to the title. Godey also determined what was proper reading for women in the nineteenth century and the magazine focused on fashion, household hints, recipes, some light fiction, and articles that steered clear of controversy. Editor Sarah Buell Hale also advocated education for women and dress reform, though everything was couched in a nonthreatening style.

When Curtis began publishing the *Ladies Home Journal*, his wife, Louisa Knapp Curtis, continued to serve as editor, as she had done for the original supplement. Although it seemed outrageously ambitious, their goal was to attract one million subscribers. To accomplish this, they began to attract well-known and popular authors to contribute to the pages of the magazine. Writers such as Louisa May Alcott and Mark Twain enticed subscribers, even when the already high yearly rate of fifty cents per subscription was raised to one dollar in 1889.

That same year, Louisa Curtis retired and the Curtis' son-in-law, Edward Bok, a Dutch immigrant, took over as editor. Under his direction, the magazine continued to flourish with the addition of regular advice columns written by women, and well-written feature articles. The articles covered a wide range of issues, some of which other women's magazines had avoided because of their controversial nature. For example, Helen Keller's article on neonatal blindness was a remarkable departure from the usual fare, because in most cases, the genesis of neonatal blindness was parental venereal disease. Although the *Journal* lost some subscribers because of Keller's article, overall women were receptive to intelligent discussions of a variety of issues. Bok also refused to accept certain kinds of advertising that he deemed inappropriate for a woman's magazine.

By 1903, under Bok's direction, the *Ladies Home Journal* surpassed the Curtis' original goal of one million subscribers. By then, the *Journal* had also outlived *Godey's Ladies Book*, which ceased publication in 1898. Other women's magazines also made their appearance at about the same time as the *Journal*, including *Good Housekeeping* (1885) and *Vogue* (1893). None of the other magazines had quite the broad appeal of *Ladies Home Journal*, but all of them helped to keep women informed of the changes that most affected their lives. As the magazines themselves matured, they became more responsive to women. The editors might not particularly agree with a trend or issue, but even in their negative reaction they were providing a service to their readers. For example, when Betty Friedan wrote *The Feminine Mystique*, the editorial board of the *Ladies Home Journal* rejected her thesis, primarily because it appeared to devalue the roles of mother and housekeeper in which most of its readers were engaged. But even when they negatively critiqued Friedan's book, they were informing many more readers about the issues involved than the book itself could reach. *The Ladies Home Journal* continues to be a forum for issues confronting American women, from politics to religion to health to child-rearing. As its readers have grown in sophistication and knowledge, so also has the magazine. Today, few issues are considered too controversial to find a place in its pages.

1885: William Stead Exposes Widespread Trafficking in Young Girls

(Social Reform)

In 1885, Englishman William T. Stead brought to the attention of a shocked public, first in England and then in America, the extent of the practice of buying and selling young girls for sexual purposes.

When William Stead first described the practice of "white slavery," Americans were shocked not just by the extent of the practice, but by minimum legal age of consent in most states, which, in some cases, was as low as ten years old. The shock turned into action under the leadership of the "Social Purity" movement, a loose alliance of reformers who sought to curb the excesses caused by human passions, in particular the abuses associated with sex. They successfully opposed the movement to regulate prostitution in favor of a strict legal stand against the practice altogether, and they successfully lobbied state governments for an increase in the age of consent. Connecticut changed its laws in 1895 to raise the age from fourteen to sixteen, while Maine's went from ten in 1887 to thirteen, and then to fourteen just two years later. Arkansas raised its minimum from twelve to sixteen in 1893, and by 1900 just two of the remaining states and territories still had age-of-consent laws below the age of fourteen. Twelve states and territories raised the legal age of consent to eighteen.

The Social Purists would have liked to raise the age of consent to twenty-one, but legislators feared that juries would not convict a man who had had sex with a woman of 20. Nevertheless, with the widespread rise in the minimum age of consent, the Social Purity movement had won an important victory, a victory that raised the protection of young girls above the pleasures of men.

The Social Purists won an equally important victory in their struggle against prostitution, although the measure of their success was what did not happen rather than what was done. Since the 1850s, when Dr. William Sanger had published a detailed study of the "world's oldest profession," the American medical profession had been calling for effective medical regulations, instead of what appeared to be ineffective criminal sanctions, in order to curb disorder and disease. Their efforts gradually made headway, having been endorsed in 1867 by the prestigious magazine, the *Nation,* and by the *New York Times,* and in 1876 by the conservative *New York Tribune.*

The intent of the medical reformers was not to condone prostitution but to limit its apparently inevitable impact. The Social Purists would have none of it. They campaigned tirelessly against all suggestions of accommodation, and in the end they had their way. By the late 1880s, almost no doctor in the country was willing to publicly advocate regulation of prostitution. Prostitution in America remained thereafter an illegal activity.

1885: Annie Oakley Joins Buffalo Bill's Wild West Show

(Entertainment)

Already famous for her unsurpassed marksmanship, in 1885, Annie Oakley joined Buffalo Bill Cody's Wild West Show and soon rose to international stardom. Through her mastery of this stereotypically masculine activity, she demonstrated to the Victorian world what women were capable of.

Annie Oakley stood less than five feet tall and weighed less than one hundred pounds, but her steady hand and keen eyesight made her a legend of the Wild West.

She was born in Ohio, one of eight children whose father died when she was still young. At one point, her mother was reduced to putting her into an orphanage, but little Phoebe was so unhappy she ran away from her foster home. When her mother remarried, she was able to rejoin her family permanently. She enjoyed hunting in the woods, and contributed to the family finances by selling the game she brought down.

So skilled was she as a marksman that when she was only fifteen she won the marksmanship championship of Cincinnati. She so impressed the man she beat, the showman Frank Butler, that he proposed marriage to her, and she accepted. Thus began a lifelong partnership that was as happy in private as it was successful in public.

Annie dropped the name Phoebe and took the name Oakley when she married, and she and Frank began touring together as Butler and Oakley. Their success as a shooting exposition brought both of them, but especially

Annie, to Buffalo Bill Cody's attention. He invited her to join his famous Wild West Show. Frank Butler took the situation gracefully, assuming the role of his wife's manager, and the couple continued to live and work together contentedly.

While with the Wild West Show, Annie Oakley rose to international stardom. She was so good that she could hit a moving target while riding a galloping horse, she could hit a dime in mid-air, and she regularly shot a cigarette from her husband's lips as part of her act. Audiences in the United States and abroad loved her, and she was presented to both Queen Victoria and the Crown Prince of Germany. The latter was so impressed with her skill (as well as his own bravery) that he insisted she try the cigarette trick with him. Fortunately for international relations, she shot straight.

Annie Oakley's happy career came to an abrupt end in 1901 when the Wild West Show's train wrecked in the Virginia mountains. Badly injured, she retired, only reemerging to do special shows to entertain the troops during World War I. In 1922, she suffered an even worse injury in a car crash in

Florida which left her paralyzed. She returned to her birthplace in Ohio, and died at the age of sixty-one. Frank Butler died three weeks later.

1888: The Formation of Illinois Women's Alliance

(Work, Equal Rights)

Reacting to the hostility of the male-dominated craft unions of the American Federation of Labor, women trade unionists in 1888 brought thirty women's organizations together into the Illinois Women's Alliance.

As the nineteenth century progressed, women's participation in the labor force increased steadily. The majority of female employees were young, single immigrants. Generally relegated to unskilled, machine-tending roles, they rapidly became disillusioned by the indifference and even hostility of the male trade union movement to women's needs. In response, working women in Illinois created an embracing organization to work for their own interests. Reaching out to existing working class and middle class women's organizations, they forged an unprecedented alliance dedicated to improving the conditions of women and children in the workplace.

The women of the alliance advanced an ambitious program. They called for factory inspections by women "responsible to women's organizations," and regulation of the sweatshops where so many women labored. They demanded an end to child labor, the institution of compulsory education, and the construction of new schools. In 1892, in cooperation with Hull House and the General Federation of Women's Clubs, they won an eight-hour day for women and children, and restrictions on the employment of children.

Despite this significant victory, the alliance did not long endure. Under the pressure of the depression of 1893–94, it split apart, no longer able to bridge the gap between middle- and working-class women. The surface issues concerned strategy, but these manifested deeper fissures. Middle-class women regarded work as an object of pride, a source of independence and personal fulfillment. For their less well-to-do sisters, work was just work, nothing more than a source of income, which was generally shared with parents, siblings, or spouses. The endless drudgery was far more often a source of grinding frustration than a source of personal fulfillment.

The alliance disintegrated in 1894, but its spirit did live on. The influx of young women from southern and eastern Europe around the turn of the century included many who were already politicized and ready to forge a new alliance with the middle-class feminists of America. In 1903, the two groups came together again in the Women's Trade Union League (WTUL), which, from the beginning, had the dual purpose of promoting reforms in the workplace and working for a broader program of women's rights. Their ideology and actions were more militant and their collabo-

ration was longer lasting, but they were moving along a trail the members of the Illinois Women's Alliance had already explored. This was particularly evident during the garment workers strikes of 1909–11, when women from the financially and socially powerful families of Harriman, Belmont, Morgan, and others boycotted clothing manufacturers who refused to bargain with the WTUL. Wealthy members of the WTUL provided the strike funds, acted as press liaisons, and even went on the picket line and were arrested with the workers.

The alliance between upper-, middle-, and working-class women worked better at some times than at others. Eventually class distinctions once again became seemingly insurmountable and the alliance disintegrated. But for many years the only viable union affiliation for women trade unionists was the WTUL, and, just as the Illinois Women's Alliance had demonstrated that class lines could be overcome, the WTUL demonstrated the same point in its heyday, opening the way for similar alliances for other causes.

1889: Jane Addams Founds Hull House in Chicago

(Social Reform, Cultural Life, Work)

Hull House, a settlement house offering a broad range of cultural and social services to the poor and immigrant residents of Chicago's teeming nineteenth ward, founded by Jane Addams and Ellen Gates Starr, opened its doors on September 18, 1889.

While Hull House was not the first settlement house in America, it did become the prototype for future ones, primarily because of the vision and dedication of its principle founder, Jane Addams. Jane Addams graduated from prestigious Rockford Seminary in Illinois in 1882. Raised by her widowed father from the age of two, Addams was devastated when, a few weeks after her graduation, he died suddenly. A chronic back problem that required surgery, a period of aimless wandering through Europe, and then two years spent in Baltimore with her stepmother, who spent most of her time playing matchmaker on Jane's behalf, persuaded Addams that her life badly needed focus. A previous effort to find that focus by enrolling in medical school proved unsuccessful, and after one year she resigned. It was not until she and her college roommate, Ellen Gates Starr, were touring Europe once again that Addams had what she later described as an epiphany. It suddenly seemed very clear that her privileged, middle class, educated background carried with it a responsibility to use her privilege to help those less fortunate. Starr held similar views and together they vowed to open a home where poor people could come to get practical assistance for the problems they struggled with and where immigrants could come to learn how to assimilate into American life and culture.

Within two years, Addams and Starr opened the doors of Hull House, a former suburban mansion built by a wealthy realtor in Chicago. As Chicago grew and expanded in the late nineteenth century, the once-bucolic area of which the Hull mansion was a part, had turned into one of the city's most crowded districts. Hull House proved to be an enduring and important part of Chicago and American life for two reasons. First, it provided Chicago's most needy and desperate residents with a haven that offered them a variety of programs that not only addressed their immediate concerns, but provided them with cultural enrichment as well. Hull House offered its constituents medical services, child care, English classes, legal aid, day nurseries, sewing classes, vocational skills classes, citizenship classes, a cooperative residence for working women, a variety of clubs and activities for children, and rooms where groups like labor unions could hold their meetings. It also offered or sponsored art exhibits, plays, concerts, and lectures. By 1893, when the nation was entering a sustained depression, about two thousand Chicagoans attended one or more Hull House functions every week. It was an invaluable service in an era when the city itself provided little or no services to its residents.

Second, Hull House served a broader function and one which had more profound and further reaching effects for all Americans. It was the genesis of a new profession—social work—that attracted some of the best minds of the progressive era. Hull House was an on-going experiment in social services that led, naturally, to pressure for social legislation. Activists including Julia Lathrop, Florence Kelley, Edith and Grace Abbott, Sophonisba Breckinridge, Alice Hamilton, George Mead, Charles Beard, and John Dewey, all were involved in Hull House at one time or another. They, along with Jane Addams and the residents themselves, became advocates and activists working for reforms in child labor, sanitation, housing conditions, and work conditions. Taking aim at the causes of poverty, they persuaded the Illinois legislature to enact legislation mandating factory inspections, and to establish the nation's first juvenile court system. They also advocated required schooling for children, recognition of labor unions, industrial safety laws, and protection for immigrants against exploitation, all of which ultimately were adopted not only in Chicago but across the nation.

1889: Nellie Bly Goes around the World in Seventy-two Days

(Work, Cultural Life)

Investigative reporter Nellie Bly, in Europe during World War I, became the first woman to cover the Eastern Front.

L ong before Barbara Walters established herself as the preeminent woman journalist of the late twentieth century, Nellie Bly made her own headlines as the first woman investigative reporter. From beginning to end, Bly's career garnered her as many headlines as the stories she reported on. Her first reporting job, for the *Pittsburgh Dispatch* in 1885, happened serendipitously when twenty-one-year-old Jane Cochran wrote an indignant letter to the editor, taking the newspaper to task for printing an article opposed to woman suffrage and to women who wanted to work outside of the home. So impressed was editor George Madden that he promptly hired Cochran. She chose "Nellie Bly" as her by-line, and a journalism career was launched.

Bly rejected typical ladies' page stories and instead went after exposés: working conditions in factories, slum conditions, problems of working girls, divorce—the more controversial the better. The *Dispatch* sent her to Mexico in 1886 and published her letters about political corruption, the slums, and the disparity between rich and poor. For her efforts, the Mexican government expelled her from the country. Rather than return to Pittsburgh, Bly went to New York where she barged her way into Joseph Pulitzer's office and promptly landed a job with the city's most innovative and widely-read newspaper, the New York *World*. She persuaded Pulitzer to let her go undercover as a patient in a mental hospital on Blackwell's Island (now Roosevelt Island), New York. Her exposé of the horrid conditions made headlines, and a subsequent investigation into the hospital's treatment of patients resulted in long-overdue reforms.

In the years that followed, Nellie Bly repeated her formula for undercover investigative reporting to expose inequities. At one point, she had herself arrested for theft, experiencing first-hand the indignities suffered by women prison inmates. She also exposed worker exploitation by the owners and managers of a sweatshop and caught a corrupt lobbyist red-handed when, believing that Bly was a supporter of reform legislation, attempted to bribe her.

In what was her most famous venture, Pulitzer sent Bly on an around-the-world trip to see if she could outdo Phineas Fogg's eighty-day record in the fictional Jules Verne novel *Around the World in Eighty Days*. She traversed the globe, from New York to Singapore to Hong Kong to Tokyo to San Francisco, making the entire trip in seventy-two days, six hours, and eleven minutes. The public was mesmerized by accounts of the daring exploits she sent back to the *World*.

Parades were held in her honor, songs and dances were named for her, Nellie Bly toys and games were created, and a line of Nellie Bly clothing was offered to an adoring public.

Her final journalistic adventure took place after her elderly husband's death ended their fifteen-year marriage in 1910. Traveling in Europe when World War I erupted, Nellie Bly became the first woman to cover the Eastern Front—a female war correspondent at a time when female reporters were routinely relegated to write about issues related to home, family, and fashion. Her exclusive stories again made front pages, but it also marked the end of Bly's career as a journalist. When she returned to the United States in 1919, Bly found that she no longer fit in with the type of sensational journalism encouraged by the Hearst chain. She retired the following year.

1890: The General Federation of Women's Clubs Is Founded by Jane Cunningham Croly

(Cultural Life, Social Reform)

In 1889, Jane Cunningham Croly, who had founded *Sorosis,* a club for women professionals, twenty-one years earlier, invited several women's clubs to celebrate the club's anniversary. The following year, Croly was instrumental in bringing together a number of women's clubs under an umbrella organization called the General Federation of Women's Clubs (GFWC).

Beginning shortly after the Civil War, women across the country began organizing local clubs, primarily to promote cultural events. The models for the first clubs were *Sorosis,* a club for journalists and professional women started by Jane Cunningham Croly in New York in 1869 to protest the exclusion of women from the National Press Club, and the New England Women's Club, organized in the same year by several upper class Bostonians. At first, the club movement focused more on cultural affairs, with clubs dedicated to weekly lectures, book discussions, and similar pursuits. For many women, the clubs were a form of higher education. They tended to be middle and upper class and to be fairly exclusionary. Gradu-

ally, though, many clubs took on an increased concern for civic events. By the late 1880s, there were thousands of local women's clubs operating in cities and towns across the nation. For women of the late nineteenth century who did not necessarily advocate the agendas of either the enormous temperance movement or the ever-growing suffrage movement, women's clubs represented an opportunity to participate in public affairs without abandoning their traditional values rooted in their domestic roles as wives and mothers.

When June Cunningham Croly invited women's clubs to join the General Federation of Women's Clubs in 1890, it marked a turning point for thousands of middle-class women who thereafter would have a respectable alternative for expressing their views on social issues. Croly believed that, through the GFWC, women could apply their influence to effect a variety of social reforms. Croly's vision was quickly realized when the GFWC became involved in improving public education and expanding public libraries. These and other noncontroversial activities, including beautification of the environment, building hospitals and playgrounds, and supporting women's colleges and social settlement houses led to a national agenda that eventually embraced woman suffrage, temperance, and support of the progressive movement agenda. Regarding the latter, the GFWC in 1899 was responsible for establishing a national model for juvenile courts, and in 1906, it was an important factor in the passage of the Pure Food and Drug Act that led to establishment of the Food and Drug Administration. Local clubs were also involved in factory inspections, child labor conditions, the improvement of tenement housing, availability of municipal services, graft, and conservation. Thus, the middle and upper classes moved from weekly book reviews into social activism almost seamlessly and without feeling as though they had abandoned traditional values.

By 1915, the GFWC boasted more than two million members. Among other accomplishments, the GFWC can take credit for establishing over 75 percent of the nation's libraries. Although its membership has declined since 1915, it still counts more than 500,000 members representing 8,500 local clubs, and is the largest "nondenominational, nonpartisan volunteer service organization in the world."

1890: Suffragists Unite under the Banner of the National American Woman Suffrage Association

(Equal Rights, Social Reform)

In 1890, the National Woman Suffrage Association and the American Woman Suffrage Association merged under one banner, the National American Woman Suffrage Association (NAWSA), with Elizabeth Cady Stanton as its first president.

By 1890, with the trend in the women's movement pointing toward unification, leaders in both major suffrage groups culminated a series of merger discussions by announcing the formation of the National American Woman Suffrage Association. In the 1870s and 1880s, the most significant feat of the suffrage movement had been simply enduring rejection after rejection from politicians at the local, state, and national levels. The impetus for a merger between the two suffrage organizations came, interestingly enough, from the daughters of the original founders, Harriet Stanton Blatch, the daughter of Elizabeth Cady Stanton, and Alice Stone Blackwell, the daughter of Lucy Stone. At the time of the merger, Stanton and Susan B. Anthony were still involved in suffrage, and Stanton especially had to be won over to the unification. But the advances made by women in the post–Civil War decades had wrought changes that made a merger desirable.

By 1890, there were more women in high schools than there were men, and women were attending the majority of colleges. Nearly one-third of college students were women, and one-third of all professional workers were women. The women's club movement had united under the banner of the General Federation of Women's Clubs, and the Women's Christian Temperance Union was moving into its most powerful phase. Suffrage, no longer an isolated vehicle for change, was now part of a larger women's movement. The new, educated, younger, more active constituents of the women's movement began to exert an increasingly dominant influence over the suffrage movement. While Stanton and Anthony were elected the first and second presidents of NAWSA, their influence was clearly on the wane and would quickly be replaced by a new generation.

Anthony, in particular, found the new direction NAWSA was taking to be a bitter pill to swallow. She succeeded Stanton as president in 1892. The very next year, Anthony was forced to bow to the influence of the NAWSA members who wanted to cease holding the annual conventions in the nation's capital. Anthony, a long-time advocate of a federal suffrage amendment, knew well enough that removing the central activity of NAWSA to a venue outside of Washington, D.C., meant that the organization was going to abandon the federal amendment as its primary goal. When Colorado granted woman suffrage in 1893, it encouraged those who favored a state-by-state approach, and for the next quarter century, NAWSA would pursue hundreds of state campaigns, with less than a handful of successes in that time.

Anthony remained president of NAWSA until 1900, when she was eighty years old. In the final years of her presidency, with little ability to stem the new tide, Anthony watched NAWSA become more and more conservative, with an increasingly nativist tone that encouraged the playing down of civil rights in order to cultivate southern membership, favoring educational requirements for suffrage, and advocating immigration restriction. In 1896, after a bitter and prolonged internal struggle, NAWSA formally disassociated itself from Elizabeth Cady Stanton's *The Woman's Bible*, a radical critique of the Bible. Stanton argued, through an annotated exposition of the Bible, that its interpretation and language had aided in the oppression of women over the centuries. When it was published in 1895, NAWSA officials, including Anna Howard Shaw, moved immediately for NAWSA to disassociate itself from the book. Despite An-

thony's impassioned pleas, the majority sided with Shaw.

After Anthony stepped down as president, Carrie Chapman Catt took over the post. Catt, whose reputation for administration was sterling, was very much an advocate of challenging state constitutions rather than seeking a federal amendment. Catt was adept at developing personal relationships with politicians, but under her leadership, NAWSA began to stagnate as the frustration of losing campaign after campaign wore down the membership. For her part, Catt always professed that she expected to be in the fight for suffrage for the rest of her life—a pronouncement that suggested she had little hope that suffrage would be achieved in her lifetime.

By 1917, Catt reversed herself, announcing what she called her "Winning Plan" for suffrage—a return to the pursuit of a federal suffrage amendment. In large part, Catt and NAWSA changed directions because of a challenge from the younger, more activist National Woman's Party (NWP), founded by Alice Paul, a young veteran of the English suffragette movement, who was the heir of the Stanton-Anthony wing of the suffrage movement.

Within five years of the founding of the NWP, and within two years of

NAWSA's return to the pursuit of a federal amendment, suffragists secured passage of the Nineteenth Amendment.

1891: Impressionist Mary Cassatt Is Invited to Paint a Mural for the World's Columbian Exposition

(Cultural Life)

In 1891, the president of the Board of Lady Managers of the upcoming World's Columbian Exposition, while traveling in Europe, invited American artist Mary Cassatt to paint a mural for the Woman's Building. The mural, painted over two seasons while Cassatt and her mother lived in France, arrived in the United States in time to grace the Woman's Building at the opening of the exposition in 1893.

When Mary Cassatt, at the age of eighteen, announced to her family that she intended to become an artist, her industrialist father immediately objected, proclaiming that he would "rather have you dead!" Cassatt, nevertheless, persuaded her family to let her move to Paris in 1866, where she lived with friends of the family. For four years, Cassatt studied art and painted on her own. When the political situation in France grew uneasy, with the approach of the Franco-Prussian War, her family insisted she return home. Paintings completed during that period revealed that Cassatt had not yet matured as an artist. Undaunted, she returned to Europe in 1872. For the next two years, she traveled to Italy, Spain, Holland, and France, painting and studying the works of the masters. By 1874, she had begun to develop the style that would eventually influence her greatest paintings. It was in 1872, also, that Edgar Degas, the leader of the new group of independent French artists who referred to themselves as Impressionists, noticed her work and invited her to join them. For the next four years, she did a series of impressionist paintings that began to attract more and more critical attention. Her first American exhibit came in 1876, and in 1879, Cassatt accepted an invitation from American painter J. Alden Weir to exhibit her works with the newly formed Society of American Artists. Cassatt's exhibition marked the introduction of impressionist paintings to America.

In the late 1870s and 1880s, as she gradually turned to her major themes of women and children, Cassatt also began to advise American friends on art purchases. In particular, she was instrumental in directing Louisine Havemeyer, who is often credited with introducing America to Cassatt, to the impressionists. As a consequence, Havemeyer built one of the most impressive art collections ever held privately. When Havemeyer died in 1929, she left her entire art collection to the Metropolitan Museum of Art in New York, transforming that institution overnight into a leader in the field of impressionist art. In addition to her Cassatts, Havemeyer, at Cassatt's direction, had also purchased dozens of Degas, Cezannes, Manets, and Monets, as well as works by Courbet, Corot, Goya, El Greco, and Bronzino. It was a stunning gift to a museum that had been severely criticized for its refusal to purchase modern paintings.

In 1891, Cassatt was approached by Bertha Palmer, a Chicago businesswoman and heiress who had, with her husband, built a real estate and hotel empire, the crown jewel of which was the Palmer House. Palmer was the president of the Board of Lady Governors for the upcoming World's Columbian Exposition, scheduled for 1893. The exposition became a powerful force for focusing the world's attention on the status of women, and much of that was due to Palmer's strong role in overseeing development of the event. She considered Cassatt an American treasure and could think of no one better suited to paint a mural for the Women's Building at the exhibition. Cassatt agreed, and over the next two years, while she was living at Chateau Bichiville in France with her mother, she completed the project. Although Cassatt did not return to the United States to deliver the mural, it was in place by the time the exhibition opened. At an event where so much attention was focused on women and their status, it seemed entirely fitting that perhaps the finest American painter at the time should contribute to the exhibition.

Mary Cassatt returned to the United States only twice more for brief periods in 1898 and again in 1908. She continued to paint until blindness forced her to stop. At the age of eighty-two, Cassatt died in France in 1926. Her contributions to the art world and her enduring themes of mothers and children continue to keep her name in the forefront of American artists.

1892: Illinois Becomes the First State to Limit Work Hours for Women

(Work)

In 1892, the Illinois state legislature passed the first laws limiting the number of hours women could be required to work.

During the heyday of the progressive movement, at the turn of the century, American government's approach to social issues changed dramatically, if not fundamentally. Up until this period America held rigorously to the philosophy known as *laissez faire*, or "let it be." In other words, the government that governed best governed least. But faced with the massive changes in the conditions of life brought by the industrial revolution, in particular by the concentration of wealth and power in the hands of a few individuals and corporations, Americans gradually abandoned the hoary myths that workers and bosses bargained equally in setting terms of employment and that consumers had

the freedom to choose among alternative products whose quality and value they could easily see. Giant corporations set their terms and workers could take them or leave them, while industrial-scale distributors packaged foodstuffs and clothing that urban consumers had little knowledge of and few alternatives to.

In the progressives' struggle for the nation's soul, they generally found the national level a difficult forum, for there their fragmented coalition opposed the wealth of vested interests across the country. Consequently, the reformers won many of their early victories at the state level, where a well-organized local organization could give local businesses a run for their money. The struggle for restrictions on child labor, for instance, was won on the state level during the first decade of the twentieth century, when the number of states limiting child labor went from less than half to all but one. Similarly, Utah first established the eight-hour day (for miners), while Maryland pioneered the creation of workers' compensation insurance laws.

It was in this climate that progressive women in Illinois undertook to reform women's labor laws. The Illinois Women's Alliance of middle-class and working-class activists led the way, and they were joined by the General Federation of Women's Clubs and the members of Hull House. They lobbied the state legislature and appealed to the electorate for a whole range of reforms, including factory inspections, compulsory education, new schools, sweatshop regulations, an end to child labor, and an end to police abuse of arrested women. The Illinois state legislature's law limiting women's labor to ten hours a day in 1892 was their crowning achievement.

If the ten-hour day for women culminated the reform effort in Illinois, it was just the first victory at the national level. Massachusetts and New York quickly adopted similar statutes, and by 1917, thirty-nine states had adopted or strengthened laws protecting women. Eight had gone even further, setting minimum wages for women. As so often happened in the progressive era, what began as a daring experiment in one state eventually became the norm for the nation.

1893: Mary Elizabeth Lease Runs for the U.S. Senate

(Equal Rights)

Long a leading spokeswoman for the Populist party, Mary Elizabeth Lease became one of the first women to run for a major office when she accepted the party's nomination to run for the U.S. Senate in Kansas.

After starting her career as a teacher in the northeast, Lease moved west to Kansas in 1870. She married three years later, and soon had four children to raise. But life as a poor farmer in Kansas and Texas radicalized her. By the early 1880s, she emerged as a leading orator of the Populist party, and became famous for urging farmers to "raise less corn and more hell." Critics played on her name "Mary Ellen," dubbing her "Mary Yellin'."

Lease's involvement with the Populist party grew steadily as the party itself grew in the 1880s. She edited labor newspapers and gave over 150 speeches in support of populist causes. In 1892, she was prominent enough to give the seconding speech for the nomination of James B. Weaver as the party's candidate for president. The following year she secured for herself the party's nomination to run for the U.S. Senate from Kansas, which was one of the states in which women already had the vote. While she lost the election, her candidacy was a victory in and of itself.

After the election, Lease continued to broaden her career. She gave more speeches in favor of her favorite causes—Populism, prohibition, suffrage, and Irish nationalism. She branched out into writing, publishing *The Problem of Civilization Solved* in 1895, and beginning regular contributions on political topics to the *New York World* the next year. Her public service included selection as the orator for Kansas Day at the 1893 Columbian Exposition in Chicago, a gubernatorial appointment to the Kansas State Board of Charity, presidency of the National Society for Birth Control, and active support for Teddy Roosevelt and the Progressive party in the election of 1912.

Lease's contribution to the Populist movement was unquestionable, although many of her allies found her as difficult a character as her enemies did. She refused to be a "team player." She never distinguished herself as a thoughtful strategist, and she even alienated her friends by supporting Republican William McKinley over William Jennings Bryan in 1896. But friend and foe alike could agree on her strengths as well. In the end, they were her real legacy.

1895: The Henry Street Nurses Settlement Is Founded by Lillian D. Wald

(Social Reform Professionalization)

With financial backing from Mrs. Solomon Loeb and her banker son-in-law, Jacob H. Schiff, a philanthropist, Lillian D. Wald and a friend, Mary Brewster, opened the Henry Street Settlement House on New York City's Lower East Side in September 1895.

As a young medical student at the Woman's Medical College in New York in 1893, Lillian Wald, the daughter of genteel, middle-class Jewish parents, agreed to organize home nursing classes for immigrant families on the Lower East Side. A chance house call to a woman in one of the many deteriorating tenement buildings, proved to be a seminal experience for Wald. She recruited a fellow nurse, Mary Brewster, and together they set up a nurses' settlement house in temporary quarters on the top floor of a Jefferson Street tenement. Wald and Brewster wanted to bring health care to the poor and indigent residents of the Lower East Side. More than that, however, they wanted to do so as members of the community, to, as Wald said, "contribute to it our citizenship."

Wald's ability to network and to persuade people of the worthiness of her cause brought her into contact with the Loebs and the Schiffs, who soon became supporters and enabled the fledgling community house to move into its permanent quarters on Henry Street. This ability to draw support stayed with Wald throughout her career, as she launched program after program. Indeed, one friend commented that every time she sat down next to Wald, "it costs me $5,000." By 1913, the Henry Street Visiting Nurses Association consisted of ninety-two nurses, with branches in upper Manhattan and in the Bronx. The nursing staff, which was organized into specialized departments, made approximately two hundred thousand house calls per year. The settlement expanded to include not only house calls and follow-up visits for patients discharged from hospitals, but also maintained convalescent facilities and first aid stations.

The idea of the visiting nurses spread rapidly to other communities across the country and a new profession, public health nursing, came into being. Wald envisioned a nationwide service organization dedicated to the idea that many people not ill enough to require hospitalization nevertheless did need medical care that, because of their means, might not be available to them. Wald determined that the organization should be professional, independent of religious or governmental ties, and should impose fees "on terms most considerate of the dignity and the independence of the patient." Besides establishing public health nursing and the Visiting Nurses Association, Wald was instrumental in establishing the first public school of nursing program in the United States, in New York City. She was also largely responsible for the establishment, in 1910, of the nursing and health departments at Teachers College of Columbia University. In 1912, the American Red Cross, at Wald's urging, established the Town and Country Nursing Service. In recognition of her monumental efforts to create a public health nursing profession and organization, Wald was chosen as the first president of the National Organization for Public Health Nursing in 1912.

From a humble beginning in a Jefferson Street tenement, to her famous Henry Street Settlement House, Wald helped to launch a nationwide medical service that significantly altered the lives of hundreds of thousands of American women. Women went into the public health nursing profession by the thousands, bringing medical care to families not only in the inner cities but in rural areas that were badly in need of attention.

1895: The First American Women's Amateur Golf Championship Takes Place at the Same Time as the First Men's Championship

(Sports)

In November 1895, at the same time that American men played their first amateur golf championship at Newport, Rhode Island, thirteen women competed at the Meadow Brook Country Club on Long Island to determine the first female champion.

Golf is a very old game. The Chinese National Golf Association claims that the Chinese invented it in the third or second century B.C.E., and the Romans may have brought a version with them to Britain before the fourth century C.E. A figure playing golf is portrayed in a stained glass window dated 1350 in Glouchester Cathedral in Scotland, and the Scottish parliament passed a law against the game in 1457. Gutta percha balls replaced feather balls in 1848, and rubber-cored balls replaced them in turn in 1899. Steel shafts for clubs replaced wood in the 1930s.

Women's participation in golf is also quite old. Mary, Queen of Scots (1542–1587) played the game, and, having been educated in France, called the boys who chased balls "cadets," which eventually became our term "caddy." The first known tournament played by women was played by town fishwives at the Musselburght Golf Club in 1911, and the English Ladies' Golf Union was formed in 1872. It held its first national championship on June 13, 1893.

The U.S. Golf Association (USGA) was formed in 1894, and from the beginning it accepted female as well as male members. When the next year, the men held a championship tournament, so, too, did the women. Mrs. Charles Brown won, with an 18-hole score of 132.

In 1946, Patty Berg led women

professional golfers in organizing the Women's Professional Golfers' Association, which started the U.S. Women's Open tournament in the same year. In 1950, Berg helped launch the Ladies Professional Golf Association (LPGA). This organization continued the annual Women's Open until the USGA took over sponsorship in 1953. The LPGA started its own annual tournament in 1955, and the number of events increased steadily until by 1978, there were three dozen similar events on the association's calendar with a total purse of $3,400,000.

Golf, even more than tennis, was an activity in which late-nineteenth-century women found an entry into modern competitive sports. But unlike tennis, in golf they were building on a centuries-old tradition of women's participation, a tradition that helps to explain women's acceptance in a position of full equality to men.

1898: Charlotte Perkins Gilman Publishes *Women and Economics*

(Equal Rights, Cultural Life)

Already a noted novelist, in 1898, Charlotte Perkins Gilman published a book exploring the effects of industrialization on women and advocating economic self-sufficiency as the necessary basis for women's independence and equal rights.

Born into the prominent Beecher family in 1860, Charlotte Perkins Gilman learned early the drawbacks of women's economic dependency. Her father neglected his wife and children, and they were forced to live off the generosity of their relatives. From this early experience came a lifelong emphasis on economic self-sufficiency for women.

Charlotte's concern for self-sufficiency was coupled with a creative talent, possibly inherited from her great aunts, Catharine Beecher and Harriet Beecher Stowe, that showed itself first in artistic ways. She attended the Rhode Island School of Design and went on to work as a commercial artist and art teacher before marrying Walter Stetson at the age of twenty-four. She bore a daughter, but then fell into a profound post-partum depression that was only lifted when she separated from her over-protective husband and moved to California. Eventually Gilman divorced Stetson and sent her then nine-year-old daughter to live with Stetson and his new wife, an action that scandalized most of Gilman's friends, since women did not relinquish their children under any circumstances in those days.

In California, Gilman turned her creative energies to speaking and writing. Her first novel, *The Yellow Wallpaper*, published in 1892, was a powerful portrayal of the onset of insanity based on her own experience of depression. Its radical feminist thesis and surreal style put it decades ahead of its time, a prescience that was to characterize much of Gilman's later work.

In 1895, Gilman moved to Chicago and lived for a time at Hull House. Here she gained an appreciation of economics on the social rather than personal level. In 1898, Gilman published her most famous work, *Women and Economics*. In it, she advocated economic independence for women, and also called for communal solutions to individual needs. The book was translated into seven languages, and brought her both widespread recognition and the financial security that

she had so desperately searched for ever since she was a young child. Lauded at the time of its publication, *Women and Economics* became almost instantly a major contribution to women's rights. A review in the *Nation* called it the "most significant utterance on the subject since Mills' *Subjugation of Women*."

In 1900, Gilman married her younger cousin, and in the following decades she continued to write both fiction and nonfiction works. Adding to both her body of work and her reputation, Gilman wrote *Concerning Children* (1900), *The Home* (1903), *Pure Sociology* (1903), *Human Work* (1904), and *Man-Made World* (1911). From 1909 to 1916, she published the aptly named magazine *Forerunner*, which she financed largely by herself. She used it as a platform to publicize her progressive ideas, including communal childcare and kitchens, that, many years later, would become reality as daycare centers and takeout restaurants (although few were conscious of the connection at the time).

After the First World War, Gilman appeared to lose her place in the forefront of American society. Her social activism and feminism seemed outdated to the new generation of women, as did her resistance to the loose sexual mores of the "Roaring

Twenties," which she argued would end up emphasizing women's sexuality and contributing to their further dependency. Her husband died in 1934 and the following year Gilman took her own life after being diagnosed with breast cancer, but not before she published her autobiography, *The Living of Charlotte Perkins Gilman.*

1899: Florence Kelley Accepts a Position with the National Consumer's League

(Social Reform)

A divorced mother of three who had previously been a factory inspector for the state of Illinois, in May 1899, reformer Florence Kelley accepted an offer to become general secretary of the recently organized National Consumer's League (NCL).

A chance meeting in Europe in 1883 with M. Carey Thomas, the president of Bryn Mawr College, changed the direction of Florence Kelley's life and indirectly contributed to some of the most far-reaching social reforms of the progressive era. Kelley, the product of an upper-class Philadelphia family, graduated from Cornell University in 1882. After being refused admission to the University of Pennsylvania law school because she was a woman, Kelley left on an extended tour of Europe. It was there that she met Thomas, who told Kelley about her own experiences being denied entrance to a university because of her sex. Thomas had then gone to the University of Zurich, which accepted women, and Kelley decided to enroll there also. In Zurich, Kelley became a convert to socialism, primarily because it helped her to understand why working women and children were subjected to so much abuse, and why nonwhites were subjected to racial bias. Kelley married a fellow socialist, a young Russian medical student, and the couple and their first child moved to New York in 1886. After two more children and a disappointing association with the Socialist party, Kelley took her three children to Illinois, where a divorce was easier to obtain. By 1891, she and her children were residents of Hull House, and Kelley struck up lasting friendships with Jane Addams, Julia Lathrop, and Alice Hamilton, all of whom were involved in the sweeping social reforms taking place in the late nineteenth century. Kelley's growing interest in child labor led to her appointment as factory inspector by the Illinois Bureau of Labor Statistics. She was also asked to conduct a survey of city slums. The results of her combined efforts galvanized Hull House workers, including Jane Addams, to a greater awareness of the industrial conditions within the city. In 1893, the Illinois legislature passed significant reform legislation that limited the hours that women could work, prohibited child labor, and placed controls on tenement sweat shops. Governor John Peter Altgeld appointed Kelley chief factory inspector with a staff of twelve and a budget of $12,000, responsible for enforcement of the new legislation.

Kelley finally earned her law degree in 1894, graduating from Northwestern University. She might have

remained in Illinois had Altgeld's successor reappointed Kelley. Instead, she decided to move with her three children to New York. Long a believer in controlling child labor through the buying public, Kelley jumped at the chance to work for the newly organized National Consumer's League as its first general secretary. For nearly thirty years, Kelley was the NCL. Her program involved targeting the middle- and upper-class women consumers, educating them to boycott products made with child labor. The NCL published a "White List" of companies whose production methods met the NCL "Standard of a Fair House." By 1907, the program was successful enough that manufacturers vied for the privilege of issuing their goods under a "white label" that consumers were educated to seek out when making purchases.

In addition to her service with the NCL, Kelley was instrumental in the successful prosecution to *Muller V. Oregon* in 1908, which regulated working hours for women. She lobbied as well for creation of the federal Children's Bureau, with her good friend Julia Lathrop, and continued to lobby for factory inspection and minimum wage laws that several states ultimately adopted. Kelley was also an advocate of woman suffrage, though she withheld her support for an equal rights amendment in the 1920s, fearing that it would undercut the protective legislation that she had worked her entire life to help secure. She attempted to win support for a federal child labor amendment to the Constitution, and, never one to pull punches, characterized those who opposed her as "rabbit-hearted," and angrily demanded to know why "seals, bears, reindeer, fish, wild game in the national parks, buffalo, migratory birds, all found suitable for federal protection; but not the children of our race and their mothers?"

Kelley's enduring legacy, however, remained her advocacy of intelligent purchasing and the use of the boycott by consumers and her contribution to the ferment that led to so much New Deal legislation, especially protective legislation.

1900: The Rise of Social Feminism

(Social Reform)

By 1900, middle-class women seeking an outlet for their reform impulses began to join women's associations in unprecedented numbers. The associations allowed them to pursue their specific reform interests while not requiring them to address the larger question of women's rights generally.

As the requirements of family life changed with technological developments, industrialization, urbanization, and immigration, middle-class women in the late nineteenth century, had more opportunity to concern themselves with issues beyond the needs of their immediate families, and indeed, in many cases, felt compelled to help find solutions to an entirely new set of problems that were associated with these profound changes in society. The issues with which the social feminists were concerned dealt primarily with social justice and social reform, issues that settlement houses had addressed for nearly two decades. By 1900, the people of the settlement houses had spread out, forming a variety of associations and creating a dynamic reform network that included the Association of Collegiate Alumnae, the General Federation of Women's Clubs, the Women's Christian Temperance Union, the National American Woman Suffrage Association (NAWSA), the National Consumer's League, and the National Women's Trade Union League, among others. The suffrage movement itself, which did not necessarily attract reform-minded women, owed some of its resurgence to the social feminists, many of whom held overlapping memberships in two or more associations. Operating almost like an interlocking directory, the women's associations supported each other's causes in order to secure support for their own cause.

The social feminists, sometimes referred to as the New Women, tended to be educated and members of either the middle or upper middle-class. Their particular status gave them more influence than they might otherwise have enjoyed. Their concern for achieving the social reforms they believed were necessary for the good of society caused many of them to endorse the suffrage movement when they might not have been otherwise so inclined. Thus, NAWSA showed an increase in its membership from the late nineteenth century, when there were less than 13,000 recorded members, to 1910 when there were more than 75,000 NAWSA members. In the eyes

of the social reformers, the *quid pro quo* for supporting suffrage efforts was the greater ease with which social reforms could be enacted when women had political power. For the most part, the radical feminists, such as those who belonged to the National Woman's Party, were the only suffragists who demanded woman suffrage simply because women were citizens and were, therefore, entitled to the vote regardless of how they intended to use it. The social feminists, on the other hand, needed the feeling of usefulness and accomplishment that went along with securing reforms.

In the post-suffrage conservatism of the 1920s, social feminists found that very few of the reforms they envisioned were accomplished as a consequence of having the right to vote. Without the unifying and underlying cause that had actually held the social feminists together, despite their disparate goals and causes, the apparent unity they had briefly enjoyed before suffrage was secured fell apart. Politicians in the early 1920s reacted to their fear that women would vote as a bloc, and passed legislation such as the Sheppard-Towner Act of 1921. When it became apparent that this threat would not materialize, the politicians stopped paying attention. The irony of the social feminists' willingness to support suffrage in order to achieve their own goals was that without the suf-

frage cause, there was no unity and little reform.

1900: *Sister Carrie* Reveals the Harsher Side of Urban Living

(Cultural Life, Social Reform)

Theodore Dreiser's first novel, *Sister Carrie*, published in 1900, so shocked reader's sensibilities with its realistic portrayal of a young woman whose struggle to climb out of poverty leads her to abandon accepted standards of morality, that its publication was discontinued and it was withdrawn from circulation.

The initial response to Theodore Dreiser's novel *Sister Carrie* was condemnatory and defensive, as the reading public and critics alike refused to accept Dreiser's portrayal of Caroline Meeber, Sister Carrie, as an average young woman who discards conventional morality in order to gain financial advantage. Dreiser's Sister Carrie, based loosely on the experiences of his own sister Emma, arrives in Chicago in 1889, determined to make a life for herself. Her initial experiences and appearance, as Dreiser describes them, mirrors that of most late nineteenth century urban working women. Moving from menial job to menial job, there was a good deal of fluidity between blue-collar and white-collar work. A young working woman might move from factory to mill to shop clerk to piece work, almost interchangeably and with little change in status, recognizable in her "course woolen garments,…shabby felt sailor hat,…cheap piece of fur,…knitted shawl, and gloves." Sister Carrie, tiring quickly of the low wages and the drabness of her life, seeks to change all that by entering into liaisons with a series of men, each of whom offers more than the last. Her success in the theatre, in the nineteenth century considered a bastion of immorality, leaves her at last wealthy but no happier in her personal life.

Dreiser, the first of the American naturalist school of writing, which included authors such as Jack London, Upton Sinclair, John Dos Passos, and Ernest Hemingway, refused to condemn Sister Carrie for abandoning conventional morality, a factor which did not sit well with critics. Instead of meeting with disaster, as Victorian morality demanded, Carrie continued to rise up the ladder of success. Dreiser challenged norms of the day, refusing to accept that the same set of moral standards could be applied to all circumstances. He also challenged the views that society held about women like Carrie. Always fascinated by the uses and abuses of wealth and power, Dreiser wanted to expose the hypoc-risy with which society viewed women of a certain class. He also wanted to show urban life with all its rough edges, including how cruel and demeaning it could make life for those who lived on the edge of poverty.

The first edition of *Sister Carrie* was heavily expurgated before it was published. It had sold less than five hundred copies when, stung by the critic's lash, the publisher recalled the book, claiming that the public was simply not ready to read about urban life with its lack of morals. Although subsequent editions of *Sister Carrie* were released in the interim, it took nearly eighty-one years for Dreiser's novel to be published in the form he intended.

1901: The Invention of the Electric Washing Machine

(Family Life)

In 1901, the technological innovations of running water, electric heaters, and the electric motor came together in a machine that helped revolutionize American women's lives, the washing machine.

Laundry was "the white woman's burden...the bane of American housemother's professional life" according to Marion Harland, a prolific writer of household advice around the turn of the century. Washing clothes took up as much as one third of a woman's time if she didn't have servants, and most women didn't. The electric washing machine profoundly changed the way that middle-class American women spent their time.

The invention of the washing machine was one example of the technological changes that revolutionized women's lives between 1870 and 1920, and have continued to simplify them to today. Small electric water pumps led to the introduction of running water, while small electric heaters meant that the water could be hot or cold, which made possible kitchen sinks, toilets, bathtubs, and showers, as well as washing machines and ultimately dishwashers. Small electric motors powered vacuum cleaners, ventilation fans, sewing machines, and compressors in refrigerators, and eventually electric appliances like can openers, bread makers, juicers, and food processors. Electric heaters ironed clothes and cooked food, on burners and in ovens. Rubber tile floors made kitchen clean up easier, along with white tile walls and chemical cleaners. Commercial canning and refrigeration made possible preserved processed foods and fresh meats in all seasons, while modern transport and industrial marketing replaced the weekly baking day with packaged breads. Chores that had once taken hours were now done in minutes; tasks that had once left women drained were now incidental.

Technology meant that wealthy women needed fewer servants at a time when good help was getting harder and harder to find, while women of lesser means were freed from many of the jobs that had previously defined their existences. In the first case, machinery made possible the relaxing of social distinctions, as wealthy women no longer had to maintain the air of authority over a staff of dozens. In the second case, machinery made possible the widening of horizons, including participation in leisure activities, study, and social involvement. Technological change made possible the "New Woman" of the 1890s, as well as the "Flapper" of the 1920s. It released women into the work force and set the basic conditions of modern life.

The industrial revolution occurred in two phases. The first, from 1760 to 1870, was the age of coal and iron, factories and railroads. It revolutionized production, but left daily life in most ways unchanged. The second industrial revolution, in contrast, brought steel and electricity, oil and chemicals, and it altered the most fundamental aspects of human life. The impact of apparently minor technological innovations on women's lives and opportunities, their behaviors and attitudes, has been in fact so huge that it is almost impossible to perceive. Women's lives today differ more in their most basic conditions from those of their grandmothers' than in any other three generations in history. The full consequences of these changes remain to be seen.

1902: Fannie Farmer Opens a Cooking School in Boston

(Cultural Life)

In 1902, Fannie Merritt Farmer, one of the first advocates of healthy eating, opened her own cooking school in Boston, Massachusetts. Miss Farmer's School of Cookery focused on educating housewives, rather than addressing professional chefs, unlike most cooking schools at that time.

Fannie Merritt Farmer's career as a dietitian, nutritionist, writer, and cooking teacher began almost accidentally in the late nineteenth century. Afflicted by polio as a teenager, Farmer's education stopped with high school. When her father began having difficulty finding adequate work to support the family, Farmer became a mother's helper, the only job that she could find with her level of education and her polio-induced diminished use of her left leg. Although she had never cooked at home, with the encouragement of her employer, Farmer learned the basics and became adept at preparing meals.

When Farmer was learning to cook, the accepted standard of measurement for putting recipes together was "a pinch," "a handful," or a "heaping teaspoon." Farmer began to pay more attention to precise measurements when one of her young charges asked her how such measurements were defined. It opened up a whole new way to approach food preparation, not only for Farmer, but ultimately for millions of cooks, both household and professional. In 1887, at the urging of both her employer and her family, Farmer enrolled in the Boston Cooking School. After graduating two years later, she stayed on as assistant principal and by 1894, she was the head of the school. When she left the Boston Cooking School in 1902, it was to open her own.

Whereas the Boston Cooking School taught professional cooking to women who wanted to find employment as cooks or who wanted to teach cooking, Farmer was more interested in reaching the average housewife. Her popular lectures, given in the mornings to housewives and in the evening to professional cooks, were routinely reported on in the *Boston Transcript*, as well as many other newspapers throughout the country. Gradually, her central focus became the development of diets for the sick and convalescent. Farmer became convinced that recuperation had much to do with diet, a novel concept at the time. She taught classes to nurses throughout New England, she trained hospital dietitians, and she became the first professional nutritionist to lecture at Harvard Medical School. Dr. Elliot P. Joslin, who was then only beginning his pioneering work in diabetes, was interested in Farmer's ideas

about nutrition. Much later, he credited her with providing the "stimulus which started me in writing about diabetes." The Joslin Clinic in Boston is today the foremost medical institution dealing with diabetes and still devotes much of its program to instructing patients in proper diet. In 1904, Farmer published what she always considered her most important cookbook, *Food and Cooking for the Sick and Convalescent.* But the cookbook that really made her name appeared even earlier. *The Boston Cooking School Cook Book* was published in 1896, and has since gone through numerous editions and sold nearly four million copies. It is an irony that Farmer would probably enjoy, since her publisher, Little Brown, was so certain that there was no appreciable market for a cookbook that they required Farmer to pay the publication costs. The book was intended to provide not just recipes, but a sound foundation on the nutritional values of foods. The new approach to food preparation, along with providing precise measurements in recipes, made both cooking and promoting family health much easier for generations of women. Farmer's ideas did not catch on immediately, but by World War II, most people involved in cooking and nutrition recognized and accepted the value of her methods and diet advice. Although she died in 1915, Fannie Farmer's cookbooks, ideas, and her school outlived her. The Fannie Farmer cookbooks are still used by millions of homemakers.

1903: The National Women's Trade Union League Is Founded

(Social Reform, Work)

Following a meeting of the American Federation of Labor (AFL) in 1903, where it became apparent that the union relegated women workers to a second-class status, Mary Kenney O'Sullivan and Leonora O'Reilly founded the National Women's Trade Union League (NWTUL), with the goal of improving wages and working conditions for women.

Mary Kenney O'Sullivan and Leonora O'Reilly were separated by hundreds of miles, but united in a common goal of bringing relief to working women. O'Sullivan, from Chicago, had organized the Woman's Bookbinder Union no. 1 in the 1880s. O'Sullivan lived at Hull House with Jane Addams even after her marriage to a Boston labor activist. Eventually they moved to Boston. When her husband was killed in an accident, and with three children to support, O'Sullivan returned to union work. O'Reilly, a native New Yorker who had worked in the garment industry from early childhood, was a member of the Knights of Labor in the 1880s and one of the organizers of the United Garment Workers in 1897. The two came together as members of the American Federation of Labor at its annual meeting in 1903. Disillusioned by the lack of commitment to women in the AFL, O'Sullivan and O'Reilly organized the National Women's Trade Union League.

The league, whose motto was "The Eight Hour Day; A Living Wage; To Guard the Home," embraced both women in the work force and middle- and upper-class women whose sympathies lay with working women.

These so-called "allies" to the NWTUL proved to be valuable, especially during strikes, because they had the resources and the desire to support the efforts of strikers, providing both personal and financial contributions. Moreover, the allies tended to be better educated and better able to communicate the ideas of the NWTUL to the public. At the same time, the allies educated league working members for leadership roles. Leonora O'Reilly was responsible for bringing Mary Elizabeth Dreier and Margaret Dreier Robbins into the trade union movement. Margaret Robbins eventually established an annuity for O'Reilly so that the latter could quit her ten-hour-a-day factory job and devote herself full time to union activity. The allies were particularly important during the garment industry strikes from 1909 to 1911. Dreier, Robbins, Alva Belmont, and other influential women led the effort to provide the necessary support for the striking women.

At its first convention, the league proposed six primary goals, including equal pay for equal work, woman suffrage, full unionization, an eight hour day, a mandatory minimum wage, as well as all of the economic benefits subscribed to in the AFLs economic program. The NWTUL chapters were organized in eleven cities by 1911, from Boston to Denver, Colorado. After the Triangle Shirt Waist fire, the league took the forefront in conducting investigations into the conditions that led to the fire, with the result that legislation requiring corporations to maintain minimum safety precautions was enacted.

After World War I, with the postwar conservatism adversely affecting labor unions, the NWTUL never again achieved the kind of influence it enjoyed during the progressive era. It continued to exist as an organization dedicated to improving the working conditions for women, though, with Rose Schneiderman at its helm, until just after World War II.

1903: Mother Jones Leads a Caravan of Children to the President's Oyster Bay Home

(Social Reform, Work)

In 1903, in an effort to draw attention to the plight of the youngest industrial workers—children—labor organizer Mother Jones led a caravan of striking children to the home of President Theodore Roosevelt in Oyster Bay, New York.

Although children were not ordinarily the focus of Mother Jones' union activity, perhaps the fate of her own four young children prompted her to take up their cause when, at the age of seventy-three, she led striking youngsters from the textile mills of Kensington, Pennsylvania, to President Theodore Roosevelt's home in Oyster Bay, New York. Mary Harris "Mother" Jones, an outspoken, energetic woman born in Ireland in 1830, spent the first forty years of her life in a most conventional manner. As a young child, she moved to Toronto, Canada, with her family, attended school, and became a teacher herself, teaching for a short time in a convent school in Michigan before settling in Chicago, where she opened a dressmaking business. At the beginning of the Civil War, Mary Harris married an iron worker from Memphis, Tennessee. Her husband, a member of the Iron Molder's Union, introduced Mary to the concept of unionism, just then beginning to take hold among American workers. Shortly after the war ended, in 1867, a yellow-fever epidemic that swept through Memphis destroyed her young family. Her husband and their four small children all fell victim to the disease. Jones returned to Chicago to cope with her profound grief, and returned as well to dressmaking. The extravagances of her wealthy customers sensitized Jones to economic and social inequities, but it was not until after the Chicago Fire of 1871 burned her out of her home and business that she began committing herself to the labor cause.

Her early association with the Knights of Labor, the leaders of which she tended to look upon as saints, brought her into contact with those who were fighting for better wages, shorter hours, and improved working conditions.

From 1877 on, Mother Jones, as she became known to almost everyone in the union movement, moved from area to area, organizing workers, encouraging them to stand up for their rights and to strike against unfair employers. Gradually, she became associated with the miners and began organizing for the United Mine Workers, participating in the coal strikes of 1900 and 1902. She led the miners' wives on marches, in the course of which they fought strikebreakers using their brooms and mops. Jones was one of the union advocates who was not satisfied with the settlement agreed upon when Theodore Roosevelt intervened to end the strike, faulting the negotiators for not insisting on union recognition.

Her dissatisfaction with the coal miners' settlement and Roosevelt's role might have prompted her to initiate the march on Oyster Bay the following year. But in truth, Jones would probably have undertaken the march in any case, for one of her talents was her ability to win publicity and attention from the government for the workers' cause. Publicizing the evils of child labor by bringing the striking children directly to Oyster Bay accomplished exactly that. Although the Owens-Keating Child Labor Law would not be enacted for another fourteen years, Mother Jones was one of those responsible for making the public aware of the horrendous conditions under which children had to work for wages that amounted to little more than a pittance.

1904: Ida Tarbell Publishes the *History of the Standard Oil Company*

(Social Reform)

In 1904, the muckraking journalist Ida Tarbell brought together a series of articles she had written for *McClure's Magazine* in a two-volume work entitled *History of the*

Standard Oil Company. Basing her profile of John D. Rockefeller's massive monopoly on meticulous research and solid analysis, she contributed substantially to the investigation and eventual breakup of the company under the Sherman Anti-Trust Act.

Ida Tarbell did the research and much of the writing that went into her famous exposé for a series of articles for *McClure's Magazine*, where she worked as an editor. *McClure's* was the first and most influential of the muckraking journals that appeared around the turn of the century. These magazines found a lucrative market in showing the sordid side of the gilded age, combining thorough investigations with sensationalistic presentation that contrasted the ideology of human progress through capitalist competition with what seemed to be the realities of human misery and monopolistic practices. They found a ready audience in the new middle-class readers, who were concerned about the social welfare of the masses and their own quality of life. Both appeared threatened by the dark manipulations of the great monopolists.

Tarbell went to work alongside many more prominent muckrakers, but she benefited both from her obscurity and from the fact that she was a woman. Presenting herself as a naive female desiring only to publicize the achievements of the great company, she gained access to records that re-

vealed special favors from the railroad companies and from politicians. Overall, she so effectively showed the monopolistic practices of Rockefeller's company that her work led to more official investigations, the application of the Sherman Anti-Trust Act, and the breakup of the Standard Oil Company. Tarbell's work, as much as any other, vindicated the muckrakers' faith that public exposure could materially promote the public good.

Tarbell came to write her history with a strong background. Her family had made its fortune from the Pennsylvania oil fields discovered in 1859, and she graduated from a coeducational college in 1880. She worked briefly as a teacher and then as editor of a monthly magazine for eight years, after which she studied history at the Sorbonne in Paris. She began writing for *McClure's* upon her return in 1894, and she published her first book, a biography of Napoleon that sold more than one hundred thousand copies, in 1895. She drew on both her family's experience in business and her scholarly studies to prepare her *History*, and drew upon it in turn in subsequent works. She published eight books about Abraham Lincoln alone, as well as more contemporary studies of tariffs and scientific management, and did significant primary research on women in the American Revolution.

Two years after her success with Standard Oil, Tarbell joined several of her colleagues in leaving *McClure's* in order to purchase the *American Magazine*. She served as coeditor until 1915, and then traveled on the lecture circuit. During World War I, she served on the Women's Committee of the Council of National Defense. After-

wards, she covered the Versailles peace conference as a reporter, and in 1919 President Woodrow Wilson appointed her as a delegate to an International Industrial Conference. In 1921, President Warren G. Harding appointed Tarbell to a commission on unemployment, and during the twenties she was active in the peace movement. She warned of the rise of fascism in Europe following a 1926 interview with Mussolini, and reiterated her fears in her 1939 autobiography *All in a Day's Work*.

1906: Congress Passes the Pure Food Act

(Social Reform)

On June 29, 1906, Congress passed the Pure Food Act, also known as the Pure Food and Drug Act, which prohibited the sale or transportation of adulterated, misbranded, poisonous, or deleterious food, drugs, medicines, and liquor.

Ever since the Civil War, when nurse Annie Whittenmyer began arguing for better and more varied diets for patients in hospitals, interest in regulating the production of foods and medicines grew in the public perception as a necessary social reform. Harvey Wiley, who eventually became

the chief chemist of the U.S. Department of Agriculture, credited Whittenmyer for his decision to make the study of food additives and food production his life's work. When Wiley became chief chemist, his campaign for food and drug regulations began to build momentum. Turning to the women of the United States, Wiley cast the problem as one of family safety, requesting their assistance in forcing legislation that would make food processing and the production of medicines safer for American families.

Women responded with enthusiasm to Wiley's campaign. The Food Consumer's League, organized in the 1890s, appointed Alice Lakey as chair of the food investigation committee, charged with raising public opposition to the use of aniline, a commonly used coal by-product used in making food coloring dyes. Following another avenue, Florence Kelley, as the head of the National Consumer's League and a former state factory inspector in Illinois, began speaking out on behalf of increased food and drug legislation at the city, state, and federal levels. Her campaign continued, on and off, for the next twenty-five years. Even after passage of the Pure Food Act, Kelley sought to bring more and more products within the scope of the legislation.

The Women's Christian Temperance Union (WCTU) came into the fight in 1902, responding angrily to a Wesleyan University professor's accusation that the WCTU consistently lobbied against beer but said nothing about medicines containing ten times more alcohol. The WCTU quickly began an educational campaign against the use of medicines containing alcohol and against the mislabeling of patent medicines. The WCTU was helped along in its campaign between 1903 and 1906 when a number of women's magazines, including *The Ladies Home Journal* and *Collier's*, began publishing frequent articles relating the dangers of patent medicines, untested home remedies, and medicines containing large amounts of alcohol of which the consumer might not be aware.

By 1905, advocates of food and drug regulation had picked up political support in both the House and the Senate. Senator Porter McCumber sponsored the first bill calling for regulation, but when the Senate session ended before action was taken, the bill died. Coincidentally, in 1906, author Upton Sinclair published *The Jungle*, which related in graphic detail the horrific practices employed at Chicago slaughterhouses on beef products intended for human consumption. Public concern for regulation now became a groundswell of demands for instant reform. Three separate bills were immediately introduced into Congress. Senator Albert Beveridge of Indiana introduced legislation for government meat inspection that was passed and signed into law June 30, 1906. At the same time, Senator Weldon Heyburn of Idaho and Congressman William Hepburn of Iowa both introduced strong food and drug bills. Congress passed a combined version of the Heyburn-Hepburn bills on June 29, 1906. President Theodore Roosevelt signed the bill into law immediately. While a Pure Food and Drug Act was inevitable eventually, even with Sinclair's exposé of the slaughterhouses, legislation might have taken considerably longer had it not been for the widespread grassroots movement for such legislation that began with Annie Whittenmyer during the Civil War.

1907: Margaret Sage Founds the Russel Sage Foundation

(Social Reform)

In 1907, the childless widow of the financier Russel Sage, Margaret Slocum Sage, created a foundation named in his honor and dedicated to promoting social improvements through funding of both social research and social action.

Margaret Slocum graduated from Emma Willard's Troy Female Seminary in 1847 and went on to become the wife of one of the wealthiest men in America. When he died in 1906, she began to use the wealth she inherited for a variety of charitable purposes. By the time she died in 1918, she had given away approximately $80 million, a total that put her in the same league as the famous philanthropist Andrew Carnegie.

Sage's alma mater was one of the prime beneficiaries of her largesse. She gave it a vocational school for women, and she donated an island estate to the U.S. Military Academy at West Point. But the chief recipient of her funds was the foundation she established in her husband's honor, the Russel Sage Foundation.

Created in the heyday of sociology's "scientific charity" movement, which aspired to direct charitable giving according to objective criteria of utility, the foundation supported a tremendous amount of research into poor households. Among the studies commissioned by the foundation were Katherine Anthony's *Mothers Who Must Earn*, Edith Abbot's *The Delinquent Child and the Home*, Elizabeth Beardsley Butler's *Women and the Trades*, and Mary Van Kleeck's *Working Girls in Evening Schools*. These and other monographs provided incredible detail about the inner workings of poor, often immigrant households. They were used at the time to help the foundation manage its philanthropy, and in the decades since, they have given historians unparalleled insight into a strata of society whose lives generally passed unrecorded.

Because of the central role of women in these poor households (and vice versa), the foundation's activities had particular importance for women. They and their children were beneficiaries of the foundation's aid, and it is their lives that are particularly well-documented in the foundation's studies. The foundation aided women more directly as well, funding a number of women's organizations among its many causes. Others include city planning, prison reform, education, and folk arts. For both the depth of its studies and the consequent wisdom of its disbursements, the Russel Sage Foundation exemplifies the positive contribution of carefully planned charitable activities in improving the lives of ordinary people in America.

1908: U.S. Supreme Court Upholds Protective Legislation in *Muller v. Oregon*

(Social Reform, Work)

In 1908, the U.S. Supreme Court upheld the right of states to pass protective legislation in the case of *Muller v. Oregon*.

By the mid 1880s, social reformers had begun advocating and working for enactment of protective legislation in order to insure the welfare and safety of women and children working in factories. Unions had failed to take women into the fold in any meaningful way. Therefore, female workers had no institutionalized method of securing safety and fairness. Moreover, protective legislation served the purpose of organized labor because it offered a way to prohibit the infiltration of women into skilled jobs. By designating certain jobs as dangerous to a woman's health and safety, unions could preserve those jobs for male union members.

At the same time, the social reformers were acting in what they sincerely considered the best interests of women and children. As more and more information came out regarding unsafe working conditions and long hours for low wages, social reformers met with greater and greater success in securing protective legislation. Massachusetts passed a ten-hour work day law in 1887, and by 1914, twenty-seven other states had enacted similar legislation. In addition, many states passed legislation establishing minimum wages.

The state of Oregon passed ten-hour day legislation and, when a laundry owner forced his female employee to work longer than ten hours, he was arrested for violation of the law. The laundry owner sought to challenge the state's right to prevent women from working as many hours as they wished, and brought suit in the case of *Muller v. Oregon*. The suit worked its way through the lower courts and finally came to the Supreme Court, which handed down its decision in 1908.

The Court's decision in *Muller v. Oregon* was a landmark decision for two reasons. First, in upholding the right of the state of Oregon to pass legislation regulating the number of hours women could work, proclaiming that "sex is a valid basis for classification," the Court was, in effect, endorsing the concept of protective legislation. This was a clear victory for social reformers because, in most cases, protective legislation did what the reformers intended it to do—it provided protection for the health of female employees, improved the conditions under which they worked, limited their hours, and raised their wages. While future court decisions would invalidate some protective legislation, for the moment, the social reformers had won.

The second reason that *Muller v. Oregon* constituted a landmark decision was that it was the first instance of so-called "sociological jurisprudence." Florence Kelley, the head of the National Consumer's League, worked closely with the counsel for the state of Oregon, Oliver Wendell Holmes, in preparing the case. Holmes, soon to be sitting on the Court himself and destined to become one of the Court's ablest and most influential chief justices, gathered data from a variety of sources to demonstrate the vulnerability of female employees. Holmes argued his case using statistics to demonstrate the relationship between long hours of work and the declining health and morals of female employees. The Court was receptive to Holmes' line of argument, declaring that women's physical well-being "becomes an object of public interest and care in order to preserve the strength and vigor of the race." A precedent had been set in allowing the introduction of sociological data to support or refute a piece of legislation, and for the first time, real world experience won out over disconnected legal dogma.

1908: The American Home Economics Association Is Founded

(Family Life, Cultural Life)

In 1873, chemist Ellen Richards began a life's work to apply innovations, inventions, and discoveries in science and technology to the task of homemaking. A reflection of that work was the establishment in 1908 of the American Home Economics Association.

Convinced that the family home was the civilizing center of society, Ellen Richards devoted nearly four decades to capitalizing on scientific and technological developments that could release women from the drudgery associated with homework and enable them to become more involved with creative and challenging work. Her beliefs, in part, stemmed from her

Vassar education, where she had the good fortune to study astronomy with Maria Mitchell. After leaving Vassar, Richards' planned to teach astronomy in Argentina, but war in that country prevented her from doing so. Like so many creative individuals before and after, Richards had the ability to turn adversity into opportunity. She applied to the Massachusetts Institute of Technology (MIT), founded only five years earlier, and was accepted into their chemistry program, tuition free. Working under the assumption that MIT believed she had a promising future in chemistry, Richards was chagrined to learn later that she was allowed to matriculate *gratis*, so that the administration could claim she was really not a student if anyone raised objections to a woman in the graduate program. In 1873, she left MIT without her doctorate, only because the department heads did not want the first science Ph.D. to go to a woman. A short time later, Richards married a young MIT professor of metallurgy, Robert Richards. While her husband worked on his metallurgy research, she acted as his chemist, performing such outstanding work that she was the first woman elected to the American Institute of Mining and Metallurgical Engineers.

Calling on the assistance of the Woman's Education Association of Boston, Richards was able to raise funds for the Woman's Laboratory of MIT. The Woman's Laboratory helped female students who wanted to enter MIT's science program, but who had an uneven science background. For the seven years of its existence, Richards remained second in command at the facility she had organized. After years of contributing to the MIT science program, the university gave Richards a faculty appointment in 1884, a post she retained for twenty-seven years.

The opportunity to begin to put into effect some of her ideas about technology, science, and homemaking came in 1899 with a series of summer seminars that Richards started for persons interested in understanding the tremendous impact that industrialization and urbanization was having on their lives. Richards believed that homemakers, who in generations past learned timeless skills from mothers and grandmothers, had to learn an entirely new set of skills commensurate with the changing world. Generational knowledge had to be supplemented with new knowledge, methods, and skills, for the modern homemaker to absorb and manage the changes in, for example, food and nutrition. Seminar attendees adopted the name "home economics," and, under Richards' direction, helped to plan out curriculum for high schools and colleges in the new discipline, that included hygiene and sanitation as components of the new programs. In 1908, the American Home Economics Association was founded, dedicated to the "improvement of living conditions in the home, the institutional household, and the community." The *Journal of Home Economics*, underwritten by Richards, presented scholarly research with which the new professionals could improve and expand the formal programs that eventually filtered down to the average homemaker, providing her with the tools to make informed decisions for home and family.

1909: Sigmund Freud Visits Clark University

(Family Life)

In September, 1909, the Viennese doctor and psychologist Sigmund Freud traveled to Clark University in Worcester, Massachusetts, to deliver a series of lectures introducing the psychological system that he called psychoanalysis.

Freud's trip to America and his appearance at Clark University reflected the influence his system had on leading American thinkers and also served to widen its audience considerably. Arguing that both healthy and pathological psychological phenomena represent displacements, or sublimations, of unacceptable instinctual drives, his work alerted people to the power of hidden psychological proc-

esses and gave them a sophisticated set of concepts with which to understand them. His theories spread rapidly from medical and intellectual circles to become a central feature of sophisticated popular culture in the 1920s.

The most obvious impact of Freudianism on American culture in the 1920s was its promotion of sexual liberation. Freud put infantile sexuality at the center of his theories about personal development, and he insisted on the tremendous role it played in adult life. While he himself advocated discipline and restraint as necessary to preserve civil order and sublimate sexual energy into creative activity, he had opened a Pandora's box whose forces he could not so easily control. With the Victorian morality that had guided their parents' generation apparently discredited, young women of the "Flapper" era felt free to explore and enjoy their sexuality. While some older feminists warned that sexual liberality merely changed the terms, rather than ended the importance, of sex in defining the social role of women, younger women took their new-found freedom to be an important component of what it meant to be a modern woman. Sexual liberation formed part of a wider rejection of the stifling Victorian tradition that confined women to a limited and secondary role in society.

Of course, Freudianism itself was a product of the Victorian era, and while its frank acknowledgment of human sexuality helped liberate American women, in other ways it continued, and indeed strengthened, the diminution of women. Freud definitely saw women as an inadequate version of men, and in his system, women are thought to believe the same. "Penis envy," a girl's supposed disappointment that she does not possess the prominent male organ, formed the basis of the "Elektra complex," by which a girl's identity is formed. Whereas Freud thought boys go through an "Oedipal complex" in which they initially desire to mate with their mother, and eventually reconcile themselves to their secondary place to their father, he thought girls go through a stage when they want to *be* their father, and must learn to satisfy themselves with their father's love. He saw this biologically ordained frustration as the root of "female masochism" and the source of women's supposed perennial discontent.

As time went by, Freudianism became even more committed to the gender-role status quo. The sexual liberation advocated by early Freudians had always assumed that heterosexual marital relationships were the norm, and that other forms of sexuality were in one way or another pathological deviancy. In the 1940s and 1950s, this view was intensified by a new view of women's sexuality in which immature "clitoral" orgasms were contrasted with mature "vaginal" orgasms. Female sexual satisfaction, the neo-Freudians argued, depended on a direct link to procreation, one stating that "the woman needs to have in her unconscious mind the knowledge that for her the sex act, to yield maximum satisfaction, terminates only with childbirth or the end of the nursing period." Even as sexual researchers were proving the physiological role of the clitoris in all female orgasms, and that lesbians were the most sexually satisfied women they surveyed, Freudian psychology became a purportedly scientific buttress to the old notion that women were biologically fated to psychological instability and social subordination.

By allying themselves with the status quo, Freudians set themselves up for a fall during the next cultural upheaval. When this arrived in the late 1960s, the new feminists saw Freudianism as one of their principal opponents. Drawing on the extensive scientific evidence that already existed and creating new interpretations as they went along, they helped debunk Freudianism as a scientific discipline and reduce it to the first among equals in the universe of psychologies.

On balance, Freud's fundamental contribution, the realization that the human mind unconsciously redirects instinctual drives into both healthy and dysfunctional emotions and behaviors, moved our understanding of psychology to a new level of sophistication. But much of the specific content of Freud's theories, in particular many of his notions about women, proved to be reflections of his time and culture rather than the timeless insights he thought them to be. As always in science, the creation of a new paradigm raises as many new issues as it resolves.

1909: The "Uprising of 30,000"

(Work)

The influx of radicalized young women from Eastern Europe and the intransigence of American factory owners combined to create an increasingly volatile labor situation in New York that climaxed in 1909 with a general strike led by the International Ladies' Garment Workers Union (ILGWU).

The workers who created ladies' garments, mostly men, began to organize into small, informal groups in the late nineteenth century. They came together in June 1900, spurred on by the United Brotherhood of Cloak Makers Union in New York, with the immediate purpose of forming a national union to promulgate a national union label and to find a way to resist injunctions against striking garment workers. Garment workers were also concerned with finding a way of ending the "Home Contract" system of production. In this system, independent contractors, usually women, worked at home for a pittance, about 30 cents a day. The women and men who held the preferred positions as workers in the shops opposed the contract system because the owner's exploitation of the "home contract" women facilitated the exploitation of those who worked in factories.

With two thousand delegates meeting in New York on June 3, 1900, the American Federation of Labor (AFL) issued a charter to the new International Ladies' Garment Workers Union. The union leadership remained predominantly male during its first decade, even though most garment workers were women. Like most union officials, the AFL and the male unionists believed that women were incapable of handling union hierarchy. Moreover, the belief persisted that women would not support union actions because their primary careers were marriage and not industrial work.

The increase of young, radical immigrant Jewish women, however, began to exert an influence to change this perception. Typical of them was Clara Lemlich, a refugee from Russia who came to New York at the age of fifteen in 1903 and became a founding member of ILGWU's Local no. 25 in 1906. She participated in innumerable strikes and demonstrations, and was arrested seventeen times in 1909 alone. When on November 22, 1909, she joined several thousand other young women at the Cooper Union meeting hall, she listened to several hours of boring speeches calling for a general strike. Able to endure them no longer, Lemlich marched to the front of the hall, boldly took the podium, and eloquently spoke in favor of the general strike. The crowd roared its agreement, and thirty thousand garment workers walked off their jobs.

In the days that followed, the women of the Women's Trade Union League and the Socialist party came to the strikers' aid. They established twenty strike halls, and helped with organizing picketing, strike support, and dealing with police brutality. At first the enthusiasm and dedication of the strikers appeared unstoppable, but the solidarity of the Jewish immigrants did not embrace Italian, native-born, nor African-American women. In the end the strike failed. But the strike succeeded in establishing the ILGWU as a major union, and more women were organized as a result than had ever before been unionized in the United States.

The infamous Triangle Fire, in which 147 garment workers—mostly young Italian and Jewish immigrants—died because of the total lack of regulations governing work place safety, drove even more women into the union the next year. The ILGWU won a fourteen-week strike in 1916 and went on to pioneer union-sponsored health centers and other benefits. It benefited from the prosperity of the war years, and while it languished (like other unions) in the 1920s and 1930s, it revived in succeeding decades. The proportion of women remained high, around 75 percent of the rank and file, although the leadership reverted to be predominantly male. Nonetheless, the union provided an important impetus to the organization of women in labor.

1910: Frances Elisabeth Crowell Is Appointed Executive Secretary of the Association of Tuberculosis Clinics in New York City

(Medicine, Family Life)

Working as a special investigator for the Association of Neighborhood Workers in New York City, Frances Elisabeth Crowell was appointed executive secretary of the Association of Tuberculosis Clinics in New York City in 1910, a post she held until 1917, and from which she helped to launch the international public health movement.

When Frances Elisabeth Crowell graduated in the first class from St. Joseph's Hospital School of Nursing in Chicago in 1895, she made the decision to move from the city to a small town in Florida where there seemed to be more opportunity to engage in front-line nursing. The Pensacola Infirmary catered primarily to seaman on the Florida coast, and as a consequence treated a broad spectrum of ailments, ranging from venereal diseases, to tropical diseases including yellow fever, to various other epidemics. Three years after joining the staff at the Pensacola Infirmary, Crowell took an unusual step for a nurse, not to mention an unmarried woman—she purchased a half interest in the infirmary. When, in 1900, the infirmary moved to larger quarters and became a charter corporation, Crowell played a prominent role in the newly named St. Anthony's Hospital. Buying into partial ownership of the infirmary reflected long-held concerns Crowell had regarding the financial security of working women. Many of her nursing journal articles dealt with that issue over the years.

In an effort to expand her skills, Crowell enrolled in the New York School of Philanthropy—the predecessor to the Columbia University School of Social Work—to study social work. When she graduated in 1906, Crowell worked as a special investigator for the Association of Neighborhood Workers, before accepting a position as the executive secretary of the Association of Tuberculosis Clinics in New York in 1910. Throughout this period, Crowell was still an active administrator at St. Anthony's in Pensacola. Ever concerned about the quality of nursing care available to patients, Crowell started a nurses training program to provide qualified nurses and quality care to patients at St. Anthony's.

In 1917, the Rockefeller Foundation appointed Crowell to a commission that it was sending to France to help set up medical services. In France, Crowell organized nursing schools and, virtually singlehandedly, established the public health nurse as the first-line of defense in antituberculosis programs. Her work in initiating the public health movement in France earned her a Legion of Honor from the French government. Crowell worked exclusively in France until 1922, when the Rockefeller Foundation asked her to set up similar public health programs throughout the continent. For nearly twenty years, Crowell traveled throughout Europe, meeting with heads of government, medical professionals, and members of the Rockefeller Foundation board of directors, assessing the training programs for nurses in various countries and providing advice on maintaining quality public health programs. When World War II began, Crowell worked as an advisor to the Red Cross. Caught up in political events in Italy, Crowell had to take refuge in a convent for the duration of the war. Because of her years of service in establishing the public health movement, civilians throughout Europe were able to fall back on a structure of health service already in place when the war began. Were it not for Crowell, it is likely that civilians would have suffered during World War II and after even more than they did.

1911: Dr. Alice Hamilton Publishes the First Study of Occupational Disease

(Social Reform)

Appointed by the Governor of Illinois to become the first director of that state's Occupational Disease Commission, Dr. Alice Hamilton published in 1911 the results of an intensive study of occupational diseases that helped to define the field of industrial toxicology and led to passage of worker's compensation legislation.

Alice Hamilton fulfilled a long-time dream when, in 1897, she became a resident of Jane Addams' Hull House, then a center of groundbreaking research and social reform. Born in 1869 in Indiana, Hamilton knew she wanted to study medicine. Elizabeth Blackwell, the first woman graduated from medical school, had received her medical degree nearly forty years earlier, but little had been done since then to encourage women to go into medicine. Following Blackwell's trail, Hamilton applied to several medical schools before settling, as she described it, at "a little third-rate medical school" in Indiana. Shortly thereafter, the University of Michigan accepted her application to enroll at their coeducational medical school, and she jumped at the opportunity. With her M.D. in hand in 1893, Hamilton went to Europe to study bacteriology at the Universities of Leipzig and Munich. Hamilton was allowed to sit in on classes provided that she remain "inconspicuous" to the male students and faculty.

In 1897, Hamilton was appointed a professor at the Woman's Medical School of Northwestern University. As a resident of Hull House, she was able to draw on her training as a bacteriologist, reaching the conclusion that many of Hull House's constituents were contracting diseases from the noxious chemicals to which they were exposed in the industries in which they worked. Standard practice at the time, with no worker's compensation laws or safety standards to protect employees, dictated that once illness outstripped productivity, the employee was fired and replaced with any of the thousands of workers looking for jobs. Responding to the situation, the governor of Illinois appointed an Occupational Disease Commission in 1910, with Hamilton as its Director. Her report in 1911, focusing in part on the effects of lead poisoning in the factory system, quickly became a model for future investigations. At once, Hamil-

ton was established as one of, if not the, leading toxicologist in the United States. It also led directly to enactment of worker's compensation legislation in Illinois, establishing a precedent that illness resulting from work entitled an employee to some compensation from the employer.

From 1911 to 1921, Hamilton served as a nonsalaried researcher at the request of the U.S. Commissioner of Labor, who asked that she duplicate her Illinois study on a nationwide level. During World War I, Hamilton also worked tirelessly for peace.

Ironically, the war also presented new opportunities for women, including Hamilton. Her investigations into the toxic contamination to which workers were exposed in munitions factories helped to further establish her credentials as the leading expert on industrial toxicology. As a consequence, in 1919, Hamilton became the first woman to received an appointment to the Harvard Medical School faculty. Her iconoclastic sense of humor at the irony of being a female faculty member of a medical school that did not admit women until World War II caused her always to insist that her Harvard appointment was less taxing on the board of directors since she was the only candidate for the position.

The work that Alice Hamilton did in the field of toxicology helped to establish it as an important medical specialty. Hamilton's studies in industrial toxicology and the seminal contributions they made in helping to secure legislation protecting workers both from exposure to harmful chemicals and the economic hardships of enduring industrially caused diseases, remain a lasting contribution to a still-controversial subject.

1911: The Triangle Fire Kills Scores of Young Women Workers

(Social Reform, Work)

On March 25, 1911, a fire in the Triangle Shirtwaist Company in New York City claimed the lives of 146 young women workers, mostly immigrants, trapped behind locked exit doors or forced to jump to the street ten stories below in desperate attempts to escape the burning building.

Only a year before the disastrous Triangle fire, employees at the factory had returned to work after a failed strike, called to protest both low wages and dangerous conditions. The Triangle strike, part of an industry-wide walk-out of eighteen thousand workers from over five hundred shirtwaist makers' factories, had begun in November 1909 and ended in February 1910, when workers returned to their fifty-nine hour work weeks, the same low wages, and the same dangerous conditions. Some of the strik-ing women were not allowed to return to the Triangle. As it turned out, they were the lucky ones.

On March 25, 1911, a cigarette dropped in a pile of trash by one of the few male employees set off a rapidly expanding blaze that quickly tore through the several floors of the Triangle company, located on the upper floors of the Asch Building in New York's Washington Square Park. Because it was Saturday, payday at the Triangle, and management did not want workers leaving even a few minutes early to get a jump on their one day off, all but one of the exit doors were locked. As the employees became aware of the fire, some were fortunate enough to get to elevators that were still operating, and a few managed to get out of the unlocked door before fire blocked that exit. Others were able to jump to a building across the alley, and some escaped to an enclosed courtyard below. Those in the courtyard survived only because firemen chopped through locked doors on the street level. But for 146 young women, there was no escape. More than fifty bodies were found piled behind locked doors. Scores of desperate girls and women chose to jump from the upper windows rather than succumb to the flames in what by then had become an inferno. No one who jumped from the building survived the fall to the sidewalks below, and some were impaled on iron fences surrounding the Asch Building.

Despite the irresponsible action of the company managers and owners who had locked exit doors, a subsequent trial exonerated all concerned from any wrongful death convictions. A member of the all-male jury later explained that there was a feeling among the jury that the young women, who they deemed to have less intelligence than people in other occupations might have, probably panicked and therefore caused their own deaths. Little consideration was given to the locked doors and dangerous working conditions that had been allowed to flourish.

Devastated by the loss of life, Rose Schneiderman and other Women's Trade Union League members dispatched a committee of fifty garment workers to the state legislature in Albany to present a petition asking for an investigation into the fire and for new laws regulating safety conditions in order to prevent future catastrophes. Responding to the petition, Senator Robert F. Wagner, who would later help to write the Wagner Labor Act during the New Deal, and Alfred E. Smith, the future mayor of New York and presidential candidate, proposed the formation of the New York State Factory Investigating Commission, commonly referred to as the Triangle Fire Commission. After a four-year investigation, Chairman Wagner and Vice Chairman Smith, along with the field investigators, one of whom was future Secretary of Labor Frances Perkins, called for a series of new regulations governing factory safety. The thirteen-volume report included recommendations for sixty separate laws, fifty-six of which were enacted by the legislature. Out of the Triangle

Shirtwaist Company fire, New York emerged with the most comprehen-

sive laws governing factory safety standards of any state in the union.

1911: Kansas City, Missouri, Passes the Nation's First Mother's Pension Law

(Family Life)

After much lobbying by advocates of protective legislation and by progressive reformers, Kansas City, in 1911, became the first city in the nation to pass a law that provided funds for widows, deserted wives, or other single women to raise their children at home.

For years a major concern of both the protective legislationists and the progressive reformers dealt with the difficult question of who was responsible for widows with young children, deserted wives and mothers, and other single mothers with no means to support themselves or their children. In 1909, these concerns were formalized at a Conference on the Care of Dependent Children at the White House in Washington, D.C. Called by President Theodore Roosevelt, the conference discussed the social consequences of paying mothers a pension so that they could keep their children at home, rather than having to institutionalize them. Most of the supporters of a mother's pension law considered it an entitlement, not charity. Common to the approach to social problems of the time, a coalition of women's organizations, clubs, social workers, politicians, and trade unionists lobbied legislators for appropriate legislation.

In 1911, Kansas City, Missouri, became the first city in the nation to make provisions for those eventualities. Illinois followed later that year, passing a statewide mother's pension provision. By 1919, thirty-nine states had enacted some kind of mother's pension law. In all states that had mother's pension laws, eligibility extended to widowed mothers with children fourteen years of age and under. Because in most states children over fourteen years old were considered capable of holding a job, no provisions were made for older children. In some states, but not all, divorced mothers, women whose husbands deserted them, and women whose husbands were in prison were also eligible for pensions.

Despite efforts to persuade politicians and the public that pensions should be considered an entitlement, most people looked upon them as charity. Women who applied for funds often had to endure the close scrutiny of city and state employees whose goal it was to disallow anyone who did not precisely fit the designated cri-

teria. Thus, recipients were constantly harassed by investigators checking to make sure the home environment was up to speed and that no other source of income was available to the recipient. These constraints were imposed despite the reality that mother's pensions were usually not enough to maintain a home without supplemental income. Moreover, many southern states would not even entertain applications from African-American women.

Even with all of the drawbacks associated with the mother's pension programs, they still constituted the best hope for women left alone to care for children. Until the enactment of the Social Security Act of 1935, it was the first and only acknowledgment from governments at various levels that they did have some responsibility for the well-being of all their citizens.

1912: The Heterodoxy Club Holds Its First Meeting

(Cultural Life, Equal Rights)

Responding to the concerns of her friends and colleagues about the changing status of women in the early twentieth century, journalist Jennie Marie Howe organized a

New York–based club, Heterodoxy, to give modern women a place to voice untraditional ideas without risking reprisal.

One of the more unusual organizations in the history of American women was a club founded by New Yorker Jennie Marie Howe, a journalist, in 1912. Howe's purpose in founding Heterodoxy was to give women a place to express themselves without having to worry about inviting scorn or misunderstanding from either public or private quarters. In order to protect themselves, the club limited itself to a handful of hard and fast rules, one of which was that no minutes would ever be recorded. Meeting places and times, and activities of the club were also unrecorded.

Heterodoxy was not an entirely secret organization, however. It did have a public image. At first, it was viewed as a prosuffrage organization, but through a series of public forums, Heterodoxy transformed its image into that of a frankly feminist club. That transformation became apparent especially between 1912 and 1914, when the forums ranged from one entitled "Twenty-five Answers to Antis" (referring to antisuffragists), to "What is Feminism?" Not surprisingly, most of the club members were also members of a suffrage organization, usually the National American Woman Suffrage Association. Unlike most clubs, Heterodoxy members were all professional career women, whose various jobs kept them so busy that the club, which existed until 1942, never held a meeting when more than half the current membership was present. Members included writers, journalists, physicians, lawyers, stockbrokers, and theatre people. Although all of them tended to be more liberal than conservative, their political identities were also varied, with both Republicans and Democrats, Socialists and Prohibitionists, anarchists and radicals all counted among the 105 members, who included people like radical labor organizer Elizabeth Gurley Flynn, economist and writer Charlotte Perkins Gilman, lawyer and socialist Crystal Eastman, and choreographer Agnes de Mille. A book of letters currently in the archives of the Schlesinger Library in Cambridge, Massachusetts, each one written by a member of Heterodoxy as a commemorative to Jennie Howe, provides ample testimony about the importance of having such an organization where members could both express and be exposed to the broadest range of ideas on almost every social cause and condition.

Probably the one issue on which club members could not find a common ground for discussion was World War I, when pacifists and interventionists argued so bitterly that some members actually felt compelled to resign from the club.

While meetings continued to take place throughout the 1920s and 1930s, the necessity for such a forum became less and less acute. Gradually membership fell off and the club finally discontinued its luncheon meetings in 1942.

1912: Juliette Gordon Low Founds the Girl Scouts of America

(Cultural Life)

When Juliette Gordon Low met Sir Robert Baden-Powell in 1911, she was so taken with the concept of the Boy Scouts, which Baden-Powell had founded three years earlier, that she began making similar plans for girls. Returning to America, Low established the first Girl Guide unit on March 12, 1912, in Savannah, Georgia.

Juliette Gordon Low met Sir Robert Baden-Powell on one of her many trips to Europe. A native of Savannah, Georgia, Low's own childhood was a privileged one, marked by private schools and numerous opportunities to pursue interests including painting, playwriting, and acting. Although none of her interests led to lifelong commitment, Low continued to develop new talents throughout her life. Her habitual trips to Europe began when she was still fairly young. Her marriage to a wealthy Savannah resi-

dent, William Mackay Low, who also spent considerable time in Europe, allowed her to continue her travels. The marriage, unfortunately, was not a particularly happy one. The Lows had no children, Juliette was increasingly plagued by ear problems developed from childhood, and her husband was not faithful. After eighteen years of marriage, William Low died in 1905, leaving the bulk of his estate to his mistress. It took several years for Juliette to secure a settlement that gave her financial independence.

Low's friendship with Baden-Powell, based on shared interests, led her to become well-acquainted with his Boy Scout program. Immediately, she could see that a similar organization for girls would be beneficial. At one of her several homes, Low organized the first troop among poor Scottish girls. In London, she organized two more troops. Returning to America, Low set out to establish Girl Guide troops in Savannah. On March 12, 1912, she organized sixteen Savannah girls into two patrols. From that small beginning, the girl scout movement expanded rapidly. She began talks with founders of the Campfire Girls, which had been established in 1910, with an eye toward combining the two groups, as the Girl Scouts of America. Although the merger did not take place, Low renamed her Girl Guides Girl Scouts. In 1915, the Girl Scouts of America was officially organized, with Juliette Low as the first president.

Low did not consider herself a feminist by any means, and she probably did not favor woman suffrage. But she did have a vision for girls that included self-reliance, independence, and a willingness to do something every day for someone else. This became the heart of the girl scout movement. Low traveled throughout the country enlisting volunteers, many of whom came to agree with Low, despite their initial intention to resist. For many privileged young women, volunteering for the Girl Scouts became a way to fill their time productively. Girl Scout camps were built across the country, and the young scouts learned survival training and an appreciation of nature. Domesticity was by no means ignored, though, and the first merit badges were earned for skills developed in categories including cooking and housekeeping. By 1919, there were Girl Scout troops in almost every state and in Hawaii. Although most of the scout leadership came from the upper and middle classes, the Girl Scouts were open to girls from all economic backgrounds. Moreover, race and ethnicity were not barriers to joining the Girl Scouts.

Throughout its existence, the Girl Scouts has retained its central focus on self-reliance and independence, an appreciation of nature, and the development of homemaking skills. But it has also expanded to include exploration and consideration of a variety of career choices, encouraging its young members not to exclude a career because of their sex. Millions of girls have been members of the Girl Scouts since its founding in 1912, and it remains the largest female voluntary organization in the world, with a small nucleus of paid professionals.

1912: Alice Paul Leads a Protest at Woodrow Wilson's Inauguration

(Equal Rights)

Determined to serve notice to incoming president Woodrow Wilson that women expected him to act on the suffrage issue, Alice Paul organized a huge suffrage parade to take place on March 3, 1914, the day before Wilson was scheduled to take the oath of office.

Alice Paul, whose experiences with the English suffragette movement had persuaded her that a federal suffrage amendment was the quickest way for American women to get the vote, took over NAWSA's Congressional Committee in January 1913. Paul believed that federal suffragism, to succeed, would require the support of the president of the United States. Over the objections of some of NAWSA's more conservative members, Paul scheduled the great Washington suffrage parade for March 3, 1914, the day before Woodrow Wilson would take the oath of office. In addition to serving notice on Wilson that the suffragists would have to be reckoned with, the timing of the parade was also selected to insure the maximum audience and maximum press coverage.

The parade was a monument to Paul's organizational abilities. Eight thousand marchers, twenty-six floats, ten bands, six chariots, and five units of cavalry for crowd control participated in the parade. The eight thousand marchers included representatives from every occupation and profession in which women were engaged, every local, state, and national suffrage organization, most of the voluntary and women's club associations, and several prosuffrage congressmen and senators.

Congress, on March 1, had passed a special resolution instructing the Washington Superintendent of Police to "prevent any interference with the suffrage marchers." The superintendent, who did not approve of the parade, insisted that the matter should be handled by the War Department, and the War Department denied responsibility. Paul contacted Secretary of War Henry L. Stimson through his sister-in-law, suffragist Elizabeth Rogers, and Stimson agreed to position the Fifteenth Cavalry on the city's western perimeter, in the event they might be needed. It proved to be a prescient move on Paul's part.

An estimated half-million people lined Pennsylvania Avenue for the suffrage parade. Very quickly, the crowd became uncontrollable, as disinterested police failed to stop the ill-behaved. Within a half-hour, crowds had spilled out into the line of marchers until it was virtually impossible to distinguish marchers from spectators. A near riot broke out, with sporadic acts of violence against the suffragists. When Genevieve Stone, the wife of Congressman Claudius Stone, appealed to the police for help, a nearby officer responded by saying, "if my wife were where you are, I'd break her head." A contingent of Boy Scouts from Philadelphia did try to assist the beleaguered suffragists, but order was not restored until the Fifteenth Cavalry arrived. In all, 175 calls for ambulances were made, and over 200 people, mostly suffragists, were treated at local hospitals. Fortunately, no one was seriously injured.

The parade accomplished its goals. When Wilson arrived at Union Station as the parade was underway, he was somewhat surprised that no welcoming crowd had gathered for his arrival. Indeed, from where his party stood, the streets of Washington looked deserted. When one of his people asked where everyone was, he was told, "over on the Avenue, watching the suffrage parade." It was, as Paul had hoped, the first issue confronting Wilson on his arrival in Washington. Within days of the parade, a delegation of suffragists was able to secure their first meeting with the new president. Secondly, the publicity that was generated as a result of the riot led to an outpouring of public sympathy for the suffragists and, by extension, for their cause. Contributions to the suffrage movement increased markedly, including a $1,000 donation from the editor of the *Washington Post*. A special Senate investigation was held to determine why the riot had occurred and the Superintendent of Police was fired. Finally, the suffrage parade was the first shot fired in the final suffrage battle that would culminate in 1919 with passage of the Nineteenth Amendment. It was also recognition that a new generation of suffragists, much more willing to take direct aggressive action to secure a federal amendment, had arrived.

1912: The U.S. Children's Bureau Is Established

(Social Reform, Family Life)

Responding to pressure from progressive social reformers, the federal government created the U.S. Children's Bureau in 1912, with a broad mandate to investigate conditions surrounding "infant mortality, birth rate, orphanage, juvenile courts, desertion, dangerous occupations, accidents, and diseases" affecting children's lives and welfare.

For years, social reformers had advocated restrictions on child labor, as well as enactment of legislation that would provide a more secure environment for all children. Florence Kelley, the head of the National Consumer's League, had long been an advocate on behalf of children, objecting strenuously to their exploitation as child laborers. Kelley was one of those who has lobbied for creation of a children's agency and for a federal child labor amendment, often pointing out the irony that while congress was willing to provide protection for every other species of fish and game, it refused to provide protection for children and their mothers. In 1912, President William Howard Taft signed legislation creating a new federal agency, the U.S. Children's Bureau.

Taft appointed the well-known sociologist Julia Lathrop to become the first head of the bureau.

Julia Lathrop, a graduate of Vassar College in 1880, had been a member of Jane Addams' inner circle at Hull House for more than twenty years when Taft selected her to become the first presidential appointee to head a federal agency. In Chicago, Lathrop had taken particular interest in the mentally ill, and like Dorothea Dix, undertook an exhaustive study of conditions in Illinois. Governor John Peter Altgeld appointed her to the Illinois Board of Charities. In a treatise based on her research, entitled *Suggestions for Visitors to County Poorhouses and Other Public Charitable Institutions* (1905), Lathrop vigorously denounced the practice of housing the young and the old, the sick and the insane, in the same facilities. Along with colleagues including Grace Abbott, Lathrop was one of those who established the country's first graduate school in social work at the University of Chicago in 1903.

Lathrop's friendship with Florence Kelley ignited her own interest in children's welfare, and her desire to promote restrictions that would eliminate child labor. Under Lathrop's direction, a primary focus of the Children's Bureau was the crusade against child labor. But the Children's Bureau pursued a broad range of interests. With a staff of fifteen and a budget of $25,000, Lathrop investigated infant mortality in selected cities across the country. The investigations led to appeals for uniform birth registration procedures previously lacking, and to the initiation of bureau-sponsored maternal education programs that offered instruction and advice in prenatal care, infant feeding and care, and medical consultation for women who had little or no access to such care.

When Taft was succeeded as president by Woodrow Wilson, the new president reappointed Lathrop, enabling her to continue the work already begun at the bureau. Additional studies on maternal mortality, the effects of nutrition on child develop-

ment, juvenile delinquency and juvenile courts, illegitimacy, child labor, and mother's pensions were all published, providing a wealth of information for reformers, agencies, and citizens alike. In 1916, the first National Baby Week was held, with the goal of getting information into the hands of parents. In that same year, congress passed the first child labor law, the Keating-Owen Child Labor Act, which forbade interstate shipment of goods produced by child labor. Enforcement of the new law fell to the Children's Bureau. Lathrop immediately established the Child Labor Division and sought out another Hull House colleague, Grace Abbott, to head the new division. Although the Supreme Court struck down the Owens-Keating Child Labor Law in 1918 (*Hammer v. Dagenhart*), Abbott remained at the Children's Bureau as Lathrop's assistant. In May 1919, Lathrop and the Children's Bureau held a national conference on child welfare standards in conjunction with the "Children's Year" activities. Two years later, the enormous amount of research conducted by Lathrop and others, as well as their active campaign on behalf of federal aid to states for maternal and infant care, led to passage of the Sheppard-Towner Act.

When Lathrop resigned as head of

the Children's Bureau in 1921, she was succeeded by her assistant, Grace Abbott. Abbott continued the programs set in place by Lathrop with the result that much of the groundwork had already been laid for the Roosevelt administration to enable them to enact a variety of health and welfare programs under the New Deal, including the Social Security Act. During World War II, the Emergency Maternity and Infant Care Program insured departing servicemen that their pregnant wives and newborn children would be provided with the best medical care available.

The Children's Bureau continued to initiate programs promoting the health and welfare of its constituents, including programs that focused on qualitative issues such as rehabilitation from crippling diseases including polio, and to make its expertise available both domestically and internationally. In the 1980s, under the Reagan administration, most of the funding for bureau programs was discontinued.

1913: Elizabeth Gurley Flynn Organizes the Paterson Strike

(Work)

Sparked by an attempt by mill owners to increase the workload of silk weavers and dyers, workers in Paterson, New Jersey, struck in a massive labor action that drew the attention and support of leading socialists and radical intellectuals.

A lmost twenty-five thousand workers labored in the mills of Paterson, New Jersey, most of them young immigrant women from southern and eastern Europe. For their labors, they received between six and seven dollars a week. Already on the edge of destitution, they reached their limit when the mill owners proposed to increase their work without increasing their pay. Led by Industrial Workers of the World (IWW) organizers Bill Hayward and Elizabeth Gurley Flynn, and the syndicalist Carlo Treesca they went on strike in February 1913, convinced that it would be "far better to die fighting than die working." (Bailyn, p. 685)

As the weeks stretched into months, the Paterson strike became a *cause célèbre* for radical intellectuals. The town was just a short ride from their haunts in Greenwich Village, so many made the excursion to see the struggle between labor and capital in person.

John Reed, in particular, was moved by what he saw, and he inspired his compatriots to join him in a massive production to support the strikers. What Reed hoped to do was create a symbiosis between the practical radicalism of the workers and the theoretical radicalism of the intellectuals and artists. To do so, he wrote and organized a play that would employ the strikers themselves to enact the events of the strike, perhaps the first example of "guerrilla theatre."

On the appointed day in June 1913, one thousand workers crossed the Hudson from Paterson and marched up Broadway to Madison Square Garden. There, before an audience of fifteen thousand, they put on the show, dramatizing all the bitterness of the walkout, the picketing, the harassment by the police, and a violent clash with scabs in which one striker was killed. The audience, many of whom were workers admitted for a quarter, joined in booing the police, chanting strike slogans, and singing the "International." It seemed for a moment that this artistic experience had finally bridged the gulf between workers and intellectuals.

Unfortunately, the production, which was to have refilled the strike fund, netted only $150. Since, as Elizabeth Gurley Flynn observed, "bread was the need of the hour, and bread was not forthcoming," the strike failed. The skilled workers broke ranks first, and the unskilled workers soon followed, without having won a single concession from the owners. By the end of the summer, the women and girls of Paterson were back at work in the mills, with no better prospects for their future than they had had when the strike began.

1915: The Woman's Peace Party Is Founded

(Social Reform, Peace)

In 1915, in response to the war in Europe, which had begun the previous year, several notable American women, including Jane Addams, Charlotte Perkins Gilman, Alice Hamilton, Florence Kelley, Edith Green Balch, and Carrie Chapman Catt, founded the Woman's Peace party (WPP).

With greater and greater influence placed upon international peace as a goal of the women's movement in the early twentieth century, nearly every significant women's organization had a "peace department." The issue attracted the most notable women reformers. Jane Addams and Alice Hamilton from Hull House; Charlotte Perkins Gilman, author of *Women and Economics;* Florence Kelley of the National Consumer's League; and Crystal Eastman, a radical young lawyer who authored New York state's first worker's compensation law, were among the founders of the party. In January 1915, eighty-six delegates representing nearly every major women's organization in the country convened for the first WPP meeting. The delegates wrote a pacifist platform that represented, as they said, "the mother half of humanity." From its inception, the slogan of the WPP was "Listen to the Women for a Change."

The WPP was the first major, all-female U.S. peace organization. Its members, most of whom could not yet vote, advocated woman suffrage and an equal right to participate in government. The war in Europe seemed to these women, to underline the failure of government policies enacted by male leaders only. A number of women, led by Jane Addams, went to the International Woman Suffrage Association conference at The Hague, in April 1915, meeting with women leaders from other nations. Delegates to the conference included those from nearly all the belligerent countries. A peace committee then began a round of travels to the capitals of Europe, where they met with various governments, pleading with them to enter into negotiations to bring the hostilities to an end. Addams also called upon President Woodrow Wilson to mediate an end to the war.

Once the United States entered the war, the WPP nearly faltered. Suffragists, such as Carrie Chapman Catt, did not want to jeopardize suffrage in order to openly oppose government policy. Others, like Jane Addams, remained adamantly pacifist despite the fact that her reputation suffered greatly for it. In an atmosphere of "100 percent Americanism," initiated to solidify support for the war, neither the government nor the public was willing to suffer quietly those whom they considered traitors. In the end, most WPP members followed their consciences in deciding whether or not to oppose the war, but formally the organization worked to bring an end to the "war to end all wars" without criticizing government policy.

When the war finally did end, the American WPP joined with its European counterparts to form the Women's International League for Peace and Freedom (WILPF), the name that it still retains. Over the decades of its existence, the WILPF has been involved in an unremitting campaign to bring about peace and justice. The WILPF has been influential in a variety of peace campaigns, including securing a nuclear test ban (1963), a protest against U.S. involvement in the Vietnam War (1964), the Nuclear Weapons Freeze Campaign (1979), the Conference on Racism (1979), the Stop the Arms Race Campaign (1980), the March for Jobs, Peace, and Freedom (1983), the Listen to Women for a Change campaign (1983), the Campaign for a Comprehensive Test Ban (1984), the International Cruise Missile Alert (1985), and the Campaign to Stop "Star Wars" (1987). As a tribute to its most illustrious founder, the educational affiliate of the WILPF is the Jane Addams Peace Association.

1916: Jeannette Rankin Becomes the First Woman Elected to the U.S. Congress

(Equal Rights, Politics)

Jeannette Rankin, a suffragist and life-long pacifist, ran for a congressional seat in her home state of Montana two years after women in that state were enfranchised. In November 1916, Rankin was the first woman elected to the U.S. House of Representatives.

Jeannette Pickering Rankin served two terms in the Congress of the United States. On each occasion, she had to choose whether to stand on principle in support of her long-held conviction that pacifism was the only road to true peace, or to make a popular choice and vote with the majority. In each instant, Rankin stood on principle.

Rankin began working on behalf of woman suffrage in her home state of Montana in 1910. From 1910 to 1914, she worked full time for the suffrage movement. In 1914, the year Montana enfranchised women, she was elected legislative secretary for the National American Woman Suffrage Association (NAWSA).

As a candidate to fill one of Montana's two at-large congressional seats,

Rankin ran as a progressive Republican. The women of Montana owed a great deal to Rankin for her efforts in securing the vote, and she was well-known and respected throughout the state. When she announced her candidacy, therefore, she had the support of women from both political parties. Even so, the campaign required her to travel hundreds of miles to remote towns in Montana, persuading women to vote not only for the first time, but for a woman as well.

Much of Rankin's first term in congress was spent on legislation affecting women's lives. She was a member of the committee charged with writing a constitutional amendment that would give women the vote. Rankin was more than diligent in her work for health reform legislation for women

WHAT EVERY AMERICAN SHOULD KNOW

aimed at lowering the infant mortality rate. The Sheppard-Towner Act, passed in 1921, appropriated matching funds for states that wished to participate in building clinics that would provide for prenatal and infant care.

But within days of being sworn in as a congresswoman in 1917, Rankin was faced with a conscience vote. President Woodrow Wilson, in the face of renewed submarine warfare by Germany against nonmilitary ships, asked congress to declare war. Part of Rankin's campaign pledge had been to keep America out of war. Wilson himself had campaigned on the promise of keeping the nation out of war, but as events in Europe went from bad to worse, Wilson's opinions changed, as did popular opinion. Rankin had to choose to stand on principle as a pacifist or to support the president. In the hours before the vote, several suffrage delegations appealed to her to support Wilson for fear that she would harm the suffrage cause with a negative vote. Carrie Chapman Catt, the president of NAWSA, put as much pressure on Rankin as she could, arguing that since the president had more than enough votes to carry the declaration of war, her vote would not help her cause. Catt warned her that it could only hurt the suffrage cause and it would cause Rankin to lose her con-

gressional seat in the next election. Only Alice Paul, founder of the National Woman's party, advised Rankin to vote her conscience, regardless of the consequences. When the vote was finally taken, Jeannette Rankin was one of fifty members of congress who voted against a declaration of war. As Catt had predicted, Rankin lost her congressional seat as well as a bid for a senate seat.

For nearly twenty years thereafter, Rankin stayed out of the political limelight. As World War II approached, though, she ran for congress once again. Running on a pacifist platform, Rankin garnered the benefit of the isolationist feelings that still ran high in the Great Plains states in 1940, and once again was elected. Once again, very soon after taking her seat, she was confronted with a vote of conscience. On December 8, 1941, President Franklin Roosevelt asked congress to declare war in the wake of Japan's sneak attack on Pearl Harbor a day earlier. The attack on Pearl Harbor had immediately wiped away any isolationist thoughts as far as most Americans were concerned. Rankin, however, as despicable as she thought the attack had been, could not renounce her pacifism. She was the lone opponent of Roosevelt's request for a declaration of war.

1916: Georgia O'Keeffe's Works Are Exhibited by Alfred Stieglitz

(Cultural Life)

In 1916, photographer and modern art sponsor Alfred Stieglitz showed several paintings by Georgia O'Keeffe in a three-artist exhibit at his avant-garde "291" gallery in New York.

Although she seemed out of step with contemporary art for most of her life and career, artist Georgia O'Keeffe became one of America's most famous female artists with a distinctive style that celebrated a particular aspect of the American landscape. Determined from an early age to chart her own course as an artist, regardless of how her work was viewed by others, O'Keeffe was known for her starkly beautiful southwestern landscapes that often featured skulls, horns, and pelvises. "When I was still a little girl," she once said, "I used to think that since I couldn't do what I wanted to…at least I could paint as I wanted to and say what I wanted to when I painted."

O'Keeffe was born in Wisconsin in 1887 and studied art at the Art Institute of Chicago and the Art Students' League in New York. Her early work featured New York skylines, but her most popular works from the early period were her flower pictures, dominated by huge red poppies or sometimes just a fragment of a flower. In all of her work, O'Keeffe defied accepted notions of perspective, with sometimes a single petal dominating an entire canvas. Her intent was to magnify the commonplace that was often overlooked. Until 1916, O'Keeffe supplemented her art work by teaching and working in advertising. But that year, the photographer Alfred Stieglitz took notice of her work and arranged to have her paintings included in a three-artist show at his New York studio. It launched O'Keeffe's career as an artist. At the same time, it was the beginning of a thirty-year relationship with Stieglitz that ended with his death in 1946. Stieglitz and O'Keeffe, nearly three decades apart in age, married in 1924. At best, their marriage would be described today as an open marriage. Both O'Keeffe and Stieglitz engaged in numerous affairs, he usually with younger women and she often with other women. But at the heart of their relationship was something that defied even unconventional behavior, for throughout their marriage, while O'Keeffe painted, Stieglitz photographer her. A collection of over 500 photographs depicts what one critic has called "the greatest love poem in the history of photography."

O'Keeffe's love affair with the southwest began in 1929 when she visited New Mexico. Thereafter, she would return periodically until 1946, when she moved there. After 1946, her work was dominated by a distinctly southwestern influence. Her most memorable paintings featured bleached-white animal bones dominating a vividly stark landscape against a brilliantly-hued sky. Between 1946 and 1971, O'Keeffe exhibited her paintings at some of the nation's outstanding galleries and museums. In 1969, she was elected to the American Academy of Arts and Letters, and in 1977, President Jimmy Carter presented her with the Medal of Freedom in honor of her contributions to American art. Although she continued to paint well into her nineties, O'Keeffe became more and more reclusive after Stieglitz's death. She died at her secluded home, called Ghost Ranch, in New Mexico in 1986.

1916: The "Birth Control Sisters" Are Arrested for Opening a Clinic in Brooklyn

(Family Life)

In October 1916, Margaret Sanger and her sister, Ethel Byrne, opened a birth control clinic in the Brownsville section of Brooklyn, New York. After just ten days, authorities closed down the clinic and arrested Sanger and her sister for violating the Comstock Law.

When Margaret Sanger and her sister, Ethel Byrne, opened the first birth control clinic in Brownsville in 1916, they anticipated being closed down by the police and being tried, and possibly imprisoned, for violating the decades-old Comstock Law. What they did not know was how many women might take advantage of the limited window of opportunity they were offering, to get advice on birth control and contraceptives. The response was overwhelming. In the ten days that the clinic remained open, nearly five hundred women came in looking for information. That turnout, as much as anything else, convinced Sanger that she was correct in her long-held conviction that women wanted to be able to control their own reproductive capabilities.

Sanger's experiences growing up in an Irish-Catholic family in New York were the motivating forces behind her lifelong crusade for birth control. Her mother had eleven children and several miscarriages, and the toll on her health led to an early death at the age of forty-nine. Her older sisters were expected to, and did, sacrifice their own dreams in order to step in and provide the physical and financial support to keep the family going. Sanger escaped the same fate by accepting her sisters' offer to pay for col-lege teacher training. Quickly discovering that teaching was not her desire, Sanger enrolled in nursing school. While there, she met and married William Sanger, an architect and artist. Although she knew that she did not want to emulate her mother's life, Sanger was not yet at the point where she could break away from a lifetime of learned middle-class values. She moved to Westchester with her husband and had three children. A fire that destroyed their newly built home caused Sanger to recognize the precariousness of a life built on acquiring things. Her urgent need to be involved in activities that would make a difference was so great that Sanger's husband agreed to move to New York with her to save their marriage.

The marriage did not survive in the end, but Sanger had at least saved herself.

From 1910 to 1914, she threw herself into a series of radical causes, working with people like the labor leaders Elizabeth Gurley Flynn and "Big Bill" Hayward. She also discovered her own capacity for sexual expression, mainly outside of the bonds of marriage. This discovery provided Sanger with a profound sense of personal power and convinced her that women needed above all to achieve sexual liberation, because that alone would release repressed or misdirected energy. At the same time, Sanger worked as a visiting nurse on New York's Lower East Side. Confronted with case after case of abortions gone awry because there was no adequate information or help available, Sanger found her life's work.

Sanger had already run afoul of the Comstock Law in 1912, when she had written an article on syphilis for *The Call*, and the post office ruled that it could not be mailed because the article was obscene. Sanger was determined to remove the stigma of "obscenity" that zealots had attached to birth control and contraceptives. She began publishing a distinctly feminist newspaper, *The Woman Rebel*, that the post office also refused to mail, even though the paper contained no explicit advice on birth control. Indicted for violating the Comstock Law, Sanger left for Europe in 1914. While there she investigated various methods of birth control and contraception. Several months into her European sojourn in 1915, Sanger learned that her five-year-old daughter had died of pneumonia. Her sense of guilt was profound and she returned to the United States. Public sympathy for her was such that the authorities decided to drop the pending charges against her.

Undaunted and ever more determined to pursue her crusade, in part to commemorate her daughter, Sanger and her sister opened the first birth control clinic in America, in Brownsville, Brooklyn. She was arrested for once again violating the Comstock Law and convicted. Her conviction was not without victory, however. Judge Frederick Crane, while upholding the Comstock Law, acknowledged that it was just because doctors could prescribe condoms to prevent venereal diseases and he broadened the interpretation to include the right of doctors to prescribe contraceptives to women to prevent disease as well.

After that, Sanger changed her strategy, seeking to elicit the support of the medical profession. The new strategy meant having to leave behind her radical feminist beliefs and associates. But in moving toward a middle-class constituency, Sanger was able to garner badly needed financial support from socialites and philanthropists. This infusion of money allowed her to establish the American Birth Control League, the forerunner to Planned Parenthood. Her new support network allowed Sanger to keep open the Birth Control Clinical Research Bureau in New York, the first doctor-staffed birth control clinic in the United States. The clinic kept fastidious records demonstrating the safety of contraceptives and refuting the contention of some medical experts that certain contraceptives caused diseases such as cancer. By 1938, after the obscenity definitions in the Comstock Law were altered by federal courts, Sanger and her associates succeeded in opening a network of three hundred birth control clinics nationwide. It was a phenomenal achievement. Sanger retired with her then-husband Noah Slee shortly thereafter. Her suc-

cessors, in an effort to gain even more middle-class support, gradually phased out the term "birth control" in favor of "family planning," and in 1942, the Birth Control League officially became the Planned Parenthood Association.

Margaret Sanger did more than almost any other American to open the way for women to determine their own destiny by having the option of choosing how many children they would bear and when.

1917: The American Women's Hospitals Service Helps Female Physicians Serve in World War I

(Equal Rights)

At the second annual meeting of the American Medical Women's Association (AMWA) in June 1917, the American Women's Hospitals Service (AWHS) committee was established. Since women physicians were prohibited from serving in the military, the AWHS sponsored an all-female medical force that provided professional services during World War I.

Despite their desire to contribute their professional services during World War I, women physicians were prohibited from serving in the U.S.

military. Shortly after the United States entered the war in April 1917, the American Medical Women's Association held its second annual conven-

---

tion, from June 5–7, 1917. The focus of discussion for women who wanted to contribute to the war effort, or who simply wanted to donate their professional services in an emergency, was how best to circumvent the current government policy that precluded women physicians from military service. The doctors voted to establish a committee of the AMWA, the American Women's Hospitals Service, whose mandate would be to organize an all-female force of doctors, nurses, and ambulance drivers who to set up and service dispensaries in outlying areas along the French war zone to serve the civilian population.

The AWHS barely had time to organize and establish a few dispensaries when the war ended in November 1918. It quickly changed its mission to help in the reconstruction of Europe following the war, maintaining the dispensaries and providing needed medical care for the civilian population throughout the continent. It expanded its scope of operation, and in 1923, at the height of its overseas service, the AWHS provided medical care to more than twelve thousand Turkish refugees in a clinic set up on the Greek island of Macronissi.

Under the direction of Dr. Esther Pohl Lovejoy, who served as AWHS chairwoman for nearly fifty years, the committee in 1931 turned its attention back to the United States. It provided crucially needed medical care for the Appalachian area of the United States. Prior to the establishment of AWHS clinics throughout Appalachia, that region of the country had been woefully neglected by medical practitioners. In the 1930s, for the first time, Appalachian families could depend on at least some access to medical care on a regular basis, although the level of care that the women physicians could provide remained rudimentary for many years. Nevertheless, it represented major progress for Appalachia.

Despite the years of service, both overseas during wartime and at home, provided under the auspices of the AWHS, when World War II broke out the same military restrictions were imposed. Women doctors were not allowed in the regular military services until 1943, and when the war ended, the restrictions were once again imposed. It took another decade before women physicians were allowed to join the military with commissions and full rank.

1917: Isadora Duncan Appears at the Metropolitan Opera House in New York

(Cultural Life)

In 1917, after returning from South America, modern dance genius Isadora Duncan began her only successful American tour with a series of performances at New York's Metropolitan Opera House.

Isadora Duncan, whose innovative dance style featured fluidity and a reliance on instinctive body movement as an expression of creativity, spent most of her life in Europe, where her avant garde renditions were far more appreciated than they were in America in her lifetime. Duncan, a San Francisco native born in 1877, routinely rejected systems, structure, and pedantic rituals in favor of a highly individualistic dance style that met with substantial resistance from the traditional dance community. With very little formal training in dance, but with enormous encouragement from her unconventional mother, Duncan cast aside the restraints of ballet technique and costuming, originating her own free style based on natural movement. Profoundly influenced by na-

ture, Duncan tried to capture the emotional intensity that she found there. An ardent student of Greek civilization, she performed barefoot and in flowing tunics that accentuated the spirit of freedom that she strove to capture in her performances.

Her career as a dancer began in Chicago and New York, and although a 1902 dance debut earned her some praise for artistic merit, Duncan left the following year to tour Europe with Loie Fuller's company. Finding Europeans much more receptive to her creative efforts, Duncan opened her first dance school in Germany. For the next several years, she crisscrossed the European continent performing and building a reputation as both an innovative dancer and an eccentric personality. Scandalous love affairs with stage designer Gordon Craig and Singer sewing machine heir Paris Singer produced two children, both of whom died in a tragic drowning accident in 1913. When World War I erupted, Duncan returned to the United States, but efforts to establish a dance school in New York failed.

In 1916, Duncan undertook a tour of South America, again meeting with success, and the following year she reached the pinnacle of her American success, appearing at the Metropolitan Opera House in New York and in San Francisco with warm receptions in both places. After the war, she returned to Europe, operated dance schools in Paris and Athens, and married a young Russian poet, her only marriage, in 1922. Tragedy continued to follow her, however; three years after their marriage, her husband committed suicide. In 1927, after a rave performance in Paris, Duncan was killed in a freak accident when her long, flowing scarf caught in the wheels of the convertible she was driving and instantly broke her neck.

For Duncan, the purpose of creating dance was to convey the deepest concerns of humanity. Her natural sympathy for those who tried to step outside the bounds of tradition and established order was often reflected in her dances, in which she used the social and political themes of the times. One of her most successful dances was *La Marseillaise*, performed in 1915; in 1917, she performed a dance entitled *Marche Slave*, which portrayed the Russian peasant's struggle for independence. Throughout her career, Duncan sought to discover the basic dance, a dance rooted in biology and spiritualism, that she was convinced would convey both nature and the human spirit. Her contributions to the evolution of modern dance have reverberated through both time and place, helping to establish the genre of interpretive dance and breaking down all constraints inhibiting creativity and expression in modern dance.

1919: The League of Women Voters Is Founded

(Equal Rights, Social Reform)

At the final meeting of the National American Woman Suffrage Association on March 24, 1919, with the federal suffrage amendment virtually guaranteed, Carrie Chapman Catt proposed a new organization, imploring the delegates, "Let us then raise up a league of women voters…a league that shall be nonpartisan and nonsectarian in nature." Picking up on Catt's rhetoric, delegates voted to call the new organization the League of Women Voters (LWV).

The League of Women Voters evolved directly from the National American Woman Suffrage Association. When Carrie Chapman Catt addressed the NAWSA delegates at its final meeting in March 1919, she was able to persuade many delegates to reconvene as the LWV. Initially, however, about 90 percent of NAWSA's membership felt that the LWV was not necessary and would serve little purpose, now that the Nineteenth Amendment was nearly in place. Catt was elected president-for-life of the LWV, an honor bestowed upon her by the grateful NAWSA members who believed that she was largely responsible for securing woman suffrage. But the actual first-term president was Maud Wood Park, a long-time member of NAWSA's leadership.

Catt outlined three goals for the LWV. First, they had to guarantee that all women would be enfranchised by continuing to press for ratification of the Nineteenth Amendment. Second, the LWV had to take the lead in eliminating any remaining legal discrimination against women. Finally, the LWV had to be involved in making sure that democracy was secure enough to take the lead in providing for a secure world.

During the conservative 1920s, the LWV lobbied for a variety of legislation focusing on protection for women and children and on good government. In all, the LWV lobbied for thirty-eight separate pieces of legislation, but saw success on only two issues In 1922, congress passed the Cable Citizenship Act. Prior to passage of the Cable Act, American women who married noncitizens could conceivably lose their own citizenship if their husbands were deported. The Cable Act guaranteed independent citizenship for married women. In 1924, the Sheppard-Towner Act was passed, which provided medical care to women and children.

As the 1920s evolved, the LWV moved from a feminist agenda to a club movement with a civic goals agenda, partially because the women's movement itself was split over the issue of equal rights and civic goals seemed more attainable. The LWV supported voter registration drives almost from the start in an effort to convince potential voters of their responsibility to democracy. The slogan they adopted in 1928 remained in vogue for many years thereafter: "Democracy is a Bandwagon and There Are Too Many Empty Seats." The LWV also lobbied on behalf of women jurors. From the earliest days of nation-

hood, women were denied juries of their peers because women could not serve on juries. The LWV succeeded in several states in securing the right of women to serve on juries. But as late as 1961, three Southern states still refused to allow women to serve on juries, and the Supreme Court upheld their right to impose restrictions.

The LWV continues to sponsor and publish research designed to educate the electorate, including its national publication *The National Voter*. In recent years, the LWV has maintained a high profile in presidential elections by sponsoring the presidential debates that so many Americans have come to rely on. The debates remain the only formal forum for bringing together candidates from the major parties in face-to-face confrontation. In some elections, the debates have significantly influenced the outcome of the election.

1919: The Nineteenth Amendment Is Passed by Congress

(Equal Rights)

On June 4, 1919, the U.S. Senate passed the Nineteenth Amendment, which, after ratification by the states, would give the women of the country the right to vote.

After nearly a century of struggle, Congress passed the Nineteenth Amendment to the U.S. Constitution, giving women the right to vote. The amendment was ratified a year later, allowing women to vote in their first presidential election in 1920. With one exception, the women who had started the long suffrage campaign in 1848 at Seneca Falls, New York, never lived to enjoy the fruits of their labor. Only Charlotte Woodward, who was nineteen when she attended the Seneca Falls Convention, voted in 1920 at the age of ninety-three.

Since 1848, the woman suffrage movement found itself divided over policy, reunited, and divided again in the final crucial years of campaigning. The first split in suffrage ranks occurred immediately after the Civil War in 1868 over the issue of the Fourteenth and Fifteenth Amendments. The radical feminists believed that women had to put their political rights first, ahead of any other issue, or they would fail to achieve their goals. They refused to support the Fourteenth or Fifteenth Amendments because they effectively excluded women from voting rights. The Fourteenth Amendment specifically included a reference to "males" in the text, the first time that such exclusionary wording appeared in the Constitution. The Fifteenth Amendment prohibited denial of voting rights because of "race, color, or previous condition of servitude." Social feminists believed that women had no right to jeopardize voting rights for black Americans, even if the rights applied only to males.

By 1890, suffragists concluded that they had to shelve their differences in order to build a strong organization that would be taken seriously and would be a force to be reckoned with. When the American Woman Suffrage Association and the National Woman Suffrage Association joined forces to become the National American Woman Suffrage Association, suffragists began a long series of state campaigns, the goal of which was to change state constitutions in favor of woman suffrage. Several western states did allow woman suffrage, but progress was slow, painstaking, and costly. In 1914, another split in the suffrage movement occurred when a new generation of radical feminists put their efforts into securing an amendment to the Constitution. Under the leadership of Alice Paul, the radical feminists eventually formed the National Woman's Party. Putting pressure on President Woodrow Wilson and the Democratic Party, the NWP picketed the White House and the Congress, and campaigned against Democrats.

World War I proved to be another critical turning point for suffrage. Woodrow Wilson did not include suffrage on his list of emergency war measures— a list of issues that the administration would deal with exclusively until six months after the war ended. The NAWSA agreed to suspend their activities until the war was over, in much the same way that suffragists had done during the Civil War. Only the NWP refused to place women second, even to a war emergency situation. They continued to picket the White House and embarrass an administration that claimed to be fighting a war for democracy. Further embarrassment occurred when NWP members were arrested and imprisoned for their activities. In 1918, Woodrow Wilson made a dramatic appearance before the Congress, announcing that suffrage would now be considered an emergency war measure and making an impassioned plea for Congress to pass the legislation without which he would not be able to construct an effective world peace. Women— both the radical feminists and the social feminists— had forced the issue and insured, with the president's active support, that the amendment would be passed by Congress. It was, as Alice Paul noted on the day Wilson appealed to Congress, "only a matter of time."

Passage of the Nineteenth Amendment immediately placed women on a much higher political plane. While the playing field was not yet level, women now had a better chance to level it.

1919: The National Federation of Business and Professional Women's Clubs Is Founded

(Equal Rights, Work)

In 1919, Lena Madeson Phillips founded the National Federation of Business and Professional Women's Clubs (BPWC) of the United States of America, to promote opportunities for women in professional and white collar jobs.

When Lena Madeson Phillips founded the National Federation of Business and Professional Women's Clubs, she issued a challenge to her colleagues and peers: "Make no small plans. They have no power to stir the blood." It was a powerful challenge to women at a time when, in most professions and in many white-collar jobs, women were still not welcome. The majority of members in the BPWC worked in white-collar jobs and most of those worked as clerical help. But they were joined by some professional businesswomen as well, and over time more and more businesswomen joined the organization. Unlike the American Association of University Women, the BPWC did not require that its members be college graduates. And unlike many other women's organizations at the time, the BPWC was an early and constant supporter of the equal rights amendment.

Throughout the 1930s and 1940s, one of the issues that the BPWC focused on particularly was the right of married women to remain in the work force. In white-collar jobs, the standard of the day was for women who married to resign their positions. The BPWC maintained that marriage did not hamper a woman's ability to perform her job. During the Roosevelt years, the BPWC found an ally in Eleanor Roosevelt, and frequently used her influence, as well as the influence of other prominent women, to lobby for more appointments for women in high-level government jobs. The BPWC was the first woman's organization to maintain a talent bank of qualified women who were ready and able to accept professional appointments to high-level positions. Moreover, they used the pages of the organization's publication, *Independent Woman*, to lobby and network effectively to promote their status in the workplace.

By the 1970s and 1980s, the BPWC was more focused on developing its influence as a lobbying group on behalf of white-collar women workers. It achieved the distinction of being the largest organization representing white-collar workers, with over 150,000 members and 3,500 local organizations and chapters. Besides developing political skills, the BPWC also committed itself to expanding educational opportunities for women, as well as professional development opportunities. The BPWC established a National Council on the Future of Women in the Workplace, which was chaired by Democratic party leader and women's rights activist Eleanor Holmes Norton. Under Norton's leadership, the council investigated new patterns for women in the workplace, focusing on such issues as pay equity, child care, and technological changes in jobs associated with white-collar women workers. It also sponsors the National Business Women's Week, held the third week in October; promotes education and research affecting women's employment; and sponsors scholarship and loan programs for women.

1920: Paramount Pictures Makes Lois Weber One of the Highest Paid Movie Directors

(Cultural Life, Work)

In 1920, Famous Players–Lasky Productions, which ultimately became Paramount Pictures, signed female director Lois Weber to a multipicture directing deal, agreeing to pay her $50,000 and one-third of the profits per film, making her one of the highest paid directors of the day.

Women involved in the modern day film industry still have difficulty gaining acceptance as directors, a position that has traditionally been reserved for men. Even women who direct successful films—economically and/or critically—are held to a different standard and are frequently judged by the Hollywood community using criteria not imposed upon male directors. A case in point is Barbra Streisand, whose two directorial efforts have both been well-received by critics and filmgoers alike. *Yentl* and *The Prince of Tides*, both money-makers, the yardstick generally applied when the decisionmakers are determining the fate of a director, and both earning high marks from critics, did little to change Hollywood's opinion of Streisand as an unprofessional interloper in the field of directing. Other women directors of successful films (for example, Joan Micklin Silver, the director of *Hester Street*), have often faced the same impediments to securing funding for new projects, regardless of their track records. It is sometimes surprising, therefore, to learn that successful women directors are not new to Hollywood.

Lois Weber began directing movies as early as 1912, and was a much sought after director. As a principle of Rex Pictures, Weber helped to build up the production company to the point where Universal Studios released Rex Pictures nationally. The films she directed proved to be extremely popular because she tackled themes and subjects no one else would. Her film *Where Are My Children?* (1916) was a movie about birth control, then a subject that very few people were willing to even talk about. In 1920, Jesse Lasky, of Famous Players–Lasky Studios, signed Weber to direct films for them, agreeing to pay her $50,000 and one-third of the film's profits for each film. The deal made Weber one of the industry's highest paid directors and affirmed her status and reputation as a first-rate director.

At the same time that Weber was making her best films, another woman, Dorothy Arzner, was also beginning to establish herself as a director. Arzner quit her premed studies at the University of California to go into the movie business. Starting off as a typist, she worked her way up to script girl, scenario writer, and then director. Her first film, *Fashions for Women* (1927), was a great success, but it immediately pegged her as a director who did "women's movies," a category that Arzner was entirely happy with. In her view, since women made up the majority of filmgoers, directors who could make films that the audience would appreciate ought to be in demand. During her career, Arzner worked with some of the best actresses to come out of Hollywood, including Clara Bow, Rosalind Russell, and Katharine Hepburn. *Christopher Strong*, directed by Arzner in 1933, was Hepburn's second movie. The strongly feminist story of a woman pilot who has an affair with a married man that brings her face-to-face with society's double standard is still considered a minor classic. Arzner's career spanned nearly thirty years, and she lived long enough to see her films honored by the Director's Guild, as well as several film festivals.

The third notable woman director of pre-1960s Hollywood was Ida Lupino. Lupino, a film actress from England, was under contract first to Paramount, from 1933, and then to Warner Brothers, until 1947. As an actress, she was considered one of the best by the critics and was extremely popular with the public. But acting alone did not satisfy Lupino. In 1949, she formed her own independent production company, The Filmmakers, and over the course of the next five years, wrote, acted, produced, and directed several films including *Hard, Fast, and Beautiful, The Bigamist,* and *The Hitchhiker.* Although she always professed not to be a feminist, perhaps because that was so anathema to so many in Hollywood, Lupino's films generally contained a powerful critique of home-versus-career confrontations. Lupino did not limit her directing skills to the movies. She was one of the first big directors to make the transition to television in 1959. Lupino directed episodes of "The Twilight Zone," "Alfred Hitchcock Presents," and "Thriller," and she continued to act as well. In the 1960s, she and her husband, Howard Duff, starred in a comic series about a husband-wife private detective team that aired for several seasons.

Weber, Arzner, and Lupino all represented women who were able to tap into the emotional wellspring of contemporary society to direct films dealing with important questions that faced then, and still face, American women. Among the three of them, they directed well over one hundred films.

1920: Edith Wharton Wins a Pulitzer Prize for *The Age of Innocence*

(Cultural Life)

Expatriate writer Edith Wharton was awarded the Pulitzer Prize for literature in 1920. Her book *The Age of Innocence*, a brilliant novel mourning the passing of an era while at the same time delineating its excesses and foibles, forever established Wharton's credentials as a writer.

E dith Wharton wrote about what she knew best—upper-class society in an age of innocence, the late nineteenth century. As the daughter of a wealthy New York society family, Wharton, who was born in 1862, grew up surrounded by comfortable gentility and an abundance of culture and manners. For several years before her tenth birthday, the family lived in Europe as a consequence of economic losses suffered during the Civil War. Her father taught her to read and to love books. In each of the countries in which they lived, he also supplied the youngster with a tutor, who taught Edith the native language. Thus, by the time she reached her teenage years, Wharton had developed an intellectual agility not generally acknowledged in a world dominated by a focus on social accomplishments. Although she had written a slim volume of poetry at the age of sixteen, which she had privately published, Wharton did not give serious thought to becoming a writer until three years into her marriage, an unsuccessful one, to a retired Boston banker thirteen years her senior. For several years, the childless couple lived a fairly idle existence making the social rounds between New York, Boston, Newport, and Europe. For Wharton, the "moral solitude" of those years led to bouts of depression, finally alleviated when she began writing seriously.

Wharton wrote several short stories, some of which were published in *Scribner's, Harper's,* and the *Century.* Her first book, a collaboration with an architect friend, entitled *The Decoration of Houses* (1897), was a protest against the excessive and usually bad taste exhibited by many in her social set, and an appeal to return to a cleaner style and classic values. Wharton did not publish her first novel, *The Valley of Decision* (1902), until she was forty, but after that she wrote almost one book a year for the remainder of her life. Her first acclaimed novel, *The House of Mirth* (1905), revealed Wharton as a keen observer of the manners and morals of late-nineteenth-century society. Most of the novels that followed dealt with the same issues of class, taste, and the corruption of values with which Wharton was so intimate. A marked deviation was the publication, in 1911, of *Ethan Frome,* a story set in rural poverty that focuses on a doomed triangle. An instant classic, *Ethan Frome* was for decades required reading in high school literature classes. Her signature novel, *The Age of Innocence,* won the Pulitzer Prize for Wharton and a place in American belles lettres. Returning once again to the world of late-nineteenth-century society, Wharton's attention to the descriptive details of an era ended forever by the guns of World War I, won for her the accolade from Edmund Wilson that she was not only a pioneer "but the poet of interior decoration."

Wharton spent most of her remaining years in Europe, following her husband's hospitalization and death. Although she was elected to the National Institute of Arts and Letters in 1930, and the American Academy of Arts and Letters in 1934, her writing after *The Age of Innocence* never again approached the brilliance of her most critically productive period. But her contributions to literature and especially her observations of the pressures placed on women by society, even in the wealthiest milieus, by then had already placed Wharton in the company of America's best writers. While Wharton was the first American woman to win a Pulitzer Prize for literature, she would not be the last. With the ground broken, the Pulitzer Committee honored poet Edna St. Vincent Millay three years later in 1923. Other American women who have won Pulitzer Prizes for literature include Pearl Buck, Toni Morrison, and Alison Lurie.

1921: Congress Passes the Sheppard-Towner Act

(Social Reform, Health Care)

In the wake of passage of the Nineteenth Amendment, and fearful that women would use their new voting rights to retaliate against congressmen unresponsive to women's issues, Congress passed the Sheppard-Towner Act, which provided funding to help reduce maternal and infant mortality.

When the Nineteenth Amendment was ratified there was an expectation on the part of many politicians that women were going to use their combined vote to vote against elected officials who failed to support legislation favorable to women. As a consequence, the Congress was quick to demonstrate its willingness to listen to their new female constituents and to vote for measures that women supported. The most impressive piece of legislation passed by Congress in this context was the Sheppard-Towner

Act, intended to reduce the rate of childbirth-related mortality and infant mortality. It was the first federally funded health care act ever passed by Congress. Under the terms of the act, Congress appropriated $1.25 million to establish prenatal clinics and public health centers in any community for which the state was willing to provide matching funds.

The legislation had a great deal of support among various women's groups. Mary Anderson and Julia Lathrop of the Children's Bureau pointed out that infant mortality in the United States had reached 250,000. Florence Kelley of the Consumer's League also fought hard for passage of the bill, which she considered a culmination of forty years of work on behalf of women. Several national women's magazines ran timely articles on the subject as well. In the event that any congressmen did not understand the ramifications of opposing the Sheppard-Towner Act, Harriet Upton, the vice-chairperson of the Republican party, made it clear that women would not forget that opposition at the polls. An overwhelmingly large vote in favor of the legislation in both the House and the Senate seemed to signal that congressmen heard and understood the message.

But the Sheppard-Towner Act was not without its critics. The National Woman's Party considered it special interest legislation that would perpetuate women's second class status. Birth control advocate Margaret Sanger also found it inadequate, because it did not provide for birth control information. As Sanger noted disdainfully, the clinics would teach a woman how to take care of her seventh child but not how to prevent an eighth. But the strongest opposition came from the American Medical Association (AMA). Prior to 1921, the idea of well-patient doctor visits— that is, checkups to prevent medical problems from developing— were not a part of medical responsibility. The clinics were mandated to correct this for mothers and children, but physicians worried that health care was being removed from their control and taken over by the government.

The clinics that were established because of the Sheppard-Towner Act did provide information and health care to hundreds of thousands of mothers and their young children. The clinics were generally staffed by women doctors and nurses, and most were located in rural areas where there was little access to health care on a regular basis. Ironically, the success of the clinics and the potential lucrativeness of this type of service provided by private physicians also brought about the demise of Sheppard-Towner funding. By 1929, Congress, under continued pressure from the AMA and less fearful that women would retaliate in any organized fashion, voted to terminate the program. The program nevertheless caused

physicians to absorb preventative health care and well-baby visits into their private practices. Medical practices expanded thereafter to include office visits for well-patients of all ages.

1921: The Women's Bond Club of New York Is Founded

(Professionalization, Work)

In 1921, a group of pioneering Wall Street women, including Betty Cook, Mary Riis, and Louise Watson, organized the Women's Bond Club of New York for women working in the financial industry.

Relatively few women worked on Wall Street, or anywhere in the financial industry, in the early twentieth century. Victoria Claflin Woodhull and her sister, Tennessee Claflin, had opened their own investment brokerage in the late 1860s, but while they did rather well with help from their mentor, Cornelius Vanderbilt, Wall Street looked upon them as an anomaly. The first modern woman to work on Wall Street was probably Betty Cook, a Cornell University graduate who went to work for Hemphill Noyes

in 1908, and remained with that firm and its successors for nearly half a century. Besides developing her own financial expertise, Cook worked hard to recruit young women to the industry and to help them advance. The measure of her success in bringing women to Wall Street could be determined during World War I, when several firms established "Women's Departments." The management of the firms involved apparently believed that women would be more credible selling Liberty Bonds to other women.

The women's departments, in any event, achieved remarkable success in selling the bonds crucial to the support of the war effort. In the process, the women financiers developed a collegial relationship and became the nucleus for what they began to refer to informally as the Women's Bond Club.

In 1921, Betty Cook and several colleagues, including Mary Riis and Louise Watson, decided to charter the Women's Bond Club and expand their weekly luncheons into official gatherings for Wall Street women. Mary Riis, the widow of photojournalist Jacob Riis, was the former head of the women's department at Higginson Securities, before she became a mainstay of the Shearson bond department. Louise Watson, a Bryn Mawr graduate, in 1917 was allowed to join the prestigious training program of the Guaranty Company, which later became J. P. Morgan/Guaranty, only after she agreed to pay for her own training. After going through the program, Watson quickly established herself as Guaranty's leading salesperson. Not only was she the first woman in the training program, but she was undoubtedly the first committed socialist and suffragist as well. Watson later became the first modern woman to establish her own investment advisory firm.

Under Betty Cook's tenure as president of the Women's Bond Club, the organization developed the programs and philosophy that have remained largely intact over the past seventy-three years. Committed to helping women in the conglomerate Wall Street industries and to fostering and recognizing the professional contributions of women in finance, the club holds frequent educational seminars on both professional and personal financial topics. It invites speakers from both within and outside of the financial industry and provides an opportunity to develop the networks that are crucial to success. For more than a decade, the Bond Club has reinforced those ideas in a public way by sponsoring an annual Merit Awards Dinner, in which a member of the financial community is chosen Merit Award Woman of the Year, and a woman not necessarily in finance is chosen as the Women Helping Women winner. Most recently, the Woman of the Year Merit Award went to Denise Boutross McGlone, the Chief Financial Officer of Sallie Mae Corporation, while Faye Wattleton, formerly of Planned Parenthood, won the Women Helping Women award.

Since its founding, the Women's Bond Club has developed a reputation as not only the oldest women's financial organization in the country, but also the most prestigious. Where once members had to cajole potential speakers into talking to the "girls," the WBC now attracts speakers from all over the world, including recently, vice-presidential candidate Geraldine Ferraro and former Japanese Minister of Finance Toyoo Gyohten.

1921: Betty Crocker First Appears

(Family Life)

In 1921, General Mills launched one of the longest and most successful advertising and marketing campaigns in history, by introducing the image of a fictitious woman named Betty Crocker as a human face for the international corporation.

Marjorie Child Husted invented Betty Crocker while working as the head of the home service department of the Washburn-Crosby flour milling company of Minneapolis, Minnesota. She had her employees use the name as a common signature to consumer inquiries, and after the company merged with General Mills, the name became the foundation of a corporate image. In 1921, Neysa McMein drew the first picture of Betty Crocker, and over the course of decades, the fictitious woman's face became one of the most familiar household symbols in America.

The stories of all three of the women connected with this marketing campaign reveal much about America in the early twentieth century. McMein, the artist, was a successful fashion designer and illustrator who had done covers for major magazines before the First World War. She was at the height of her commercial success when she contracted to create the image for General Mills. She went on to do patriotic posters for the government during World War II. McMein was a talented commercial artist who achieved success as an independent contractor at a time when business was supposed to be a man's world.

Marjorie Husted was even more of an anomaly for her time. Head of her department while still in her twenties, she stayed with the company through the merger and went on to ever greater successes. She rose to hold a series of top executive positions within General Mills, and eventually left to start her own consulting firm.

Ironically, the most enduring legacy of these two business women's careers was an image of traditional female domesticity. Betty Crocker was designed to give a giant food conglomerate a human face, to present an image that women would trust when shopping for processed foods. Her appearance changed over the decades, reflecting changes in fortune and fashion, but always carefully designed to reinforce the impression that a woman could be stylish and a homemaker, up-to-date and yet fulfilled in her traditional role. She reflected and reinforced the ambivalence many American women felt toward their dual role in society, their desire to be fresh and independent and their duty to home and family. Always changing yet always the same, Betty Crocker reflected and reinforced the ambiguous place of women in American society.

1921: The Miss America Pageant Attracts Atlantic City Tourists

(Cultural Life)

In an effort to keep tourists in Atlantic City, New Jersey, after the Labor Day weekend, promoters organized a second Rolling Chair Pageant in September 1921. The Rolling Chair Pageant had had a successful first outing the year before. To attract even more tourists, organizers decided to include a beauty pageant in this second one, the first Miss America Pageant.

The boardwalk of Atlantic City is famous for many things, not the least of which are the rolling chairs pushed along by enterprising individual for the convenience of tourists who hire the chairs both to get where they want to go on the extended boardwalk, or simply to enjoy the view. Hoping to keep tourists in Atlantic City beyond the normal end-of-summer Labor Day weekend, the city organized a Rolling Chair Pageant in 1920. The chairs, decorated much like floats in a parade, rolled along the boardwalk in a long line, with prizes awarded to the most creative chairs. The following year, organizers decided to include a beauty pageant in the Rolling Chair Pageant. Thus, the Miss American Pageant was born.

A reporter for the *Atlantic City Press*, Herb Test, hired to publicize the event, invited city newspapers to ask their readers to send photos for consideration. The winner of each city contest would be brought to Atlantic City, all expenses paid, to participate in the pageant—to become, as Test titled it, Miss America. On September 6, 1921, sixteen-year-old Margaret Gorman, of Washington, D.C., became the first Miss America, picked from among hundreds of finalists from all over the country. In addition to her title, Gorman was awarded a statuette valued at $5,000.

The pageant was held yearly after that, with the exception of the years between 1927 and 1933, when pageant officials gave in to critics who termed it an immoral display. Pageant officials raised the level of the competition after 1933, hoping to remove some of the carnival atmosphere that still surrounded it. In 1938, a talent aspect to the contest was introduced. In 1939, only states, cities, and recognized regions could send contestants to the pageant. Moreover, contestants had to be at least eighteen years old and swear to the fact that they had never been married. In 1941, the contest officially became the Miss America Pageant. The following year, the winner was sent on tour to help raise money for war bonds, a tradition that was followed until the war ended. Thereafter, in times of war, Miss America has often accompanied USO (United Service Organization) shows on tours to entertain American servicemen. By the end of the 1940s, the Miss America Pageant also awarded college scholarships to winners and runners-up.

The man most associated with the Miss America Pageant, Bert Parks, became the host in the 1950s when the pageant began to be televised. At the same time, the pageant theme song, "There She Is, Miss America," was introduced and has remained ever since a part of the ceremonies.

From the beginning, the pageant had critics, some more vigorous than others. Early critics objected to what they viewed as an immoral display. With the women's movement of the 1960s, criticism was renewed, this time on the basis that the pageant, and all beauty pageants, were sexist and objectified women. Opponents of the Vietnam War objected to sending Miss America to entertain troops, claiming that it was an endorsement of the war. Through it all, the Miss America Pageant had weathered the storms and continues each year to proclaim someone Miss America. The pageant, and those who participate, have made efforts to upgrade the affair from a simple contest of attractive women to one that includes real talent, poise, and the ability to express oneself intelligently. The scholarships awarded by the competition have made the pageant the largest private endower of scholarships for women.

1921: M. Carey Thomas Opens the Bryn Mawr Summer School for Women in Industry

(Social Reform)

M. Carey Thomas, the driving force behind Bryn Mawr College, initiated a unique summer program for women blue-collar workers in 1921, when she organized the Bryn Mawr Summer School for Women in Industry.

MCarey Thomas, educator, feminist, and president of Bryn Mawr College, brought to that institution her own personal standard of excellence, for which she expected everyone else associated with the college to strive, whether faculty, student, or support personnel. Thomas shaped Bryn Mawr in an effort to make it the elite of the elite women's schools. In her view, Bryn Mawr had to maintain standards equal to or better than those of the most demanding men's colleges. Few women who passed through Bryn Mawr's halls would argue that the Thomas stamp remained on them long after they left.

Between 1921 and 1938, hundreds of working women who passed through Bryn Mawr, however briefly, were also touched by the forceful and often controversial Thomas. Thomas, along with Professor of Social Welfare Hilda Smith, organized the Bryn Mawr Summer School for Women in Industry in an effort to bring to working women some of the education they were not privy to because of their economic backgrounds. The hope was that a summer of instruction in a variety of fields, including economics, history, and politics, would help better to prepare the participants to step into leadership roles in organizing and sustaining unions.

While women workers were never well-represented by established unions, in the post–World War I era their participation plummeted to new lows. To be sure, all unions were experiencing drastic declines in the new conservatism of the 1920s, but women's unionization dropped to less than 3 percent, with only one woman in thirty-four protected by union membership. At the same time, the Women's Trade Union League had begun to shift its focus from organization to education, so the prospects of becoming unionized were dimmer for women workers than they had been in several decades. Finally, the protective legislation laws enacted under the aegis of the progressives tended to segregate women further, prohibiting them from many jobs that required night work, for example. In trades where few women worked anyway, protective legislation tended to favor male employees, since there were fewer restrictions placed on them.

The Bryn Mawr program was financed by union funds, which enabled approximately sixty women workers to spend between six and eight weeks each summer on the Bryn Mawr campus. The program mirrored the Brookwood Labor College program, which also began in 1921. While Brookwood concentrated on training its coeducational classes for union activism, Bryn Mawr's focus was more humanistic. For most of the women workers who participated in the summer school program, their lives were changed immeasurably and, perhaps just as significantly, the lives of the faculty members with whom they came into contact were also changed. The summer school in many ways was a politicizing experience for faculty members previously insulated from the reality of working-class lives and work. Many of the women workers who participated did move into union leadership roles, with several becoming vice-presidents of national unions. Many of the faculty members turned to public service careers, either in addition to or in place of their academic careers. Notable in the latter category was Esther Peterson who, years later as the head of the Women's Bureau, would be instrumental in the estab-

lishment of the President's Commission on the Status of Women in the Kennedy administration.

1922: Ida Husted Harper Completes the Six-Volume *History of Woman Suffrage*

(Cultural Life)

The six-volume *History of Woman Suffrage*, started in 1876 under the able direction of Elizabeth Cady Stanton and Susan B. Anthony, was finally completed in 1922 when editor Ida Husted Harper published the final two volumes.

The *History of Woman Suffrage* took almost as long to write as the suffrage campaign took to secure the Nineteenth Amendment. Part of the reason, of course, was that the history could not be completed until woman suffrage was ratified and a constitutional amendment passed. But the overriding consideration was that the volume of information that was part of the official record of the suffrage campaign was simply more than anyone had anticipated. The task, in the end, was so monumental that it is to the great credit of the editors and their

dedication that it was finished at all.

Elizabeth Cady Stanton, Susan B. Anthony, and Matilda Joslyn Gage decided in 1876 that the history of their campaign to win the vote needed to be recorded. But even they, who had already been involved in the suffrage movement for a quarter century, anticipated two or three short pamphlets that they believed would not take more than a couple of months. Dividing up the work in a manner playing to each of their strengths, Anthony was in charge of finding a publisher, while Stanton and Gage were to gather information, sort it out, and write the history. The first three volumes took fourteen years to complete, and on several occasions disagreements among the three principals involved created strain and tension. Moreover, Lucy Stone, the founder of the conservative American Woman Suffrage Association, refused to contribute information, feeling that the AWSA should write its own history. But when the first three volumes appeared, totaling just over three thousand pages, they represented one of the most extraordinary accounts of a political or social movement that had ever been recorded. A wealth of letters, speeches, convention notes, petitions, and personal memoirs were all tied together with narrative that conveyed the passion with which Stanton and Anthony pursued suffrage. The first three volumes covered the years from 1848 to 1883. When Matilda Gage died, Anthony asked her friend and biographer Ida Husted Harper to edit the fourth volume, from 1883. After Anthony died, Harper completed the last two volumes, ending with passage of the Nineteenth Amendment in 1920.

Although the final three volumes are not nearly as well done as the first three, primarily because Harper lacked the intensity of a Stanton or an Anthony, the entire six-volume collection remains the single best source for information about the suffrage movement and the ideas, beliefs, and thoughts of those who participated. More than a record of the activities of the leadership, the *History* is a record of the countless women who labored for years with the one goal of securing for themselves the right to vote.

1922: Emily Post Publishes *Etiquette*

(Cultural Life)

In 1922, Emily Post published the book that made her name synonymous with good manners for decades to come.

Emily Post was born into circumstances that laid the foundations for her later role as arbiter of social correctness, but the route by which she came to that role belied her image as a stuffy conservative. She came from a wealthy New York family, was raised by a governess, attended elite finishing schools, and debuted into New York society with all the pomp and circumstance befitting a Gilded Age society princess. She married at twenty in 1892, and spent much time traveling in Europe and at various fashionable vacation homes while mothering her two sons. On the surface, her life seemed charmed.

In reality, though, her life was far less perfect. Her husband carried on affairs with other women, of which Emily was aware. Instead of pretending ignorance, as many women would have done, she decided to leave him, even though she knew the cost would be heavy. In 1905, she won a divorce, but lost the luxurious lifestyle in which she had always lived. She went from riches not to rags, but to a life of work and purpose.

At age thirty-three, the newly independent Post took up writing in order to support herself. She wrote magazine articles and novels about the rich, as well as articles on travel and interior decoration. For almost twenty years she labored with modest success, but in 1922, she struck gold. Her book on etiquette appeared just in time to become a handbook of good manners in a decade of tumultuous social change. In it, she steered a middle course between highbrow conservatism and the realities of change. She managed thereby to teach the children of old families how to accommodate the new social forms, the rising members of the *nouveau riche* how to fit into their new social strata, and the mass audience of middle-class readers some semblance of the old social graces.

Post revised and updated her book often, adapting it to the changing circumstances of the Depression and later the Second World War and postwar world. In 1932, she began to supplement it with a daily newspaper column that was carried by over two hundred papers, and she spoke regularly on radio. She died at the age of eighty-eight in 1960, but even after her death, and despite the social and cultural convulsions of the 1960s and 1970s, her work remained popular. By 1980, the book had gone through one hundred printings, and it continues to sell well. By creating an etiquette that maintained the veneer of polished society while being flexible enough to accommodate changing mores, Post provided generations of Americans with a manual of apparently timeless manners in a period of unparalleled social flux.

1923: The U.S. Supreme Court Strikes Down Minimum Wage Laws

(Work, Social Reform)

In 1923, the U.S. Supreme Court declared, in the case of *Adkins v. Children's Hospital*, that imposing minimum wage laws for women was unconstitutional.

When Florence Kelley heard in 1923 that the U.S. Supreme Court had struck down minimum wage laws for women, she noted somewhat bitterly that the Court had really proclaimed "the inalienable right of women to starve."

Minimum wage laws were a crucial part of efforts to enact protective legislation since the early twentieth century. Rooted in the shockingly low wages paid to women and children in some factories and in the so-called "sweated" trades, the minimum wage laws were an effort to eliminate the exploitation of workers largely unprotected by any other means. Labor unions, for example, routinely ignored women workers. When protective legislation advocates, like Florence Kelley of the National Consumer's League, succeeded in securing at least lukewarm union support for minimum wages for women and children, it was

not because the unions had had a true change of heart. Rather, organizations like the American Federation of Labor decided that supporting protective legislation for women and children only would eliminate the need for unions to accommodate women, while at the same time protecting jobs for male union members.

In 1908, the courts ruled that imposing regulations governing women's work was allowable because of their unique vulnerability. Between 1912 and 1919, fourteen states, primarily in the midwest and far west, and the District of Columbia passed minimum wage laws for women. Employers continued to oppose minimum wage laws in the courts, with mixed results initially. The argument used by employers was that, while women might be considered a vulnerable segment of the working population, the imposition of minimum wages unfairly prohibited women from freely negotiating their own work contracts. In 1917, in the case of *Stettler v. O'Hara*, the Court upheld the minimum wage law by a narrow margin. But five years later, in the case of *Adkins v. Children's Hospital*, the Court, by a five to three margin, struck down the minimum wage law that had been passed for the District of Columbia in 1918. In the *Adkins* case, the Court ruled that the recent suffrage victory had made special protective legislation for women unnecessary. Surprisingly, Justice Oliver Wendell Holmes, who earlier had proclaimed that the Court had an obligation to give protective legislation the benefit of the doubt, sided with the opposition in *Adkins v. Children's Hospital*. Adopting a strict-constructionist point of view, Holmes argued that "the criterion for constitutionality is not whether we view the law to be for the public good."

The *Adkins* decision effectively overturned all of the minimum wage laws that had been enacted in the previous decade. Efforts to formulate a minimum wage law for women that would stand up to constitutional scrutiny continued to prove futile for protective legislationists throughout the 1920s and 1930s. In the early years of the New Deal, several states tried once again to pass minimum wage laws for women. Once again, the Court overturned these laws in the case of *Morehead v. New York ex.rel. Tipaldo* (1936). But in 1937, the Court reversed itself in the case of *West Coast Hotel Co. v. Parrish*. In this case, the Court declared that economic regulations were not necessarily unconstitutional where it could be shown that such laws served the public interest. The key to the Court's decision to uphold the minimum wage law in this case was that its decision was gender-neutral—that is, minimum wage laws that served the public interest were constitutional, but they were constitutional for both men and women. This proved to be a crucial decision, for it opened the way for passage of the Fair Labor Standards Act in 1938, the key provision of which established a minimum wage for *all* workers.

1924: The National Congress of Parents and Teachers Is Founded

(Education, Family Life)

In 1924, the already quarter-century-old National Council of Mothers, founded to encourage mothers to become involved in the public education of their children, changed its name and focus to the National Council of Parents and Teachers, commonly referred to as the Parent-Teacher Association, or PTA.

In 1897, Phoebe Apperson Hearst and Alice McLellan Birney organized a "mother's congress" to encourage mothers to take an active role in the public education of their children. Out of that meeting the National Council of Mothers was born. The first president of the organization was Birney. Birney, the wife of Theodore Weld Birney, a grandson of abolitionist James Birney, developed her interest in parental contributions to public education when she was raising her own two daughters. Appalled by the lack of literature available to guide parents and disturbed over the way that many children were warped by parental ignorance, Birney began investigating how mothers could be educated to the idea of the importance of the child. She conceived the idea of a great gathering of women to discuss

the situation, and succeeded in winning the support of Hearst, a wealthy advocate of improved education on all levels. Over two thousand women met in Washington, D.C., on February 17, 1897, for a "mother's congress" that culminated in the founding of the National Council of Mothers. While Birney served as president, the organization was largely funded in the early years by Hearst.

Under Birney's direction, the PTA developed as a series of local organizations, composed of mothers, to engage in child study, to support local child welfare bodies, and to encourage greater parent and teacher cooperation for the well-being of the children. Since its inception, the goals of the PTA have changed little. It remains the largest and most powerful child advocacy group in the country.

In 1924, the National Council of Mothers became the National Council of Parents and Teachers, a move to acknowledge the responsibility of fathers to their children's education. A few years later, in 1927, the National Congress of Colored Parents and Teachers was founded by Selena Sloan Butler to foster improvements in segregated schools, primarily those in the South.

Both organizations maintained similar objectives, focused on securing strong relationships between parents and teachers, as well as on maintaining higher standards for children in all areas affecting their lives, from the home to school to health care to the legal system. The influence of the national PTAs has been felt in some of the legislation affecting children. Specifically, laws governing the attendance requirements of children in schools and the passage of child-labor welfare laws were all heavily influenced by the support of the PTAs. In 1970, the National Council of Parents and Teachers and the National Council of Colored Parents and Teachers united forces, reflecting the changes in segregation that came about as a result of the Supreme Court's decision in *Brown v. Board of Education*. Membership in the PTA numbers in the millions and, while members tend to be predominantly female, recent sensibilities have seen more and more participation by men.

1925: Florence Sabin Is Elected to the National Academy of Sciences and to Membership in the Rockefeller Institute

(Medicine, Work)

Florence Sabin, one of the foremost scientists of her day, whose work in immunology, hematology, and embryology led to a more precise understanding of human cell embryology that paved the way for immunological discoveries, became the first woman elected to the National Academy of Sciences in 1925, and the first woman elected full membership in the Rockefeller Institute that same year.

Florence Sabin, who was once proclaimed by the Rockefeller Institute "the greatest scientist of our time," spent her life studying the human cell and teaching others the methodology she developed. A Smith College graduate in 1893, Sabin was determined to go into medicine. Lacking the funds immediately, she spent two years in Denver, Colorado, teaching mathematics, and another year at Smith College in their zoology department. In 1896, she was a member of the fourth class admitted to the Johns Hopkins Medical School. As such, she was afforded the best medical education then available in the United States. Her career in medicine coincided with the emergence of anatomy as an experimental science through studies in embryology and histology. An excellent student, Sabin won one of four highly coveted internships at Johns Hopkins with the preeminent internist William Osler. But her real mentor was Franklin Mall, a professor of anatomy, with whom she worked for many years.

In 1902, she became the first woman on the Hopkins medical faculty, and when she was promoted to full professor in 1917, that too was a first. Sabin's work focused on the origins of blood cells and the lymphatic vessels. She provided the histological evidence that reversed accepted medical theory about how lymphatics developed, leading to a series of widely cited papers and a chapter in the influential *Manual of Human Embryology*. She also developed the process by which cells could be studied in a living state so that vital processes could be observed.

Sabin's twenty-five-year career at Hopkins was marred only by the fact that, although she had worked as Mall's assistant and had taught the histology course at Hopkins, when Mall died in 1917, one of Sabin's former students was chosen to succeed him as chairman of the department. Although she had been a quiet advocate of women's rights since her Smith College days, she refused to let Hopkins' sex discrimination alter her attitude toward teaching. Her students noted that after each lecture, Sabin would tear up her lecture notes, so that she would have to rework the lecture anew each year, thereby avoiding the potential of ignoring new developments. To students unaccustomed to female professors, Sabin proved to be an outstanding teacher. Her personal dignity and enthusiasm conveyed themselves to her students, many of whom went on to become leading figures in immunology, anatomy, and hematology.

In 1924, Sabin was elected president of the American Association of Anatomists, and the following year she was the first woman elected to the National Academy of Sciences. That same year, the Rockefeller Institute elected her to full membership, the first such position held by a woman. She spent thirteen years at the Rockefeller Institute, continuing her work in embryonics and cell development. When she retired in 1938, she returned to her native Colorado.

1928: Margaret Mead Publishes *Coming of Age in Samoa*

(Cultural Life)

Anthropologist Margaret Mead, whose work did more to shape modern thought and public opinion on attitudes toward families, children, and male and female relationships, launched her professional career with the publication of her most famous book, *Coming of Age in Samoa*, in 1928.

Margaret Mead was undoubtedly the best known anthropologist of the twentieth century. Throughout her professional career, she was a tireless advocate and popularizer of cultural anthropology. After graduating from Barnard College in 1923, Mead studied at Columbia University with Ruth Benedict and Franz Boas. Her field work in the South Pacific, which prepared her to write her dissertation, led to publication of *Coming of Age in Samoa* in 1928.

Mead's observations of native cultures contradicted some of the western world's most cherished notions of child-rearing, family relationships, and the role of women in society. In contrast to modern Western society, Mead's studies of life in Samoa strongly suggested that adolescence need not be an especially difficult time, that matrilineal societies allowed women and children greater freedom, producing greater self-respect, and that gender roles were not innate, but rather culturally determined. These views were particularly troublesome to Western politicians and religious leaders alike, who had assumed for decades that both colonization and missionary outposts were beneficial because of western superiority over the "heathen" cultures they sought to change. Mead returned to the South Pacific several times during the 1930s, publishing two more books, one focusing on child-rearing (*Growing Up in New Guinea*, 1930), and a comprehensive volume, *From the South Seas* (1939). What made her work there particularly valuable was that it was the last opportunity to study these cultures untainted by the intrusion of World War II.

During the war, Mead worked for the Office of War Information. Ironically, just as the army notoriously misused its personnel, so the OWI misused Margaret Mead. At a time when information on the South Seas was desperately needed to develop a strategy against Japanese aggression, the westerner who probably knew more about the South Seas than anyone else alive was assigned the task of writing about British and American relations. This lack of recognition of Mead's anthropological contributions was not the only one. In her decades-long association with the Museum of Natural History in New York, only belatedly in 1964, did she earn the title of full curator. Similarly, when Columbia University finally gave her an academic position, it was as an adjunct professor. Mead never held an important position in anthropological societies, and the National Academy of Science did not see fit to make her a member until 1973. Yet her reputation among the public continued to grow. She lectured widely; was a frequent contributor to radio, television, and the print media, and helped to establish the United Nation's emergency relief agency, UNESCO, as well as other relief agencies. Mead remained active until her death in 1978.

1929: Women Inspectors in an Elizabethton, Tennessee, Textile Factory Go on Strike

(Work, Social Reform)

On March 12, 1929, women inspectors at the American Glazstoff factory in Elizabethton, Tennessee, walked off their jobs to protest low wages. Joined by workers at the nearby American Bemberg plant, the strikers formed a local of the United Textile Workers.

When women workers at the German-owned American Glazstoff rayon plant in Elizabethton, Tennessee, were faced with wage cutbacks, a group of young women inspectors decided their only recourse was to walk off the jobs and go on strike. On March 12, 1929, the women walked out of the plant. Very quickly, they were joined by workers in the nearby German-owned American Bemberg plant. Seeking to shore up support as quickly as possible, and contrary to accepted beliefs about women workers (despite their long history of strikes and union endorsements), the workers formed a local of the United Textile Workers, which belonged to the American Federation of Labor. Picket lines were set up near

the plant. The factory owners, after a brief time, obtained a court injunction prohibiting the strikers from picketing near the plants. Nevertheless, the strikers continued to picket. Moreover, when the governor of Tennessee sent National Guardsmen in to escort strikebreakers into the plants, the strikers defied the National Guard as well. In a bizarre twist of events, some local businessmen, hoping to intimidate the strikers, kidnapped one of the organizers. Before long, the strike spread to other textile plants throughout the South, an indication of the unrest that already existed and would continue to exist, with predictable results, until after World War II.

Although women in Elizabethton made up only 37 percent of the work force, they continued to be the prime movers and supporters of the strike. The young women strikers symbolized, in many ways, the modern women of the 1920s, with smart, store-bought fashions and an undisguised enjoyment of the latest commercial products available. Plant owners and local businessmen tried to compromise the strikers by insinuating that many of them were engaged in illicit activities including prostitution, but the ruse was not taken seriously. Unfortunately, although the resolve of the strikers was solid, the United Textile Workers union was not as determined. Six weeks after the strike began, on May 26, 1929, the union negotiated a settlement in which the companies had to make no concessions to the strikers. Strike leaders were blacklisted and received no support from the union. The German owners, however, recalled the unpopular plant managers, raised wages, and instituted a counseling and welfare system for the workers. For the strikers themselves, a sense of empowerment was a long-lasting consequence of the strike. Many of the strikers were convinced that they had accomplished something positive for the generations of workers who would come after them.

1929: Women Pilots Organize the Ninety-Nines, Inc.

(Professionalization, Work)

On November 2, 1929, twenty-six women pilots met in a hangar at the Curtiss Flying Service in New York, to create an organization for women pilots. Called the Ninety-Nines, because that represented their charter membership, the organization signaled the growing interest of women as professional aviators.

In the fall of 1929, after the first Women's Air Derby, a major cross-country race for women pilots, several of the pilots expressed an interest in creating an organization that would provide support for women in aviation. Clara Trenchmann of the Curtiss Flying Service on Long Island in New York persuaded several of her colleagues to write letters to each of the 129 registered licensed women pilots, asking for their views on such an organization. Ninety-nine women responded with enthusiasm. Twenty-six of the ninety-nine charter members of the Ninety-Nines, Inc., met at one of the Curtiss hangars for the first meeting on November 2, 1929. The organization dedicated itself to "assist women in aeronautical research, air racing events, the acquisition of aerial experience, and the administration of aid through aerial means in times of emergency."

By the time the Ninety-Nines organized, women had already begun to take aviation as a profession seriously. Constraints against women participating in the military in anything other than nursing roles up to World War II prevented women from becoming as involved in professional aviation as men were. But women aviators nevertheless remained a vital part of flying. Amelia Earhart achieved the status of a national hero with her trans-Atlantic flight, and her last around-the-world

effort. Other women, like Jacqueline Cochran, were responsible for the hundreds of women pilots who flew noncombat missions in World War II, as members of the Women's Air Service Pilots. Some women, like Olive Ann Beech, ran their own aviation-related businesses. For years, Beech ran Beech Aircraft and was a prominent figure at the management level of the aircraft industry. For years, commercial flying was prohibited to women pilots. That, too, changed as a consequence of the renewed women's movement of the 1970s, when commercial airlines began accepting women as copilots, navigators, and finally pilots. Although women have been allowed to fly noncombat planes in the military for many years, it was not until 1993 that women members of the service academies were given the option of taking fighter pilot training after graduation.

Many of today's women pilots are included among the 6,500 members of the Ninety-Nines, which is headquartered in Oklahoma City. The organization is still dedicated to supporting women pilots around the world in all endeavors.

1930: The Association of Southern Women for the Prevention of Lynching Is Founded

(Social Reform, Civil Rights)

In 1930, Texan Jesse Daniel Ames organized the Association of Southern Women for the Prevention of Lynching (ASWPL) in order to put an end to the mob violence committed in the name of southern women.

Like many women who found themselves in similar circumstances, Jesse Daniel Ames gradually developed a feminist sensibility when she was left with three small children to raise on her own after the death of her physician husband in 1914. Along with her mother, who had also been recently widowed, Ames started a small business that provided an income for the family. Both she and her mother also became involved in the suffrage movement and were largely responsible for Texas becoming the first southern state to ratify the Nineteenth Amendment. Ames organized the Texas League of Women Voters in 1919, serving as its first president, and assumed—as did many others—that women would use their new voting power to band together in order to secure the kinds of social and political reforms for which they had advocated securing the vote. Very quickly, in Texas and throughout the nation, it became apparent, though, that women were not forming the effective coalitions that might have resulted in real change.

At the same time, Ames began to become increasingly uncomfortable with the persistence of southern white males engaging in mob violence that all too often ended with the lynching of African-American males, particularly since the justification for such violence was often the protection of white women. By 1924, Ames had become Texas director of the Commission on Interracial Cooperation (CIC), an organization based in Atlanta, and five years later, she was named the national director of the CIC. African-American women within the CIC had, for years, made the argument that if southern white women wanted lynching to stop, it would be stopped, and not before. Now with Jesse Daniel Ames directing the CIC, that argument could be tested. The year following her move to Atlanta, Ames and twenty-six like-minded southern women, founded the Association of Southern Women for the Prevention of Lynching.

The ASWPL remained active for twelve years until 1942. During that time, Ames and her colleagues traveled throughout the South speaking out against mob violence, lynchings, and most of all, against the hypocritical justification used by those who initiated the violence. Armed with the facts garnered from studies of the situation, Ames was able to point out that fewer than one-third of all lynchings happened because of rape or even the accusation of rape. To Ames, it seemed clear that the root of mob vio-lence was the link between sexual and racial repression in the South. The myth of the black rapist and the pure southern lady produced a false chivalry that was as harmful to white women as it was to black men. Leaving the racists with no place to hide, Ames also denounced the acceptance of white men lynching black men while at the same time sexually exploiting black women.

Ames, with a message that struck at the heart of racial and sexual repression, drew the wrath of local officials throughout the South. But she also secured the support of influential women's groups, including the Methodist women, and gradually began to see a change in the incidence of lynchings. The year 1940 was a turning point in the campaign, for in that year not one lynching occurred. By 1942, with World War II underway, the ASWPL dissolved.

1931: Jane Addams Is Awarded the Nobel Peace Prize

(Cultural Life, Social Reform)

In 1931, the Nobel Committee chose Jane Addams and Nicholas Murray Butler, the President of Columbia University, as cowinners of the Nobel Peace Prize. Addams, the first woman so honored by the Nobel Committee, won the award because of her years of dedicated work on behalf of world peace.

Jane Addams may be better remembered for her work in the field of social reform, but she devoted much of her adult life to the cause of world peace. Indeed, her experiences at Hull House with its micro-internationalism, led to the publication of *Newer Ideals of Peace* in 1907, a volume in which Addams discussed the ethnically diverse neighborhoods of Chicago's Nineteenth Ward. Addams argued that the ability of the residents to overcome their cultural differences held the potential for becoming a force for world peace. When World War I began in Europe in 1914, Addams focused all her energies on peace. As chairwoman of the Woman's Peace party and president of the International Congress of Women at The Hague, Addams worked tirelessly to promote the idea that the belligerent nations, if offered a face-saving alternative to war, would agree to mediation. Efforts to enlist American President Woodrow Wilson's support for a conference of mediation failed, but Addams was determined to continue her quest for a mediated end to the war. Although she had severe reservations about Henry Ford and his so-called "Peace Ship," she nevertheless agreed to join that group of mediation advocates. Illness forced her to withdraw at the last moment, perhaps fortuitously, since the peace voyage ended prematurely when the idiosyncratic Ford lost interest and cut off funding.

All too quickly, the United States itself was embroiled in the war and Addams redoubled her efforts to work for peace. Very few Americans chose to renounce U.S. participation in the war, and those that did were subjected to almost universal vilification. Overnight, it seemed, Americans forgot the years that Addams had spent working to improve the lives of immigrants and the underprivileged. Very few of her colleagues at Hull House supported Addams' point of view, although they certainly did not subject her to the level of abuse with which she was often greeted by others. When the Daughters of the American Revolution revoked her membership, the undaunted Addams commented that she did not realize that her lifetime membership was contingent on her good behavior. Despite these rebuffs, Addams could not and would not compromise her principles. The closest she came to war work occurred as a result of her admiration for the work that Herbert Hoover had done as head of the Belgian Relief Project in 1915. When Hoover became the head of the Food Administration, Addams toured the country lecturing on the merits of food production and conservation in order to provide help to victims of the war.

Addams' quest for what William James called the "moral equivalent of war," led her to accept the presidency of the Women's International League for Peace and Freedom in 1919. For the next fifteen years, she presided over the league's conferences held in world capitals from Zurich to Dublin. She paid little attention to the continuing, if sporadic, attacks leveled at her by the Daughters of the American Revolution and the American Legion throughout the 1920s, but events did, at times, seem overwhelmingly against any real or effective peace, as when

the United States refused to join the League of Nations.

Despite the few critics who continued to question her patriotism and motives, Addams regained her favor with the public and throughout the world. A true luminary of the twentieth century, Addams' name consistently appeared first on lists of America's greatest women. Her years of work on behalf of peace were recognized with the ultimate accolade when the Nobel Prize Committee named Addams a cowinner of the Nobel Peace Prize in 1931, citing her lifelong efforts to bring about peaceful solutions to world conflict. In a gesture that confirmed the committee's wisdom in the award, Addams immediately donated her half of the prize money—$16,000—to the Women's International League for Peace and Freedom.

1931: The Society of Industrial Engineers Awards the First Gilbreth Medal to Lillian Gilbreth

(Work)

In 1931, the Society of Industrial Engineers established the Gilbreth Medal Award, both to honor motion study pioneer Frank Gilbreth and to recognize individuals in the field who had built on Gilbreth's work. The first recipient of the medal was Lillian Gilbreth, the widow and partner of Frank Gilbreth, who had continued to make her own unique contribution to the field despite the constraints of raising twelve children.

L illian Gilbreth's background pre-pared her for only one of the two careers she eventually found herself engaged in. As the oldest of eight children, she had had to take responsibility for younger siblings from time to time because of her mother's ill health. Thus, she was at least partially prepared when she and her husband had twelve children of their own. Gilbreth's parents, although they were well-off and considered one of the prominent families in Oakland, California, hesitated when Lillian wanted to attend the University of California at Berkeley. With the idea of becoming a teacher, Gilbreth majored in English Literature. She was the first female to be chosen as commencement speaker. Two master's degrees, one from Columbia and one from Berkeley, followed, and she was about to begin work on a doctorate when she met Frank Gilbreth and married him in 1904.

For the next seventeen years, Lillian Gilbreth worked as her husband's partner in the motion study business they built up, taking time out in between for her twelve children. The Gilbreths pioneered in the application of motion study. As a team, they made motion study a respectable branch of industrial engineering, and when Frank Gilbreth died in 1924, his wife took over the business. Working alone, the task was infinitely harder, not because she had not acquired the necessary expertise over the previous twenty years, but because clients that she and her husband had worked with decided arbitrarily that she could not do the job alone. For several years, trying to raise twelve children and restart a business left Gilbreth on financially shaky ground.

She used her own family as the basis for an engineering specialty that, up to then had been ignored. Gilbreth wrote about her home methods in a book entitled *The Home Maker and Her Job* (1927). She quickly became the leading expert on the scientific management of the home, filling requests from universities and hospitals to organize departments of home economics. She also taught at Purdue University, becoming a professor of management in 1935.

In 1931, the Society of Industrial

Engineers, which had created the Frank Gilbreth Medal for outstanding contributions to the field of industrial engineering and motion study, selected Lillian Gilbreth as its first recipient. By then, the motion study concepts developed by the Gilbreths had become part of the accepted methodology for industrial engineers, industrial psychologists, and personnel specialists.

Lillian Gilbreth continued to work and write into her eighties. But it was not until the 1950s, when her son, Frank Gilbreth, Jr., and her daughter, Ernestine Gilbreth Casey, wrote two memoirs of their lives with their parents, that the Gilbreths became household names. The memoirs were humorous and obviously loving accounts of life with two industrial engineers as parents. *Cheaper by the Dozen* was published in 1948, and *Belles on Their Toes*, which told Lillian's story after her husband's death, was published in 1950.

1931: Dorothy Thompson Interviews Hitler

(Work, Politics)

In 1931, while on a working trip to Europe, journalist Dorothy Thompson interviewed Adolf Hitler, who was then considered an up-and-coming political power in Germany. Convinced from speaking with him that the German people could not possibly take Hitler seriously, Thompson initially dismissed him as insignificant.

Dorothy Thompson was one of the few American journalists who fought for U.S. intervention in the war in Europe. One of the most influential journalists in the late 1930s, and some argued the most prominent American woman in the world, second only perhaps to Eleanor Roosevelt, Thompson used her radio show, and newspaper and magazine columns, in addition to the lecture circuit, to urge Americans to fight Nazism before it was too late.

Thompson's first job was as publicist for the New York Woman Suffrage Association. After suffrage had been passed, and with World War I ended in Europe, Thompson took a trip to Europe, in the course of which she managed to secure an interview with Irish independence leader Terence MacSwiney, and covered a strike of Fiat workers in Rome. Both stories were carried by the Independent News Service (INS), which brought Thompson to the attention of publisher Cyrus Curtis. By 1924, Thompson was the Central European bureau chief for two Curtis publications, the *Philadelphia Public Ledger* and the *New York Evening Post.* A second marriage to novelist Sinclair Lewis brought Thompson back to the United States. For a brief time, the constraints of motherhood and marriage prevented her return to Europe, but by 1930 she was back.

In 1931, Thompson interviewed Adolf Hitler for *Cosmopolitan* magazine. Profoundly unimpressed with Hitler, Thompson characterized him as an "inconsequent…ill-poised, insecure," a man of "startling insignificance," who, she believed, would never be able to seize real power. Watching events as they unfolded, Thompson quickly changed her mind about Hitler, and between 1933 and 1941, she became the foremost advocate of U.S. intervention to stop Nazi aggression. Her expulsion from Nazi Germany in 1934 was a newsworthy occurrence, enhancing her reputation as a serious journalist and political commentator. Thompson wrote a regular column for the *New York Herald Tribune* beginning in February 1936, entitled "On the Record." She was also a regularly featured commentator on NBC radio. Undaunted by attacks from the isolationists and America First-ers, Thompson continued to lobby for the United States to intervene in Europe.

By the late 1930s, as well, Thompson began to publicize the plight of refugees. Privately, she helped many European acquaintances secure American visas, often providing them with temporary shelter. Publicly, she called for a defined U.S. policy to deal with the growing problem. Thompson was influential in bringing about the international conference on refugees at Evian-des-Bains in France in July 1938. The conference, called by Franklin Roosevelt, led to the formation of an Intergovernmental Committee on Refugees. Honored at a dinner in New York for her efforts, Thompson received messages from both Roosevelt and Winston Churchill.

Once the United States did enter

the war after the bombing of Pearl Harbor in 1941, Thompson reached a turning point in her career. Thompson spent the war years almost on the fringes of world events. After the war, in probably her most controversial period, Thompson took up the cause of the Arabs in the Middle East. Her advocacy brought her into direct conflict with Zionists. Eventually, her contin-ued support of Arabs brought her into conflict with the American media and the public as well who believed that her journalistic independence had been compromised. Although she continued to write until her death in 1961, Thompson's reputation and influence was never again what it had been in the pre–World War II years.

1932: Amelia Earhart Flies the Atlantic Ocean Solo

(Cultural Life, Technology, Exploration)

On May 21–22, 1932, Amelia Earhart flew her Lockhood Vega monoplane from Harbor Grace, Newfoundland to Culmore, Ireland—the first woman to fly solo across the Atlantic Ocean.

Amelia Earhart had earned her reputation as one of America's foremost aviators in 1928 when she, accompanied by pilot Wilmer Stulltz and mechanic Lou Gordon, became the first woman to fly across the Atlantic. On that trip, however, Earhart had done nothing more than keep the flight log. Always uncomfortable with the immediate fame resulting from the flight, Earhart never missed an opportunity to let people know that she had not piloted the plane. The public did not care. She was dubbed "Lady Lindy," a reference to pilot Charles Lindbergh, a nickname at which she bristled every time it was used. She was a strong believer that women deserved to be acknowledged independently for their accomplishments.

Earhart's flying career began in 1921. From then on, she eagerly embraced every opportunity to promote flight. But even before that, as a volunteer at a Canadian military hospital during World War I, Earhart fell in love with the idea of flying when she heard firsthand of the exploits of the pilots of the Royal Flying Corp. After her 1932 Atlantic solo flight, for which she received a Distinguished Flying Cross from Congress and the French Legion of Honor, and encouraged by her husband, publisher George Putnam, Earhart became the first pilot to fly solo from Honolulu to the American mainland in 1935. That year, she also made the first nonstop flight from Mexico City to Newark, New Jersey.

Aside from the challenges of frontiers unconquered, Earhart was convinced that her flights were advancing transportation and air safety. Her dedication to this pursuit helped persuade her to accept a position as a career counselor to women students at Purdue University. The post carried with it the title of special advisor in aeronautics, for which the Purdue trustees established a fund for aeronautical research. She was also provided with a Lockheed Electra, so well-equipped that Earhart called it her "flying laboratory." It also made it possible for an around-the-world flight. In 1936, Earhart began preparing for a final "long flight."

On June 1, 1937, Earhart and pilot-navigator Fred Noonan, left Miami, Florida, on the first leg of a round-the-world flight. On July 2, the most difficult stretch of the trip was supposed to carry them from Lae, New Guinea, to the tiny Pacific island, Howland, 2,556 miles away. The Coast Guard had constructed a landing strip specifically for Earhart on Howland. The island itself was a mere two miles long by a mile wide. Crossing the International Dateline toward Howland, where it was still July 2, Earhart and Noonan began sending ever-fainter messages indicating that they were having trouble finding the island, according to official reports from the Coast Guard cutter *Ithaca*. They never landed at Howland and no trace was ever found of Earhart's plane.

Since the disappearance, persistent rumors have circulated about Earhart's true mission on her final flight. Recent research has produced persuasive evidence that these rumors were, in fact, true. Amelia Earhart was not only flying around the world; she was also on a mission to monitor the military buildup of the Japanese in the Pacific. She was apparently either shot down or forced to land by Japanese military personnel. Eyewitness accounts and a photograph place Earhart in Saipan two months after that fateful day. Beyond that, any explanations are still speculation.

Amelia Earhart was just forty years old when she disappeared. During her brief career as an aviator, she did indeed advance transportation in flight and air safety. She may also have made the ultimate sacrifice for her country. Beyond that, she inspired a generation of women, newly emancipated, to pursue their own independence.

1932: Frances Perkins Becomes the First Woman Cabinet Officer

(Equal Rights, Work)

When Franklin Delano Roosevelt was elected president in 1932, one of his first cabinet appointments was the unprecedented selection of a woman. Frances Perkins, a long-time advocate for working women, who had experience in both social work and labor, was sworn in as secretary of labor on the day that Roosevelt took the oath of office, and continued to serve in that capacity until 1945.

Hiring a woman for the position of secretary of labor in 1932 established a new precedent. Frances Perkins, Roosevelt's choice, was eminently qualified for the post. A graduate of Mount Holyoke College and Columbia University, with years of experience in social work and labor reform, she earned her reputation for thoroughness early on as a researcher for *The Survey*. Later, she turned to social work and in 1926, Al Smith, the governor of New York, appointed her to chair his state's industrial board. When Roosevelt was elected governor of New York in 1928, he appointed her the first woman state industrial commissioner.

The fact that she was a woman created controversy. One reporter asked her if being a woman was going to put her at a disadvantage in Washington. "Only," she replied, "when climbing trees." Despite her background, it still took some behind-the-scenes maneuvering on her behalf by Eleanor Roosevelt and Molly Dewson, one of the Democratic party's canniest politicians, to persuade both Roosevelt and the public that appointing Perkins would be a wise move. Dewson, in particular, saw to it that Perkins' name was before the public as much as possible, with magazine and newspaper articles. She also solicited letters from public figures who urged Roosevelt not to overlook Perkins. Roosevelt, already predisposed to appointing women to his administration, had no problem bringing Perkins on board, but the nomination carried with it some risk. In particular, organized labor was not at all enamored of the idea of a woman heading up the Department of Labor. The president of the Congress of Industrial Organizations (CIO) referred to Perkins disparagingly, and William Green, the president of the AFL, went into an absolute rage when he heard that she had been nominated.

Years later, William Green praised Perkins as one of the best secretaries of labor that had ever held the post. Indeed, she proved to be one of

Roosevelt's most valuable domestic assets. She was instrumental in developing and securing passage of the Wagner Act, the Social Security Act, and the Fair Labor Standards Act, all of which enormously influenced the course of labor relations in America. Perkins was also responsible for innovative ideas to help working people, including unemployment insurance, minimum wages, and maximum hours. She was a fierce advocate for child labor legislation. Perkins accomplished all of this while raising a daughter, protecting her from the glare of publicity, and caring for a permanently hospitalized husband whose bouts of severe depression prevented him from functioning on his own. Much of her support and encouragement came from other women, both friends and acquaintances, who provided her with invaluable advice and friendship. Perkins was always very aware of her responsibility as a woman to represent all women to the best of her ability. "I have always felt that it was not I alone who was appointed to the cabinet," she noted in a 1933 speech, "but that it was all the women in America."

1933: Sodium Pentathol Is Introduced as an Anesthetic

(Medicine, Family Life)

Sodium pentathol, a fast acting suppressant of the central nervous system, rapidly became the anesthetic of choice during labor and childbirth after its introduction in 1933.

The words "labor" and "childbirth," relatively benign in themselves, have more often than not masked a painful reality throughout history. Some women experience relatively easy labors, but most experience childbirth as acutely distressing, often with hours of painful contractions leading up to delivery, and the delivery itself a time of intense pain. Whether because of a physical malfunction during the pregnancy or because of body chemistry or physiology, women have frequently had to endure excruciatingly painful deliveries. The search for an appropriate anesthesia, therefore, has occupied some medical researchers throughout the history of medicine. Anesthesia as a medical necessity has long been an accepted practice, and as long as sedatives have been available, some women have needed to use them. At the same time, as long as sedatives have been available, some women without a compelling medical condition have wanted to use them. The advances of modern medicine have made this not only easy but common.

Even before the discovery of sodium pentathol, doctors sedated some women with opiates, although the debilitating effect on both mother and child lingered for days. In contrast to the opiates, however, the introduction of sodium pentathol made available a relatively benign anesthetic with few side effects. Introduced in carefully controlled dosages intravenously, sodium pentathol, absorbed into the system quickly, induces a deep but temporary sleep, and its effects dissipate rapidly once the flow of medication is discontinued. Its effects on mother and baby are noticeable, but they are not nearly as pronounced as those of the sedatives used earlier. The increasing armory of pharmaceutical palliatives has led to the increasing use of drugs in the course of labor, until by now, despite the holdouts in the "natural childbirth" movement, the use of anesthesia is almost universal at some point before delivery.

Ironically, its very attractiveness has made sodium pentathol into something of a problem. Its lesser impact is the direct effect of sedation. Now almost all deliveries in modern hospitals involve some degree of sedation, although the "epidural," which involves local anesthesia delivered into the lower body to reduce rather than eliminate pain, is by far more common than the use of general anesthesia. The greater impact of sedation has been the dramatic increase in Caesarian sections. Once an emergency procedure used only in cases of extreme danger to mother or baby, it has become a common, and indeed routine, means of delivery. Some women prefer it both because they can avoid the pain of childbirth and because they can actually schedule the day and the hour of their delivery. Doctors like it because it makes the timing of delivery more predictable, and make it easier for them to avoid problems that might lead to lawsuits. Nonetheless, Caesarian sections are surgical procedures and have the effect of separating women from the traditional process of childbirth. Like so many modern inventions, sodium pentathol is a two-edged sword: it has removed some of the painful experiences from life, but it has also put greater distance between people and their experience of life.

1935: Mary McLeod Bethune Accepts a Government Position as Minority Affairs Advisor

(Social Reform)

In 1935, Mary McLeod Bethune, one of the most prominent African-American women of the twentieth century, became director of the Office of Minority Affairs of the National Youth Administration (NYA). It was the highest such office created for an African American by the Roosevelt administration, and Bethune became one of a handful of advisors to Roosevelt on minority affairs.

Mary McLeod Bethune, the seventeenth child of former slaves, probably would have succeeded in life under any circumstances, but she was fortunate enough to be provided with a scholarship from a young Colorado Quaker, whom she had never met. Bethune left home at the age of twelve and headed for Scotia Seminary in North Carolina. When she graduated from Scotia, Bethune earned another scholarship to the Moody Bible College in Chicago. Her plans to become a missionary in Africa were shattered when she could not find a parish that would sponsor her. From 1894 to 1904, Bethune taught at a series of schools, entered into a short-lived marriage, bore her only child, a son, and moved with him to Florida where she began the task of building an outstanding boarding school for African Americans.

Bethune's school in Daytona started out as a boarding school for girls only. Scraping together every dime she could earn or raise, she put her students in uniforms to hide any disparities in economic status. Bethune was able to solicit funding from Procter and Gamble, as well as from

John D. Rockefeller. By 1925, Bethune's school had grown so much that she began talks with the local Cookman Institute, an all-male school, that ultimately ended with their merger. The combined schools became Bethune-Cookman College in 1929, and the high school aspect of the school was phased out by 1936. After the merger, Bethune stayed on as president until 1942.

Bethune's concerns did not rest with building the school. When African Americans were denied treatment at white hospitals, Bethune helped to organize a hospital that trained African-American nurses and had a biracial medical staff. She was also instrumental in founding two of the most influential African-American women's organizations, the National Association of Colored Women and the National Council of Negro Women. She also served on committees of the National Association for the Advancement of Colored People (NAACP) and the National Urban League. She was a life member of the Association for the Study of Negro Life and History.

Through her work with the National Council of Negro Women, Bethune met and befriended Eleanor Roosevelt. That friendship led to Bethune's becoming a member of Roosevelt's "Black Cabinet," the group of advisors whose council he sought on minority affairs. When Roosevelt created the Office of Minority Affairs of the National Youth Administration in 1935, he turned to Bethune, appointing her director. Initially reluctant to accept the position, even though she knew it was tailor-made for her, Bethune eventually accepted. As with all her other endeavors, Bethune threw herself totally into the job, traveling hundreds of thousands of miles, meeting not only with African-Americans, but with Native Americans and Mexican Americans as well. She was a constant advocate for the NYA, setting up more schools for minorities in order to provide them with the education and training they so badly needed. More often than not, at meetings of the Black Cabinet, it was Bethune who controlled the agenda and pushed for integrated programs. During World War II, Bethune was a member of the Advisory Committee of the Women's Army Corps, and again lobbied for an integrated corps. In 1945, President Harry S Truman appointed Bethune to the first conference of the United Nations, making her the only nonwhite woman with official status. In addition, Bethune was a founder of the Central Life Insurance Company, which provided insurance to African-Americans, something that white insurance companies had refused to do for decades. In 1952, Bethune was the only woman president of a national insurance company in the United States.

1935: Billie Holiday Records with Teddy Wilson

(Cultural Life, Entertainment)

Called the most important female jazz artist of all time, Billie Holiday's professional career came into its own when she did a series of recordings with Teddy Wilson and his jazz band in 1935.

Billie Holiday, who was probably born on April 7, 1915, did not know her own birthday, and grew up as the lonely daughter of a domestic servant. Moving from Baltimore to New York when she was about twelve, she had already been earning much of her own living for two years, and she continued to work as an errand girl, maid, and then dancer to support herself and, increasingly, her sickly mother. When working as a dancer in a Harlem nightclub, she got the opportunity to sing, and the audience's response was overwhelming. In her words, "The whole joint quieted down. If someone had dropped a pin, it would have sounded like a bomb." She began singing for a few dollars and tips from midnight to the morning hours in 1931, when she was still a teenager. From the start, she maintained a noticeable dignity and wore gardenias in her hair—her trademark thereafter—for which she was derisively referred to as "Lady" by the other nightclub employees. In 1933, jazz enthusiast John Hammond arranged for Holiday to record without credit on a Benny Goodman record. But it was not until 1935, when, with Hammond again the facilitator, she cut her first credited records with Teddy Wilson and his jazz band, that Holiday's career became established.

The same year, 1935, she opened at Harlem's famed Apollo theatre, further establishing her stature as a leading jazz singer, and the next year she made her first starring record. She toured with both Count Basie and Artie Shaw in 1937 and 1938, and continued to sing in New York nightclubs and cut records for the next decade. From 1939 to 1941, Holiday sang at a Greenwich Village club called the Cafe Society Downtown. During those years, she recorded two of the songs that are still closely identified with her, "Strange Fruit," an antilynching song, and "God Bless the Child." She won the Esquire Jazz Critics Poll in 1944 and the Metronome Vocalist of the Year award in 1945. She made a movie that year as well, and toured America and Europe with a number of major artist in the late 40s and early 50s. She wrote her autobiography, *Lady Sings the Blues*, in 1956, and it was made into a motion picture in 1972, thirteen years after her death.

Behind her public and artistic successes, though, Holiday led a troubled personal life. She felt the sting of racial discrimination when she toured, despite her success, and was routinely denied service and accommodations. Even her stint in Hollywood was marred by the role she was given, that of a maid. She was disappointed in business and love by a series of lovers/managers who exploited and then abandoned her, and she was profoundly affected by the death of her mother in 1945. Her refuge from these problems became alcohol and drugs, but they compounded the situation. Arrested in 1947 for narcotics violations, she was barred from performing in New York from then on, which consigned her to lesser known locales. Periodic stints in a sanitarium and two more drug arrests in 1949 and 1956 failed to cure her of her heroin habit, and her final arrest came in 1959 when she was literally on her deathbed.

Despite, or perhaps because of, her personal travail, Billie Holiday sang with a unique beauty and poignancy. Jazz greats who recorded with her inevitably praised her inventiveness with melody and timing, compelling interpretations, and intuitive inflections, all of which combined to create her distinctive style. Her voice transported those who flocked to her live appearances, disregarding her personal and legal troubles, and it lives on in her recordings today.

1935: Congress Enacts the Social Security Act

(Social Reform)

In 1935, Congress passed the Social Security Act of 1935, the most comprehensive piece of social legislation to come out of the New Deal. Included in the Social Security Act were provisions for dependent women and children, the first time that guarantees were available to them, and included education benefits for children as well as mother's pensions.

Prior to passage of the Social Security Act of 1935, the government failed to acknowledge that the country had long before outgrown the idealized concept of Jeffersonian agricultural self-sufficiency of the eighteenth and nineteenth centuries. In an industrial society that periodically fell victim to the vagaries of severe market fluctuations, and whose workers had only rented apartments or mortgaged homes rather than the family farm to see them through economic difficulties, social reformers had long argued that some kind of government-guaranteed security was crucial. The New Deal, mandated to reform a crippled system that had been devastated by depression, represented an opportunity to insure that future generations would not be left unprotected when disaster struck.

The primary provision of the Social Security Act was to provide retirement pensions for workers who had reached age sixty-five or older. The provision covered both male and female workers. But in addition, it provided coverage for dependent wives and mothers with young children. This was really a victory for those women who had worked for decades trying to secure protective legislation for women and children. The protective legislationists, like Florence Kelley, Mary Anderson, and Mary Elizabeth Dreier, all of whom were close colleagues of First Lady Eleanor Roosevelt, had worked with the administration to secure these provisions. Next to the dramatic decrease in the number of women workers over the age of sixty-five, the greatest impact that Social Security had on the lives of Americans was the support of dependent widows and children, and the educational benefits that these children gained access to. But it took another forty years and the renewed feminist movement of the 1970s, for the government to make changes in the Social Security Act that afforded protection for homemakers who had spent years, sometimes decades, raising children and maintaining a home, only to be left without retirement protection when they were involved in a divorce.

Despite the criticisms of the system in its current form, Social Security has probably had as significant an economic impact on the lives of women as any other social reform enacted in the twentieth century.

1935: The National Council of Negro Women Is Organized

(Social Reform)

Organized in 1935 by Mary McLeod Bethune, Mary Church Terrell, Charlotte Hawkins Brown, and Mabel Staupers, among others, the National Council of Negro Women (NCNW) was created as an umbrella organization to unify efforts by African-American women to affect national public policy.

On December 5, 1935, after several years of planning and discussion, Mary McLeod Bethune called together a meeting of representatives of African-American women's organizations, for the purpose of founding an umbrella organization, the National Council of Negro Women. Before 1935, the National Association of Colored Women (NACW) was the most influential organization for African-American women. When Bethune had been struggling to establish her school in Florida, which ultimately became Bethune-Cookman College, she turned to the NACW for help. Bethune quickly perceived, though, that the NACW lacked enough of a feminist focus, in both structure and national influence, to make itself truly effective. Women interested in forming a new umbrella organization with whom Bethune spoke were also concerned that

the African-American women's club movement might be split as a consequence. When Bethune was appointed by the Roosevelt administration to direct the Office of Minority Affairs of the National Youth Administration, the time seemed right to proceed.

Bethune had won the support of fourteen women's groups, all of which sent representatives to New York to meet with Bethune on December 5, 1935. The NCNW was organized, as Bethune said, "to harness the great power of nearly a million women into a force for constructive action." Charlotte Hawkins Brown, the president of the North Carolina Federation of Women's Clubs, expressed concerns about the reaction of the NACW, which, she assumed, would be negative. But for those who were inclined to take the side of the NACW, Brown pointed out that the older organization never discussed issues related to the status of women in American life, nor did it establish committees for the specific purpose of evaluating the status of African-American women. The purpose of the NCNW, on the other hand, was to unite national organizations into a powerful force that could draw on the expertise of its member organizations and disseminate information necessary to achieve the goal of uplifting African-American women.

Bethune, the first president of the NCNW, spent its first years making the organization credible among other women's organizations and in the eyes of politicians with whom they lobbied for change. It became an advocate for a broad range of issues that directly affected African-American men as well as women. Most of its focus involved questions of acceptance, whether by labor unions, government as an employers, or the military. By the time Bethune turned over the presidency in 1949, the NCNW had achieved its initial goal of establishing itself as an influential organization directly accountable to millions of African-American women.

1935: Sulfonamides Are First Used Against Puerperal Fever

(Medicine, Family Life)

In 1935, sulfonamide drugs were first used to cure puerperal fever, otherwise known as "childbed fever," a leading cause of death among adult women since the beginning of recorded history.

Oliver Wendell Holmes' *The Contagiousness of Puerperal Fever,* published in 1853, had taught American doctors the importance of cleanliness when attending to women delivering babies. Although not readily adopted, eventually the medical profession did realize the wisdom of taking precautions, and in the decades after, cleanliness and sterile techniques became routine and deaths due to puerperal fever declined dramatically. Yet when a woman did contract the disease, there was little doctors

242

could do to help her. Once contracted, the disease was generally fatal.

The first step toward a cure rather than prevention came in 1879 when Louis Pasteur isolated a dotlike microorganism in the discharges of a woman with the fatal fever. Called *hemolytic streptococcus*, it was related to the streptococci that caused tonsillitis, scarlet fever, and fulminating surgical infections, all of which were often fatal. Other common organisms like *staphylococci, anaerobic streptococci, Escherichia coli, Clostridium welchii*, and, very occasionally, the bacillus of tetanus were also identified as causes of the fever, but the *hemolytic streptococcus* was the most common.

The real breakthrough against this killer of women, however, came in 1935, when doctors at Queen Charlotte's Isolation Hospital in London successfully administered sulfonamides to cure women infected with *hemolytic streptococcus*. Later, the same chemotherapy was used against other common causes of the illness, and in the 1940s, penicillin became available to cure the cases caused by *staphylococci*. After the 1940s, infection and death from puerperal fever were almost unknown in American hospitals. The occasional outbreaks were seen mainly as an embarrassment to the obstetric unit, for they evinced a breakdown of preventative measures that had come to be relied upon far more than the cure.

In more recent years, there has been some increase in the disease, caused mainly by strains of *staphylococci* that are resistant to antibiotics. The main measures against these have been to reduce the indiscriminate use of antibiotics, since it is this overexposure that leads to resistant strains. But, despite the appearance of these mutant strains, puerperal fever poses only a shadow of the danger to women that it once did.

1936: Margaret Mitchell Publishes *Gone With the Wind*

(Cultural Life)

After nine years of writing and rewriting several thousand pages of an untitled, unorganized novel, Margaret Mitchell's Pulitzer Prize–winning classic novel of the Old South, *Gone With the Wind*, was published by the Macmillan Company in 1936.

As far as Margaret Mitchell was concerned, her epic novel of the Old South was never written for publication. Mitchell, an Atlanta native whose family lived the plantation life for decades, began writing her novel in 1926, when an ankle injury forced her to retire from journalism. Although she had been a well-respected columnist writing under her "Peggy Mitchell" byline, Mitchell never considered herself a good writer. Mitchell was also not the eccentric recluse she was made out to be after publication of *Gone With the Wind*. Although she hated publicity about herself, Mitchell, perhaps recalling her own days as a journalist, was invariably cheerful and responsive with reporters.

Encouraged by friends who knew of her ever-growing manuscript to send it to a publisher, Mitchell always declined. But when a representative from Macmillan, who had heard of the manuscript, approached Mitchell on a visit to Atlanta, she showed up in his hotel room with stacks of paper tied in bundles. A brief moment of doubt caused Mitchell to send a telegram to the editor after he had left, telling him she had changed her mind and asking that he return the manuscript. Riding the train back to New York, the editor had read enough to know that he wanted to publish her story, and persuaded Mitchell to move ahead with the project.

When *Gone With the Wind* was published in 1936, it became an instant bestseller, with an incredible one-day record of fifty thousand volumes sold. The novel, whose name was taken from a poem by Ernest Dawson, followed two story lines. The first was the immutable bond between southern belle Scarlett O'Hara and the land that she grew up on, the family plantation, Tara. The second was the powerful love story of Scarlett and an iconoclastic war profiteer named Rhett Butler. In the process of telling these two stories, Mitchell also related the stories she had grown up with, handed down from generation to generation. Inarguably, her view was a nostalgic one with which critics could find fault, since it romanticized plantation life in the Old South, and therefore masked the national tragedy of slavery. But most critics overlooked this, and the public, in particular, responded in an overwhelmingly positive fashion.

A large part of the appeal of *Gone*

With the Wind rested with the character of Scarlett O'Hara. Critics enjoyed portraying Scarlett as the classic self-centered, shallow southern belle with little or no concept of honor or values. Readers, however, saw something different in Scarlett. They saw Scarlett as a strong-willed, indomitable force, evolving from a self-centered girl into a proud, unyielding woman who responded to the tragedy of war by doing what she had to in order to save herself, her family, and her land. It was a characterization that resonated with the millions of American readers who were enduring their own struggles with the depression and who could sympathize with a woman willing to give up everything for the land that was an inseparable part of her.

Gone With the Wind won a Pulitzer Prize in 1937. It was also made into one of the most successful motion pictures of all time. So great was public interest in *Gone With the Wind* that thousands of letters were sent to Hollywood executives, newspapers, and magazines, offering suggestions on who should be given the two primary roles, of Scarlett and Rhett Butler. Interestingly, most of the letter-writers immediately identified Clark Gable as the ideal Rhett Butler, but Scarlett was a more difficult part to cast. Hundreds of established actresses and hopefuls auditioned for the part, including Bette Davis, Katharine Hepburn, and Joan Crawford. In the end, a new English actress, Vivien Leigh, won the role of Scarlett. The 1939 premiere of *Gone With the Wind*, held in Atlanta, remains one of Hollywood's most elaborate and memorable events. Like the novel itself, the movie was the first blockbuster, remaining for decades the number one choice of all-time favorite film by moviegoers, a testament not only to the movie, but to Margaret Mitchell and one of the most enduring and intriguing heroines of modern fiction.

1936: Eleanor Roosevelt Transforms the Role of First Lady

(Social Reform, Politics)

By 1936, Eleanor Roosevelt had transformed the position of First Lady, taking an activist role in the twelve years that Franklin Delano Roosevelt served as president. Through networking, politicking, and publicity, she kept social reform in the forefront of New Deal legislation.

By virtue of her husband's four successive terms as president, Eleanor Roosevelt served as First Lady longer than any other woman in the nation's history. Because of the term limitations later placed on the presidency by constitutional amendment, she will always hold that distinction, unless further constitutional amendments change things. By the time that Roosevelt assumed the role of First Lady, she had developed a network of political, social, and personal friends that allowed her to take full advantage of her position in order to promote the ideas and legislation she believed in.

Prior to Roosevelt, First Ladies were largely confined to hostessing official Washington events, occasionally becoming a spokesperson for a particular cause. They little resembled modern First Ladies. They did not hold news conferences, they did not actively advocate causes, they did not represent their husbands on trips abroad or domestically, and they most certainly did not have opinions for public consumption. Eleanor Roosevelt changed all that. Because her husband had polio that severely limited his ability to get around freely, Roosevelt trav-

eled tens of thousands of miles during her twelve years in office, sending back official reports that the president could incorporate into his decision-making process. During World War II, Eleanor visited almost every theatre of war, meeting with American troops and reporting back on the state of affairs. Reporters covering the White House in those years were accustomed to hearing Franklin Roosevelt start a sentence by saying "My Missus says...."

Earlier in the New Deal, Roosevelt became the advocate of groups likely to be overlooked in the new legislation designed to alleviate the country's suffering. She insisted that a percentage of all New Deal programs had to be earmarked specifically for women's jobs and women's projects. She maintained almost constant contact with the head of the Women's Work Division of the Federal Emergency Relief Administration, Ellen Woodward. And she took a particular interest in the fate of the National Youth Administration, insuring that that agency would maintain a better sex and race ratio than other agencies seemed able to do. She had no qualms about donning a helmet to go down into the coal mines and inspect conditions there, or inviting African-American students from Nannie Burroughs' school to the White House, both of which generated a good deal of criticism. Indeed, most of the hate mail that Roosevelt received came from those who objected to her efforts on behalf of African-Americans. It was she who was responsible for the belief that developed among African-Americans that the New Deal had addressed their concerns, thus prompting one of the biggest single voting bloc switches in modern political history, turning African-Americans from the party of Lincoln to the Democratic party in the 1936 election. But far from being a cynical ploy to generate votes, the First Lady was a true believer in equality and civil rights. Her anger at the Daughters of the American Revolution (DAR), of which she was a member, when they refused Marian Anderson's request to hold a concert at Constitution Hall, was such that Roosevelt resigned from DAR and persuaded Secretary of the Interior Harold Ickes to allow Anderson to hold her concert at the Lincoln Memorial. When the military raised concerns about the ability of African-American pilots to fly planes, Roosevelt promptly dispelled their stereotypical biases by flying with black pilots. Although the Army Air Force did not integrate during the war, African-American fighter pilots assigned to a segregated fighter unit carried out their assignments with as much courage and skill as any other pilots in the service.

Roosevelt held news conferences at which only women reporters were allowed access, thereby promoting the careers of women journalists whose newspapers needed the crucial coverage. Moreover, her long-standing friendships with some of the most influential women of the twentieth century, including Jane Addams, Lillian Wald, Mary McLeod Bethune, Rose Schneiderman, and Mary Anderson, helped them to achieve mutual goals providing jobs and social services to women. This was especially important during the depression when, as Roosevelt well knew, it was the women who had primary responsibility for holding together families despite severe economic dislocation. She also helped to promote the careers of talented women, most especially that of Frances Perkins who became the first woman to serve in a cabinet position.

In addition to all of her other activities, both official and unofficial, Roosevelt wrote a daily column, *My Day*, in which she gave advice and encouragement to readers across the country. She wrote articles for national magazines, including *Woman's Day* and the *Ladies Home Journal*, and she had a weekly radio show, again offering advice and encouragement for the myriad problems people faced during the hard years of the depression and World War II.

Throughout her tenure as First Lady, Eleanor Roosevelt was subjected to criticism—some of it cruel references to her appearance and her voice, both of which were distinctive—but she never allowed her critics to determine her activities. She received thousands of letters as First Lady, most of them complimentary, and many of which she tried to answer personally, often including a small check or the name of a particular person who might be helpful in a job search. She never overlooked an opportunity to turn a critic into a friend, thus she spent as much time responding to unfavorable letters as she did favorable ones. The contributions she made to women throughout the world, to enhance their image, power, and self-esteem, have made Roosevelt one of the truly remarkable women of the twentieth century. Indeed, even decades after her death, Eleanor Roosevelt is still considered one of the most admired women of the century.

1936: The Federal Court Rules that the Comstock Law Definition of Obscenity Cannot Include Birth Control

(Family Life, Equal Rights)

In a case initiated by Margaret Sanger's Committee on Federal Legislation for Birth Control, a U.S. Federal Court ruled in 1936 that new information required a re-evaluation of the 1873 Comstock Law, which had outlawed the distribution of birth control or contraceptive materials through the mail. *United States v. One Package* was a clear and significant victory for the birth control movement.

For more than sixty years, the Comstock Law prevented American women from receiving information on birth control and contraceptives through the U.S. mail. Numerous people had been prosecuted under the law, including the radical Emma Goldman, by zealous enforcers who equated birth control with obscenity. When the Comstock Law was passed, physicians and the American Medical Association were in the forefront of those who supported the legislation. Because of the enormous amount of education and research carried out by people like Margaret Sanger, and because a prohibition against sending contraceptive and birth control information through the mails no longer served the purposes of the AMA, physicians, for the most part, now favored the dissemination of such information. So it was something of an irony that physicians' hands were tied because of a law that the AMA had endorsed more than half a century before.

For years, Sanger conducted guerrilla warfare against the legal system in an effort to overturn the most harmful impediments to establishing a meaningful birth control movement. From smuggling illegal diaphragms into the United States, to testing the constitutionality of laws outlawing contraceptives, Sanger campaigned vigorously to secure reproductive control for women. Sanger's Committee on Federal Legislation for Birth Control initiated a legal suit to test the Comstock Law when it sent contraceptive material through the mail, confident that the material would be seized by the Post Office. The resultant suit, *United States v. One Package*, was decided by a federal court in 1936. In its decision, the court ruled that new clinical information regarding contraceptives forced a reinterpretation of the Comstock Law. Birth control, the court declared, was not synonymous with obscenity, and henceforth, mailing contraceptive information intended for use by physicians would no longer be illegal.

The court's reversal of the Comstock Law interpretation and its new ruling regarding appropriate birth control materials, cleared the way for a resolution passed the following year by the American Medical Association. In 1937, the AMA voted to recognize contraception as a legitimate medical service that should be taught in medical schools. Sanger's goal of winning over professional medical support for birth control had come to pass. Birth control had achieved the legitimacy necessary for its success.

1938: Pearl Buck Wins the Nobel Prize for Literature

(Cultural Life)

In 1938, Pearl S. Buck won the Nobel Prize for Literature, just eight years after she published her first book. She was the first American woman to win this honor, and the only one until Toni Morrison joined her in 1993.

Pearl Buck's parents were missionaries, so while she was born in West Virginia, she grew up in China. After attending Randolph-Macon Woman's College in Virginia, she returned to Asia to work as a teacher, which she did until she married an American agriculturalist, John Buck, in 1917. She moved with him to northern China where she lived among the peasantry and gained much of the knowledge that would inform her greatest book. She bore one child, who was retarded, and adopted another while teaching at the University of Nanking.

Buck began writing in 1922 while nursing her ailing mother, and her first story was published by *Asia Magazine* in 1925 when she returned to the United States to get help for her daughter. She earned a master's degree from Cornell University and returned to teach at two universities in China in addition to Nanking. She continued to teach there until 1931 despite the growth of antiforeign feelings, which resulted in 1927 in the loss of the manuscript of her first novel when she and her husband had to flee their home and hide with friends to avoid an uprising. She published her first novel, *East Wind: West Wind* in 1930, and the next year brought out her masterpiece, *The Good Earth*. This book brought her instant success: it won the Pulitzer Prize, was made into a play and an Academy Award–winning film, was translated into dozens of languages, and sold millions of copies. Buck herself was suddenly rich and famous.

She wrote two more books in the three years she remained in China, and left both the country and her long-estranged husband in 1934. Marrying her publisher in 1935, she began to churn out books and articles at an amazing rate over the next forty years. She produced one book in the year of her marriage, two in the following year, translated two volumes from Chinese in 1937, and in the following decades produced as many as five books in a single year. She published extensively in popular magazines, and wrote on topics ranging from children's books to widely read commentaries on Far Eastern affairs. Her work was imbued with her belief in toleration and internationalism, and her views made her more controversial as time went on. During the McCarthy era she published under a pseudonym (successfully), but went back to her own name when she saw that they were still well-received.

Buck's liberalism was not limited to her writing. She created the East and West Association in 1941 to sponsor cultural exchanges, and she served for ten years as president of the Author's Guild, an organization dedicated to free speech, in the late 1950s and early 1960s. She created a foundation to care for the unwanted children of Asian mothers and American fathers, and went beyond that measure by adopting a half-dozen mixed-race children herself. She also supported care for the mentally retarded, and in her works, she dealt with many women's issues.

Buck's politics, as well as her readiness to publish whatever she wrote, earned her numerous critics, but in both her writing and her life she proved to be irrepressible. Either her social activism or her cultural contributions would have constituted a tremendous legacy; the combination marks her as one of the truly remarkable American women of the twentieth century.

1938: The Fair Labor Standards Act Establishes Minimum Wages

(Work, Equal Rights)

In 1938, Congress passed the Fair Labor Standards Act (FLSA), which established minimum wages and maximum hours in businesses engaged in interstate commerce. It also prohibited child labor, defined as anyone under the age of sixteen, in the same industries.

The depression years were difficult ones for most people who normally held industrial jobs. Working women were caught in the double bind of needing to work more than ever because of the overall state of the economy and the probability that one or more contributors to the family income were unemployed, and a public perception that women should not be taking a job that a man could do. Those women who did find themselves employed during the depression were likely working for seriously reduced wages. In some textile mills in the South, women worked for five cents an hour, and some unscrupulous manufacturers would hire women apprentices with the provision that they would not begin earning wages until the apprenticeship was completed. When that time approached, the apprentices would be fired. So, for these

and other reasons, advocates of protective legislation and minimum wage laws continued to lobby for those reforms even at the height of the depression.

Minimum wage laws had been on the protectionists' agenda since the turn of the century. Indeed, many states had passed minimum wage laws, and sometimes ten-hour workday laws, only to have the Supreme Court declare them unconstitutional. As late as 1935, the Supreme Court was still finding fault with establishing wages and hours when it struck down the National Industrial Recovery Act (NIRA), a New Deal effort to revive the economy that included establishing wage and hour guidelines according to industry. Almost immediately, the Roosevelt administration responded with new legislation to take the place of the NIRA. The Fair Labor Standards

Act was passed by Congress in 1938.

Under the terms of the FLSA, which applied to all workers in specified industries without differentiating on the basis of sex or age, a minimum wage of twenty-five cents per hour was established. Over a seven year period, this would increase to forty cents per hour. At the same time, a maximum work week of forty-four hours was imposed. This would decrease to forty hours over time. The FLSA prohibited the employment of children under the age of sixteen. The administration and everyone else waited, of course, for the Supreme Court to rule on the constitutionality of the new legislation before relying on its permanency (though the FLSA had to be observed by all parties in the meantime). As everyone expected, the wait was relatively short. In 1941, the Court ruled, in the case of *United States v. Darby*, that the FLSA did not violate the constitution.

After nearly four decades of effort, a minimum wage law protecting women and men was in place. The FLSA was not without some flaws. It did not cover, for example, domestic work or farm work, which meant that African-American women were largely left out of the loop. In 1930, 90 percent of African-American women employed worked either as domestic or farm laborers, when they could find employment. For most African-American women, the 1930s were spent unemployed. Moreover, they were least likely to be included in federal relief programs. On the plus side, whereas previous wage and hour restrictions applied only to women and only covered about 12 percent of the adult female work force, the FLSA covered 57 percent of women workers and 38 percent of male workers. Of course, the elimination of child labor, which had been fought for for so long, was finally accomplished as well.

1939: Karen Horney Publishes *New Ways in Psychoanalysis*

(Family Life)

In her second book, *New Ways in Psychoanalysis*, Karen Horney opened the feminist challenge to classical Freudianism. She rejected the portions that treat women as a somehow dysfunctional version of men, and stood the notion of "penis envy" on its head by suggesting that childbirth and breastfeeding are such fulfilling experiences that men may suffer from "womb envy."

Born in Germany in 1885, Karen Horney was educated at her mother's insistence over the strenuous objections of her father, earning a medical degree from the University of Berlin in 1911. She practiced psychiatry in that city for the next two decades, while raising her three children. She emigrated to America in 1932, settling first in Chicago and two years later in New York.

Her move to New York resulted from her growing differences with the Chicago Institute for Psychoanalysis, but she soon found herself at odds with the psychoanalytic establishment in New York as well. Her first book, *The Neurotic Personality of Our Time* (1937), advanced her view that many psychological problems reflected cultural practices, challenging the orthodox view that held culture as a relative constant and focused instead on how well an individual adapted to his or her surroundings. This book was challenging without being especially disputatious but her second book provoked a storm of controversy. Building on the ideas developed in the first work, Horney pushed farther her challenges to Freudian orthodoxy, especially in relation to women.

In 1941, the New York psychoanalytic establishment responded to her heresy by disqualifying her from acting as a training analyst, which is the highest institutional position psychoanalysts can achieve in their careers. Horney responded by joining with several colleagues to form a new association, the Association of the Advancement of Psychoanalysis. She edited the association's journal and served as dean of its affiliated training program, the American Institute for Psychoanalysis, from its founding until her death in 1952.

Horney's iconoclastic positions alienated her from the psychoanalytic establishment of her time, but she won the support of a considerable body of professionals then and influenced succeeding generations of psychologists. Her willingness to challenge Freud directly, her insistence that culture be seen as a variable rather than a constant in psychological analysis, and her favorable view of female sexuality all formed a legacy that presaged and contributed to the radical revisions of psychological understanding in the succeeding generation.

1939: Marian Anderson Sings at the Lincoln Memorial

(Social Reform, Cultural Life)

Marian Anderson, considered the greatest contralto of her generation and perhaps of the twentieth century, scheduled to sing at a concert in Washington, D.C., at Constitution Hall, was denied permission by the hall's owners, the Daughters of the American Revolution. With the assistance of first lady Eleanor Roosevelt, Anderson sang instead at the Lincoln Memorial on Easter Sunday, 1939.

When the Daughters of the American Revolution denied Marian Anderson permission to hold a concert at Constitution Hall because of her race, they could not have guessed how much their actions would advance the cause of civil rights in America. Anderson, at the time, had already achieved remarkable success in Europe, where there was less hostility toward African-Americans. In the early 1930s, Anderson made several tours of Europe, during which she performed before royalty and at some of the most prestigious concert halls in Europe. Composer Jean Sibelius was so overcome by her sheer talent that he wrote a composition especially for her.

In between European tours, Anderson had the opportunity to meet with First Lady Eleanor Roosevelt in 1936. The two women struck up a friendship that was to last for the remainder of their lives. Three years later, after performing before integrated audiences in the United States to rave reviews, Howard University sponsored a concert featuring Anderson. Attempts to secure Constitution Hall for the performance were rejected by the Daughters of the American Revolution. When Eleanor Roosevelt heard about DAR's action, she was outraged and ashamed. A member of DAR, Roosevelt was offended that they could treat anyone, least of all Marian Anderson, so disrespectfully. In protest, Roosevelt publicly resigned her DAR membership, leaving no doubt as to her reasons.

It was Roosevelt's idea to reschedule the concert at the Lincoln Memorial, an altogether appropriate venue under the circumstances. With the assistance of Secretary of the Interior Harold Ickes, permission was obtained to hold the concert on Easter Sunday, 1939. Other Americans publicly added their sponsorship to the concert, including Supreme Court justices, cabinet members, and prominent women such as Clare Booth Luce and Katharine Hepburn. Anderson sang before an audience of seventy-five thousand people that day. Her initial disappointment in being rejected by DAR was evident for, as she noted, "It was a thing for which I had wished for a long, long time." But her gratitude to Roosevelt, who she characterized as "an extraordinary person," was equally evident. She realized that Roosevelt's gesture allowed her the opportunity to make a significant statement at a time when African-Americans had few opportunities to do so. The Anderson concert is often described as the first modern civil rights protest. Anderson, through her grace and extraordinary talent, helped to break down racial barriers in classical music. She was, moreover, a symbol of African-American womanhood throughout the world.

1939: Grandma Moses' Paintings Are Exhibited at the Museum of Modern Art

(Cultural Life)

In 1938, Anna Mary Robertson Moses, known as Grandma Moses, sold several of her primitive paintings to an art collector. He was so impressed with the paintings that in 1939 he included them in an exhibit at the Museum of Modern Art in New York.

Grandma Moses, perhaps the foremost of the American primitive painters of the twentieth century, did not begin her career as an artist until after her seventy-seventh birthday. A farm wife born on the eve of the Civil War in rural New York, Moses married at the age of twenty-seven and bore a total of ten children, five of whom survived infancy. Having moved to Virginia with her farmer husband, she moved back to her native New York after her husband's death in 1927. But it was not until 1937 that she took up painting, and then only because arthritis had made needlework too uncomfortable to continue. With no thought that she was painting for anyone other than herself and perhaps her family, Moses used old pieces of board painted white as her canvasses. Her works featured happy scenes of rural life, ranging from various depictions of farm chores, to apple pickers in orchards, to homey scenes of Christmas.

Two years after she began painting, Moses took several of her works to a Woman's Exchange, as did many of her neighbors in the depression years, hopeful that she might be able to use them for barter. Spotted by an art collector, her paintings and their simplistic depictions of rural life, im-

mediately attracted his attention. After buying as many of her paintings as he could, the collector made them part of an exhibit at the Museum of Modern Art in New York in 1939. Moses' paintings were popular with both the public and with critics, who were taken with her primitive style. In 1940, at the age of eighty, Grandma Moses had her own one-woman show and drew both national attention and critical acclaim. Grandma Moses continued painting for another twenty years, until her death in 1961, never straying from the style that had made her famous. Over the years, her popularity increased and the value of her paintings grew accordingly. She finished nearly 1500 paintings before her death at the age of 101. Ironically, while her paintings were critically received and she attracted numerous imitators, her family never took her seriously as an artist, never quite able to believe that her stick figures and unsophisticated use of color were considered works of art by collectors around the world.

1940s: Dorothea Lange and Margaret Bourke-White Win Honors for Photographic Essays

(Cultural Life, Work)

Two of America's premier photographers of the twentieth century, Dorothea Lange and Margaret Bourke-White, were honored for their work in the early 1940s. Dorothea Lange became the first woman to be awarded a Guggenheim Fellowship in 1941, and Margaret Bourke-White became the first female war correspondent in 1942, as the official photographer for the U.S. Air Force.

For almost four decades, from the late 1920s through the 1960s, two of the world's best photographers were American women. Dorothea Lange and Margaret Bourke-White created brilliant photographs that captured the pain, despair, hope, determination, and humanity in the faces of Americans during two of the most trying experiences of the twentieth century: the Great Depression and World War II. Both women were frequent contributors to *Life* magazine's pictorial cavalcade. A Margaret Bourke-White photograph was chosen to grace the cover of the very first issue of Life in 1936. As a consequence, hundreds of millions of people around the world have seen one or more photographs taken by Lange and Bourke-White.

Dorothea Lange always wanted to be a photographer from the time she was a child growing up in New York City. She completed a degree in teacher training but never taught, and very briefly studied photography at Columbia. But a move to San Francisco, marriage, and two children ended her formal training. In San Francisco, Lange gained a reputation as a portrait photographer. Her own success did not insulate her from the misery of others, and as the depression deepened in the early 1930s, Lange began photographing the faces of white-collar workers who, for the first time in their lives, were unemployed. A 1934 exhibit of those photographs led to a job with the Farm Security Administration. Given the task of putting on film the lives of farm workers, she helped the rest of America see how bleak farm life had become. Her 1939 book of photographs, *American Exodus: A Record of Human Erosion,* won critical acclaim as well as popular success. Lange, the first woman to win a Guggenheim Fellowship, turned her camera toward another subject shortly after World War II began. As a photographer for the War Relocation Authority (WRA), she recorded the internment of Japanese-Americans in detention camps. While the WRA expected her photos to reflect their point of view, Lange chose instead to record from the point of view of those imprisoned. As a result, she left the WRA and went on to another agency for the duration of the war. After the war, Lange's work appeared regularly in *Life* magazine, and the final few years of her life were spent pulling together a collection to be placed on exhibit at the Museum of Modern Art, the first woman to be so honored. Lange died in 1965, but five years earlier, one of her most poignant photographs from the depression years—*Migrant Mother*—was chosen as one of the fifty best photographs of the century.

Margaret Bourke-White helped to invent the genre of photographic essay. As one of *Life* magazine's original staff, she not only produced the first cover photograph of the first issue of *Life,* but her photos were regularly featured there thereafter. As a young photojournalist, Bourke-White focused on an area generally considered to belong to men: industry. In 1929, *Fortune* magazine hired Bourke-White as a staff photographer. A self-proclaimed feminist since her early youth, Bourke-White never refused a job because it was "inappropriate" for a woman. She traveled to Russia several times, and in 1931, her first book, *Eyes on Russia,* was well-received by many Americans suffering the ravages of the depression. Eventually, Bourke-White published two more collections of photographs focusing on the Russian people. Not yet in her mid-thirties, Bourke-White could already claim a solid reputation with a number of publishers. She, like Lange, spent part of the depression years traveling America, especially in the South, recording the lives of the desperately poor. For Bourke-White, this sojourn was more than a journalistic exercise, for it opened her own eyes to subjects far more interesting than the dispassionate industrial photographs with which she had earlier been preoccupied. In this, Bourke-White was influenced by her association with Erskine Caldwell, with whom she collaborated on several projects and eventually married. They did two subsequent depression books, including the remarkable *Have You Seen Their Faces?*, published in 1937, which elevated her photography to new heights.

When World War II began, Bourke-White immediately began lobbying for a war correspondent slot, and in 1942, she became the first woman provided with credentials from the army identifying her as a war correspondent. As with everything she did, Bourke-White threw herself wholly into covering the war, bringing back the faces of American servicemen, sometimes at the risk of her own life. During the North African invasion in 1942, she was on board a ship that was torpedoed, and when Patton's army crossed the German border,

Bourke-White crossed with them. When Bourke-White sent back extraordinary photos of Buchenwald, *Life*'s editors had to decide whether to go with the long-standing tradition of not printing the most excruciating scenes of battle, or to break with that rule and print what they knew to be the most compelling photos of the war. Bourke-White's photos ran in *Life*. After the war, Bourke-White continued her quest for photos that told entire stories. In India, she took the last photo of Gandhi before his assassination, she covered rebellion in South Africa, and she covered the Korean War. Altogether, before her retirement, Bourke-White spent thirty-three years as *Life*'s leading photographer.

Both Bourke-White and Lange showed the world pictures of itself and in the process revealed their own humanity.

1941: Women Are Accepted into the Armed Forces in Roles Other than Nursing

(Work, Equal Rights)

During World War II, for the first time women were accepted into the military in a variety of roles heretofore forbidden to them. No longer confined to nursing duties, women were employed in almost every occupational category except combat.

Since the turn of the century, women have served in the military as nurses in formally organized, permanent military units. In 1901, the Army Nurse Corps was established, followed in 1908 by the Navy Nurse Corps. For the next thirty years, with one brief exception, women were allowed to serve in the military only in the role of nurses. During World War I, a loophole in the legislation affecting military personnel allowed the government to enlist women as navy yeomen, filling jobs as telephone operators and clerks in order to relieve male personnel for active duty. Despite the outstanding service performed by the female yeomen during World War I, that loophole was soon closed. Unofficially, of course, women have served the nation in a variety of military capacities as far back as the Revolutionary War, when women traveled with Washington's army as nurses and quartermasters. In that war and in the Civil War, numerous instances of women disguising themselves as men in order to join combat units have been recorded.

When the United States entered World War II, women began to be officially accepted into military units in roles other than nursing. Representative Edith Nourse Rogers of Massachusetts sponsored legislation to establish a women's army corps, and on May 15, 1942, President Franklin Roosevelt signed PL-554, creating the Women's Auxiliary Army Corps (WAAC), which had partial military status. In 1943, Congress abolished the WAAC in favor of the Women's Army Corps (WAC), which had full military status with rank and benefits equal to those of male personnel. On July 30, 1942, PL-689 created the WAVES (Women Accepted for Volunteer Emergency Service). WAVES had the same status as male reservists. Mildred McAfee, the president of Wellesley College, became the first director of the WAVES, with the rank of Navy Captain. Women in the U.S. Coast Guard, called SPARS, from *Semper Paratus* (Always Prepared), the Coast Guard motto, were also accepted on the same basis as male reservists in this military branch, created four months after the WAVES. The Marines did not create a women's corps until February 1943, nor did they assign a distinctive name to their female marines. Marines were simply marines.

Most African-American women

who served in the military belonged to the WAC. The WAC accepted both white and black enlistees, although, like the men's service, there was segregation within the corps and, of course, discrimination. In the Navy, plans to increase African-American enrollment to 10 percent never reached fruition, and by 1945 there were still less than fifty African-American WAVES. Even fewer African-Americans served with either the SPARS or the marines.

In all of the women's branches of the military service, women freed up men for combat posts during World War II. They performed any job that was not classified as combat. Although there was considerable doubt in the beginning regarding women's abilities to perform military jobs, when the military brass discovered how efficiently these women performed their jobs, generals asked for more women to take the place of men, who could then be freed up for combat. Dwight Eisenhower, as Supreme Allied Commander, asked for more WACs than belonged to the entire corps. Over the course of the war, approximately 350,000 women joined various branches of the service. At peak strength, 271,000 women were members of the military. Of this number, approximately 4,000 were African-Americans, not because they were any less patriotic, but because there was simply less opportunity.

The controversy over whether women should be allowed to take on combat roles continues to exist, although there are signs that even those barriers are crumbling. In 1993, women aviators were given permission to fly fighter jets. Breaking down the combat job barrier is considered important because top level command posts in the military have always gone exclusively to individuals with combat experience.

1941: World War II Increases the Demand for Women Workers

(Work)

Confronted with an immediate outflow of male workers into the military services, and the necessity to maximize production in order to supply a vastly increased army, World War II provided women workers with more opportunities in a greater variety of fields than they had ever previously enjoyed. By 1945, women made up more than half the labor force in the United States.

Many of the new opportunities opened up to women as a result of the United States' entry into World War II would turn out to be temporary. But in very profound ways, the war initiated changes in the American work force and in the lives of women from which there was no going back.

The immediate problem facing the American government was that of quickly producing the tools necessary to challenge effectively the German and Japanese armies, both of which had been stockpiling for years. Everything from uniforms to bombers had to be produced. The Roosevelt administration was asking for, among other things, fifty thousand new airplanes each year—a task that many industrialists feared was impossible. To make matters worse, the attack on Pearl Harbor had destroyed a significant portion of the American navy. Battleships, destroyers, troop ships, aircraft carriers, supply ships—the necessity for more of everything was daunting, to say the least.

In order to accomplish the monumental production task, industrialists turned to a previously untapped labor source: middle-class women. The de-sire to contribute to the war effort and reasonable compensation attracted hundreds of thousands of women who had never before been involved in the industrial work force. As an example of how capable the new labor force was, by 1944, industry was turning out 120,000 new airplanes every year, far exceeding the initial requests that everyone assumed would be impossible to fulfill.

Between 1940 and 1945, the number of women in the American work force increased from twelve million to nineteen million. Former barriers to employment, including marital status and age, were removed from many jobs, including teaching. While "Rosie the Riveter" was a highly publicized icon symbolizing the willingness of women to participate in the war effort, women were entering a number of previously restricted jobs, and in some cases, by the war's end, the job category had been transferred from male to female. During the depression, white-collar jobs, including bank tellers, cashiers, and office clerks, were considered male jobs. By the end of the war, these jobs had become female jobs. One of the biggest changes came about in government employment. Previously, most government employees were men. Over the course of the war, women moved into government jobs in unprecedented numbers, and the government became the single largest employer of female workers.

Domestic service largely disappeared during the war as thousands of African-Americans, who had made up the vast majority of domestic servants, left these jobs in order to work in other areas, particularly defense factories. Fully half the African-Americans who had held domestic service jobs quit in order to take more lucrative and higher status jobs. As a consequence, the remaining domestic servants could ask for higher wages and better work conditions.

Professional women also found themselves in demand for the first time. Military commissions for female physicians who wanted to enter the service, real lawyer jobs for women who previously could count on only legal secretary work even with their law degrees, administrators, teachers, and journalists—in all of these professional occupations, women found themselves able to move beyond previous, underemployed levels.

The shape of the work force and its impact on women was felt in other ways as well. The percentage of married women entering the work force increased by more than one-third, from 18 to almost 25 percent. This trend continued even after the war ended. At the same time, women were experiencing on a large scale the double phenomenon of taking sole responsibility for making family decisions regarding everything including the allocation of financial resources, to earning a paycheck over which they had sole discretion. Before the war, most women said they wanted only to work outside the home until the war was over and the soldiers returned home. By the end of the war, their lives and sensibilities had changed so markedly that more than half now wanted to remain in the work force for both personal fulfillment and to continue earning their own money. For young, single women, work was also changed immutably. Many of them traveled away from home for the first time in order to take advantage of job opportunities. The whole notion of delaying marriage and family in order to have a career, however brief, also took hold among many women.

In significant ways, then, the war changed American women in their outlook toward family issues, in their desire to earn their own way, in their willingness to take advantage of new opportunities, and in their refusal to return to prewar sensibilities. At the same time, some things in the area of employment did not change in any fundamental way. Job categories tended to still move along two tracks, with some jobs classified as male and some as female, with very little oppor- tunity for women to cross over these arbitrary lines. Wages for male workers in equivalent jobs also continued to be higher than wages for female workers. By and large, however, women did make significant gains as a consequence of the war.

1942: Planned Parenthood Adopts a New Name over the Objections of Margaret Sanger

(Social Reform, Family Life)

In 1942, the American Birth Control League changed its name to Planned Parenthood Federation of American, over the objections of birth control pioneer Margaret Sanger. The change was made by the ruling majority of the Birth Control League because they believed that "Planned Parenthood" had a more positive connotation that would make it more acceptable to the American public.

Margaret Sanger spent most of her life fighting for the right of American women to have free and open access to birth control information. She raised money, defied authorities, challenged laws, and even went to jail for the cause she believed in so passionately. In 1921, she coined the term "birth control," and conse- quently harbored a proprietary feeling about the name of the organization she founded, the American Birth Control League. By 1942, however, control of the league was no longer in Sanger's hands. By then it had become a predominantly male-led organization, although that seemed not to have been a major factor in deciding to change the name.

Birth control, for many people in America, would always have negative associations. Moreover, religious groups, notably the Roman Catholic church, considered it a mortal sin to practice birth control. Finally, proponents of the name change argued that the organization had long since stopped being solely concerned with birth control. In addition to distributing contraceptive information, a number of infertile couples had also been counseled at birth control clinics. Nevertheless, Sanger raised predictably loud public objections when the decision was made. But in 1942, the American Birth Control League officially became the Planned Parenthood Federation of America. The two most prominent names associated with Planned Parenthood since the 1940s have been Dr. Mary Calderone and, more recently, Faye Wattleton.

Planned Parenthood now maintains approximately 750 centers around the country, dispensing not only contraceptive information, but information about abortion, sterilization, infertility, and menopause. One of the fastest growing Planned Parenthood constituencies in recent years has been unmarried teenagers. Planned Parenthood, aware that teen pregnancy and sexually transmitted diseases are on the rise, has spent a considerable amount on campaigns directed at teenagers. But teenage pregnancy is not the only issue that has kept Planned Parenthood on the front lines. Acquired Immunodeficiency Syndrome (AIDS), now into its second decade as the deadliest sexually transmitted disease in history, now occupies a primary place on the Planned Parenthood agenda. But by far the most controversial service provided by Planned Parenthood—advice on abortion—has led to confrontations in recent years that have literally placed the organization under siege. It seems likely that the confrontations between those who advocate or support abortion and those who call themselves right-to-life advocates are likely to continue.

1942: The WASPs Are Created by Jackie Cochran and General "Hap" Arnold

(Equal Rights, Aviation)

After proving her ability to fly in England, female pilot Jackie Cochran sought to establish a women's air force shortly after the United States entered World War II. Refused permission to organize as a branch of the U.S. military, Cochran and General "Hap" Arnold created the Women's Air Service Pilots (WASPs) in Sweetwater, Texas, in 1942.

Decades before World War II began, women had been flying airplanes. In 1911, seven years after the historic flight at Kitty Hawk, the first American woman, Harriet Quimby, earned her pilot's license. By the time America entered the first world war, eleven women held pilot's licenses, but many, many more were flying without a license. Women pilots were prominent during the barnstorming 1920s, and at least one woman, Mabel Cody, owned her own Flying Circus. By 1929, the first women pilots' air race had been established, attracting some women who wanted the prize money, but many more who wanted to demonstrate their skills as pilots. Perhaps the most famous woman pi-

lot, Amelia Earhart, made her historic solo flight across the Atlantic in 1932.

Another female pilot, Jackie Cochran, had won seventeen speed races by 1940, including beating out a field of male aviators in the 1936 Bendix Transcontinental Air Race. When World War II erupted in Europe, Cochran immediately began thinking about a women's air force, and contacted Eleanor Roosevelt to enlist her support in bringing the idea to fruition. For two years, Cochran lobbied politicians to no avail. Finally, in the summer of 1941, frustrated with American neutrality that kept it on the sidelines while nations fell to fascism, Cochran contracted to fly a bomber from Canada to England, and joined the British Air Transport Authority, as a captain. She then began recruiting other American women pilots. Until December 1941, they flew all types of military aircraft, from the giant bombers to small experimental fighters. When Pearl Harbor was attacked, bringing the United States into the war, Cochran returned to the United States. With the help of Air Corps General "Hap" Arnold, she created the Women's Air Service Pilots, in Sweetwater, Texas.

The WASPs was not a military organization. Women who wanted to join had to have their own pilot's license and at least two hundred hours of flying time. They had to pay their own way to Sweetwater, and initially they had to supply their own wardrobe because uniforms were not issued until the lack of them created problems for the women pilots. They also had to undergo a six-month-long training program. As civilians contracting with the Army Air Corps, the WASPs lived in military housing and followed military orders. But they had no military rank nor benefits, including insurance. When a WASP died in the line of duty, as thirty-eight of them did, their families were expected to pay for funeral expenses. In one instance, a WASP head-of-household

supporting several children died in a plane crash. Although she had over 2,500 hours of flying time with the WASPs, her comrades had to take up a collection to send her body back home.

For nearly three years, the WASPs flew every type of military aircraft that male pilots flew. Primary tasks included breaking in and delivering new planes, towing glider planes for the male cadets learning to fly, towing targets for gunnery practice, and flying tracking planes for artillery students learning to follow planes at night. WASPs also had to test out planes that cadets reported with mechanical problems. In an effort to reproduce the reported problems, the WASPs put the planes through dangerous maneuvers, obviously at the risk of their own lives.

Toward the end of 1944, Cochran, believing that the WASPs had more than proved their value to the war effort, appeared before Congress to demand that it either make the organization a military branch or disband it. Already under pressure from male pilots looking ahead to flying jobs in the post-war environment, Congress refused to upgrade the WASPs to military status. By Christmas 1944, the over one thousand WASPs were on their way home.

1945: Eleanor Roosevelt Joins the U.S. Delegation to the United Nations

(Social Reform)

Following the death of President Franklin Delano Roosevelt in 1945, his successor, President Harry S Truman, appointed Eleanor Roosevelt to the U.S. delegation to the United Nations, then in the process of being organized.

When Franklin Delano Roosevelt died on April 12, 1945, Eleanor Roosevelt wasted little time in vacating the White House and returning to her Hyde Park cottage, Val-Kill. Reporters, soliciting her about future plans, were told that she was now retired from public life. "The story," she said, "is over." If anyone, including herself, actually believed that this most dynamic of women would remain out of the public eye, they were wrong. Roosevelt wrote long letters to Truman, encouraging him to go forward with civil rights, to maintain the Fair Employment Practices Commission, and to work for a foreign policy where atomic weapons would not be negotiating chips in international relations. Late in 1945, Truman appointed Roosevelt to the U.S. delegation to the United Nations. On New Year's Eve, she flew to London for the initial meeting of the United Nations.

Despite her long experience in politics, many of the old hands in the State Department doubted Roosevelt's ability as the only woman delegate to rise to the occasion as a diplomat. They might have better spent their wasted energy on more productive concerns. For two years, in exhausting meetings in Geneva, Paris, New York, and San Francisco, Roosevelt chaired the Human Rights Commission. An endless series of quarrels developed between those who wanted human rights to revert to individual nations and those, like Roosevelt, who wanted a universal declaration of human rights. Indeed, Roosevelt was the main proponent of the universal declaration. Facing down communists who consistently impugned the motives of the United States—although never Roosevelt's—the document that eventually was brought forth from the Human Rights Commission stood as a beacon for all the world to emulate and aspire to. The United Nations Declaration of Human Rights was a victory of human rights over states' rights. On December 10, 1948, the Universal Declaration of Human Rights, fundamentally the creation of Eleanor Roosevelt, was adopted. In honor of her monumental effort to secure the declaration, Roosevelt was accorded a standing ovation by the full United Nations body. Even those critics who had been most adamantly opposed to Roosevelt's appointment to the United Nations retracted their criticism. Notably, her old adversary from New Deal days, Senator Arthur Vandenberg of Michigan, declared, "I want to say that I take back everything I ever said about her, and believe me, it's been plenty." The woman who had often been a figure of scorn and ridicule by conservative opponents during the New Deal was quickly becoming a national heroine. Shortly after her death in 1962, Roosevelt became the posthumous recipient of the first United Nations Human Rights prize. "What other human being," Adlai Stevenson asked at her memorial service, "has touched and transformed the existence of so many?"

1946: Emily Greene Balch Is Awarded the Nobel Peace Prize

(Social Reform)

For her lifetime of work on behalf of peace and freedom, in 1946 Emily Greene Balch became only the fourth woman and the second American to receive the Nobel Peace Prize.

Since its inception in 1901, the Nobel Peace Prize has been awarded to only four women, two of whom were Americans. Jane Addams was the first American woman so honored in 1931, and Emily Greene Balch became the second American woman Nobel Peace Laureate in 1946. Not surprisingly, the paths of these two women crossed frequently from the early years of the twentieth century until Addams' death in 1935.

Like Addams, Emily Balch's life was profoundly altered by the degree of poverty she found when working at a settlement house that she had helped to found in Boston, Massachusetts. It caused the Bryn Mawr graduate to redirect the focus of her life to the study of economics, in the hope that she could contribute to solving the multiple problems associated with poverty. Her career eventually took her to Wellesley College, where she taught economics and sociology for nearly two decades. Balch threw herself into a number of causes during that period, including the cause of peace.

When war broke out in Europe in 1914, Balch was one of fifty-two American women, including Jane Addams, who traveled to Holland the following year to attend a world conference of women at The Hague. The focus of deliberation at the conference was world peace and how women could influence the course of events. After the conference, an international coalition of women traveled throughout Europe, visiting the capitals of nearly all the belligerent nations, meeting with kings and government leaders, in an effort to bring all the parties together to mediate a peace settlement. The failure of the mission did not detract from the significance of women stepping beyond their traditional roles in an effort to secure world peace.

When the United States finally became a party to the war, Balch was one of a handful of activists who refused to abandon their pacifist beliefs. Like Jane Addams' experience, her reputation suffered greatly. In Balch's case, the board of trustees of Wellesley terminated her teaching position, despite the overwhelming support of her expressed by both faculty and alumnae. Thus, in 1918, in her early fifties, Balch found herself without a job and without a pension after twenty years at Wellesley. Turning adversity into opportunity, Balch turned to writing to support herself, and began an association with the Women's International League for Peace and Freedom, which she had helped to found, that would last the rest of her life.

As World War II approached, Balch was faced with another dilemma. This time, however, recognizing early on the dangers inherent in fascism, Balch could not remain neutral. "Neutrality in the sense of treating the aggressor and his victim alike is morally impossible," she concluded, thereby choosing to support the Allied war effort to defeat Germany, Japan, and Italy. While she did not abandon her goal of securing world peace and freedom, during the war her focus was on freedom. Balch became an advocate of Japanese-Americans interred in the United States during the war, and of Jewish refugees fleeing Nazi Germany. For her unstinting efforts on behalf of these groups, the Nobel Peace Prize Committee chose Balch to receive the 1946 Nobel Peace Prize. Characteristic of Balch, she donated the prize money to the work of the Women's International League for Peace and Freedom.

1947: Farnham and Lundberg Publish *The Modern Woman: The Lost Sex*

(Family Life, Cultural Life)

In 1947, Marynia Farnham and Ferdinand Lundberg published a widely read book, *The Modern Woman: The Lost Sex*, in which they argued that American women needed to return to their natural domestic roles after the wartime emergency. Using popularized Freudian analysis as the basis for their theories, Farnham and Lundberg represented one of many voices urging women to renew domestic pursuits.

Most Americans during the depression years of the 1930s counted themselves lucky to have one breadwinner gainfully employed. The issue of whether or not women should work outside the home was a nonissue in an economy that had hit rock-bottom and was recovering only at a snail's pace. With the emergency created by World War II, everything changed. Suddenly it was a patriotic necessity for women to accept work in war-related industries and to fill in for their absent fathers, husbands, brothers, and sons who were in Europe and the Pacific. Concern about what would happen after the war, when men would return to their jobs, came from both government and private sources. A wave of articles in women's magazines, intended to ease the transition of women back into the home, began to extol the virtues of domesticity. Some women, like Frieda Miller of the Woman's Bureau, continued to insist that women, like men, needed to find self-worth in areas away from the family. But these voices grew fainter and fainter. In the postwar years, it was psychiatry that provided the definitions of what was acceptable female behavior. *The Modern Woman: The Lost Sex*, published in 1947, became a primer for those who advocated a domestic role for women.

The authors of *The Modern Woman: The Lost Sex* lent the weight of their professional backgrounds to the theories they put forth so assuredly. Marynia Farnham, a psychoanalyst, and Ferdinand Lundberg, a sociologist, argued that the independent woman was a contradiction in terms. Feminism, they stated, was an illness and the antidote could be found only in accepting domestic roles. In fact, Farnham and Lundberg were particularly aggressive in their condemnation of feminism, characterizing it as a "neurotic reaction to natural male dominance." In the authors' view, feminists proved Freud's "penis envy" theory, because such women were rejecting their instincts and trying to become men. Feminism was nothing less than a psychological disorder whose symptoms included hatred of fathers, rejection of mothers, and aggressive behavior.

Farnham and Lundberg defined real women as self-accepting, dependent on men, sexually passive, and totally fulfilled by child-bearing and child-rearing. Among their proposals was a plan for the government to reward child-bearing with subsidies, and to provide funds for therapy for feminists who, by virtue of their beliefs, were maladjusted human beings.

Other books supported Farnham and Lundberg's theories on women, including psychoanalyst Helen Deutsch's two-volume work, *The Psychology of Women* (1944), and Barnard sociologist Mirra Komarovsky's *Women and the Modern World* (1952). Lacking an equally aggressive countervailing opinion, it is not surprising that women who chafed under the model of perfect domesticity felt alone and isolated in their discontent.

1949: Babe Didrikson Zaharias Is Named Woman Athlete of the Twentieth Century

(Sports)

At the height of her spectacular career in sports in 1949, Babe Didrikson Zaharias received the signal honor of being voted the outstanding woman athlete of the twentieth century by the Associated Press journalists, after having been named Outstanding Woman Athlete of the Year on six different occasions. Almost forty years later, with the twentieth century drawing to a close, no other woman has come close to challenging Zaharias' standing.

Babe Didrikson Zaharias was perhaps best known by her later fans as a phenomenally talented golfer who won almost every tournament she entered. In her most successful year as a golfer, in 1947, Zaharias won her seventeenth consecutive gold medal tournament. The following year, in 1948, Zaharias was the principal founder of the Ladies' Professional Golf Association, still the most prestigious women's golf association and the most prominent vehicle for women golfers to attain both standing in their sport and financial success as a consequence.

Babe Didrikson was born in 1911 in Texas, and received her nickname because of comparisons made of her natural athletic ability to that of Babe Ruth. But even before that, she was known as the "Texas Tomboy," because of her spectacular multi-event performance at the 1932 Amateur Athletic Union (AAU) Championships. As a high school student in Port Arthur, Texas, she was known as an outstanding basketball player. But by the time she attended the AAU Championships in 1932, she was a virtual one-woman team, placing first in five events and second in two others. In addition to basketball, she excelled in baseball, javelin, eighty-meter hurdles, shotput, high jump, and discus. At the 1932 Los Angeles Olympics later that same year,

Didrikson won two gold medals, setting an Olympic record in the eighty-meter hurdles, and winning in javelin as well. She also tied for first in the high jump.

Taking up golf in 1934, Babe met her future husband, former pro wrestler George Zaharias, at a 1938 tournament. Thereafter, Zaharias became his wife's manager and greatest fan. Although she concentrated primarily on golf in her later career, Babe also won prizes for tennis, diving, and bowling. Her fans became used to the idea that any sport that Zaharias tried, she would excel at. Her critics, few though there were, did chide her for being arrogant and for her lack of femininity. But Zaharias, the first woman athlete to earn nearly a million dollars from golf, had little time for critics.

In 1952, Zaharias' formidable career was cut short when she was diagnosed with cancer. After undergoing an initial surgery that year, she was able to return to golf briefly. Even then, she won national championships in 1953 and 1954. A second surgical procedure brought her career to an abrupt halt. In the brief time she had left, Zaharias wrote her autobiography, *This Life I've Led*, published in 1955. She died a year later at the age of forty-five.

Besides her outstanding athletic talent and her career in sports, Zaharias contributed something as well to understanding cancer. Rather than hide her disease, Zaharias went public—one of the first to do so. Cancer, at that time, still carried a stigma and most people did not wish to divulge their illness as a consequence. Zaharias founded a Cancer Research Fund, promoted cancer education, and attended as many charity golf tournaments as she could. Honored by numerous cancer societies and public health agencies, Zaharias was a role model for both women who wanted to compete in professional sports and people stricken with cancer. Her obvious enjoyment of competition during her sports career became a model of grace under pressure during her battle with cancer.

1950: Margaret Chase Smith Delivers "A Declaration of Conscience" Speech

(Politics)

Disturbed by the increasingly irresponsible accusations being leveled by her fellow Republican Senator, Joseph McCarthy, Senator Margaret Chase Smith, on July 1, 1950, at great political risk to herself, denounced McCarthy and his tactics on the floor of the senate in a speech that became known as "A Declaration of Conscience."

Senator Margaret Chase Smith, a Republican from the state of Maine, was the first woman to be elected to both the House of Representatives and the Senate. A former schoolteacher from Skowhegan, Smith first went to Congress in 1940, winning the congressional seat previously held by her late husband. In 1948, Smith decided to make a run for the U.S. Senate, to replace the retiring incumbent. In order to do so, she had to oppose the Republican party, for whom she was not even a second choice for the nomination. Both a former governor and the current governor wanted the nomination. In all, she faced three opponents in the primary and in the end the voters of Maine endorsed Smith by choosing her with more

votes than the other three candidates combined. As a senator, Smith joined other freshmen senators, including John F. Kennedy and Richard M. Nixon. For more than thirty years, she represented the people of Maine with unquestioned integrity and dedication. As a senator, Smith eventually served on the Rules Committee, the Appropriations Committee, and the Armed Services Committee, all three of which carried significant clout.

Margaret Chase Smith generally did not seek out the limelight, but she found herself in it on several occasions in her political career. Her 1960 campaign for reelection was widely covered because it was the first time that two women ran head-to-head for the same Senate seat. In 1964, fearful that the right wing was overtaking the Republican party, Smith announced her candidacy for president. In a year in which Republicans seemed to outdo each other in making excessive statements to prove their conservatism, Smith's was one of a handful of moderate Republican voices that tried to keep the party from moving to the extreme right. Her twenty-seven first ballot votes were insignificant compared to the groundswell for Barry Goldwater, the eventual nominee, but Smith once again came away with integrity and principle reaffirmed.

Throughout her career, Smith never toed the party line. She voted for as many Democratic proposals as some of her Democratic colleagues. A consistent supporter of the National Institutes of Health, Smith was just as insistent on not giving in on votes for increases in Defense Department spending on experimental weapons systems. She was also one of the Republicans who sided with the Democrats in rejecting two of President Richard M. Nixon's controversial Supreme Court nominations.

But Smith's most courageous stand came during her first term as senator, shortly after Senator Joseph McCarthy of Wisconsin began making wild accusations about so-called communists in the State Department and other gov-

ernment agencies. As McCarthy continued to make his charges and as the media began to churn the waters further with daily headlines, the Senate Foreign Relations Committee appointed a subcommittee to investigate the charges. On June 1, 1950, Margaret Chase Smith rose in the Senate chamber to deliver a speech. It was, she said, her "declaration of conscience." Smith denounced the tactics used by McCarthy to smear his opponents and to gain notoriety for himself and his reelection campaign. She decried his willingness to place in jeopardy the smooth working of the various government departments, especially the State Department, that McCarthy had attacked so indiscriminately. And she sympathized with those who had already been smeared by McCarthy's unfounded innuendoes and accusations. That her outspoken denunciation of McCarthy was an act of political courage, there is no doubt. For others who had tried—and would in the future—to defend those accused by McCarthy, found themselves the targets of his invective. Part of McCarthy's success in persuading people that some of what he said must be true was his simple audaciousness in accusing even the most reputable people. One of his targets, for example, was George Marshall, the general-turned-statesman who had formulated the Marshall Plan to bring relief to people in Europe. The Foreign Relations subcommittee report, issued on June 20, 1950, declared that it found absolutely no proof to sustain any of McCarthy's accusations. Yet, by that time, McCarthy and a willing public had already become determined to save the United States from the communists working within. When Smith ran for reelection in 1954, McCarthy endorsed her opponent in an effort to discredit his Senate adversary. But the Maine electorate stood behind Smith and she won reelection with 82 percent of the vote.

Smith remained in the Senate until 1972, when she was defeated in a close race. By then, she had become known as the Conscience of the Senate, the woman who could always be counted upon to do not the politically expedient thing, or even the politically correct thing, but the right thing. It is a measure of the respect that her colleagues held for her, even her adversaries like Everett Dirkson, who had opposed Smith when she fought to have the rose declared the national flower. Dirksen dearly wanted the marigold, but Smith won, and was forever after associated with the rose. When word was received of her death some years later, an anonymous member of the Senate placed a single red rose upon the desk Smith had occupied. It was a fitting tribute to a woman who had inspired so many others with her perseverance, her integrity, her simple presence for so long in the halls of Congress, and always her dignity.

1950: Althea Gibson Breaks the Color Barrier in Professional Tennis

(Civil Rights, Social Reform)

In 1950, Althea Gibson became the first African American to play in the U.S. Open national championship games at Forest Hills, effectively desegregating professional tennis for both men and women.

Althea Gibson, by all measures, should not have succeeded in escaping the poverty of her Harlem childhood. Growing up in the Harlem of the late 1930s and 1940s, Gibson developed a "tough kid" attitude that led to school truancy and episodes of running away. At various times in her rough and tumble childhood, Gibson was a client of the Society for Prevention of Cruelty to Children, and a recipient of the welfare system. Her saving grace always was her determination and her athletic ability. After she won the Police Athletic League and the Parks Department paddle tennis competitions, musician Buddy Walker, recognizing her innate talent and ability, took her to the Harlem River Tennis Courts, where she began to learn the game of tennis. Before long, the Harlem Cosmopolitan Tennis Club collected donations for her to become a member and to take tennis lessons. In 1942, she won the Girl's Singles New York State Tournament, sponsored by the all-black American Tennis Association (ATA). She won several more ATA tournaments in 1944 and 1945, but her game was badly in need of more discipline and more coaching.

When wealthy businessmen offered Gibson a home, secondary schooling, tennis instruction, and an encouraging and supportive atmosphere, Gibson was on her way. She graduated from Williston Industrial High School in South Carolina, acquired the skills she would need both on and off the courts to win big-time tennis tournaments, including self-respect and self-discipline, cooperation and poise. From 1947 to 1956, Gibson won ten consecutive ATA national women's singles tournaments. In 1950, Gibson enrolled at Florida A&M University. Efforts to bring Gibson into the still-segregated grass-court invitationals met with resistance. But when tennis champion Alice Marble declared in the July 1950 issue of *American Lawn Tennis* magazine that Gibson was "not being judged by the yardstick of ability but by the fact that her pigmentation is somewhat different," the Orange Lawn Tennis Club extended an invitation. In turn, this led to an invitation to the 1950 national championship games at Forest Hills, the most prestigious American tennis tournament. Gibson was the first African American of either sex to play at Forest Hills. A year later, in 1951, Gibson became the first African American of either sex to play at Wimbledon, the world's premiere tennis tournament.

Still lacking the confidence needed for success, victory in these tournaments continued to elude Gibson until 1956, following a State Department–sponsored tour as a member of the U.S. team in Southeast Asia. She won the Indian and the Asiatic women's singles titles, as well as several European titles. With renewed confidence, she returned to Wimbledon in 1956, winning the women's doubles championship that year. The following year, 1957, was to be Gibson's year. She won the single's title at Wimbledon, the women's doubles title, and national clay court and Forest Hills singles titles. Gibson returned once more to Wimbledon in 1958, and once again won the singles and doubles titles. When she retired in 1959, Gibson had accomplished what no other African-American woman had ever done. She integrated tennis for all time, she won the national singles championships at Forest Hills, and she won the Wimbledon singles and doubles titles in back-to-back years. The Associated Press voted Gibson Woman Athlete of the Year in 1957 and 1958. Gibson was also named to the Lawn Tennis Hall of Fame and the Black Athlete Hall of Fame.

1950: Gwendolyn Brooks Wins a Pulitzer Prize for *Annie Allen*

(Cultural Life)

In 1950, Gwendolyn Brooks became the first African-American, male or female, to win a Pulitzer Prize. Brooks won her Pulitzer for a book of poems entitled *Annie Allen*.

Poet Gwendolyn Brooks began writing poetry when she was just seven years old. At the age of eleven, she began collecting her poems in notebooks. Brooks grew up in Chicago surrounded, fortunately, by loving parents and relatives who encouraged the youngster to write. As a student at an all-white school in Chicago, Brooks might have felt more isolated than she was, were it not for her discovery of other poets, including T. S. Eliot, Wallace Stevens, and Ezra Pound. But meeting Langston Hughes when she was sixteen was a highpoint in the young poet's life. Hughes read some of her poetry and encouraged her to continue writing. For the next several years, Brooks continued to write and develop her craft. She also graduated from junior college and married.

Despite her writing skills, developed over the course of nearly twenty years, as a poet Brooks was still the isolated child in the all-white school. An opportunity to sit in on a class in modern poetry in 1941, taught by Inez Cunningham Stark, proved to be a turning point for Brooks. For the first time, she was able to talk with other poets about her work, about their work, about poetry. It was, for Brooks, an exciting time. Within two years, she won her first award for poetry, from the Midwestern Writer's Conference, the result of which was the publication of her first book of poetry, *A Street in Bronzeville*. The book was well received critically. Brooks had begun to establish an identity among African-American poets and writers.

In 1946 and 1947, Brooks was the recipient of several prestigious grants, including two Guggenheim fellowships, and grants from the American Academy of Arts and Letters and the National Institute of Arts and Letters, which allowed her to concentrate fully on her next volume of poetry. In *Annie Allen*, Brooks described the human condition with an eloquence and simplicity that won her a Pulitzer Prize in 1950. Her style, a wholly self-invented form of sonnet and ballad, brought to life the voices of the voiceless, the children of poverty.

Brooks continued her writing for the next seventeen years. But 1967 became another turning point. That year, Brooks attended the Fisk University Black Writers Conference and came away transformed by black pride. There she met writers like LeRoi Jones, who was taking his writing to the people, by which he meant African-Americans. Brooks' primary audience had always been the white middle class, the establishment culture. Fisk gave her an entirely new world view, a new focus for her poetry. For the next several years, Brooks became more and more involved with the black power movement and the celebration of black culture. *In the Mecca, Riot, Family Pictures,* and *Beckonings,* all written between 1967 and 1973, reflected Brooks' new perspective directed toward a black audience.

Gwendolyn Brooks gave to African-Americans in particular, but to a wider audience as well, a new sensibility of the people in her everyday life in the African-American community. In 1968, the state of Illinois designated Brooks as its poet laureate for life. She was the first African-American woman to be chosen as poetry consultant for the Library of Congress. She continues to reach out to young people, direct-ing and funding yearly Poet Laureate Awards for high school students in Illinois.

1951: Marianne Moore Wins the Pulitzer Prize

(Cultural Life)

In 1951, the poet Marianne Moore won the Pulitzer Prize for her volume, *Collected Poems.*

Marianne Moore's mother was a widow from Missouri who supported Marianne and her brother by working as a teacher in Pennsylvania. Moore followed in her footsteps by teaching business courses to Native Americans after graduating from Bryn Mawr in 1909, but her true calling was poetry. When she, her mother, and her brother moved to New York a few years later, Moore worked first as a librarian, and then as editor of a literary magazine. While earning money in these positions and living with her mother and brother, she began to pen the poems that would bring her increasing recognition over the next four decades.

After moving to New York, Moore quickly established herself as part of the literary scene in Greenwich Village. Recognition of her work from this circle, however, did not come until almost a decade later. In 1924, she won a prize of $2,000 from *The Dial* magazine, and the next year she was invited to become its chief editor. With this dual recognition, her literary career began to take off. She published two books of poetry each decade from the 1920s to the 1940s, and she became a noted essayist and translator from French as well.

It was only after the Second World War, however, that her work began to be recognized as first rate. She was selected for the National Institute of Arts and Letters in 1947 and won the Pulitzer Prize for her seventh book, *Collected Poems*, in 1951. The next year she won the National Book Award, and the year after that she received the National Institute's Gold Medal. In 1955, the public recognition climaxed when she was elected to the American Academy of Arts and Letters. She continued to work for more than a decade thereafter, polishing her words and refusing to release anything she felt was not ready, right up until her death in 1972.

The recognition that perhaps meant the most to her came from the leading writers of her time, however. Ezra Pound and William Carlos Williams both highly praised her work, and T. S. Eliot gave her the best praise of all. Marianne Moore was, he said, "one of the few who have done the language some service in my lifetime."

1952: Playwright Lillian Hellman Testifies before the House Un-American Activities Committee

(Civil Rights)

Summoned to appear before the House Un-American Activities Committee (HUAC) in 1952, playwright Lillian Hellman refused to provide information about the political affiliations of her friends and colleagues in Hollywood. Her refusal caused her to be blacklisted in Hollywood and for some years following that, one of the most respected writers, both in Hollywood and in other theatres, was unemployable in the movie industry.

One consequence of the post–World War II hyperbole about the dangers of domestic communist activity was that the Dies Committee, also known as the House Un-American Activities Committee, was given permanent status as an investigative body to pursue allegations of communism in government employment. HUAC lost little time in establishing its on-going committee hearings, which gave the appearance, at least, of an all-out effort on behalf of the American people to rid the government of communists. During the depression, when the bottom was falling out of the economy and people were left without resources, capitalism seemed a less viable economic system than it had in the past. As a consequence, many people began looking for other answers, including socialism and communism. Most people were fairly quickly disenchanted with communism because of the repressiveness of the Russian political system. When Russia became an American ally during World War II, no one thought twice about previous or current affiliations with the communist party in America. That all changed once the war ended.

Consequently, actors, directors, writers, and producers—were all summoned to appear before the committee and asked to compromise either themselves because of past affiliations or any of their colleagues or friends who might or might not have been associated with communists in the past. The fear that gripped the country over this issue, and especially the fear of being accused of having communist connections, caused many people to name names simply to demonstrate that they themselves had nothing to hide. Robert Taylor, a screen idol with a reputation as a take-charge strong man, who had made a film extolling the virtues of Russia as part of the war effort, was called to testify before the committee. Taylor's defense for making the pro-Russia movie was to blame the studio bosses who, he said, had forced him to do the movie.

To defy the committee was to take an enormous risk with one's livelihood. But there were those in the Hollywood community who stood on principle and refused to implicate others in order to save themselves. The playwright Lillian Hellman was one such person. She refused to apologize for her past or to renounce her friends. Hellman, the author of such hits as *The Children's Hour, The Little Foxes,* and *Watch on the Rhine,* was an early opponent of fascism. She herself had made two trips to Russia during the years when Russia was a western ally. But to the members of the Dies Committee, who questioned whether she had formal ties to the communist party, either then or at present time, Hellman steadfastly refused to provide information. In a much-publicized statement, Hellman declared, "I will not cut my conscience to fit this year's fashions."

Hellman's courage in standing up to the committee inspired others to do the same. Nevertheless, for her personally and for her long-time companion, mystery writer Dashiell Hammett, the consequences of refusing to become an informer meant blacklisting in Hollywood. For many years, Hellman wrote screenplays under an assumed name. By the time of her death in 1984, Hellman's name and reputation had been fully restored.

1952: Marilyn Monroe Achieves Stardom in *Gentlemen Prefer Blondes*

(Cultural Life)

Playing the role of sexy Lorelei Lee in the movie *Gentlemen Prefer Blondes* in 1952, actress Marilyn Monroe, who had been signed as a starlet in 1946 by Twentieth Century Fox, achieved star status with the newfound responsibility of living up to the image created for her by Hollywood.

Since 1910, when independent movie producers, in an effort to break the control of the Motion Picture Patents Company, also known as "the Trust," began publicizing previously anonymous actresses in order to build up a public following, women actresses have played an important part in the development of the movie industry and of Hollywood. From the first popular women stars, Mary Pickford, Lillian Gish, and Clara Bow, women have helped to make the movies a true national pastime. But the star system that developed along with the studios also dictated that female stars adhere to certain rules to protect their carefully cultivated studio images. Those who resisted were labeled box office "poison," and the studios effectively punished them by refusing to assign them movie roles. Stars like Bette Davis and Katharine Hepburn, both of whom tried to retain some control over their careers, were considered such for short periods. Determined to extract as much as possible from each movie produced, the studio heads had to walk a tight line between making their female actresses as alluring as possible to the public, without offending sensibilities and, more importantly, without offending the movie censors. But throughout Hollywood's history, certain female stars have been able to come across as frankly sexy and sexual without losing the support of the public. Mae West was probably the first overtly sexy star. Part of her image was that of a dumb blonde, but gradually she became better known for her wise-cracking double entendres. Mae West continued starring in films through her forties, fifties, and even into her sixties, and for several years she earned more than any other actor—male or female—in Hollywood.

Marilyn Monroe began her career projecting a similar Mae West image as the sexy but dumb blonde. Monroe, however, cultivated that image both on and off screen, whenever she appeared in public. Signed by Twentieth Century Fox in 1946, Monroe's first real break came in the 1950 film *The Asphalt Jungle*, in which she played a disturbed babysitter. Although she was a talented actress, even this serious role did little to convince her public that Monroe was anything more than a sexy blonde with aspirations beyond her abilities. Her breathless, little girl

voice, and accentuated figure that was both a promise and a threat, made her a creature of desire to men and a potential rival to women. As Gloria Steinem observed, Monroe represented to women—especially to women in the 1950s—"the fear of a sexual competitor, who could take away men on whom women's identities and even livelihoods might depend; the fear of having to meet her impossible standard of always giving—and asking nothing in return."

In a career that lasted little more than a dozen years, Monroe made films that, on second and third consideration, demonstrated a talent that was far more complex and memorable than she was credited with at the time. In such movies as *Gentlemen Prefer Blondes, The Seven Year Itch, Some Like It Hot, How to Marry a Millionaire, Showgirl, Bus Stop,* and *The Misfits,* Monroe showed herself at her best, and sometimes her worst. At the height of her popularity, she received over five thousand fan letters a week, and her picture graced the covers of fan magazines with regularity. But if she was a success with the public, the critics tended to be less kind. Monroe never believed that she was being taken seriously by anyone. A series of failed marriages with Arthur Miller and Joe DiMaggio, along with increased bouts of depression, drug abuse, alcoholism, and affairs—including ones with John and Robert Kennedy—took their toll. On August 4, 1962, Monroe died of a drug overdose.

1953: The Kinsey Report Reveals Changing Sexual Mores and Practices

(Family Life, Cultural Life)

In 1953, Professor Alfred C. Kinsey, Wardell B. Pomeroy, and Clyde E. Martin published *Sexual Behavior in the Human Female*, the second half of a two-part report, the first half of which was published in 1948 under the title *Sexual Behavior in the Human Male*. The first wide-ranging survey of sexual practices made since 1928, the Kinsey Report, as it became known, provoked widespread controversy.

Few academic studies have provoked as much controversy as the Kinsey Report. Alfred C. Kinsey, for whom the reports were named, was a professor of zoology at the University of Indiana when he undertook his investigation of sexual practices and mores in the United States. Working with two colleagues, Wardell B. Pomeroy and Clyde E. Martin, at the university's Institute for Sex Research in Bloomington, Indiana, Kinsey worked up an elaborate series of questionnaires intended to elicit information on a wide range of sexual behavior, such as petting, marital and extra-marital intercourse, female orgasm, oral sex, and masturbation. Eventually, the Kinsey team questioned 5,300 white males and 5,490 white females from a variety of backgrounds.

From the start of the survey, Kinsey and his colleagues met with enormous resistance from public officials who took a dim view of the nature of the project. Impediments ranging from police interference, to attempts to exert influence over university officials to halt the study, to last-ditch efforts to stop publication of the findings, were a constant source of distraction. At the same time, the publicity that was generated and which grew with each effort to stop the survey, probably helped to pique more curiosity about the final results.

In 1948, the first half of the survey, *Sexual Behavior in the Human Male*, was published, followed in 1953 by *Sexual Behavior in the Human Female*. The conclusions drawn in the Kinsey Reports were based on the statistical analyses of the information gathered from the questionnaires. Controversy followed publication as it had the entire study. In particular, Kinsey questioned traditional views on American sexual mores and offered lengthy opinions on questions such as oral sex and female orgasm, both of which were taboo subjects for public discussion at the time. Kinsey argued that normality ought to be defined according to behavior and not according to some theoretical imposed dogma, handed down by religion and psychoanalysis.

Kinsey's study of sexual mores was not the first to make people sit up and take notice. In 1918, sociologist and former penal reformer Katherine Bement Davis began a several-year study of the sexual practices of white, middle-class women, both married and single. Some of her findings supported the conventional wisdom regarding women's sexuality in the early twentieth century. For example, more than half the women surveyed had strong emotional relationships with other women, although only one in five respondents had homosexual relationships. Interestingly, very few women had premarital heterosexual relationships. What was revealing about Davis' survey was that married women, for the first time, were expressing marital sex as something other than duty. It was clear that women who used contraceptives viewed sex as a pleasurable experience, entirely normal and satisfying. The survey also dashed some of the misconceptions held regarding the consequences of frequent intercourse. Many sociologists, including Davis before she started her survey, held the view that frequent intercourse led to poor health and sterility. Both were proven untrue, according to the results of the survey. Finally, Davis' survey was noteworthy for another reason. It focused, for the first time, on what was referred to as "normal" people. That is, surveys of this nature, in the past, had focused on abnormal or deviant behavior. For information, surveyors questioned what they considered abnormal or deviant people, usually prostitutes and delinquents. Davis' field of respondents was drawn from membership lists of women's clubs and from alumnae lists, that is, college women.

Several years after the Kinsey Reports, another and equally controversial sex survey was conducted by William Howell Masters, a gynecologist, and Virginia Masters, a psychologist. What made the Masters and Johnson Report different was that, in addition to having people fill out questionnaires, they also conducted clinical tests using polygraphlike instruments to measure human sexual response in the laboratory. Their pioneering reports became the basis for reevaluating sexual responses of women and of homosexuals. In *Human Sexual Response* (1966), they described the physiological responses during four phases of erotic arousal for males and females. *Human Sexual*

Inadequacy (1970) examined the treatment of sexual problems, such as impotence and frigidity. And *Homosexuality in Perspective* (1979) argued that homosexual behavior could be altered if the subject so desired. Like Kinsey, Masters and Johnson were criticized, especially in their case, for using clinical tests, which they acknowledged probably altered the outcome, since those participating in the survey knew they were being monitored.

All of these surveys, however controversial, helped to alter perceptions of women's sexuality. Davis' data pointed to a real revolution within the confines of marriage, as the attitudes of women toward sex differed markedly from Victorian notions. Kinsey's surveys confirmed, to most observers, the existence of female sexuality, and Masters and Johnson made a strong case for the equality and even the superiority of female sexual responsiveness. Long-held notions about female passivity were finally put to rest.

1955: Rosa Parks Refuses to Give up Her Seat to a White Passenger on a Montgomery Bus

(Civil Rights, Social Reform)

On December 1, 1955, Rosa Parks of Montgomery, Alabama, boarded a bus to make the trip from her job to her home. Discriminatory practices on the Montgomery bus system frequently meant that African-American riders had to give up their seats to white riders. When Parks was told to give up her seat by the bus driver, she refused. Parks was arrested on the spot, and within three days, a massive boycott was initiated by Alabama African-Americans against the bus company.

When Rosa Parks refused to give up her bus seat on December 1, 1955, many people interpreted her action as a spur-of-the-moment decision made out of weariness after a long day's work. As a consequence, to outside observers, Rosa Parks for a long time remained a peripheral, almost accidental, figure in the history-making Montgomery bus boycott. Credit for initiating, sustaining, and successfully concluding the boycott went to civil rights leaders, including Martin Luther King, Jr., who not only emerged as the leader of this particular movement, but also began his own journey, which was destined to change the face of America.

The truth was that Rosa Parks had long been involved in efforts to change the Montgomery bus system. She hated having to enter the front door of the bus to pay a fare, and then get off and enter the bus again from the rear door; she hated the policy requiring African-Americans to give up their seats in the event that white people were standing; and she hated the disrespect with which African-Americans were treated by drivers who felt no compunction about leaving people standing in the roadway after they had paid their fares, or ejecting people who were not deferential enough. Parks had also just competed a summer seminar 'at the Highlander Folk School in Grundy County, Tennessee. Highlander sponsored seminars for both African-Americans and whites seeking to bring equality and civil rights to fruition. So when the opportunity to act presented itself, Rosa Parks, a mild-mannered seamstress in her mid-forties, was equal to the challenge.

When Jo Ann Robinson, a professor at Alabama State College, who had also been involved in efforts to change the public transportation policy, heard about Parks' arrest, she immediately swung into action. Robinson ran off fifty thousand flyers calling for a general boycott of all Montgomery buses the following Monday, December 5, 1955. So began a year-long struggle between public officials in Montgomery and African-Americans who chose to walk or carpool rather than take the segregated buses.

From the start, the bus boycott was a monumental success. Strike leaders, again motivated by Robinson and other women, organized the Montgomery Improvement Association (MIA) to di-

rect strike strategy, and elected Martin Luther King, Jr., the young pastor of the Baptist church, to become president. The primary support for the strike came from thousands of women who chose to walk, sometimes as much as twelve miles a day, or to carpool, in order to realize success. One elderly woman promised King that she would walk every day until the strike ended. When King protested that her feet must be tired, she acknowledged that they were, and added, "but my soul is rested." Such determination could scarcely fail to bring success. When the Supreme Court ruled, in *Browder v. Gayle* in November 1956, that Alabama's state and city bus segregation policies were unconstitutional, the MIA called off the boycott, almost one year to the day after it had begun. The Court's decision also gave civil rights leaders the motivation to continue their activities in other area.

1956: Josephine Bay Becomes the First Woman to Head a Member Firm of the New York Stock Exchange

(Equal Rights)

In 1956, Josephine Perfect Bay was elected without opposition to be president of A.

M. Kidder & Company, and thus became the first woman ever to lead a member firm of the New York Stock Exchange.

Born in 1900, Josephine Perfect remained single until she was forty-two, when she married a prominent financier. Despite the fact that her husband was a millionaire, she did not retire into a life of luxury and privilege, but instead involved herself, with her new mate's full support, in his business affairs. Privately, she served as his advisor, later recounting that "time and time again," he "would discuss a business problem with me—urging me to take the opposite viewpoint to help clarify his thinking." Publicly, she participated directly in the world of business, achieving the post of chairperson of the board of American Export Lines, and along with it a reputation as a shrewd businesswoman.

This reputation served her well when her husband died after a decade of marriage. He left her a third of the stock of A. M. Kidder & Company, and she proceeded to use that considerable clout to become the chairperson of the board and president of the company. Since the corporation was a member of the New York Stock Exchange, it was thus that in the middle of the conservative 1950s that a woman first took a place as an equal member of that venerable and inestimably influential institution.

Josephine Bay was liberated in word as well as in deed, and her advice to other women was prophetic. Women should not settle for being "just sweet and naive things...mere passive coupon clippers." Instead, she insisted, they should be "active investment owners," which would benefit not only them but would make "our economy...more vibrant and more venturesome." Given the tremendous influx of young upper-middle class women from top colleges and universities into the financial and corporate world since the 1970s, Josephine Bay's form of liberation is one that truly has been fulfilled. While the "glass ceiling" still prevents many women from reaching the very upper reaches of the corporate world, there is no question that their role in major corporations is immeasurably greater than it was when Josephine Bay led the way.

1956: The La Leche League Is Founded

(Family Life)

In 1956, at a time when bottlefeeding of infants was the norm in American families, seven young mothers who preferred breastfeeding began meeting regularly for encouragement and advice. Before long many friends began to join them and found groups of their own. Over the course of two decades these informal gatherings blossomed into an international organization, La Leche League, devoted to promoting breastfeeding of infants over the use of formulas and bottles.

At a church fair in the town of Franklin Park, a suburb of Chicago, in 1956, a young woman sat under a tree breastfeeding her baby. A friend approached, and they began to discuss how much they preferred breastfeeding over the use of bottles. Five of their other friends expressed similar feelings, and the small group began meeting regularly to discuss the merits of the method, share knowledge and information about it, and to give each other support in the face of the hostile reactions they sometimes encountered. The organization grew steadily over the next two decades, developing into a worldwide organization with forty thousand members in forty-eight countries and a budget of $2 million annually.

The purpose of La Leche League, and the controversy it engendered, would have been inexplicable to anyone who lived before the twentieth century, because women had since time immemorial fed their children with the food nature provides all mammals, breast milk. The only exception to this rule was the aristocratic women who, in certain times and places, employed "wet-nurses," servant women who were nursing their own babies and could therefore suckle the noble child as well. For the overwhelming majority of women, however, breastfeeding was as natural as conception and childbirth, an activity they might find pleasurable and fulfilling or painful and inconvenient, but which was an unquestionable feature of human life.

Around the turn of the century, this age-old situation began to change. Advances in sterilization and refrigeration made it possible to prepare and preserve formulas based on cows' milk, and to feed it to babies with little danger of transmitting disease. The technology had obvious uses in cases where the mother could not provide milk for some reason, but after 1920, bottlefeeding rapidly became the method of choice. In part this reflected the advice of doctors, who were trained in a way that emphasized technology over natural processes. In part it reflected the growth of the public health industry, whose nurses and social workers made their living teaching lower-class women correct bottle procedures and feeding regimens, among other things. In part it reflected the impact of advertising by companies that made money from selling something that had heretofore come for free, and to some extent it reflected the rise of professional advice-givers who sold books that advocated rigid feeding schedules that started early teaching children the tyranny of the time-clock. Last, but hardly least, it reflected the desire of many women to escape the tyranny of their own nature, just as their aristocratic forebearers had.

Like any liberation, bottlefeeding had its costs, and by the 1950s, women were beginning to feel it. Practically, they had been liberated from nursing to be enslaved by formula mixing, bottle sterilization, and, in many cases, the screams of their children waiting for the appointed time on the clock. Moreover, some realized that an important psychological bond was being lost, and medical research began to reveal that breast milk has important advantages over formula as well. After a slow start in the 1950s, La Leche League grew rapidly in the late 1960s, in membership and even more in influence. By the 1970s, its activities, and those of others inspired by it, had begun to seriously impact the profits of the great companies that sold infant formula. In response, they began marketing aggressively in Third World countries, and La Leche League has followed, campaigning actively to persuade women to continue nursing the old fashioned way. In the meantime, women in Western countries have settled on a freedom of choice arrangement, in which many use one or the other method, and many combine both. But for the active encouragement of the women in the organization, an important part of being female, and, for babies of both genders, an important part of being human, might well have been lost forever.

1959: The Lorraine Hansberry Play, *A Raisin in the Sun,* Opens on Broadway

(Cultural Life)

On March 11, 1959, *A Raisin in the Sun*, by playwright Lorraine Hansberry, opened at the Ethel Barrymore Theater, transforming forever the American theatre.

When Lorraine Hansberry's brilliant play *A Raisin in the Sun* opened on Broadway in 1959, critic Walter Kerr wrote that Hansberry had taken "the precise temperature of a race at that time in its history when it cannot retreat and cannot quite find the way to move forward....Three generations stand poised and crowded on a detonating cap." Hansberry's play altered the American theatre, forever changing what producers of Broadway productions would consider acceptable subject matter. Ironically, the play almost did not make it to Broadway because the so-called "smart money people" did not believe that the American public was ready to support a play about a black family. Hansberry had more faith, both in her creation and in the American theatre-going public. When

producers wanted to make changes that they considered necessary to make the play acceptable but that significantly altered the content, Hansberry refused, preferring instead to raise the money in other ways. With no guarantee of a Broadway house, Hansberry and her colleagues raised enough cash to take the play on the road. Its success in other cities, including New Haven, Philadelphia, and Chicago, finally convinced doubters that America was indeed ready for such a play. *A Raisin in the Sun* won the New York Drama Critics Circle Award in 1959, the first time that an African-American playwright won. Hansberry was also the youngest playwright to ever win the award, and she was only the fifth woman.

Hansberry, a native of Chicago, was only twenty-eight when *Raisin* opened on Broadway. The theme of the play was inspired by African-American poet Langston Hughes' poem "Harlem," in which he asked, "What happens to a dream deferred?...Does it dry up like a raisin in the sun?...Or does it explode?" Lorraine Hansberry would not allow her dreams to be deferred. A civil rights activist, author, and playwright, it was she who coined the phrase, "young, gifted, and black," in a speech she gave to winners of the United Negro College Fund's writing contest in 1964. By then, Hansberry already knew that she was dying of cancer. Yet she refused to allow that to stop her from achieving her goals. She managed to complete her next play, *The Sign in Sidney Brustein's Window,* and saw it open to mixed reviews in October 1964 at the Longacre Theater. The theme was a call for intellectuals to become involved with social problems, and it surprised critics to see an African-American playwright write a play about whites, perhaps because

Hansberry had become so identified with the civil rights movement. But she had learned long before that profound human suffering transcends race and class, and it was that understanding that made her works so universally accepted. Hansberry's plays also reflected her own feminist sensibilities. In most of her works, there exist female characters who, through sheer will power, hope, and aspiration, provide the cultural and emotional links that unite her protagonists with the human family.

Hansberry died in January 1965 at the age of thirty-four, a brief six years after her star rose in the American theatre. But the work she did as a playwright, as an author, as a civil rights activist, as a political commentator, and as a humanist, despite the discrimination she faced as a woman and as an African-American and despite her painful illness, is permanent testimony to the innate courage of the human spirit.

1960: The Food and Drug Administration Approves "The Pill"

(Family Life)

After extensive tests, into its effectiveness and safety, the U.S. Food and Drug Administration in 1960 approved the manufacture and sale of "the pill" as a new form of contraception. This small chemical tablet quickly became the keystone of the "sexual revolution."

People have always practiced birth control, although they have not always known it. Medieval peasants varied their age of marriage, and thus their number of children, depending on economic conditions, while monks and nuns were encouraged to practice abstinence. *Coitus interruptus* and various mechanical means have been known and practiced for centuries, passed down by word of mouth and in books on practical medical techniques.

The Victorian era may have left a legacy of sexual repression, but the reaction against it is as old as the twentieth century. Avant garde intellectuals before the First World War rebelled against it, and much larger numbers followed their example during the "Roaring Twenties." The Depression and the war against fascism put a damper on pleasure-seeking for more than a decade, and the strait-laced fifties continued this ethos, at least on the surface. But underneath, American attitudes were changing once again. Peace and prosperity reduced the need for restraint, and the pill demolished the last practical arguments in its favor.

A radically new form of avoiding pregnancy, the pill separated the act of contraception from the sexual act, even as it separated the act of sex from conception. A woman who took it once a day could engage in sex without hesitation, for it was not only the most discreet but also the most effective form of contraception. For the first time in history, women could approach sex with the same attitude as men, treating it as a form of self-validation, self-discovery, or simple recreation. The "sexual revolution" accompanied the rise of the "singles" culture that glorified young, unattached career women. The "Playboy" philosophy of the mid-1960s evolved into the tantric free sex of the hippie movement and eventually the "swinging" lifestyle of the 1970s.

At first, it appeared that most young women regarded the sexual revolution as an unqualified good, a liberation from the repression of Victorian morality. Some threw themselves into the pursuit of pleasure with abandon, while a much larger number simply incorporated sex into their romantic relationships long before they had any thoughts of marriage. However, as time went by, liberation began to reveal a down side. Even before the advent of herpes and then the AIDS crisis, feminists began to question the emotional tone of liberated sexuality. They noticed that relationships all too often satisfied the stereotypically male goals of physical release and multiple partners, while losing the stereotypically female goals of emotional intimacy and commitment. Whether or not these stereotypes do justice to the true range of feelings of either sex, there was no denying that by the late 1970s, sex was not only tolerated by a once intolerant society, it was increasingly treated as just another commodity. In the sexual sphere, the social reaction of the 1980s against the legacy of the 1960s came not only from the political right, but from the radical left as well.

1962: Dolores Huerta Helps Found the United Farm Workers Union

(Social Reform)

In 1962, Dolores Huerta, a longtime colleague of Cesar Chavez, joined with Chavez to establish the United Farm Workers (UFW) union in order to organize agricultural workers.

In the late 1950s, in Stockton, California, labor organizer Fred Ross recruited a young Dolores Huerta, persuading her to work with him in a grassroots group called the Community Service Organization (CSO). Huerta worked through the CSO in voter registration drives to get more Chicanos into the electorate. She also helped to bring public attention to the on-going police brutality against Chicanos. It was as a CSO volunteer that Huerta met Cesar Chavez. Working together, they helped to establish more than twenty CSO locals throughout the state and in Arizona. Huerta also worked as a lobbyist on behalf of Chicanos and first-generation Mexicans living in California. Her skills were amply demonstrated when she was able to persuade legislators in Sacramento to include first-generation Mexicans, regardless of citizenship, in an old-age pension program. During that period, Huerta also succeeded in getting farm workers included in disability coverage, a remarkable feat since the Chicano population was not yet organized enough to wield much political power at the polls. When the CSO objected to plans made by Huerta and Chavez to set up a rural program, they left the organization.

Chavez went first to Delano, California, and began organizing agricultural workers. In California, most agricultural workers were Hispanic in origin and represented the last large unorganized workers' group, charac- terized by extremely low wages, long seasonal hours, and horrible working conditions.

Huerta soon joined Chavez in Delano, and together they organized the United Farm Workers union. Huerta served as vice-president and chief negotiator for the UFW. In September 1965, the Delano grape strike was begun in California—an action that would last for almost five years before it was settled. In the course of the strike, a number of influential unions and civil rights organizations supported the grape pickers. They also secured the support of Robert Kennedy, which brought a great deal of national media attention to the strike. Their red flag bearing a black Aztec eagle and the word "Huelga," "strike," became a commonly recognized symbol, as did the long marches that also characterized the strike. Huerta and Chavez mounted a campaign to pressure growers into negotiating with them by organizing, as part of the strike, a nationwide consumer boycott of grapes.

Although the *machismo* culture of Hispanics militated against accepting women into their union, people like Huerta set an example of accomplishment that was hard to deny. Women ultimately became very important in the strike, establishing themselves as the chief proponents of the union's nonviolent philosophy. When the very first contract was drawn up with the grape growers, Dolores Huerta was the chief negotiator. She continued to negotiate the contracts herself for another five years.

1962: *Silent Spring* Alerts the Public to the Dangers of Pesticides

(Science, Family Life)

In 1962, biologist Rachel Carson published a book called *Silent Spring*, in which she prophesized a spring season in the not-too-distant future bereft of the birds and small animals that were being systematically eliminated because of the uncontrolled use of pesticides and other toxins destroying the earth's ecosystem.

A chance encounter with a biology teacher in her third year of college changed Rachel Carson's life forever. Nearly four decades later, a random request from a friend helped to change forever the way Americans view the environment. Rachel Carson intended to be a writer from the time she was a child. When she was ten, the magazine *St. Nicholas* published a short story she had written. So when she enrolled at the Pennsylvania College for Women, Carson chose to major in English. In her third year, required to take a biology course to fulfill her curriculum requirements, Carson was fortunate enough to be as-signed to a class taught by an extraordinary teacher, Mary Scott Skinker. Carson had always been fascinated by nature, spending hours of time as a child wandering in the woods near her home in order to study birds, plants, and other living things. When she took Skinker's biology course, she knew she had found her true calling. She quickly transferred from English to biology, and despite the bias against women entering fields of science, with Skinker's help Carson was able to secure a scholarship to Johns Hopkins, where she earned a master's degree in zoology. Carson spent her summers at the Marine Biological Laboratory in

Woods Hole, Massachusetts, which eventually led to a job with the U.S. Bureau of Fisheries in Washington, D.C., the first woman to be employed as a scientist by that agency.

Shortly after beginning work with the Bureau of Fisheries, Carson also began to write again, beginning with an article for the *Atlantic Monthly*, "Undersea." An editor for Simon and Schuster persuaded her to turn the article into a full-length book, *Under the Sea-Wind*. It was another ten years before her second book, *The Sea around Us*, brought Carson the literary success that had eluded her earlier. A Guggenheim Fellowship that year allowed her finally to take time off to concentrate on writing and eventually to leave her Bureau of Fisheries job altogether.

From the end of World War II, Carson had been interested in the proliferation of DDT use. A request from a friend who had a private bird sanctuary in Duxbury, Massachusetts, persuaded Carson that she had to write a book on the subject. Her friend, Olga Owens Huckins, noticed that birds in her sanctuary died after the area was sprayed with DDT as part of the state's mosquito control program. Huckins asked Carson if there was something she could do to change that policy. The result, in 1962, was *Silent Spring*.

Using evidence laboriously gathered for several years, Carson said that DDT and other toxins that were being indiscriminately used to control nature, were also systematically destroying the delicate ecosystem. The earth, the air, and the water were being poisoned by man, and Carson predicted that a spring would come when all birds and small animals would be gone, destroyed by the poisons. Although Carson, her research, and the conclusions drawn in *Silent Spring* were all subjected to a bombardment of ridicule and abuse by the agricultural chemical companies, the book had profound effects on the public's awareness of the environment and led directly to President John F. Kennedy requesting a special panel of the President's Science Advisory Committee to investigate the effects of pesticides. The report of the committee vindicated Carson.

Rachel Carson died from bone cancer two years after publication of *Silent Spring*.

1963: The Mary Kay Cosmetics Company Is Founded

(Work, Family Life)

In September 1963, Mary Kay Ash, backed by $5,000 in life savings and extensive experience in direct sales, founded Mary Kay Cosmetics, a small direct sales company, which she initially operated out of her Texas home.

When Mary Kay Ash retired in 1963, she intended to write a book on sales careers for women. Her own career in direct sales had been successful and she was certain that, with the right guidance and motivation, many women could enjoy the same kind of success. In the course of organizing her book, Ash realized that her own experience and what she had learned about what elements made up a successful business could be applied to her own venture.

Ash had two principles upon which she wanted her cosmetics company to be built. The first was that she wanted an organization whose members accepted as a guiding philosophy the Golden Rule. Second, she wanted her business to provide opportunity for women to achieve unlimited success. In the thirty years since its founding, the company has succeeded beyond all predictions. Traditionally, Mary Kay Cosmetics reached out to housewives seeking a nontraditional employment opportunity that would allow them to structure their work hours around family responsibilities. At a time when very few companies had even heard of flex time, Mary Kay Cosmetics was building its corporation around that concept. Moreover, women who found part-time employment or a full-time career in Mary Kay Cosmetics had an equal opportunity to reach management level, regardless of formal qualifications.

Part of the company's success is its ability to motivate its saleswomen. From its annual meetings, to which everyone is invited, to Pink Cadillac awards for achieving specific sales levels, the women who work for Mary Kay Cosmetics develop a special sense of belonging that extends beyond the usual employee-employer relationship. The sales structure is based on free enterprise and each saleswoman is, in effect, an entrepreneur. Advancement is entirely based on merit, progressing from consultant to sales director to national sales director. What helps to make Mary Kay Cosmetics unique among major employers of women in the United States, is that the success of each individual carries with it the unanticipated benefit of building self-esteem and confidence,

something that is not necessarily a by-product of other employment situations. The commune is one of the largest employers of women, with a sales force of over 375,000 in 1993. Over half of the national sales directors have earned between $1 and $4 million in commissions. A Fortune 500 company with 1993 sales exceeding $1 billion, Mary Kay Cosmetics has been listed as one of *the one hundred best companies to work for in America.*

1963: The President's Commission on the Status of Women Issues Its *American Women* Report

(Social Reform, Equal Rights)

On October 11, 1963, the President's Commission on the Status of Women, established by President John F. Kennedy in 1961, issued its report, entitled *American Women.*

While President John F. Kennedy was very dependent on women's votes, he was not at all committed to promoting women's rights. It seems somewhat ironic, then, that he should be the one to establish a Commission

on the Status of Women in 1961, particularly since former Presidents Dwight D. Eisenhower and Harry S Truman had been similarly lobbied to create a commission and both had refused. For Kennedy, there were good political reasons for doing so.

Esther Peterson, the head of the Women's Bureau, and the highest-level woman appointee in the Kennedy administration, first came forward with the suggestion. Peterson had two reasons for doing so: first, she wanted to deflect any potential pro–equal rights amendment (ERA) activity, primarily because it was still opposed by organized labor; second, Peterson wanted to see legislation enacted that would guarantee to women equal pay for equal work, a measure for which the support of organized labor would be required. Kennedy had already been criticized by women for not making any cabinet-level appointments involving women. Indeed, his record of female appointees lagged behind those of his predecessors. When Peterson suggested the commission, Kennedy viewed it as an opportunity to recoup some of his female support.

The commission, composed of thirteen women and eleven men, was chaired by Eleanor Roosevelt. It employed seven investigatory committees, on which many prominent women sat, as well as scores of consultants and Women's Bureau staff. In November 1962, Eleanor Roosevelt died. As a tribute to her memory, the commission issued its report, entitled *American Women*, on October 11, 1963, the anniversary of Roosevelt's birth.

As expected, the report declared that an equal rights amendment was not necessary at the present time because, in the opinion of respected Constitutional scholars, the Fifth and Fourteenth Amendments guaranteed equal rights to women. Attorney Marguerite Rawalt, the only pro-ERA advocate on the commission, had insisted that the wording be such that it left open the question of whether an ERA might be appropriate at a future date.

The sixty-page report did include a long list of conditions that required amelioration and made specific recommendations. Among other things, the report advocated an end to the prohibition against women jurors and restrictions on married women's rights. It supported federally and privately funded childcare centers for working mothers, joint guardianship of children, continuing education programs for women, equal employment opportunities, paid maternity leaves, equal pay laws, increased vocational training, promotion of women to high-level government jobs, more appointments of women to policymaking jobs, and continued efforts on the part of the government to insure the rights of women.

Two special consultations set up by the commission had provoked most of the controversy within the commission. Both were set up as afterthoughts, but they reflected to a great extent the concerns that would begin to emerge in the revived women's movement of the mid-1960s. The first was a consultation on "Images of Women in the Media." Sitting in on the symposium were writers including Lorraine Hansberry, the author of A Raisin in the Sun, Marya Mannes, and Betty Friedan. Hansberry complained that women were constantly objectified in media images. Mannes noted that magazines tended to portray women as housewives and mothers, neglecting all of their other roles and categories. And Friedan criticized magazines for failing to convey the idea that women had goals and ideals outside of the narrowly defined stereotypes. A second commission, "The Problems of Negro Women," chaired by the president of the National Council of Negro Women, Dorothy Height, complained that too little attention was paid to the plight of African-American families and their lack of opportunities.

While the report of the commission attracted little attention, it did result in passage of the first federal law prohibiting sex discrimination, the Equal Pay Act, by the end of 1963. Moreover, Kennedy directed executive agencies to put a stop to sex discrimination in hiring and promoting practices, and a permanent Citizen's Advisory Council on the Status of Women was created to act as a watchdog agency. Finally, individual states began appointing their own commissions to make similar inquiries on statewide conditions. But perhaps the most lasting legacy of the commission was that it served as a turning point, heralding a revitalization of the women's movement that would have far-reaching effects on American society.

1963: Congress Passes the Equal Pay Act of 1963

(Work, Equal Rights)

In 1963, at the recommendation of the President's Commission on the Status of

Women, Congress passed an equal pay act, the first national legislation for women's employment since the progressive era.

Throughout the history of industrialized America, women workers have been paid less than male workers for the same jobs. During the progressive era, in the two decades immediately before World War I, protective legislation advocates had made attempts to insure that some sort of parity would be achieved by promoting minimum wage laws for women workers. Although several states did pass such laws, the Supreme Court eventually declared them unconstitutional in the *Adkins v. Children's Hospital* case in 1923. Only one state, Wyoming, had any kind of equal pay laws on the books. In 1869, the year Wyoming became a state, its legislature passed an equal pay law for employees of the state government. Until the Equal Pay Act of 1963, no other states had entertained the notion of legislating such laws.

There were several reasons for this state of affairs, not the least of which was a culturally accepted tradition that men were entitled to earn more than women, even when they both did the same job, because men were the breadwinners and the heads of households. This was widely accepted, even in the many cases where the head of the household was a woman, who had the same economic responsibility to provide for her children that male heads of households had. During World War II, when women went into the labor force in unprecedented numbers, they were still paid about half of what male workers doing the same job received.

The Equal Pay Act of 1963 was intended to remove that disparity. The act provided for equal pay for men and women for jobs requiring equal skill, responsibility, and effort. It also prohibited employers from lowering the wages of one sex in order to avoid raising the wages of the other sex. Unions were forbidden from causing or trying to cause employers to violate the law. The circumstances under which exceptions could be made were wages based on seniority, merit, quantity or quality of production, or differentials based on any reason other than sex.

Since its inception, the Equal Pay Act has been difficult to enforce fairly because of the varying interpretations of what constitutes equal effort, skill, and responsibility. Moreover, jobs were often categorized by personnel departments as either male or female, with job descriptions that could be altered just enough to make a provable case that the jobs were not comparable. Until the 1970s, even help-wanted advertisements in the newspapers were segregated into "Help Wanted, Male," and "Help Wanted, Female," so determining equality in employment was, at best, vague and imprecise.

In the 1970s, feminists and advocates of equal rights began to look at jobs in a slightly different way that made it more possible to win suits under the Equal Pay Act. Rather than looking for precise job equality, these women began looking for comparable worth in job descriptions and wages. Where it could be demonstrated that

jobs held by men and women had comparable worth, the courts were much more inclined to rule in favor of the women litigants. In 1985, women won comparable worth lawsuits in six states, most of them involving city or state jobs, because these jobs can be more easily quantified in terms of qualifications and requirements. Lawsuits on the federal level were less successful, primarily because of the renewed conservatism of the 1980s, coupled with the Reagan administration's hostility toward such litigation. Nevertheless, comparable worth assessments hold out the best hope for pay equity in the absence of an equal rights amendment.

1963: *The Feminine Mystique* by Betty Friedan Is Published

(Family Life, Work, Cultural Life)

Betty Friedan's book, *The Feminine Mystique*, published in 1963, critiqued women's magazines, behavioral scientists, and the advertising industry, which, Friedan charged, combined to perpetuate the stereotype of women achieving total fulfillment in their roles as wives and mothers.

Betty Friedan described the problem that afflicted many women in

post–World War II America as a vague feeling of discontent and aimlessness that persisted despite having everything that both science and popular culture told them defined their most fulfilling roles in life as wives, mothers, and homemakers. It was, said Friedan, "the problem that has no name." Although the publisher of *The Feminine Mystique* expected reasonably good sales, W. W. Norton limited the first printing of the book to two thousand copies. No one, including Friedan, anticipated the explosive response to the book. Within ten years, *The Feminine Mystique* sold three million hard-cover copies and many more in paperback

Friedan herself had written for the very women's magazines that she accused of helping to circumscribe the options open to women outside of the home by determining for women from where their self-worth ought to come. Her experience as a suburban housewife and mother, and memories of her own mother's discontent at abandoning a career in favor of marriage, led Friedan to question the validity of this popular viewpoint. A survey of her Smith College class of 1942 indicated, moreover, that the problem might be more widespread than anyone suspected.

According to the popular viewpoint, scientifically corroborated by social scientists and reported in page after page of women's magazines,

from *Redbook* to *Ladies Home Journal* to *Cosmopolitan*, American women could find no greater fulfillment than in devoting their lives to their husbands and to raising their children in a nurturing environment. This "cult of domesticity" might have continued unchallenged had not the expanded opportunities for women created by World War II, and thereafter retracted, resulted in a groundswell of discontent, boredom, and loneliness. Until *The Feminine Mystique*, most women experiencing these feelings thought the problem was uniquely theirs and that they somehow lacked appreciation for all that they had. It was both a revelation and a release to discover that many women felt the same way.

In retrospect, it should not have surprised Norton that *The Feminine Mystique* would have such an impact on American women. Two previous books on the subject, *The Exurbanites* (1956) by A. C. Spectorsky and *The Split-Level Trap* (1960) by Katherine Gordon, had also sold briskly. In 1962, *Esquire* devoted a full issue to the American woman that, in many ways, sounded more like a lament for what might have been than a celebration of what was. But Friedan's book seemed to touch an untapped nerve. By going beyond descriptions like "discontent" and "boredom," and identifying what women were feeling, Friedan gave it more weight. It could not be as easily dismissed or explained. It also helped to break the long silence on issues such as unequal salaries, limited opportunities, and women's powerlessness in both family and society. Finally, women especially responded to Friedan's assertion that women could help themselves out of their malaise. They could take positive steps to reassert their identities without relying on or waiting for social scientists and women's magazines to point them in the right direction. In a very important sense, *The Feminine Mystique* was the first real clarion call of the modern women's movement.

1964: "Bewitched" Begins a Seven-Year Run as a Top-Rated Television Show

(Entertainment)

In 1964, a half-hour situation comedy about a witch who settles down to a life of suburban domesticity premiered. It ranked in the top three television shows in its first year and was still rated number thirteen after four years. "Bewitched" continued to be produced until 1972.

"Bewitched" was the perfect show for a nation on the cusp of "women's liberation." Produced by William Asher and starring Elizabeth Montgomery and Dick York as Samantha and Darren Stevens, its basic situation was that, while on the surface, Darren and Samantha were just a normal advertising executive and his homemaker wife, living a normal early-sixties suburban existence, in reality Samantha was a powerful witch, able to cast spells and work magic that could transform reality. The central concept of the show was that when, on their wedding night, Darren learns of his bride's marvelous powers, instead of thinking how they can benefit from them, he resolves that they should have no role in their lives whatsoever. Samantha's magic will not replace grocery shopping or the washing machine in her life, and it certainly will not influence his career: what he gains will be from own talents and hard work alone. Samantha, who has already decided to give up her life as a witch for a life of simple domesticity, cheerfully agrees to go along.

The comedy in the show comes from the fact that it naturally proves impossible to avoid the fact of Samantha's extraordinary powers. In the first place, Samantha sometimes lapses into magic, thinking that the use will be harmless, but inevitably creating a situation in which the consequences are bigger than she had anticipated. Furthermore, her meddlesome mother Endora (played by Agnes Moorehead) causes trouble whenever possible since she has never approved of her daughter's folly in marrying the mortal "Derwin." Occasionally, other of Samantha's relatives intervene in the Stevens' life with magic, out of spite or out of kindness, but in any case creating a situation that violates Darren's prime directive. Each show then revolves around Darren and Samantha's desperate attempts to put things back to normal, to undo whatever has been

done, to make sure no one suspects what really happened, and, most of all, to insure that whatever successes Darren has scored are only the result of his own efforts.

What made the show such an interesting commentary about the early sixties, and a portent of the women's movement that came shortly thereafter, was the fact that the husband Darren was so threatened by his wife's powers that he insisted they be bottled up entirely. His objection was not based on moral or theological grounds, but on his own psychological need to be the sole breadwinner. While Samantha's magical powers of course exaggerate the situation, how typical this situation was in the upper-middle-class families of the early 1960s, when college educated women with work experience and even advanced degrees were expected to turn off their talents and ambitions in order to play the role of suburban housewife, content to manage the household and serve as an adornment to their husbands' careers. Viewed in this light, what was really striking about Samantha Stevens was not her magical powers, but her complete and unconflicted willingness to protect her husband's fragile ego.

1964: The Civil Rights Act Includes a Prohibition against Sex Discrimination in Employment

(Equal Rights)

On July 2, 1964, the U.S. Senate passed the Civil Rights Act of 1964, the most ambitious and far-reaching piece of civil rights legislation to date. Included in the act was Title VII, which prohibited employment discrimination based on either race or sex.

Because the Civil Rights Act of 1964 was such an ambitious piece of legislation covering discrimination in public places, voting rights protection, and employment discrimination, among other things, the bill had to overcome a great deal of opposition. Octogenarian Representative Howard W. Smith of Virginia introduced an amendment to Title VII that he thought would help to ensure the defeat of the entire bill. His amendment called for the prohibition of employment discrimination on the basis of not only race but sex as well. Smith, who had appeared on "Meet the Press" a short time before, had apparently taken a serious suggestion put to him by veteran White House correspondent May Craig and decided that including a provision outlawing sex discrimination would render the bill as ludicrous to everyone else as it was to him.

The Smith amendment elicited the kind of response he had hoped for. Both liberals and women's groups, including the League of Women Voters, objected to endangering the cause of civil rights by tying it to another cause. One member of Congress voiced the fear that acceptance of such a provision might "endanger traditional family relationships." The congressman also suggested that it could affect hard-won privileges, such as alimony and child-custody. President Lyndon B. Johnson was determined that the Civil Rights Act would be passed, however, and he began to put pressure on members of Congress to secure the necessary votes. He also enlisted the help of Michigan Representative Martha Griffiths and the "Conscience of the Senate," Maine Senator Margaret Chase Smith.

The Civil Rights Act passed the House of Representatives on February 10, 1964, but its fate in the Senate was not at all certain. For eighty-three days, southern senators filibustered on the floor of the Senate in an effort to fatally delay passage. On June 10, Senate proponents of the bill mustered the necessary two-thirds majority to invoke the closure rule and bring an end to the filibuster. Finally, on July 2, the Civil Rights Act of 1964 was passed into law, complete with its Title VII provisions prohibiting employment discrimination on the basis of race or sex. The new law also provided for the establishment of the Equal Employment Opportunity Commission, charged with enforcing the provisions of Title VII. All provisions were required to go into effect one year after passage of the bill.

1964: Fannie Lou Hamer Founds the Mississippi Freedom Democratic Party

(Civil Rights)

In August 1964, Fannie Lou Hamer led a delegation of African-American dissenters, who had organized themselves as the Mississippi Freedom Democratic party (MFDP), to the Democratic National Convention in Atlantic City, demanding to be seated in place of what she considered to be an illegal whites-only Mississippi delegation.

In August 1964, Fannie Lou Hamer, a Mississippi civil rights activist, led a contingent of dissenters to the Atlantic City Democratic National Convention. With little real hope of succeeding, but intent nevertheless on pressing the issue, Hamer, the founder and vice-chairwoman of the Mississippi Freedom Democratic Party, protested before the convention and before a national television audience, the seating of the all-white Mississippi delegation to the convention. Democrats Hubert Humphrey and Walter Mondale tried to organize a compromise that would have seated two members of the MFDP, but the Democratic party refused to entertain the compromise. Fearing that it would look too reactionary, the Democratic party made an unprecedented pledge guaranteeing to the MFDP that no delegations that excluded African-Americans would be seated at the 1968 convention.

Fannie Lou Hamer, who had acted as spokesperson for the MFDP, had already been through more on behalf of civil rights than most Americans could comprehend at the time. One of twenty children of Mississippi sharecroppers, Hamer had seen as a child the myriad ways in which African-Americans were discouraged from even thinking about getting ahead in Mississippi. When her father, after years of saving, put together enough money to purchase two mules to help with the farming chores, whites poisoned the mules as an object lesson in maintaining one's place. In August 1962, inspired by civil rights activist Ella Baker, Hamer organized a voter registration drive at the Sunflower County Courthouse in Mississippi.

Registration officials spent most of the day creating new reasons why they could not register. On the way home, their bus was stopped and the driver arrested for violating a segregation law. Hamer was fired when her boss heard of her actions. She was evicted from her home. Her husband and daughter were arrested on false charges. The Hamers were billed $9,000 by the water department for a home that had no running water. Hamer became a target for violent racists, and was threatened with bodily harm and death. All of this resulted from the single action of trying to register voters. Instead of being discouraged, Hamer was fired up. As she told a congressional committee sometime later, she was "sick and tired of being sick and tired."

Hamer continued to work for civil rights in the South. The year after her efforts to register, Hamer and Annelle Ponder opened a citizenship school in their town, the reprisal for which was a severe beating at the hands of the local police. Although the Justice Department did bring charges against the five men responsible, the presiding judge at their trial directed the jury to bring in a not-guilty verdict. Still Hamer persisted. In an audacious move, she qualified to run for Congress from her home district. Although it is difficult to determine how many votes she won, because all the ballots with her name on them were disqualified, it is safe to say that she picked up a significant percentage of the votes cast.

In January 1965, Hamer challenged the legality of the Mississippi delegates to Congress on the grounds that African-Americans had been denied the right to vote. After nine months, the MFDP lost. Hamer continued to serve as vice-chairwoman of the MFDP, but over the next several years deteriorating health limited her activism. In 1977, at the age of fifty-nine, Hamer died of cancer.

1965: Helen Gurley Brown Takes Over as Editor of *Cosmopolitan*

(Cultural Life)

Helen Gurley Brown, the author of a controversial advice book entitled *Sex and the Single Girl*, in which she bluntly proclaimed that sexual activity ought to be part of a single girl's life, in 1965 became editor of *Cosmopolitan* magazine, a seventy-nine-year-old family publication in decline.

When Helen Gurley Brown published *Sex and the Single Girl* in 1962, she probably anticipated the wave of controversy that would come crashing down around the book and its author. The forty-year-old veteran of years in a secretarial pool and a somewhat shorter career as an advertising account executive was nothing if not a smart, savvy observer of office politics and social mores. Brown rejected the idea of single women leading drab lives, waiting to be rescued by the first knight who happened by. To the consternation of conservatives who worried that the modern unmarried woman was in danger of abandoning moral values, *Sex and the Single Girl* celebrated a lifestyle that acknowledged and applauded an active sex life.

When offered the opportunity to take over the helm of *Cosmopolitan* magazine, Brown jumped at the chance and immediately began to change its image. *Cosmopolitan* had existed as a family-oriented magazine since its founding in 1886. Like many magazines, however, it had fallen on hard times, with declining subscription rates and loss of advertising as television became more and more entrenched as the recreation medium of choice. But under Brown's direction, *Cosmopolitan* shed its family image in favor of one catering to the liberated single woman. Based on the success of her book, Brown correctly predicted a large, heretofore untapped segment of the population that both magazines and advertisers had overlooked—the single career woman. The "Cosmo Woman" defined a particular type of American woman, not necessarily feminist but definitely independent, open to opportunity, and willing to redefine her own image in

order to gain an advantage. Brown helped to abolish the traditional categorization of women as either married or unmarried. At least in the pages of *Cosmopolitan*, and to a large extent in popular culture, the unmarried spinster stereotype gave way to the glamorous single woman.

Brown's *Cosmopolitan* was also one of the first magazines to consciously court a precisely defined segment of the population, rather than casting a wider readership net by offering something for all readers. From its feature articles, to its monthly how-to and advice columns, to its choice of fiction, *Cosmopolitan* reached out to single working women. As a consequence, subscriptions skyrocketed and the magazine experienced a rebirth under the unfaltering hand of Helen Gurley Brown.

1966: The National Organization for Women Is Founded

(Equal Rights)

At the Third Annual Conference of the Commissions on the Status of Women, held in Washington, D.C., in 1966, a group of women, including *The Feminine Mystique* author Betty Friedan, founded an organization intended to pursue the rights of women in much the same way the NAACP pursued civil rights. The acronym for the

---

National Organization for Women—NOW—was a purposeful reminder that women were tired of waiting for equality.

The twenty-eight women, each contributing five dollars, who met together and founded the National Organization for Women in 1966, arrived in Washington to attend the Third Annual Conference of the Commissions on the Status of Women with no intentions to start a new women's organization. An on-going struggle between Michigan Representative Martha Griffiths and the Equal Employment Opportunity Commission (EEOC) precipitated the action taken by the NOW founders.

When the Civil Rights Act of 1964, with its Title VII provisions prohibiting sex discrimination in employment, went into effect in 1965, the EEOC was inundated with discrimination complaints from women. Because the EEOC considered civil rights its priority and not sex discrimination, it refused to take these complaints seriously. The first executive director of the EEOC knew that the sex discrimination provisions were added in to Title VII as a ploy to defeat the whole Civil Rights Act. He, therefore, decided to ignore complaints from women. Representative Griffiths was determined that the EEOC should treat all complaints with equal seriousness.

When the EEOC failed to do so, she took to the floor of Congress and delivered a blistering speech in which she accused the commission of refusing to enforce the law.

Griffiths' speech, delivered only days before the Conference of the Commissions on the Status of Women was due to convene, met with approval by women within the EEOC who were also distressed by the executive director's noncompliance. The EEOC women believed that if women had a civil rights organization behind them to apply pressure in the same way the NAACP did, their complaints could not be ignored. Members of the conference, filled in on the inaction at EEOC, decided to propose a resolution urging the agency to deal with sexual discrimination as it did with racial discrimination. Conference leaders ruled that the proposition was inappropriate and refused to consider it. Before the conference adjourned for the day, the twenty-eight original members of NOW had taken the first step in creating an organization that would focus on women's civil rights.

In October 1966, three hundred women and men attended the first organizing meeting of NOW. At that meeting, they elected Betty Friedan to serve as the first president, and articulated the goals of the organization. NOW's statement of purpose rejected tokenism and demanded a "fully equal partnership of the sexes, as part of the worldwide revolution of human rights." They opposed any policy or practice that denied opportunities, as well as those that fostered in women "self-denigration, dependence, and evasion of responsibility…and fostered contempt for women." They rejected the idea that men had to carry the full burden of supporting themselves, their wives, and their families, as well as the idea that women were solely responsible for the nurturing of marriage, home, and family. NOW also took issue with the idea that women had to choose between either marriage or career. "Above all," NOW declared, "we reject the assumption

that these problems are the unique responsibility of each individual woman, rather than a basic social dilemma which society must solve."

NOW organizers also put together its version of a Bill of Rights that included an equal rights amendment to the U.S. Constitution. It also included maternity leave, deductions for home and childcare expenses for working parents, government subsidized daycare, equal education, training for poor women, the right to a legal abortion, and not least, EEOC enforcement of all Title VII provisions.

With the founding of NOW, women finally had a political pressure group. In its first five years, NOW grew in membership from the original twenty-eight, to fifteen thousand. It also became the leading voice for the modern women's movement.

1967: Executive Order 11375 Broadens Affirmative Action to Include Sex

(Equal Rights)

In 1967, President Lyndon Johnson broadened affirmative action by including sex as one of the categories that employers holding federal contracts were prohibited from discriminating against. In signing Executive Order 11375, Johnson added sex to race, color, religion, and national origin.

I n the spirit of the Civil Rights Act of 1964, President Lyndon Johnson signed Executive Order 11246, which established a policy of affirmative action as a means to both eliminate discrimination in hiring and to persuade corporations to make a good faith effort to remedy past discrimination. The policy applied to specific categories, including race, color, religion, and national origin, and it forbade corporations who held government contracts from discriminating in their hiring practices against individuals solely based on one of those characteristics. Although it was by no means a panacea against discriminatory hiring practices, it did give the government leverage over corporations because the government could withdraw federal contracts. In 1968, Johnson broadened affirmative action by including sex as one of these categories.

The Office of Federal Contract Compliance (OFCC), which oversees corporate compliance with the regulations in cases where the federal contract is in excess of $1 million, can choose from several penalties, depending on the degree of noncompliance by the offending corporation. It can withhold funds until compliance has been achieved; it can prohibit the corporation from receiving future federal contracts; or it can refer the case to the Justice Department or to the Equal Employment Opportunity Commission. Corporations holding federal contracts are provided with strict guidelines and timetables under which they must reach compliance. Theoretically, such a policy should effectively prohibit discriminatory practices. In fact, the policy has not worked as it was intended to for several reasons. First, understaffing in the agencies charged with carrying out the policy have made it difficult to monitor holders of government contracts. Second, an on-going controversy over the issue of establishing numerical goals has divided both those who oppose affirmative action and some government agencies including the Justice Department. Finally, during the 1980s, the Reagan administration made efforts to weaken the regulations governing government contracts.

Hopes for a renewed effort to impose sanctions against violators and to require compliance, came in 1988 when Congress overrode Reagan's veto of the Civil Rights Restoration Act. By overriding the veto, the original intent of Congress was reestablished and actually strengthened as a result.

1968: Shirley Chisholm Becomes the First African-American Congresswoman

(Civil Rights, Equal Rights)

Shirley Chisholm, the daughter of Caribbean immigrants, ran for a newly apportioned congressional seat representing the Bedford-Stuyvesant section of Brooklyn in 1968. In order to win, Chisholm had to first defeat the Tammany Hall establishment candidate in the Democratic primary, and then the popular civil rights activist, James Farmer, the candidate of a Republican-liberal coalition ticket in the general election.

Shirley Chisholm, born in New York City, spent most of the first ten years of her life living with her grandmother in the Barbados and attending British schools. After returning home to live with her parents, Chisholm attended Brooklyn schools and graduated from Brooklyn College in 1946. She took her first teaching job in Brooklyn and within three years was director of the Brooklyn Friends Day Nursery. By 1949, Chisholm had married a New York police detective, Conrad Chisholm, and enrolled in a master's program at Columbia University. The year after she earned her M.A. from Columbia, Chisholm accepted the position of director of the Hamilton-Madison Child Care Center in Manhattan. Chisholm, a well-respected administrator and teacher, might have remained a teacher had she not joined the Bureau of Child Welfare as a daycare specialist in 1959.

Her concern for issues affecting minority women and children caused her to become active in Democratic politics on the local level. In 1964,

Chisholm ran for and won a seat in the New York State Assembly, an office she held until 1968 when she decided to run for the newly formed congressional seat representing the Bedford-Stuyvesant section of Brooklyn. Chisholm won both the primary and the general election, when she had to run against the popular civil rights activist, James Farmer. Her years spent teaching, her advocacy on behalf of minority women and children, and her ability to speak fluent Spanish, all coalesced to secure victory. In 1969, Chisholm was sworn in as the first African-American congresswoman in the nation's history.

As a congresswoman serving during the height of the Vietnam war abroad, and the social upheaval of the sixties at home, Chisholm lost little time in establishing herself as a leader of both women and minorities. An article in *McCalls* magazine in 1970 garnered national attention when she said that having endured both racial and sex prejudice, she believed that sexism was by far the more intractable of the two. She spoke out emphatically against a continued U.S. presence in Vietnam, leading marches and partici-pating prominently in rallies. She was a vocal supporter of equal rights for women and for social justice for minorities. In 1972, Chisholm announced her candidacy for the office of president, insuring that women's rights would be a major issue in the campaign. With Cissy Farenthal of Texas as her running mate, Chisholm ran an energetic campaign that, while she knew would not succeed, nevertheless brought the issues to the public. At the Democratic convention Chisholm emerged as a national spokesperson.

Although she remained in Congress throughout the seventies, Chisholm longed to return to her first love, teaching, and to writing. She chose to retire from Congress in February 1982, announcing that she had accepted a teaching position at Mount Holyoke College. Chisholm by no means left politics entirely behind. In 1984, she was a founder of the National Political Congress of Black Women. For three years, Chisholm was, according to the Gallup Poll, one of the "Ten Most Admired Women in the World," and in 1993, President Bill Clinton appointed her Ambassador to Jamaica.

1969: San Diego State University Establishes the First Women's Studies Baccalaureate Degree Program

(Education, Equal Rights)

Reflecting the growing interest in women's rights and the concern over the lack of representation in academia of women's experiences and contributions to American life and culture, San Diego State University in California in 1969 became the first university to establish a degree-granting program in women's studies.

For decades, students progressed through the American school system with little or no concept of the experiences or contributions of women to American life and culture. Ignored in much the same way that nonwhite and non-Western peoples in general have been slighted, women were relegated to a few lines, usually concerning women like Martha Washington, Florence Nightingale, Betsy Ross, and Jane Addams. With the reemergence of a women's movement in the 1960s, an increasing demand for an integration of women into the curriculum began to yield results. In 1969, San Diego State University became the first institution of higher learning to create a women's studies program as part of its curriculum.

At the university level, the initial demands for women's studies came from faculty in the humanities and social sciences, but eventually broadened to include receptive faculty in the sciences as well. For female faculty and students especially, the need for both the immediate role models within the university and the scholarly and historical role models in the literature, were all part of the same problem. Without changing the curriculum to reflect women's role in the development of culture and society, changes in women's status in contemporary society would be significantly harder to achieve. For proponents of women's studies, the biggest hurdle to overcome within the academic community were those academics who saw nothing wrong with continuing to marginalize women, arguing that no adequate scholarship existed to warrant either creating new disciplines or even changing specific course curriculums. What began as a cross-discipline effort to integrate women into the curriculum quickly evolved into an independent methodology focusing on gender.

Five years after San Diego State established the first women's studies program, nearly forty colleges and universities had similar programs, and by the end of the first decade, that number had exploded to over four hundred programs, with a full-fledged scholarly association and scholarly journals. The National Women's Studies Association held its first meeting in 1979. Even before that, *Women's Studies—An Interdisciplinary Journal* published its first issue in 1972, as did *Feminist Studies*. In 1975, what has become the leading journal in the field— *Signs: Journal of Women in Culture and Society*—began publication. A major forum for research, not just in history but in a broad range of disciplines, is the Berkshire Conference on the History of Women, an annual symposium held in the Berkshire Mountains in Western Massachusetts, begun in 1972.

From the beginning, there has been disagreement between those who believe that women's studies should be a separate discipline, and those who believe that the goal should be to integrate women's studies into other disciplines. The consensus now is that both are necessary. The work done in women's studies on the college and university level has also filtered down to high school and grade schools as well. New emphasis has been placed on the books supplied to students in public schools to ensure that not only women, but minorities as well, are reflected in the text and pictures.

1970: The Coalition of 100 Black Women Organizes to Provide Leadership

(Social Reform, Civil Rights)

A small group of African-American women met in New York City in 1970 to discuss both the problems facing them and the opportunities available to them in the wake of the civil rights movement and the women's movement. They organized, calling themselves the Coalition of 100 Black Women, with an agenda to develop leadership and to investigate opportunities.

In 1970, twenty-four African-American women met in New York City, convinced of the necessity of providing a forum for black women leaders. That forum became the Coalition of 100 Black Women, so named because the founding mothers hoped that eventually they would be able to build up the organization to include one hundred women. The coalition initiated a variety of programs to deal with what they perceived to be the most pressing problems facing African-American women, including career advancement, particularly in the corporate world, political and economic empowerment, and the crisis of the black family.

The coalition quickly reached and surpassed its original goal of one hundred women professionals. By 1977, when the dynamic Jewell Jackson McCabe took over as president, the coalition had a membership of 127 women. Four years later, there were 890 members. More importantly, the success of the New York organization had inspired women in other communities to petition for permission to organize branches. A decade later, the National Coalition of 100 Black Women had fifty-nine chapters in twenty-two states, with a total of seven thousand members. The coalition had also become a member organization of the National Council of Negro Women.

The council still operates under a four-point mandate, which includes providing effective networks among women leaders and establishing ties between the coalition and the political and corporate sectors; making black women a visible force, economically, socially, and politically; developing leadership talent within the black community; and publicizing not only the current achievements of black women, but their historic achievements as well. A significant element of their program involves acting as mentors and role models for upcoming generations of African-American professional women, with an eye toward providing the younger women with the leadership and business skills necessary both to succeed personally and influence events in a more general sense. To that end, the coalition maintains a career exploration program for promising high school students, which includes summer internships in large corporations and a career education course at Hunter College in New York.

The coalition has also established a model mentoring program at Spelman College in Atlanta, and City College of New York. The model mentoring program was picked up by chapters in other states as well.

Not yet at the quarter-century mark, the National Coalition of 100 Black Women has nevertheless been able to make itself felt in both political and corporate spheres, in many cases garnering corporate support for some of its more ambitious educational programs. Time-Warner Corporation, for example, is sponsoring the Time-Warner Time to Read Program at coalition chapters in cities such as Atlanta, Los Angeles, and Washington, D.C.

1971: *Ms.* Magazine Is Founded

(Cultural Life, Social Reform)

In 1971, writer Gloria Steinem hosted a gathering of feminist journalists and writers in her New York City home, to discuss how they could better reach out to American women to share with them the goals and hopes of the women's movement. Out of that meeting, *Ms.* magazine was created.

M s. magazine, the first national publication that was created by women specifically for women readers, was perhaps the most creative innovation to come out of the women's movement of the 1960s and 1970s. Gloria Steinem, one of the acknowledged leaders of the women's movement, invited a group of feminist writers and journalists to her home early in 1971, for the purpose of discussing ways in which they might reach out to women who were not members of any of the organizations that had sprung up to discuss the status of women and to promote women's rights. Steinem, one of the founders of the successful *New York* magazine, wanted to create a magazine that would address crucial issues and that would be directed at a very specific female audience. The idea met with enthusiastic responses, and those present, including Betty Friedan and Pat Carbine, immediately began to use their combined journalistic experience to find the necessary financial support.

The format of the new magazine was very clearly defined. It would avoid the usual advice, cooking, and beauty columns traditionally found in women's magazines. At the same time, the founders did not want a magazine that relied on dogmatic partisanship or ideological debates that would almost surely prohibit broad readership. The goal was to provide a forum for feminist trends and ideas, presented in a low-key fashion that would not alienate women who did not consider themselves feminists. One of the most innovative editorial policies decided upon was that the magazine, under no circumstances, would accept advertising that portrayed women in a demeaning way.

Steinem approached her *New York* colleague, Clay Felker, and persuaded him to include a preview copy of *Ms.* as an insert in an issue of *New York*. The *New York/Ms.* issue was released at the end of 1971. The now-famous *Ms.* first cover featured, appropriately enough, Wonder Woman. That particular issue of *New York* proved to be the magazine's all-time sales leader. Steinem and Felker had agreed on a three hundred thousand copy run that they believed would last for eight weeks, right up to the projected spring

debut of *Ms*. All three hundred thousand copies were sold in eight days. It was a stunning first outing.

Since its inception, *Ms.* editors (Steinem was the editor for the first fifteen years) have published articles on issues concerning contemporary women both at home and in the workplace. A hallmark of its editorial style was a noncondescending and forthright discussion of issues that appealed greatly to its readers. In addition, *Ms.* featured articles on women's history, poetry, and fiction by some of the best contemporary writers available.

The success of *Ms.* led to other ventures, including the Ms. Foundation for Women, Inc., organized in 1975 as a tax-exempt educational and charitable foundation that provided grants for research projects. A year later, the Free to Be Foundation was established to fund nonsexist children's programming and to promote unbiased development.

By 1982, *Ms.* boasted a solid subscription base of two hundred thousand readers. As the politically conservative 1980s wore on, however, the economic difficulties that beset the nation generally began to make themselves felt at the magazine. By 1988, the publishers had to sell *Ms.* to a more lucrative publishing company that could afford to continue publication. Although *Ms.*, under its new ownership, was redirected slightly to a more mainstream product, it nevertheless continued to promote and support women writers and women's issues as the core of its monthly content.

1971: The National Women's Political Caucus Is Founded

(Equal Rights)

A vehicle to encourage more women to participate in the political process both as candidates and as electors, the National Women's Political Caucus (NWPC) was founded by a representative group of leaders of the women's movement in 1971.

Prior to passage of the Equal Rights Amendment by Congress in 1972, women involved in both politics and the women's movement were persuaded that no real progress would be made unless and until women were more equitably represented in policy-making bodies, including both state and federal legislatures. In 1971, Congresswomen Bella Abzug and Shirley Chisholm, and activists Gloria Steinem, Betty Friedan, Dorothy Height, and LaDonna Harris founded the National Women's Political Caucus. Seeking to increase the numbers of women participating in both public and political life, the bipartisan caucus initially worked with women who expressed a desire to run for political office. Using their own political campaign experience, the founders helped to organize campaigns and to provide crash courses in politicking for the less experienced candidates. By the late 1980s, the NWPC had three hundred affiliates nationwide, and a membership of nearly eighty thousand women.

On all levels and in all political arenas, the NWPC affiliates encouraged women to become involved as officeholders, volunteers, political appointees, convention delegates, judges, and committee members. By

326

this time also, the caucus members were recruiting likely women who they believed could be groomed for public office. In addition, the caucus lobbied constantly for contributions to fund campaigns. In 1973, the caucus was a prime sponsor of the Year of the Woman Conference held in Houston, Texas. The conference, which was chaired by Bella Abzug and attended by more than twenty thousand people, was a clear sign of how far women had come politically.

Since the founding of the National Women's Political Caucus, the number of women officeholders has increased dramatically. In 1971, approximately 4 percent of all state legislators were women; by the mid-1980s, that num-ber had increased to over 14 percent. There have been more women repre-sentatives in Congress, women gover-nors and mayors, and women judges and delegates. More recently, the 1992 elections produced a bumper crop of women Senators, and the Clinton ad-ministration has appointed several women to highly visible positions, in-cluding cabinet officers Janet Reno (the first woman Attorney General), Donna Shalala (Secretary of Health, Education, and Welfare), and Ruth Bader Ginsberg, the second woman appointed to the Supreme Court. While women still fall far short of po-litical parity, they have been encour-aged nevertheless by the gains made.

1972: Title IX Prohibits Discrimination on the Basis of Sex in Federally Funded Education Programs

(Equal Rights)

The Education Amendments of 1972 prohibited discrimination on the basis of sex in federally funded or aided education programs. Title IX in the Education Amend-ments applied the ruling to a wide variety of programs, including sports programs.

When the Education Amendments of 1972 were being debated in Congress, efforts were made to exclude intercollegiate athletics from the provisions. Advocates of the exclusion were unsuccessful, and Title IX changed the face of college sports programs for women, virtually overnight. Women had always been interested in competitive and recreational sports, but different constraints at different times discouraged the widespread participation that characterized men's sports. In the late nineteenth century, conventional wisdom determined that participating in physical activity would be detrimental to a woman's more fragile constitution. Since working-class girls and women did not have access to sports in the same degree that middle- and upperclass women could have, the social rules that proscribed women's participation were directed more at middleclass sensibilities. While sports participation was encouraged, and even expected as part of men's rites of passage, and while young girls might be encouraged to take up moderate forms of physical activity, by the time girls reached their teen years, they were made to understand that it was unladylike and unacceptable for women to engage in excessive physical activity. Even well into the twentieth century, the constraints against women in sports were overwhelming, although more and more women were participating in both amateur and professional sports. Notably for women, golf and tennis proved to be avenues to both participate in career sports and to earn a respectable, even wealthy, livelihood, although that aspect is a much more recent phenomenon.

One area where women remained fairly low-key in sports participation was at the college level. With the exception of the women's schools, like Wellesley, Smith, and Mount Holyoke, which always encouraged physical activity and consequently funded athletic programs, most women attending colleges and universities found only a rudimentary physical education program, if that. Virtually all monies spent for athletic programs went to men's sports. As a result, women who wanted to compete in sports had to make do with underfunded programs characterized by shoddy equipment, shabby uniforms, and generally a competitive schedule that was more determined by the ease with which teams could get together than by any real competitive equity. Nevertheless, dedicated women coaches and players kept the programs alive in the leanest of times.

When Title IX was included in the

Education Amendments of 1972, it revolutionized women's sports programs in colleges and universities. By 1975, the growing awareness of the impact of Title IX and the guidelines set forth by the Department of Health, Education, and Welfare, produced enormous changes for women's programs. In 1970, the number of women students participating in intercollegiate athletic programs was about 7.5 percent; by 1978, that number had increased to almost 32 percent. An astounding 570 percent increase in the number of women athletes during these years, compared to the 13 percent increase in the number of male athletes, was dramatic proof of the effectiveness of the federally mandated equal funding for women's sports programs.

Opponents of Title IX, including the Reagan administration, seeking to find loopholes in the tough enforcement mechanism, finally succeeded in finding an ally when the U.S. Supreme Court virtually gutted Title IX as a consequence of its decision in the case of *Grove City College v. Bell*, in 1984. Until then, colleges were forced to abide by Title IX for fear that they would be stripped of federal funds, regardless of whether or not those funds were used for athletics, if it could be determined that the institutions were discriminat-

ing against athletic programs for women. In *Grove City College v. Bell*, the Court ruled that federal funds could be stripped only from those programs found to be discriminatory. In other words, a college that received no federal funds earmarked for sports programs and that discriminated against women in funding such programs could not be stripped of federal funds or grants used to support, for example, scientific research. It was a huge blow to women's sports programs. But advocates in Congress, refusing to accept defeat, passed a Civil Rights Restoration Act in March 1988, reinstating the former institutionwide penalty for sex discrimination. Proponents were able to build a coalition strong enough to override a Reagan veto of the act, by allowing a provision that enabled colleges and universities to refuse to provide abortion-related services without threat of penalty.

Title IX continues to underpin the athletic programs for women in colleges and universities, encouraging women to participate in sports and to compete. One irony of its success, however, is that women coaches and athletic directors have become the expendable victims of revamped programs. In 1983, the Association for Intercollegiate Athletics for Women was dissolved when women's sports came under the aegis of the male-dominated National Collegiate Athletic Association. As schools combined their athletic programs under one structure, it was more often than not the women coaches and staffs that were let go in favor of retaining the male administration and coaching staffs. Also, as salaries for coaches of women's teams increased, male coaches began to take more interest in and eventually took over many of the coaching duties previously performed by women. So, while Title IX has been a boon for women athletes and women's sports programs, the victory has been bittersweet.

1972: Congress Passes the Equal Rights Amendment

(Equal Rights)

After intensive lobbying by feminists and other proponents of equality, in 1972 both houses of Congress passed the Equal Rights Amendment. The vote in the House was 354 to 23, and in the Senate an equally impressive majority of 84 to 8 passed the legislation. Significantly, the legislation as passed included a limitation on the amount of time that Congress would allow for the requisite number of states to ratify the amendment.

In 1923, under a mandate from the National Woman's Party, of which she was the founder, Alice Paul penned the simple lines of the Equal Rights Amendment modeled on the recently passed Nineteenth Amendment: "Men and women shall have equal rights throughout the United States and every place subject to its jurisdiction. Congress shall have the power to enforce this article through appropriate legislation." The amendment, which in its final form changed only slightly, was immediately dubbed the Lucretia Mott Amendment on its introduction to Congress in December 1923. But if advocates hoped that naming the amendment after the renowned Quaker pacifist might help in eliminating some of the controversy surrounding it, it was purely wishful thinking.

From the start, the women's movement was divided over the issue of the ERA. Radical feminists, like Paul, believed that until and unless the nation was willing to guarantee equal rights to women through a constitutional amendment, true equality would be nonexistent. Moderates, including virtually the entire woman's movement, led by women such as Florence Kelley, Carrie Chapman Catt, Elizabeth Dreier, Margaret Dreier Robbins, and Mary Anderson of the Woman's Bureau, feared that adoption of an ERA would nullify all of the protective legislation for women and children that had taken years of lobbying to put into place. It was a legitimately heartfelt difference of opinion that kept the women's movement divided for several decades and caused Paul and her supporters to redefine their strategy. Whereas Paul had initially planned to mount an ERA campaign much like the suffrage campaign, resistance from other women's groups made it clear that the NWP would first have to lobby among their own and gain the support of a majority of American women.

It was not until after World War II that women's groups such as the Gen-
eral Federation of Women's Clubs and the League of Women Voters began to be persuaded that an ERA was necessary, partially because the women's movement that had provided the impetus for the Nineteenth Amendment dispersed after its passage. In the final years of the suffrage campaign, NAWSA's strategy to mobilize women was to convince them that the vote was an end in itself. Once suffrage was secured, women would not have to campaign for reform because reforms would be secured at the polls. Ninety percent of the suffragists who had put in months and years of volunteer work for the cause wanted nothing more than to return to their private lives. They were not prepared to embark on another political campaign, nor did they want to.

In the 1960s, with a reemergence of the women's movement, feminists began to focus again on an ERA. When the amendment was passed by Congress, women believed that the fight had finally been won because the majority of Americans supported the ERA. Within a year, twenty-eight states had ratified the ERA. After that, opponents began to mount a counter-campaign. Led by people like Phyllis Schlafly, the strident editor of the *Phyllis Schlafly Report* and the *Eagle Forum Newsletter*, the ERA opponents rallied support from housewives across America by playing on their fears about what a world with an equal rights amendment would look like. According to Schlafly, women would be subject to the draft. They would have to leave their homes and children while they served in the armed forces. Equality like that, Schlafly argued, would destroy the family. Schlafly also used an existing element of resentment to drive a wedge between, in her view, two diametrically opposed camps: feminists and housewives. In part, the feminists had helped to create the mistrust by not validating those women who truly wanted to be housewives. But Schlafly was more than skilled at creating a chasm where none really existed. As she toured the country speaking out against the ERA, resistance began building. By 1977, thirty-five states had ratified the ERA, but with time running out, another three states were needed for ratification. Against the objections of Schlafly's STOP ERA organization, Congress granted a four-year extension for ratification.

In actuality, once Congress had placed a limitation on the amount of time they would allow for ratification when the legislation was passed in 1972, they had really insured that with any kind of organized opposition, the ERA would have little chance of ratification. When the suffrage amendment was passed in 1919, opponents then had tried to impose a similar time limit for ratification. That effort was recognized for what it was, and Congress refused to attach limits to the ratification process. Opposition to ratification melted away almost overnight. Opponents were quite clear about the reason why they gave up the fight. With a finite amount of time to ratify the suffrage amendment, the opposition could dig in their heels and put all their resources into those states where they had the best chance of defeating ratification. Without a time limit, the opposition believed that they could not sustain the support necessary to hold out indefinitely. With the ERA, the opposition got their time limit. They had only to organize their anti-ERA campaign in key areas in order to prevent ratification in the time allowed. When the time extension ran out in 1982, ratification was still three states shy of the necessary thirty-eight.

1973: Billie Jean King Defeats Bobby Riggs in a Widely Touted Battle of the Sexes

(Equal Rights, Sports)

On September 20, 1973, tennis great Billie Jean King defeated Bobby Riggs in three straight sets in a highly publicized tennis match held at the Houston Astrodome before a record-breaking audience that included prime-time television coverage.

The tennis match between Billie Jean King and Bobby Riggs attracted so much publicity and interest among the American people because it came to represent much more than a contest between two individual opponents. Women's tennis, which had long been the poor relative to the much more lucrative and prestigious men's tennis, was trying to establish itself as an equal competitor in the sports world. In large part, that effort was a consequence of the women's movement, which was testing barriers and trying to break them down on a number of fronts, particularly equal rights. Moreover, Bobby Riggs set himself up as the perfect target. Riggs, then in his fifties, was unrelenting in his boasts that he would have the much younger King crying for mercy.

Men were the stronger and therefore better tennis players, Riggs said time after time.

Without a doubt, much of Riggs' pregame performance was little more than posturing, grandstanding for the sake of his considerable audience. The match represented for Riggs one last chance for the former tennis contender to capture a national audience. To get as much press attention as he could, he let loose a broadside against women tennis players whenever the opportunity presented itself. In almost cartoon-like fashion, Riggs represented to women everything they were trying to change, from chauvinistic attitudes toward women to a refusal to allow women to compete at the high stakes levels, whether in sports or business or any other area of life traditionally dominated by men.

At age thirty, Billie Jean King was still in the prime of her career. Beginning in 1961, King had won twenty Wimbledon titles in singles, doubles, and mixed doubles. She also won titles at the U.S. Open and the French Open. King helped to change the way people viewed women's tennis, and not because of her match with Bobby Riggs. Her style was quick and aggressive, definitely more exciting and a departure from other women players. It was a source of discontent with King, as it was with some other women players, that they remained so poorly paid in comparison to the substantial rewards associated with men's tennis. It was King who organized women players in the "renegade" Women's Tennis Association (WTA) in 1973, an unofficial union that gave women tennis players better bargaining power to gain the same advantages enjoyed by men. The WTA worked out a deal with Virginia Slims promoter Gladys Heldman to appear in that high-paying tournament, thus forcing other tournaments to increase their prize money or

risk losing the best of the women players. King became the first woman player to earn more than $100,000 in a single year. In all, King played a pivotal role in establishing women's tennis as a major sport. The Associated Press chose her as the Woman Athlete of the Year in 1967 and 1973, *Sports Illustrated* named her its Sportswoman of the Year in 1972, and *Time* magazine named her the Woman of the Year in 1976.

When the match was held at the Houston Astrodome in September 1973, it attracted the largest live audience ever to attend a tennis match. In addition, it was telecast during prime time nationwide. The match had long since become more than just a simple tennis match. Women across the country who had never before expressed an interest in tennis were rooting for King. The fact that King beat Riggs so handily before such a wide audience did more for both women and tennis in one night than King could possibly have hoped for when she accepted Riggs' challenge.

1973: *Roe v. Wade* Strikes Down Antiabortion Laws

(Equal Rights, Social Reform)

After two years of deliberation, the U.S. Supreme Court in the case of *Roe v. Wade* declared on January 22, 1973, by a vote of seven to two, that women have a constitutional right to decide whether or not they wish to continue a pregnancy and that the government cannot interfere with that right.

When the Supreme Court made its landmark decision in *Roe v. Wade*, declaring that women have a constitutional right to abortion under the personal liberty clauses of the Ninth and Fourteenth Amendments, it changed the lives of women in a more fundamental sense than any other ruling in the history of the Supreme Court. Although the practice of abortion in the United States had never been formally legalized, until about 1860, midwives, physicians, and women themselves regularly induced abortions for a variety of reasons. Generally speaking, no one perceived the act as sinful or immoral. Between 1860 and 1880, male physicians began to lobby to have abortions ruled illegal as part of their efforts to outlaw all contraception. Active in this movement was Anthony Comstock, a self-styled arbiter of morality and obscenity, for whom the Comstock Law was named. The stand taken by physicians regarding abortion remains interesting because, while in this case they were advocating government regulation of medical procedure, in other instances physicians have adamantly insisted that government had no place in health care and medical practices. It is not clear what percentage of physicians who pressed for legislation also had a hidden agenda. As licensing and professionalization was becoming more and more a requirement to practice medicine, physicians were eager to limit the acceptable activities of midwives.

Between 1860 and 1965, all fifty states adopted antiabortion legislation that made it a crime for physicians to perform abortions in all but the most extreme circumstances. Women with sufficient means could always find safe ways to obtain abortions, but for the vast majority of women, an unwanted pregnancy for any reason placed severe strains on their quality of life. Women could choose to have the child for which there might be little emotional or economic support, or they could choose to find an affordable way to end the pregnancy. Besides being illegal, the methods for undergoing an abortion were often life-threatening.

In Texas, where *Roe v. Wade* originated, a pregnant women referred to as Jane Roe, brought suit against Henry Wade, the district attorney of Dallas County, challenging the state's right to prevent her from having an abortion. Roe won in the lower court and when Wade appealed to the Supreme Court, the lower court decision was upheld. In its ruling, the Supreme Court refused to define the point at which life begins, preferring to take as a measure of when abortion could legally be prevented the point at which a fetus becomes viable and able to survive outside of the mother's womb.

The state has a compelling interest in potential human life at the point of viability and therefore the state's interest supersedes the mother's. Before that point, however, the state has no right to interfere in a woman's right to privacy.

The most vociferous critic of the Supreme Court ruling was the Catholic church. But women in general viewed the decision as a great stride forward since it overturned all of the assumptions previously held regarding the right of the government to restrict women's free choice. Since *Roe v. Wade*, several attempts have been made to overturn the court's decision. Thus far, the court has made only minor adjustments, for example in allowing states to impose waiting periods before women could obtain abortions, and in requiring that minors get permission from both parents before undergoing abortion. The fundamental right to a legal abortion has been preserved so far. But one of the serious consequences of *Roe v. Wade* has been the birth of a right-to-life movement that, in recent times, has become more and more violent.

1976: Women Are Admitted to the U.S. Service Academies by an Act of Congress

(Equal Rights, Education, Military)

After prolonged debate on the subject, Congress enacted legislation in 1975 that mandated the service academies, including West Point, Annapolis, and the Air Force Academy, begin accepting women cadets in 1976. After more than a century of exclusion, the changes were wrought primarily because of pressure brought to bear by the revived women's movement of the 1970s.

When the feminist movement was revived in the late 1960s and early 1970s, two areas where women experienced rapid success in achieving changes in the status quo were in the areas of employment and education. For example, careful scrutiny of the textbooks routinely used in grade schools revealed that sexist stereotypes abounded from the lowest grades on up. Elementary school readers used story lines and illustrations that made inappropriate distinctions between girls and boys, generally depicting boys in shop classes or athletic endeavors, and girls in cooking classes. Allocations for the funding of high school and college athletic teams were also determined to be unfair to girls. The lion's share of athletics money went both for male sports teams and for athletic scholarships for boys.

Some of the biggest changes occurred in areas of higher education, and in particular the decision to allow women entrance into all-male schools, including those in the Ivy League and the service academies. The military leaders at West Point, Annapolis, and the Air Force and Coast Guard academies, as well as the overwhelming majority of graduates of those institutions, argued against admitting women, influenced not only by conventional societal views regarding women in the military, but by the long tradition of excluding women from the academies themselves. Moreover, the cadets and midshipmen enrolled at the academies at the time overwhelmingly disapproved of women joining their elite company. Once Congress acted to change tradition, however, the military had little choice but to make the necessary arrangements.

The Air Force Academy, at Colorado Springs, Colorado, the "youngest" of the service academies, attempted from the start to instill an esprit de corps among its new female cadets and the rest of the cadet wing, by emphasizing their presence in a highly visible manner, characterizing them as an elite cross-section of American women that were joining the elite cross-section of American men chosen to enter. At West Point, New York, the administrators of the U.S. Military Academy, the nation's oldest service academy, focused more on maintaining the same standards that cadets had always had to live up to. The female cadets of West Point understood from their first days in "Beast Barracks," that no consideration would be made based on gender differences. At the Naval Academy in Annapolis, Maryland, the female midshipmen joining the brigade were expected to blend in with as little fanfare as possible, with an eye toward becoming invisible if possible. The differing strategies resulted in different experiences for the first classes of female cadets and midshipmen. The Air Force Academy maintained the lowest attrition rate, primarily because it alone devised and implemented a plan for the smooth transition from all-male to a coed student body.

The first class of women graduated from their respective institutions in 1980. They arguably had the most difficult time because of the sexist behavior that inevitably accompanied their entry into the academies. Upperclassmen often treated women more harshly in an effort to avoid being accused of favoritism. Women also had to endure sexist remarks and behavior from their fellow cadets and midshipmen. It sometimes became a contest to see how quickly a female cadet could be reduced to tears. Despite the added difficulties of being female at a military academy where the indoctrination, training, and level of academic requirement combined to weed out a significant portion of each entering class even without the added burden of being perceived as "different," the first women graduates and their successors have done well. All three service academies have had women graduating first in the class, a feat that requires not only an outstanding academic record, but military expertise and athletic prowess as well. The military careers of the first graduating class revealed little difference from their male counterpart, with the notable exception that women, until very recently, were prohibited from taking positions that were considered combat jobs, such as jet fighter pilots, traditionally a requisite for military officers to reach the highest command levels. Even this restriction has been all but removed, and women graduates of the service academies can now choose high ranking career paths.

1976: Maxine Hong Kingston Wins the National Book Critics Circle Award

(Cultural Life)

In 1976, Maxine Hong Kingston, a Chinese-American daughter of immigrant parents, won the National Book Critics Circle Award for nonfiction for her autobiographical book, *The Woman Warrior*.

Maxine Hong Kingston's childhood as the daughter of immigrant Chinese parents who ran a laundry was as stereotyped as one could imagine. Imbued with her parents' cultural beliefs in hard work, symbolism, and legend-myths, Kingston struggled to find her own life free of old world stereotypes and cultural superstitions. Despite her efforts to live in the American culture in which she was growing up, and which she ultimately perceived as hypocritical, Kingston found that she had no identity unless it included her Chinese heritage. Her autobiographical account of her girlhood and youth, living in two worlds, was published in 1975, under the title *The Woman Warrior*. It was critically acclaimed, and won the National Book Critics Circle Award for 1976. The book also resonated with minority women, particularly those whose cultural heritage was rooted in

Asia. Like other books focusing on the integration of Asian and American cultures, notably Amy Tan's best seller *The Joy Luck Club*, Kingston's *The Woman Warrior* is a valuable contribution to American ethnic heritage as well as to literature produced by women writers.

Kingston's experiences were both uniquely Chinese and typically Asian-American. Despite the diversity of Asian immigrants that have settled in America, including Chinese, Japanese, Korean, Vietnamese, Taiwanese, Indian, Pakistani, Filipino, and several others, there is a commonality that all share in their experiences as immigrants. Very few Asian women immigrated to America before the late nineteenth century. Chinese males immigrated beginning around the mid-nineteenth century, when many of them were able to find jobs on the railroads. But most Chinese immigrants expected to return to their native countries and therefore did not bring wives or children with them. As late as 1860, the ratio of males to females stood at 33 to 1. More often than not, Asian women who did immigrate did so as servants or prostitutes, frequently against their wills. They had little choice in the matter. By the end of the century, other constraints militated against Asian women immigrating, including the Chinese Exclusion Act of 1882, which barred further immigration of Chinese laborers, and the so-called Gentlemen's Agreement of 1908, which barred Japanese and Korean labor immigrants. Like the Chinese, Japanese immigrants were primarily male, with less than 5 percent of total immigrants being female in 1900. The vast majority of Asian immigrants tended to be either Chinese or Japanese, with a smattering of Filipinos, Koreans, and other Asians. Asian immigrants, like most other ethnic groups, tended to keep their traditions and cultures alive in their children through careful nurturing of old world values and customs.

For most Asian-American women, World War II had an enormous impact. Over 120,000 Japanese-Americans after the attack on Pearl Harbor were stripped of their civil rights and their possessions, forced to leave their homes on the west coast, and incarcerated in concentration camps built in remote desert areas in the western United States. Other Asian groups fared better because they came from countries that were either allies or neutrals. Many Asian women found jobs working in industry where labor tended to be scarce during the war. After World War II, assimilation tended to be easier for most Asian-Americans because of the greater opportunities in employment and education, and the easing of civil rights and social interaction restrictions. With new opportunities, Asian-American women began to expand their horizons in terms of the types of jobs they sought. Even with increased educational levels, the double impediment of being female and being nonwhite generally meant that their wages were far lower than those of a white male, for example.

With the passage of the Naturalization Act of 1965, up to twenty thousand immigrants from each country were allowed to immigrate, with preference given to reuniting families and attracting skilled and professional workers. This resulted in an increase in Asian immigration, over half of whom were women whose husbands had migrated earlier, or professional or skilled women seeking better economic opportunity. Very often, however, women doctors, nurses, teachers, dentists, and lawyers were unable to practice their professions until they could pass licensing examinations that often tended to be discriminatory.

In 1980, Asian-American women numbered just under 2 million, out of a total Asian population of about 3.7 million. As a group, Asian-American women tend to be better educated than the national average and they have a higher percentage in the work force than any other ethnic group. They also earn slightly more than the average for women wage earners, but lower than any male groups. As Maxine Hong Kingston discovered in her relationship with her mother and in her own attitude, Asian women continue to work toward assimilation while still retaining the strong cultural and traditional values of their ethnic identity, taking pains to pass them along to their children.

1977: A Year of the Woman Conference Is Held in Houston

(Equal Rights, Cultural Life, Family)

In keeping with the United Nations' International Year of the Woman, American women held a three-day National Woman's Conference in Houston, Texas, to celebrate women, assess their status, and draw up a revised plan of action to achieve future goals.

American women came away from a three-day conference in Houston, Texas, with a renewed sense of commitment to pursuing the goals that the women's movement had begun in the early 1970s. Held in conjunction with the United Nations' International Year of the Woman, the National Woman's Conference was funded in part by the federal government. One thousand, four hundred and forty-two delegates were elected at fifty-six state and territorial meetings that were open to the public. Another four hundred delegates were appointed at-large by an overseeing national commission. Referred to on many occasions by both participants and observers as a "rainbow of women," the conference truly represented every ethnicity, race, religion, income bracket, political persuasion, and occupation. Thirty-five percent of the delegates were non-white, including African-Americans, Puerto Ricans, Native Americans, and Eskimos. Twenty percent of the delegates were from low income brackets, twenty-six percent were Catholics, and eight percent were Jewish. The presiding officer and chairwoman of the conference was Bella Abzug, the former Congresswoman from New York,

who had been instrumental in securing federal funding for the conference. The conference was attended by every notable activist and feminist, including Gloria Steinem, Betty Friedan, and Eleanor Smeal. Lady Bird Johnson, Betty Ford, and Rosalyn Carter also attended. In addition, each session of the conference was attended by hundreds of observers who brought the total attendance to over twenty thousand. By an overwhelming margin, the delegates were women who were unknown outside of their own communities, lending to the conference a genuine feeling that it was a grassroots movement.

By the end of the three-day meeting, delegates had armed the women's movement with a twenty-five-point National Plan of Action, most of which was passed by significant majorities. Among the twenty-five points were a call for passage of an Equal Rights Amendment, the right to abortion on demand with federal and state funds for women who could not otherwise afford an abortion, a national health insurance plan with specific provisions for women, elimination of discrimination against lesbians, federal and state programs for victims of child abuse, rape prevention education, and shelters for battered wives. Three of those issues did touch off controversy with a fundamentalist minority objecting to abortion, lesbian rights, and the ERA. Although the theme of the conference was unity, such as that exhibited when the minority rights resolution was rewritten, strengthened considerably, and then overwhelmingly passed by all of the delegates, in retrospect the three "hot button" issues made unity difficult in the long run.

Women left Houston with a renewed purpose, convinced that the conference had marked a watershed for American women. As Ruth Clusen, the president of the League of Women Voters, observed, "Even for women who are outside organizational life, who don't see themselves as part of the women's movement, something has happened in their lives as a result of this meeting, whether they realize it or not."

1977: Iris Rivera Refuses to Make Her Boss Coffee

(Work)

In early February 1977, Iris Rivera lost her job because she refused to make coffee for her boss. Her stand became a rallying cry for female office workers across the country, initiating a series of movements against petty discriminations that revised the role of women in the workplace.

Iris Rivera, a Chicago legal secretary, took a stand: "(1) I don't drink coffee, (2) it's not listed as one of my job duties, and (3) ordering the secretaries to fix the coffee is carrying the role of homemaker too far." Her stand got her fired.

It also galvanized other secretaries. On February 3, 1977, fifty of them protested during their lunch hour in the heart of Chicago's business district, the Loop. An existing group, Women Employed, seized the opportunity to lead a series of public actions against the petty ways in which female clerical workers were made to feel inferior. They conducted a lesson for the attorneys' benefit on how to make coffee (i.e., Step 5, "Turn the switch to on"), and they presented Rivera's boss with a bag of used coffee grounds. They got Rivera her job back.

Iris Rivera's office rebellion was just the most notable instance in a subtle but sweeping change in women's attitudes about their proper role at work. Women Employed dated back to 1974, the same year that a similar group, Nine-to-Five started in Boston. Organized as community organizations rather than unions, they initiated a series of legal and popular actions that gradually changed public attitudes, employers' practices, and the laws. They used Title VII and affirmative action guidelines to force employers to reform their practices, and they used more direct and dramatic techniques as well. They popularized the slogan "Raises Not Roses" as a counter to the tokenism of National

Secretaries' Day, and they used the occasion to bestow awards to the stingiest bosses.

During the 1980s, Nine to Five developed into a national organization. It worked in particular with Service Employees International Union to help with organizing efforts, and with women in other unions to address the issue of the differences between men's and women's wages. Research conducted by these activists revealed that a major reason for the persistent differences was the gender segregation of the labor market. Against the determined opposition of the Reagan administration at the national level, labor activists pushed the notion of equal pay for comparable work, and by 1987 more than 40 states and 1,500 local governments had implemented some form of comparable worth policy.

1978: The First Woman Is Elected to the U.S. Senate in Her Own Right

(Equal Rights)

In 1978, Nancy Landon Kassebaum, whose father was Alf Landon, a Republican nominee for President of the United States in 1936, became the first woman elected to the Senate who was not the widow of a congressman. Kassebaum, a moderate Republican, represents the state of Kansas.

Nancy Landon Kassebaum holds the distinction of being the first woman elected to the U.S. Senate who did not succeed her husband into office. Kassebaum, who was elected in 1978 after she decided to make a run for the seat being vacated by the retiring Kansas senator for whom she served as staff member, has been reelected twice, in 1984 and 1990. As a senator, Kassebaum was appointed to the powerful Senate Foreign Relations Committee when her party gained a Senate majority after the 1980 elections.

Kassebaum did not enter the political arena until well after her graduation from the University of Kansas in 1952, and the University of Michigan in 1955. She worked first at the family-owned communications company, a radio station in Wichita, working her way up to vice-president. At the same time, she was raising four children. Her only real political experience was as a member of the school board in the small suburban town where she lived, although she did serve as a member of the Kansas Governmental Ethics Commission and the Kansas Committee for the Humanities.

Encouraged by her mother to make the run for the Senate, Kassebaum faced eight men in the Republican primary. She won the election, polling over 55 percent of the vote. Although it was certainly no secret that Kassebaum was Alf Landon's daughter, she steadfastly refused in her campaign to exploit her father's name for her political benefit. As a freshman senator and the only woman senator at the time, Kassebaum served on the Banking, Budget, and Commerce committees. She vigorously supported the Equal Rights Amendment, and supported as well legislation that would have made women susceptible to the draft. Kassebaum was reelected to the Senate in 1984 and 1990. In April 1991, she was named to a bipartisan committee formed to draft standards of ethics for Senate members. Her only truly disappointing vote, as far as feminists were concerned, was her support of the Clarence Thomas nomination to the Supreme Court.

Having spent several years as the senate's only woman member, Kassebaum was joined in 1992 by a bumper crop of women senators, many of whom owed at least part of their election to the national controversy that was stirred up over the Anita Hill–Clarence Thomas hearings. Among the new women senators that joined Kassebaum in 1993, were Patty Murray from Oregon, Barbara Boxer and Diane Feinstein, both from California, and Carol Mosley-Braun from Illinois. In the case of Boxer and Feinstein, it is the first time that a state has been represented by two women senators simultaneously Significantly, in April 1994, all of the women senators, joined by many of their female colleagues in the House, banded together, crossing party lines, to oppose the elevation of Admiral Thomas Kelso to a four-star rank on his retire-

ment. The congresswomen charged that Kelso's knowledge of the Tailhook Scandal, a navy gathering at which women were sexually harassed and abused, and his failure to act appropriately, militated against rewarding him on the occasion of his retirement. While the congresswomen did not emerge victorious, it sent a message that grabbed the attention of the country, that a new standard of behavior was expected and that women would continue to fight together for that standard.

1979: Judy Chicago Completes the "Dinner Party"

(Cultural Life)

In 1979, the artist Judy Chicago completed her monumental work, "Dinner Party," a celebration of women's lost history that took six years and the help of hundreds to complete.

In 1973, Judy Chicago began a monumental project that brought together her feminist beliefs and her fascination with ancient mythologies. Convinced that "myth has to be challenged before economics or sociology will change," she decided to satisfy women's "deep cultural hunger" for symbols that affirm their role in society by creating a huge triangular white table, a symbol of female sexuality and power, on a raised tile floor. On the table are thirty-nine large ceramic plates dedicated to the prehistoric goddesses. First comes the Primordial Goddess, symbolized by a cleft in a rock. Next comes the Goddess of Fertility, symbolizing birth and rebirth through bulbous podlike forms. After her comes Ishtar, the ancient Babylonian Goddess, the medium between nature and humanity, and then Kali, the Indian blood Goddess, symbol of destruction. Among the others are the Cretan Snake Goddess, and the Celts Boadicea and Saint Bridget. The collaborative nature of the project emphasized the artist's conviction that art could be used not just to express ideas and feelings but to cultivate the feminization of society.

Chicago continued and developed these themes in her later works, and she was just one of many female artists in the 1960s and 1970s who began to use ancient symbols to challenge patriarchal culture and celebrate the female half of humanity. Carolee Schneemann created a whole body of work designed to replace male perceptions of women with women's own, and to reconnect them with the primal meanings of fertility, healing, and sexuality. Her symbolic and erotic performance in 1963, when she appeared in the nude with snakes crawling across her body, anticipated the

rise of performance art in the next decade, and had the purpose of restoring women's sense of mastery over their own bodies. "In some sense I made a gift of my body to other women," she wrote, "giving our bodies back to ourselves. The haunting images of the Cretan bull dancer—joyful, free, barebreasted women leaping precisely from danger to ascendancy, guided my imagination."

So, too, has ancient symbology informed the artist Mary Beth Edelson. Her work brings together Jungian psychology, feminism, her own dreams, politics, and collaborative effort in a variety of media. She does not just capture images of her imagination, but she creates entire rituals as living works of art. Her "Gate of Horn," shown in 1977 in New York City, was an altar-like flaming ladder approached through a frame of photographs of different women's hands making the horned finger gesture. In another living piece of artwork, she staged a public ritual on Halloween commemorating the "9,000,000 Women Burned as Witches in the Christian Era" that began in a gallery and ended in the streets.

These women artists, and many others, are trying to mobilize the power of images and actions in the service of a "new history." Their work is redefining the way women see themselves by using contemporary forms to reconnect them to the primal understandings of primitive mythology.

1980: The U.S. Divorce Rate Reaches an All-Time High

(Family Life)

1980 census data published by the U.S. Department of Commerce revealed that the divorce rate in the United States had reached an all-time high of 5.3 divorces per 1,000 population, almost triple the pre–World War II divorce rate and higher than the rates of any other industrialized nations.

For most of the nineteenth century and until 1940, the rate of divorce in the United States remained relatively stable. In 1890, for example, the divorce rate per 1,000 population was less than one (.53), and in 1940, the rate was still only two divorces per 1,000 population, with the largest single increase coming in the years immediately following World War I. Since 1940, the divorce rate has grown at what some observers have called an alarming rate.

From the earliest settlements, the possibility for divorce existed in one or more colonies, but throughout the nineteenth century, divorces became more and more difficult to obtain. In the mid-nineteenth century, a few states actually had extremely liberal divorce laws. In Connecticut, for example, if a marriage partner did anything that permanently inhibited the happiness of the other partner, a divorce could be obtained. But the same moral purity campaign that resulted in passage of the Comstock Law, also influenced state legislatures to clamp down on divorce laws. Connecticut repealed its divorce law in 1882, bringing it into line with most other states.

Throughout most of the twentieth century, divorce carried with it a stigma that made the idea of terminating even a profoundly unhappy marriage something that was not lightly entered into. Women, in particular, suffered in these circumstances. Prevailing attitudes held that men were responsible for earning a living and women were responsible for maintaining a happy home and raising the children. Moreover, it was accepted that men were naturally sexually active and women were sexually passive. Society tended to view divorce, then, as something that the woman should have been able to prevent. Her failure to do so was often attributed either to her inability to keep her husband happy or to her own immoral behavior. Either way, the onus for a broken marriage fell most often on the shoulders of the woman. Divorcees automatically acquired a reputation in the community that was generally wholly unwarranted. Divorce was difficult legally and socially.

A handful of states did maintain liberal divorce laws, and some, like Nevada, became the haven for women who could afford a divorce and were willing to put up with the social stigma. After several weeks residency, Nevada granted a divorce for something as vague as mental cruelty. In the immediate post–World War II years, the Supreme Court decided a series of cases where these "quickie" divorce laws were contested. Once the Supreme Court declared that the state laws were entirely constitutional, the floodgates began to open up in other states. By the late 1960s, most states had enacted much more liberal divorce laws, corresponding to the changing attitudes people had regarding divorce. In 1969, California became the first "no fault" divorce state, a concept quickly adopted by numerous other states.

Critics often point to the emergence of a renewed women's movement in the 1960s, roughly corresponding to the growing divorce rate, and make the assertion that one affected the other. It is just as likely that the liberalization of divorce laws and changing attitudes toward divorce were more directly linked to higher divorce rates. Indeed, equal rights advocates and feminists rarely addressed the divorce issue until it became apparent that, under the new divorce laws, women and children were suffering financially. Terms like the "feminization of poverty" have only recently made women aware of how ill-protected they and their children are, as a result of no-fault divorce laws.

1981: Sandra Day O'Connor Is Appointed to the U.S. Supreme Court as the First Woman Associate Justice

(Equal Rights, Professions)

In September 1981, Reagan appointee, Sandra Day O'Connor was sworn in as the 102nd Justice—and the first woman—to be seated on the U.S. Supreme Court.

When Sandra Day O'Connor was a young lawyer fresh out of law school and seeking her first job, she was offered the kind of work that many qualified young women lawyers were offered—legal secretarial work. O'Connor, a native of Arizona, had attended Stanford University in California, graduating after five years with both her undergraduate and law degree in the top 10 percent of her class, at the age of twenty-one. She did find work as a lawyer, but she worked for only a very brief period of time. Her husband, John O'Connor, whom she had married immediately after graduating, went into the Army, and like most of her peers, O'Connor resigned her job to move to her husband's new station. Three children later, O'Connor was ready to resume her career full-time in 1965.

Back in Arizona again, O'Connor also became active in Republican politics. In 1969, she was appointed to the state senate to fill the seat of another woman. Running in her own right, she was elected in 1970 and reelected in 1972. Within five years, she had become the youngest majority leader in the senate, and the first woman majority leader in any state legislature. Her rise through the judiciary ranks was just as rapid. Running first for a judiciary seat in 1974, she was appointed after five years to the State Court of Appeals, and two years later, in 1981, President Ronald Reagan nominated her for the U.S. Supreme Court.

O'Connor was considered a moderate as an Arizona judge. With her uncontroversial record and the feeling that the time was right for a woman appointee, O'Connor's nomination hearing before the Senate Judiciary Committee proceeded without incident. Her responses to questions on issues that were considered highly sensitive, most notably the abortion question in the post–*Roe v. Wade* environment, were measured and responsive. At the same time, she refused to allow herself to be categorized as either pro- or antiabortion. Nevertheless, when she took her place on the Court, most observers believed that when confronted with the abortion issue, O'Connor would come down on the side of the antiabortionists. Indeed, it was almost taken for granted that she would weigh in with the conservatives on most issues. As has frequently happened in Supreme Court history, justices who were expected to act one way turned out to be unpredictable in their decisions. O'Connor has not consistently voted with the conservatives on the bench. Indeed, in recent years, she has often turned out to be the swing vote on the Court. When the Court had the opportunity to reverse *Roe v. Wade*, O'Connor voted with the majority in refusing to overturn the landmark decision.

O'Connor remained the sole woman Justice on the Supreme Court for more than a decade until President Bill Clinton nominated Ruth Bader Ginsberg in 1993. In her first year on the bench, Ginsberg has demonstrated her unwillingness to take on the role of the traditional silent observer as is expected of new Justices. Recent cases on sexual harassment that came before the Court prompted sharp and incisive questioning from Ginsberg, much to everyone's surprise. The particular type of case that Ginsberg chose to try out her new judicial wings—sexual harassment in the workplace—was not lost on women. Having women on the Supreme Court brings a new perspective to the Court, just as Thurgood Marshall brought when he was seated as the first African-American Justice.

1983: Astronaut Sally Ride Becomes the First American Woman to Travel in Space

(Equal Rights, Work)

Physicist Sally Ride became the first American woman to travel in space. In June 1983, Ride was a member of the crew of the Challenger spacecraft that spent six days in orbit before returning to earth.

Despite the fact that a Russian female astronaut had already successfully traveled in space without ill-effect or without disrupting her mission, the American space agency was slow to accept women into the space program. The National Aeronautics and Space Administration (NASA), founded in 1958 with initial funding of $4 billion for research and development, was created in response to Russia's startling launching of a man-made satellite, Sputnik, in 1955.

By almost any measure, the American space program was successful and reasonably safe. Yet it would take another ten years after the moon landing for NASA to accept women astronauts into the space program. When Sally Ride applied for admission into the space program in 1977, she was one of 8,000 applicants, one of 208 finalists, and one of 6 women among the 35 persons accepted into the space shuttle program in 1978. Also included in that group was Judith A. Resnick, a member of the ill-fated crew that died in the 1986 Challenger disaster.

Sally K. Ride, a Californian, came to the space program with a background in both physics and literature. At Stanford University, Ride was a double major, receiving a bachelor of science in physics and a bachelor of arts in English literature. She remained at Stanford in their graduate physics program, ultimately acquiring both a master's degree and a doctorate in that discipline. The group to which Ride belonged as an astronaut, Group 8, was composed of pilots and mission specialists. Ride was a member of the crew of STS–7 and STS–41G. (The Space Transportation System [STS] program took over from the Skylab Program in 1981.)

Because there have been so few women in the astronaut program, and because Sally Ride was the first American woman to be assigned to a crew, the publicity that surrounded her first mission almost rivaled the publicity that the early space missions generated. Despite the sometimes circuslike atmosphere that surrounded her mission—the most popular headline when the mission was launched, was "Ride, Sally Ride!"—Ride seemed to take it in stride, always careful to remind the press and the public that although she would indeed be the first American woman in space, she was part of a team. Nevertheless, it was an occasion for some celebration when STS–7 left the launch pad on June 18, 1983.

Altogether, since its inception, the space program has accepted 214 astronauts, of which 22—about 10 percent—have been women. Seventeen of the twenty-two are still in the astronaut program. With the exception of three career Air Force officers, one naval officer, and one army officer, all the women astronauts have been civilians, accepted because of their science backgrounds.

One of the most famous women associated with the astronaut program was Christa McAuliffe, the high school teacher from New Hampshire who was chosen as the first civilian to travel in space. In a much-publicized competition, teachers across the country were invited to submit an essay stating why they would like to be included in a space mission. McAuliffe, the mother of two young children, was able to convey in her essay the enthusiasm for teaching, for adventure, and for life that the entire country came to know as she progressed through her training schedule. A crew member aboard flight STS–51L, the Challenger mission that Judith Resnick was also on, McAuliffe's death in particular seemed to affect the world when the flight exploded on January 28, 1986. Astronaut Sally Ride was a member of the commission appointed to investigate the Challenger disaster.

1984: Geraldine Ferraro Accepts the Nomination as the Democratic Party's Vice-Presidential Candidate

(Equal Rights)

On July 12, 1984, Representative Geraldine Ferraro from New York accepted the nomination as the Democratic party's choice for a vice-presidential candidate in the national elections, the first woman to be so designated by a major political party.

For nearly all of her adult life, Geraldine Ferraro seemed to be constantly flying in the face of tradition and bucking the odds. As a recent graduate of Marymount College in New York, Ferraro accepted a teaching job during the day and began attending Fordham Law School at night. When she married four years later in 1960, she continued both pursuits and retained her own last name. While raising three children, she maintained a private law practice until 1974, when she became an assistant district attorney for Queens County, New York. While none of this sounds particularly unusual now, in the 1960s, Ferraro was an oddity. Women did not keep their own names when they married, nor did they continue to pursue a career (as opposed to a job) while raising children. It was particularly surprising for someone from her ethnic, religious, and politically conservative background to step away from tradition as Ferraro did.

Her case load as a district attorney was heavily weighted with child-abuse, domestic violence, and rape cases. It was for her the experience that turned her from a conservative to a liberal, by her own admission. Active in local Democratic politics, Ferraro decided to make a run for the House of Representatives four years after her appointment as assistant district attorney. Running a measured campaign, Ferraro succeeded in defeating her Democratic opponents in the primary and in repeating that experience the following November against the hand-picked Italian male candidate representing the Republican party. Her election surprised some observers who believed that a liberal Democrat could not win against a conservative Republican in the blue-collar, largely Italian neighborhoods that made up Queens' Ninth Congressional District.

As a three-term congresswoman, Ferraro earned the respect of her colleagues and the continued support of her constituents. Her voting record, with few exceptions, reflected her own liberal views and not the more conservative views of the people who continued to reelect her. While serving on the powerful House Budget Committee and receiving the endorsement of her colleagues when they appointed her secretary of the House Democratic Caucus, Ferraro also consciously aligned herself with those issues affecting women and children with which she had become involved as a district attorney. In 1980, Ferraro received another vote of confidence from fellow Democrats when she was named to chair the Platform Committee of the 1980 Democratic Convention.

In 1984, when Walter Mondale had virtually locked up the Democratic nomination, rumors began flying that he was considering not one, but three women for the second spot on the ticket: the mayor of San Francisco, Diane Feinstein; the governor of Kentucky, Martha Layne Collins; and the representative from Queens, Geraldine Ferraro. When Mondale's choice became known, and Ferraro stepped forward to accept the nomination, it was a heady moment for all women, regardless of political affiliation. For the first time, a major political party had nominated a woman to serve on the ticket as the vice-presidential candidate. Ferraro herself acknowledged how momentous an occasion it was, saying, "By choosing a woman to run for our nation's second highest office, you send a powerful signal to all Americans. There are no doors we cannot unlock."

The ensuing campaign was a difficult one for Ferraro, as her critics focused in on her husband's finances in order to detract from an otherwise popular, witty, and forthright campaigner. In the end, it is doubtful that the Mondale-Ferraro ticket could have beaten the Reagan-Bush ticket under any circumstances, for Reagan was enormously popular as president. But as much as Ferraro's nomination gave women a greater sense of self-esteem and reason for jubilation, the campaign left a bitter residue in those who felt that she was being held to a double standard, accountable for her spouse's activities in a way that male candidates were not.

1985: Wilma Mankiller Becomes Principal Chief of the Cherokee Nation

(Equal Rights, Cultural Life)

In December 1985, Wilma Mankiller, who had served as deputy chief since August 1983, became Principal Chief of the Cherokee Nation, the first time in tribal history that a woman served in either position.

When Wilma Mankiller accepted the position of deputy chief of the Cherokee Nation, she vowed to "make things happen." Two years later, only mid-way through her first term as deputy chief, Mankiller was chosen as Principal Chief, the first time in tribal history that a woman had led the Cherokee Nation. Before Europeans arrived in North America, Cherokee women were able to exercise a good deal of power, although not as chiefs. They played a crucial role in agriculture, they had the right to speak in village councils, and some Cherokee women accompanied the men when the tribe went to war. Many other American Indian tribes had similar customs, and Indian women in general had tribal powers ranging from moderate to significant. The Iroquois, for example, were organized along matrilineal lines. Women owned the longhouses, mothers arranged marriages, sons-in-law lived with the wife's family, and women managed the farming activity, which also gave them power. Among the Senecas, women were allowed to vote for male chiefs and to participate in other political activities. While it is true that women in agricultural tribes had more power than those in hunting tribes of the Great Plains, in general the role of women within Indian society was valued.

When Europeans began to make significant inroads in North America, they also began to encourage Indians to alter their culture to fit a European ideal. Gradually, the power base enjoyed by Iroquois and Cherokee women began to erode. Notions of land ownership, a concept not unlike ownership of the sun or the air to the Indians, also changed concepts of materialism over time. Missionaries and religious schools established to educate the Native Americans also imposed European culture on the grounds that it was superior. Young girls were taught homemaking skills as though they were going to inhabit societies identical to the European settlements. They were chided or even ridiculed for wearing traditional Native clothing, and for speaking in their native tongue. Finally, most Indian tribes were moved further and further west as whites advanced further into the interior. Time after time, lands would be declared to be Indian lands, only to be redesignated a short time later, particularly if the lands turned out to have additional value, as, for example, when gold was discovered. A series of treaties initiated between the Cherokees and the U.S. government in 1791 designated parts of Georgia as an independent Indian nation. When gold was discovered and the Indians protested white trespassers, it initiated a Supreme Court case, *Cherokee Nation v. Georgia*. The Court, with John Marshall acting as Chief Justice, held for the Indians. But President Andrew Jackson, who had little regard for Na-

tive Americans, refused to uphold the law. "John Marshall has made his decision," he is said to have remarked. "Now let him enforce it." The Cherokees were forced to leave Georgia, again with government assurances of new lands, and eventually they settled in Oklahoma.

Mankiller, who announced in April 1994 that this would be her last term as Principal Chief, was not yet thirty-two when she was elected the Cherokee leader in 1985. As a young child, she had left Oklahoma for San Francisco in 1957, as part of the Bureau of Indian Affairs' relocation program. Two decades later, she returned to Oklahoma with two daughters, an undergraduate degree in social sciences from the University of Arkansas, and the beginnings of a graduate degree in community planning. Despite her young age—or perhaps because of it—Mankiller did make things happen. Convinced of the value of self-help, particularly since the Bureau of Indian Affairs had traditionally not acted in the best interests of the Indians, Mankiller has pushed through new training, education, and health service programs; water line installations; and new housing and the upgrading of old housing. Before her election, she established and then managed a multimillion dollar community development department that has improved the quality of life for hundreds of Indians in rural northeastern Oklahoma. She was also a founding member of Rainbow Television Workshop, Inc., which produced programs about minorities, and she is a task force member for Save the Children, Inc.

Mankiller has had a profound influence on the lives of hundreds of Cherokee Nation members because of the work she has done on behalf of her constituents. But more than that, she is also an important role model, and not only for women. At a time when unemployment and alcoholism, the by-products of two hundred years of systematic mistreatment, seem to be the only lasting characteristics of Indian life, Wilma Mankiller's fight to restore self-esteem and dignity to the Cherokee Nation is nothing less than heroic.

1985: EMILY'S List Funds Women's Campaigns

(Equal Rights)

In 1985, Ellen Malcolm founded EMILY'S List in order to break down the barriers faced by women seeking elected office. EMILY, an acronym for Early Money Is Like Yeast (it raises dough), is a donor network that raises campaign funds for pro-choice Democratic women running for governorships, the Senate, and the House of Representatives.

Ellen Malcolm, the founder of EMILY'S List, has been active in public service for more than two decades. She was press secretary for the National Women's Political Caucus before joining the Jimmy Carter White House, as press secretary for Esther Peterson, the special assistant for consumer affairs. As a woman interested in seeing other women succeed in the political arena, and savvy in the requirements for success, Malcolm created her unique fund-raising organization in 1985. EMILY'S List operates in a deceptively simple fashion. Choosing from a roster of recommended pro-choice Democratic women, members make contributions to the candidates they wish to support, making their contributions through EMILY'S List in order to maximize political impact. Members are sent carefully researched candidate profiles, analyses, and campaign assessments to help them make informed decisions about which candidates to support. EMILY'S List also provides strategic campaign support by conducting surveys, doing political research, developing resource materials, and providing technical assistance on planning, fundraising, media, and message development.

Since its inception, EMILY's List has helped to elect several top women Democrats, most of whom credit the organization with providing the crucial funds necessary to succeed. In 1985, the List was able to raise $350,000 in campaign funds; by 1992, that figure had risen to $6.2 million, which helped to support the campaigns of 75 women candidates running for state and federal office. The candidates helped by EMILY'S List include Texas Governor Ann Richards who, with the biting humor that has become her trademark, observed, "My opponent had pockets deeper than a West Texas oil well. But I had EMILY'S List and its members on my side and I struck political gold." EMILY'S List was crucial in the campaigns of the only five Democratic women ever elected to the U.S. Senate in their own right, four of whom were elected in 1992: Diane Feinstein, Barbara Boxer, Patty Murray, and Carol Mosley-Braun. The fifth, Barbara Mikulski, was elected in 1990. At a inaugural luncheon in 1993, held by EMILY'S List for the house and senate candidates who had won their races, Mikulski told a cheering audience, "Some women spend their life waiting for Prince Charming. I spent my life waiting for Dianne and Barbara and Carol and Patty."

While the enthusiasm for the numbers of women elected to high office over the past several elections since EMILY'S List has been active suggest to some that too many women are holding public office, the statistics demonstrate that women still are in their infancy in terms of office-holding equity. Of the 435 House seats, women hold 48. They hold 7 Senate seats out of a total of 100, and there are only 3 women governors in the fifty states. EMILY'S List has become the nation's largest single financial resource for women candidates—indeed, for *all* candidates for both the House and

Senate—and it is likely to remain so. Perhaps the most unusual thing about EMILY'S List, given the tenor of modern politics, is that the candidates who are the recipients of campaign funding are not beholden to anyone for the donations. Unlike recipients of gun control funding or tobacco funding or abortion rights funding, EMILY'S List candidates are not required to either support or oppose any particular legislation. They make no promises in order to get the money and their sole obligation is to do their job with integrity and in good faith on behalf of their constituents.

1987: The National Museum of Women in the Arts Opens in Washington, D.C.

(Cultural Life)

On April 7, 1987, the National Museum of Women in the Arts opened its doors in Washington, D.C., with the goal of promoting awareness and educating the public about the achievements of women in the arts through the ages.

While Virginia Woolf lamented that what women writers needed was a room of their own in which to develop their creativity, women artists of centuries past might have wished for a museum of their own in which to display their own creativity, free from the anonymity required of them for so long. The National Museum of Women in the Arts, founded by philanthropists Wil- helmina and Wallace Holladay, opened its doors to the public on April 7, 1987. Located in the former Masonic Temple of Washington, the museum, part of the National Register of Historic Places, is dedicated to all aspects of women's art through the ages. The core of the museum collection is over five hundred pieces of art donated by the Holladays, ranging from Renaissance to contemporary art. It includes not only paintings and sculptures, but photographs, Georgian silver, and Native American pottery as well.

A measure of its overwhelming success, the museum membership in the three years between 1985 and 1988 increased by almost 85,000 subscribers, from all fifty states and twenty-four foreign countries, one of the largest museum memberships in the United States. Since its inception, the museum has regularly featured exhibits by women artists, highlighting their creative achievements in a particular time period or a particular region or creative medium. In addition, it has become the repository of perhaps the single most comprehensive research collection on women artists in the entire world. The library and research center has over five thousand volumes and eight thousand files on women artists. The museum building itself, in addition to housing women's art, has won several awards for both its interior and exterior restoration, and stands as a monument to women artists and their works.

1991: Anita Hill Testifies at the Clarence Thomas Confirmation Hearings

(Equal Rights)

In October 1991, Law Professor Anita Hill testified at Senate Confirmation Hearings for Supreme Court nominee Clarence Thomas, charging that Thomas had sexually harassed her during his tenure as chairman of the EEOC.

When President George Bush announced that his nominee to replace retiring Supreme Court Justice Thurgood Marshall would be Judge Clarence Thomas, initial response promised an uncontroversial and uncontested confirmation. Thomas, an African-American jurist, had, after all, gone through a similar process without incident not long before when he was elevated to the District Court. In the months between his nomination and confirmation hearings, rumors began circulating in Washington circles that Thomas had sexually harassed one of his assistants at the Equal Employment Opportunity Commission, nearly ten years earlier. Nevertheless, the hearings began uneventfully on September 10, 1991, and when Thomas finished his testimony several days later, the Senate Judiciary Committee seemed ready to give the nominee a green light, thus insuring full Senate support.

In the meantime, on September 12, Anita Hill, a law professor from the University of Oklahoma, contacted the Judiciary Committee's nominations counsel, Harriet Grant. Hill informed Grant that she had worked for Thomas at the EEOC in the early 1980s, and alleged that Thomas had sexually harassed her, eventually causing her to leave the EEOC and pursue an academic career. Grant assured Hill that her statement would be distributed to the Judiciary Committee members. As the hearings drew to a close, it became clear that the Judiciary members were not going to act on Hill's allegations. Judge Susan Hoechner of California, a long-time friend in whom Hill had confided about the harassment, contacted the Judiciary counsel to vouch

for Hill. Finally, on September 20, the Federal Bureau of Investigations (FBI) was asked to interview Hill and report back to the Judiciary Committee. Hill, who had, up to that point, insisted on confidentiality, agreed to go forward, even though it meant also going public.

Even after the ranking members of the Judiciary had seen the FBI report, they chose to ignore it and set a date for the confirmation vote. Senator Joseph Biden, the committee chairman, announced that as far as he was concerned, Thomas's credibility, credentials, and character were above reproach. Before the confirmation vote could take place, however, Hill's allegations became front page news when journalists Nina Totenberg of National Public Radio and Timothy Phelps of New York *Newsday* both released the story. The furor that ensued caused the committee to delay the Thomas vote, especially when seven women members of the House of Representatives marched en masse to the Senate building to protest what they believed was the committee's inappropriate response to Hill's charges.

Within days, Anita Hill appeared before the Judiciary Committee in a televised special session. In measured, unemotional tones, Hill read a lengthy statement laying out in detail her charges against Clarence Thomas. She recounted that advances on his part, which she repeatedly rejected, finally caused her to resign from the EEOC. Following her testimony, Hill was questioned by members of the Judiciary Committee, many of whom were openly disdainful of her charges, accusing her at various times of being a "woman scorned," of getting the details of her charges out of the pages of a lurid novel, and of being the tool of feminist and left-liberal groups intent on derailing the Thomas nomination. Since she herself was an African-American, Hill was spared the charge of racial bias in testifying against her former boss, although Thomas, in his rebuttal, did accuse the Judiciary Committee of holding nothing more than a "high-tech lynching."

Clarence Thomas denied all of Hill's allegations and brought forth a host of character witnesses, most of them women who had worked for him, who argued that he had never once made improper advances to them. Hill had four witnesses, all of whom testified that she had confided to them individually at the time of the harassment, in order to seek advice. In the end, the Judiciary Committee voted in favor of Thomas's confirmation.

The members of the Judiciary Committee clearly did not expect the firestorm of public reaction that attended the Hill-Thomas controversy. Although polls indicated that most women did not believe that Thomas was guilty of sexual harassment, the fact that the Judiciary Committee treated the charges so cavalierly in the beginning, compounded by their treatment of Hill when she testified, outraged many women. The issue also created overnight a new awareness of workplace relationships and questions about what constituted sexual harassment. The reverberations from the Hill-Thomas hearings continued long after Clarence Thomas's swearing in as a Supreme Court Justice, and were especially felt in the 1992 elections.

1992: The American Association of University Women Reports on Sex Bias in Schools

(Equal Rights, Social Reform)

In February 1992, the American Association of University Women issued its report entitled "How Schools Shortchange Girls." The report documented for the first time why school performance and self-esteem in girls diminishes as they approach adolescence.

Parents and educators both had for years been aware of the decline in school performance by girls, and a concomitant decline in self-esteem, as they reached adolescence. Young girls began their school careers on at least an equal footing with boys, and often exhibited an ability to grasp concepts more quickly in all categories, including reading and math skills, in the lower elementary grades. By the time they reached the sixth and seventh grades, the same girls were already exhibiting a tendency to fall markedly behind their male counterparts in math and science, and to lag behind generally in overall performance. Moreover, while boys were developing growing self-confidence, girls at the same age were becoming less con-

fident and losing self-esteem. The American Association of University Women began a project to try and determine what factors contributed to the radical performance turn-around for girls. Their report, issued in February 1992, documented a school experience for girls that was very different than the experience of the boys who sat next to them, primarily because of the unconscious ways in which teachers interacted with both sexes. Among other findings, the study showed that from the earliest grades, teachers tended to respond more readily to questions and comments from boys, pay attention to boys, call on boys even when it was apparent that both girls and boys wanted to be heard, and offer more encouragement and praise to boys.

Drs. Myra and David Sadker, professors at American University in Washington, were engaged in similar studies. In 1994, they published their findings in a book entitled *Failing at Fairness: How America's Schools Cheat Girls.* The Sadkers worked with parent and faculty groups throughout the country, alerting them to the behavior that they themselves were unaware of in their teaching and parenting styles.

As of 1994, about 5 percent of schools nationwide had initiated programs to deal with gender issues, but that number is growing rapidly. Several schools secured grants to set up pilot programs. Eliminating a significant factor in why girls fail to perform and experience a loss of self-esteem at around ages ten to twelve could have profound effects on social and cultural development for future generations.

1993: African-American Writer Toni Morrison Wins the Nobel Prize for Literature

(Cultural Life)

African-American writer Toni Morrison won the Nobel Prize for Literature in 1993. The award was made by the Nobel Committee, citing the body of her work, including her powerful novels, *Song of Solomon, Tar Baby, Beloved,* and *Jazz.*

Toni Morrison's literary voice is not only a powerful one for African-Americans and for women, but for anyone who wants to understand how forgetting the past can irrevocably alter present sensibilities about race, culture, and life, and how reclaiming one's historical and mythological heritage can restore race identity. For Morrison, as one of her biographers has noted, "the major challenge of the twentieth century in the aftermath of the civil rights movement and integration is forgetfulness." Over the course of a lifetime that began in the humblest of circumstances, to her position as one of America's foremost intellectual and literary figures, Morrison has produced a body of work second to none.

As the daughter of sharecroppers, Morrison was raised with a strong sense of her African heritage, a mistrust of whites born out of both race experiences and personal family experiences, and the expectation that she would become an educated woman. After graduating from Howard University and Cornell, Morrison worked as a book editor at Random House, eventually rising to the position of senior editor, a rarity for an African-American woman. She did not begin writing until the 1970s, when she was nearly forty, but quickly produced five novels, all dealing with family, race, and the search for identity. Beginning in 1970 with *The Bluest Eye*, Morrison wrote *Sula* (1973), *Song of Solomon* (1977), *Tar Baby* (1981), *Beloved* (1987), and *Jazz* (1992). For *Song of Solomon*, which was an instant bestseller, Morrison won the National Book Critics Circle Award and, for the first time since Richard Wright's 1941 novel, *Native Son*, a book written by an African-American was chosen as a Book-of-the-Month Club main selec-

tion. *Beloved*, called by critics Morrison's best book, both artistically and technically, earned her a Pulitzer Prize in 1984. In all of her books, one finds extraordinary black women characters. One of the most memorable in *Beloved* is a ghost who takes the form of a beautiful young woman who is representative of both the mass suffering under slavery and the individual suffering of a murdered child returning to seek lost love.

Able finally to leave her job as an editor, Morrison accepted the Albert Schweitzer Chair Professorship in the Humanities at the State University of New York at Albany. Five years later in 1989, Princeton University appointed her its Robert Goheen Professor in the Council of the Humanities. With the two professorships, Morrison also began writing critical essays for scholarly journals, and in 1990, she was the Massey Lecturer in American Civilization at Harvard University, and Clark Lecturer at Trinity College in Cambridge. Her long list of awards and honors culminated in 1993, when she was nominated by the Nobel Committee to receive the Nobel Prize in Literature.

1993: Maya Angelou Reads an Original Poem at President Clinton's Inauguration

(Cultural Life)

In January 1993, President Bill Clinton asked African-American poet and author Maya Angelou to participate in his inaugural ceremony by reading a poem that she had written especially for the occasion.

When poet Maya Angelou stood in front of the Capitol building on the special staging built for the inaugural ceremony at which newly elected President Bill Clinton took his oath of office, the words of her poem celebrating the occasion seemed to ring especially clear in the chill January air. Angelou's poem heralded what she hoped was a new day for America, a hopeful beginning of a new administration. If, at first glance, she seemed to be speaking of what a new president could do to bring the nation to full health, her words also held a deeper meaning. For while there were many problems facing the country, the fact that she, an African-American woman, whose roots were sunk deep in both slavery and poverty, took such a prominent part in the inaugural cere-

mony did not go unnoticed and in itself sent a message of hope for the future.

Maya Angelou, one of the most celebrated African-American writers of the twentieth century, spent part of her childhood in Stamps, Arkansas, a small rural town where, in the early 1930s, whites still harbored resentment that the slaves had been freed. The meanness of the people in Stamps never left Angelou, and when her grandmother took her to California when Angelou was ten, she vowed never to return there again. But for the strength of her grandmother, Angelou, who was raped when she was seven years old, might never have emerged from her self-imposed five-year silence following the trauma she sustained. Her grandmother insisted that Angelou read the classics aloud to her, the only person to whom the child would speak. By the time she was in eighth grade, Angelou was at the head of her class.

When Angelou went to San Francisco to live with her mother, a professional gambler, she achieved an early goal—Angelou became the first African-American woman to work as a conductor on the San Francisco cable cars, because she liked the uniforms. When she was sixteen, her son Guy was born. An unplanned pregnancy, Angelou nevertheless took her responsibility seriously, and credits Guy with starting her on the intellectual quest that has lasted a lifetime. She taught Guy to read when he was four and then, in order to answer his questions, she began frequenting the libraries wherever she lived so she could provide him with a proper answer.

Angelou's life, never an easy one in those days, took many strange and sometimes perilous turns. In order to support Guy, she worked as a waitress, a cook, and a madam for a short period of time, and she began to use drugs. Recognizing the dangers inherent in them, she quickly stopped. Sometime after the end of World War II, Angelou decided to study dance with Pearl Primus, and for a time she was a professional dancer, appearing in several New York theatres. She was also involved then in the emerging civil rights movement. Most importantly, she began writing poetry and short stories.

In 1961, Angelou and her son went to visit Africa and for a time they lived in Cairo and then in Ghana. In Ghana, Angelou taught at the university and continued writing. When she returned to the United States, a chance meeting with writer-cartoonist Jules Feiffer ended up with Angelou writing what was to be the first volume of her multi-volume autobiography, *I Know Why the Caged Bird Sings*. Since that time, Angelou's reputation and talent have grown together. Angelou finally came full circle, returning to the South when Wake Forest University offered her a lifetime appointment as the Reynolds Professor of American Studies, where she continues to teach today. Angelou and her remarkable journey also continue to inspire hundreds of thousands of people with her poetry and her wisdom, not only African-Americans, but anyone who has overcome adversity or who can appreciate the strength and courage that such a journey takes.

Selected Bibliography

Addams, Jane. *The Second Twenty Years at Hull House*. New York: Macmillan, 1930.

Addams, Jane. *Twenty Years at Hull House*. New York: Macmillan, 1910.

Bailyn, Bernard. *The Great Republic, A History of the American People*. Lexington, MA: D.C. Heath, 1985.

Banner, Lois W. *American Beauty*. New York: Knopf, 1983.

Banner, Lois W. *Women in Modern America: A Brief History*. New York: Harcourt, Brace, Jovonovitch, 1984.

Barker-Benfield, G. J., and Catherine Clinton, eds. *Portraits of American Women from Settlement to the Present*. New York: St. Martin's Press, 1991.

Barton, Clara. *The Red Cross: A History*. Washington, DC: American Red Cross, 1898.

Bateson, Mary Catherine. *With a Daughter's Eyes*. New York: Washington Square, 1984.

Bell, Winifred. *Aid to Dependent Children*. New York: Columbia University Press, 1965.

Bird, Caroline. *Enterprising Women*. New York: Norton, 1976.

Brooks, Paul. *The House of Life: Rachel Carson at Work*. Boston: Houghton Mifflin, 1972.

Brownmiller, Susan. *Shirley Chisholm, A Biography*. Garden City, NY: Doubleday, 1971.

Campbell, D'Ann. *Women at War with America*. Cambridge, MA: Harvard University Press, 1984.

Carson, Rachel. *The Sea around Us*. Boston: Houghton Mifflin, 1951.

Carson, Rachel. *Silent Spring*. Boston: Houghton Mifflin, 1962.

Catt, Carrie Chapman, and Nettie Rogers Shuler. *Woman Suffrage and Politics*. New York: Scribners, 1923.

Chafe, William. *The American Woman: Her Changing Social, Economic, and Political Roles.*New York: Oxford University Press, 1972.

Cheney, Anne. *Lorraine Hansberry.*Boston: G. K. Hall, 1984.

"Cherokee Nation Principal Chief Wilma Mankiller." Cherokee Nation (1994).

Chicago, Judy. *The Dinner Party: A Symbol of Our Heritage.* Garden City, NY: Anchor Books, 1979.

Clinton, Catherine. *The Other Civil War, American Women in the Nineteenth Century.* New York: Hill and Wang, 1984.

Cochran, Jacqueline. *The Stars at Noon.* Boston: Little, Brown, 1954.

Cott, Nancy, and Elizabeth Pleck. *A Heritage of Her Own.* Ithaca, NY: Cornell University Press, 1978.

Current, Richard N., et al. *American History: A Survey.* New York: Knopf, 1983.

David, Kenneth C. *Don't Know Much about History.* New York: Avon Press, 1990.

Davis, Allen F. *American Heroine.* New York: Oxford University Press, 1973.

Davis, Allen F. *Spearheads for Reform: The Social Settlements and the Progressive Movement, 1890–1914.* New York: Oxford University Press, 1967.

Degler, Carl N. *At Odds: Women and the Family in America from the Revolution to the Present.* New York: Oxford University Press, 1980.

Douglas, Ann. *The Feminization of American Culture.* New York: Knopf, 1977.

Douglas, Emily Taft. *Remember the Ladies.* New York: Putnam's, 1966.

Dublin, Thomas. *Women at Work: The Transformation of Work and Community in Lowell, Massachusetts 1826–1860.* New York: Columbia University Press, 1979.

DuBois, Ellen. *Feminism and Suffrage: The Emergence of an Independent Woman's Movement in America, 1848–1869.* Ithaca, NY: Cornell University Press, 1978.

Dulles, Rhea Foster. *The American Red Cross: A History.* Westport, CT: Greenwood Press, 1971.

Dye, Nancy Schrom. *As Equals and As Sisters: Feminism, Unionism, and the Women's Trade Union League of New York.* Columbia: University of Missouri Press, 1980.

Ehrenreich, Barbara, and Deirdre English. *For Her Own Good: 150 Years of Experts'*

Advice to Women. New York: Anchor Press, 1978.

Encyclopedia Americana, 1991 edition.

Encyclopedia Britannica, 1972 edition.

Evans, Sara. *Born for Liberty: A History of Women in America*. New York: The Free Press, 1989.

Ferraro, Geraldine. *Ferraro: My Story*. New York: Bantam Books, 1985.

Flexner, Eleanor. *Century of Struggle: The Women's Rights Movement in the United States*. New York: Atheneum Press, 1974.

Flynn, Elizabeth Gurley. *Rebel Girl, An Autobiography*. New York: International Publishers, 1973.

Foner, Philip S. *Women and the American Labor Movement*. New York: The Free Press, 1979.

Fowler, Robert B. *Carrie Catt, Feminist Politician*. Boston: Northeastern University Press, 1986.

Friedan, Betty. *The Feminine Mystique*. New York: Norton: 1963.

Friedan, Betty. *It Changed My Life*. New York: Random House, 1976.

Garrow, David. *Bearing the Cross: Martin Luther King, Jr., and the Southern Leadership Conference*. New York: Morrow, 1986.

Gibson, Althea. *I Always Wanted to be Somebody*. New York: Harper and Row, 1958.

Gilman, Charlotte Perkins. *The Living of Charlotte Perkins Gilman*. New York: Appleton-Century, 1935.

Goldmark, Josephine. *Impatient Crusader: Florence Kelley's Life Story*. Urbana, IL: University of Illinois Press, 1953.

Goldstein, Leslie Friedman. *The Constitutional Rights of Women*. New York: Longman, 1987.

Gordon, Linda. *Women's Bodies, Women's Right: A Social History of Birth Control in America*. New York: Penguin Books, 1976.

Green, Elizabeth Alden. *Mary Lyon and Mount Holyoke: Opening the Gates*. Hanover, NH: University Press of New England, 1979.

Hall, Helen. *Unfinished Business*. New York: Macmillan, 1971.

Hall, Jacquelyn Dowd. "Disorderly Women: Gender and Labor Militancy in the Appalachian South." *Journal of American History* (September 1986), 354–82

Hall, Jacquelyn Dowd. *Revolt against Chivalry: Jessie Daniel Ames and the Women's Campaign against Lynching*. New York: Columbia University Press, 1979.

Harrison, Cynthia. *On Account of Sex: The Politics of Women's Issues, 1945–1968*. Berkeley: University of California Press, 1988.

Haskell, Molly. *From Reverence to Rape: The Treatment of Women in the Movies*. 2d ed. Chicago: University of Chicago Press, 1987.

Hellman, Lillian. *Pentimento*. Boston: Little Brown, 1973.

Hellman, Lillian. *Scoundrel Time*. Boston: Little, Brown, 1972.

Hine, Darlene Clark, et al., eds. *Black Women in America, An Historical Encyclopedia*. Brooklyn, NY: Carlson Publishing, 1993.

Hoff-Wilson, Joan, and Margaret Lightman. *Without Precedent: The Life and Career of Eleanor Roosevelt*. Bloomington: Indiana University Press, 1984.

Ingrehma, Claire and Leonard. *An Album of Women in American History*. New York: Franklin Watts, 1972.

Irwin, Inez Haynes. *The Story of the Woman's Party*. New York: Harcourt Brace, 1921.

James, Edward T., et al. *Notable American Women, A Biographical Dictionary*. Cambridge, MA: Belknap Press of Harvard University Press, 1971.

Jones, Jacqueline. *Labor of Love, Labor of Sorrow*. New York: Basic Books, 1985.

Josephson, Hannah. *Jeannette Rankin: First Lady in Congress*. Indianapolis: Bobbs-Merrill, 1974.

Kennedy, David. *Birth Control in America: The Career of Margaret Sanger*. New Haven, CT: Yale University Press, 1970.

Kennedy, Susan E. *If All We Did Was to Weep at Home*. Bloomington: Indiana University Press, 1979.

Kessler-Harris, Alice. *Out to Work: A History of Wage-Earning Women in the United States*. New York: Oxford University Press, 1982.

King, Billie Jean. *Billie Jean*. New York: Viking Press, 1982.

Kirber, Linda, and Jane DeHart Matthews. *Women's America. Refocusing the Past*. New York: Oxford University Press, 1982.

Koszarski, Richard, ed. *Hollywood Directors, 1941–1976*. New York: Oxford University Press, 1977.

Kraditor, Aileen. *The Ideas of the Woman Suffrage Movement, 1890–1920*. New York: Columbia University Press, 1965.

Kraditor, Aileen. *Means and Ends in American Abolitionism*. New York: Pantheon Books, 1969.

Lanker, Brian. *I Dream a World, Portraits of Black Women Who Changed America*. New York: Stewart, Tabori, and Chang, 1989.

Lash, Joseph. *Eleanor and Franklin*. New York: Norton, 1971.

Lash, Joseph. *Eleanor: The Years Alone*. New York: Norton, 1972.

Lemons, J. Stanley. *The Woman Citizen: Social Feminism in the 1920s*. Urbana: University of Illinois Press, 1973.

Lerner, Gerda. *The Grimké Sisters of South Carolina: Pioneers for Women's Rights and Abolition*. New York: Schocken Books, 1967.

Levenson, Dorothy. *Women of the West*. New York: Franklin Watts, 1972.

Lisle, Laurie. *Portrait of an Artist: A Biography of Georgia O'Keefe*. Albuquerque: University of New Mexico Press, 1986.

Lunardini, Christine A. *From Equal Suffrage to Equal Rights, Alice Paul and the National Woman's Party 1910–1928*. New York: New York University Press, 1986.

Marshall, Helen. *Dorothea Dix: Forgotten Samaritan*. Chapel Hill: University of North Carolina Press, 1937.

Martin, George. *Madam Secretary*. Boston: Houghton Mifflin, 1976.

Martin, Mick, and Marsha Porter. *Video Movie Guide 1991*. New York: Ballantine Books, 1990.

Martin, Wendy. *An American Triptych: Anne Bradstreet, Emily Dickinson and Adrienne Rich*. Chapel Hill: University of North Carolina Press, 1984.

Melder, Keith E. *Beginnings of Sisterhood: The American Woman's Rights Movement*. New York: Schocken Books, 1977.

Norton, Mary Beth. *Liberty's Daughters: The Revolutionary Experience of American Women, 1750–1800*. Boston: Little Brown, 1980.

O'Neil, William. *Divorce in the Progressive Era*. New Haven, CT: Yale University Press, 1967.

O'Neil, William. *Everyone Was Brave: The Rise and Fall of Feminism in America*. Chicago: Quadrangle Books, 1969.

Rothman, Sheila M. *Woman's Proper Place, A History of Changing Ideals and Practices 1870 to the Present*. New York: Basic Books, 1978.

Roudebush, Jay. *Mary Cassatt*. New York: Crown, 1972.

Rupp, Leila. *Mobilizing Women for War*. Princeton, NJ: Princeton University Press, 1978.

Ryan, Mary P. *Womanhood in America: From Colonial Times to the Present*. New York: New Viewpoints/Franklin Watts, 1984.

Sanger, Margaret. *My Fight for Birth Control*. 1931. Elmsford, NY: Maxwell Reprint Company, 1969.

Schlafly, Phyllis. *A Choice, Not an Echo*. Alton, IL: Pere Marquette Press, 1964.

Sicherman, Barbara, and Carol Hurd Green, eds. *Notable American Women, The Modern Period*. Cambridge, MA: Belknap Press of Harvard University Press, 1980.

Solomon, Barbara Miller. *In the Company of Educated Women*. New Haven: Yale University Press, 1985.

Stanton, Elizabeth Cady et al., eds. *The History of Woman Suffrage*. 6 vols. New York: NAWSA, 1888–1922.

Starkey, Marion L. *The Devil in Massachusetts*. New York: Knopf, 1949.

Sterling, Dorothy. *Black Foremothers: Three Lives*. Old Westbury, NY: Feminist Press, 1979.

Sterling, Dorothy. *Lucretia Mott: Gentle Warrior*. Garden City, NY: Doubleday, 1964.

Van Voris, Jacqueline. *Carrie Chapman Catt: A Public Life*. New York: Feminist Press, 1987.

Vorse, Mary Heaton. *Labors New Millions*. New York: Modern Age, 1938.

Wald, Lillian. *The House on Henry Street*. New York: Holt, 1915.

Ware, Susan. *Beyond Suffrage: Women in the New Deal*. Cambridge, MA: Harvard University Press, 1981.

Weatherford, Doris. *American Women's History*. New York: Prentice-Hall, 1994.

Wertheimer, Barbara Mayer. *We Were There: The Story of Working Women in America*. New York: Pantheon Books, 1977.

Withey, Lynn. *Dearest Friend: A Life of Abigail Adams*. New York: The Free Press, 1981.

Woloch, Nancy. *Women and the American Experience*. New York: Knopf

Wood, Mary Louise, and Martha McWilliams. *The National Museum of Women in the Arts*. New York: Abrams, 1987.

Zophy, Angela Howard, ed. *Handbook of American Women's History*. New York: Garland Press, 1990.

Index

A

Abbott, Grace, 121, 177, 178
Abolition, 25, 34-37, 39-40, 46-48, 51-53
Abortion, 82-83
Abzug, Bella, 326, 327, 342
Adams, Abigail, 14-16
Adams, John, 14-16
Adams, John Quincy, 28
Addams, Jane, 120-121, 139, 180, 181, 224-226
Address to the Public...Proposing a Plan for Improving Female Education (Willard), 21, 22
Adkins v. Children's Hospital, 213-214, 306
Advocate, The, 43
Affirmative Action, 311-312, 317-319
Agassiz, Louis, 64
Age of Innocence, The, 199-201
(AIDS) Acquired Immunodeficiency Syndrome, 266
Alison's House (Glaspell), 79
All in a Day's Work (Tarbell), 152
Altgeld, John Peter, 139, 176
Alumnae Association, 54, 111-113
American Academy of Arts and Sciences, 63-64
American and Foreign Anti-Slavery Society, 56
American Anti-Slavery Society (AASS), 36-37, 47, 51-53, 55
American Association for the Advancement of Science, 64, 81
American Association of Anatomists, 218
American Association of University Women (AAUW), 112-113
"How Schools Shortchange Girls", 364-365
American Bemberg plant, 220
American Birth Control League, 187, 265-266
American Equal Rights Association, 89
American Exodus: A Record of Human Erosion (Lange), 259
American Federation of Labor (AFL), 88, 118, 147, 162, 220, 233
American Female Moral Reform Society, 42-43
American Glazstoff factory, 220
American Home Economics Association, 157-159
American Institute of Mining and Metallurgical Engineers, 158
American Lawn Tennis Magazine, 279
American Legion, 226
American Magazine, 152
American Medical Association, 82-83, 202-203, 249
American Medical Women's Association, 188-189
American Philosophic Society, 64
American Red Cross, 109-111, 134
American Slavery as It Is: Testimony of a Thousand Witnesses (Grimke and Weld), 48

E

F

M

N

O

T

U

Other Adams Media Books

The Remarkable Lives of
100 Women Healers and Scientists
100 Women Writers and Journalists
100 Women Artists
All by Brooke Bailey, hardcover, 208 pp., $12.00

Each 2-page spread tells the story of an inspiring trailblazer who set a new standard of excellence in her field. These exceptional collections of women feature 100 stories of ambition, adversity, and triumph.

The Book of Women
300 Notable Women History Passed By
By Lynne Griffin and Kelly McCann, trade paperback, 192 pp., $7.95

A remarkable new look at women whose accomplishments or intriguing life choices have so far gone unheralded. *The Book of Women* profiles 300 forgotten women from all walks of life, women we should have been taught about in school—and probably weren't.

The Book of African-American Women
150 Crusaders, Creators, and Uplifters
By Tonya Bolden, hardcover, 368 pp., $16.00

Right from the beginning, women of African descent have played an important and noteworthy role in the American experience. *The Book of African-American Women* explores the trials and tribulations, but most of all the accomplishments, of 150 women who have made major contributions to American history and culture.

Available Wherever Books Are Sold

If you cannot find these titles at your favorite retail outlet, you may order them directly from the publisher. BY PHONE: Call 1-800-872-5627 (in Massachusetts: 617-767-8100). We accept Visa, Mastercard, and American Express. $4.50 will be added to your total order for shipping and handling. BY MAIL: Write out the full titles of the books you'd like to order and send payment, including $4.50 for shipping and handling to: Adams Media Corporation, 260 Center Street, Holbrook, MA 02343. 30-day money-back guarantee.

ACROBAT CATS

By George Daugherty

Illustrations by Gretchen Schields

Based on the screenplay "Acrobat Cats," written by
Jacques E. Bouchard and George Daugherty
Illustrations based on storyboards by Ventezslav Vesselinov

SCHOLASTIC INC.
New York Toronto London Auckland Sydney
Mexico City New Delhi Hong Kong Buenos Aires

If you purchased this book without a cover,
you should be aware that this book is stolen property.
It was reported as "unsold and destroyed" to the publisher, and neither
the author nor the publisher has received any payment for this "stripped book."

No part of this work may be reproduced in whole or in part, or stored in a retrieval system,
or transmitted in any form or by any means, electronic, mechanical, photocopying, recording,
or otherwise, without written permission of the publisher. For information regarding permission,
write to Scholastic Inc., Attention: Permissions Department, 557 Broadway, New York, NY 10012.

ISBN 0-439-42873-4

Sagwa, The Chinese Siamese Cat, is produced by CinéGroupe in association with Sesame
Workshop based on the book written by Amy Tan and illustrated by Gretchen Schields.
© 2002 CinéGroupe Sagwa Inc. Characters and original story © 2002 Amy Tan.
Illustrations © 2002 Gretchen Schields. "Sagwa" and its logo are trademarks of
CinéGroupe Sagwa Inc. All rights reserved.

Published by Scholastic Inc. SCHOLASTIC and associated logos are
trademarks and/or registered trademarks of Scholastic Inc.

12 11 10 9 8 7 6 5 4 3 2 1   2 3 4 5 6/0

Printed in the U.S.A.
First printing, October 2002